Information Sciences Series

Editors

ROBERT M. HAYES
Director of the Institute of Library Research
University of California at Los Angeles

JOSEPH BECKER
Director of Information Sciences
Interuniversity Communications Council (EDUCOM)

Consultants

CHARLES P. BOURNE
Director, Advanced Information Systems Division
Programming Services, Inc.

HAROLD BORKO
System Development Corporation

Joseph Becker and Robert M. Hayes:
INFORMATION STORAGE AND RETRIEVAL

Charles P. Bourne:
METHODS OF INFORMATION HANDLING

Harold Borko:
AUTOMATED LANGUAGE PROCESSING

Russell D. Archibald and Richard L. Villoria:
NETWORK-BASED MANAGEMENT SYSTEMS (PERT/CPM)

Charles T. Meadow:
THE ANALYSIS OF INFORMATION SYSTEMS, A PROGRAMMER'S
INTRODUCTION TO INFORMATION RETRIEVAL

Launor F. Carter:
NATIONAL DOCUMENT-HANDLING SYSTEMS FOR SCIENCE AND
TECHNOLOGY

George W. Brown, James G. Miller and Thomas A. Keenan:
EDUNET: REPORT OF THE SUMMER STUDY ON INFORMATION
NETWORKS CONDUCTED BY THE INTERUNIVERSITY COMMUNI-
CATIONS COUNCIL (EDUCOM)

Perry E. Rosove:
DEVELOPING COMPUTER-BASED INFORMATION SYSTEMS

Robert M. Hayes:
MATHEMATICS OF INFORMATION SYSTEMS   IN PREPARATION

Automated Language Processing

Automated
Language Processing

Harold Borko

System Development Corporation
Santa Monica, California

John Wiley and Sons, Inc.   New York · London · Sydney

P
98
B6

to my children

Hilda and Martin

who may someday benefit from the
Techniques of Automated Language Processing

FIRST CORRECTED PRINTING, OCTOBER, 1968

Library of Congress Catalog Card Number: 66-26735
Printed in the United States of America

Contributors

Daniel G. Bobrow   Bolt, Beranek and Newman, Inc.
Cambridge, Massachusetts

Harold Borko   System Development Corporation
Santa Monica, California

H. P. Edmundson   Computer Science Center
University of Maryland
College Park, Maryland

Charles H. Kellogg   System Development Corporation
Santa Monica, California

Eugene D. Pendergraft   Tracor Corporation
Austin, Texas

Louise Schultz   Biosciences Information Service
Philadelphia, Pennsylvania

Sally Y. Sedelow
Walter A. Sedelow, Jr.   Department of Information Science,
Westhouse
University of North Carolina
Chapel Hill, North Carolina

Robert F. Simmons   System Development Corporation
Santa Monica, California

Ronald E. Wyllys   Department of Computer Sciences
University of Wisconsin
Madison, Wisconsin

11/21/69

Publ. (Gen'l Misc.)

163922

Information Sciences Series

Information is the essential ingredient in decision making. The need for improved information systems in recent years has been made critical by the steady growth in size and complexity of organizations and data.

This series is designed to include books that are concerned with various aspects of communicating, utilizing, and storing digital and graphic information. It will embrace a broad spectrum of topics, such as information system theory and design, man-machine relationships, language data processing, artificial intelligence, mechanization of library processes, non-numerical applications of digital computers, storage and retrieval, automatic publishing, command and control, information display, and so on.

Information science may someday be a profession in its own right. The aim of this series is to bring together the interdisciplinary core of knowledge that is apt to form its foundation. Through this consolidation, it is expected that the series will grow to become the focal point for professional education in this field.

Foreword

In a famous memorandum written 17 years ago Warren Weaver urged research to find out if the newly developed computer could be used to translate from one language into another. Weaver wisely foresaw that "such a program involves a presumably tremendous amount of work in the logical structure of languages before one would be ready for any mechanization" and pointed out that "such a program has the advantage that, whether or not it led to a useful mechanization of the translation problem, it could not fail to shed much useful light on the general problem of communication." Both prophecies have been fulfilled; there is still no system of mechanical translation, and the study of the problem has revolutionized the study of linguistics.

This book is about one of the most interesting and potentially valuable by-products of the quest for automatic translation: the lively area of basic research on how to apply computers to the study of language and how to use them in processing data presented as natural language texts.

By focusing on statistical analysis and on syntax it concentrates on the areas in which the most solid and intelligible work to date has been done. Yet it also calls attention to important and beautiful theoretical work, itself the subject of a rich and still growing literature in linguistics, computer science, and logic. It recognizes the link, both theoretical and practical, between the study of natural and artificial languages, a link both forged and required by computer systems. The vast uncharted depths of semantics are approached through the problem of question-answering. The possibilities of on-line man/machine interaction are ignored; but this area is relatively new.

The book presents the state of the art both literally and figuratively. Having itself been set in type semiautomatically, it embodies the fruits of a concrete technological experiment. Its contents reflect a state of becoming more than a state of being, research more than development, and development more than economical and reliable engineering practice. It is an account of exciting experiments and barriers overcome and an introduction to the multitudinous theoretical and practical problems yet to be faced before any but the most modest hopes can be realized.

ANTHONY G. OETTINGER
Cambridge, Massachusetts

Preface

If ever the preparation of a technical book could be called a labor of love, this book should be eligible for the appelation, for it is truly the product of the dedicated efforts of many people.

The idea for Automated Language Processing was suggested in 1964 at a time when the research efforts in information storage and retrieval were expanding at System Development Corporation. Many people in the company were directly interested in this area, and an even larger group had interests that were tangentially related. A quick and effective means of acquainting them with the state-of-the-art was needed, but no convenient compilation of relevant material was available. It was agreed that a book on the theory and techniques of information storage and retrieval procedures would be a worthwhile project for the language processing staff to undertake. Although no one member could reasonably be expected to cover the entire range of technical developments in this field, the staff as a whole is concerned with most phases of the work. This is attested by the fact that all but one of the chapter authors were connected with SDC either as employees or consultants. The single exception is Pendergraft, for SDC has had no sustained project in machine translation. SDC Management was enthusiastic in its support of the new project.

As editor, I undertook the task of organizing and delineating the topics to be covered. The results of our first efforts were not encouraging. The materials submitted were good, but they lacked sufficient scope and theoretical orientation. In a revision of our subject matter we included more of linguistics and language data processing, which, in turn, made it necessary to eliminate some chapters and to insist that others be rewritten. It is indicative of the dedication of the group that these decisions, though difficult, were understood and accepted.

Our aim from the beginning was to use the book as a vehicle to describe and demonstrate the concepts and procedures of automated language processing. In practice, this meant that the very words of the text would themselves be processed by computer and would become the data base on which to perform language processing experiments. The book was typeset by computer, and although slower than anticipated—for there is a large gap between theoretical knowledge gained in a laboratory and practical application by a production shop—it has proved to be quite feasible. As a research project, the text is also being used to study techniques for automatically indexing a book.

Many more people contributed to the book than those whose names appear in the Contents. First and foremost we are indebted to the management of System Development Corporation for their continuing support of our efforts. On a more personal note, I wish especially to thank my secretary Harriet Edgerton who learned to use a Flexowriter to be able to type the manuscript, Ann Walker, who proofread the manuscript, and Jules Farell, who spent many an evening coaxing the programs through the computer. All their help and support is gratefully acknowledged, and it is hoped that they will be able to take some pride in the final product.

Harold Borko
September, 1967

Contents

Part I

LANGUAGE DATA PROCESSING

Language is a uniquely human accomplishment, and although some lower animals may possess some rudimentary means of communication, only man has developed language to a stage where it can be recorded, stored, and retrieved. When people use language we say that they communicate, but what shall we say when one of the parties to this exchange is a computer? It is too anthropomorphic to call this interaction communication, for the term connotes understanding. When machines utilize words and symbols we say that the machine is merely processing the language data. This is an important distinction, for while the computer can process symbols, only the human operator can impart significance to the output. *Automated Language Processing* reviews the progress that man has made in programming a computer to process language.

The first chapter in this introductory portion (Part I) amplifies the meaning of language data processing. The phrase connotes the use of a computer for linguistic analysis as opposed to numerical analysis. In addition, the first chapter describes the methods and goals of language processing and provides a general orientation to the material covered in the remainder of the book. Louise Schultz, in her chapter on *Language and the Computer,* examines the behavior which is characterized as language processing and compares these functions to data processing by computer. The emphasis is upon recognizing those functions which can be automated.

Since computers are most competent in the field of mathematical data processing, a logical approach to the problems of language processing consists of developing mathematical models of language. In Chapter 3, Edmundson presents a comprehensive survey of many different logical, analytic, algebraic, geometric, and statistical theories that provide the bases for models of language. He also illustrates some of the possible interpretations of these mathematical entities.

Part I, *Language Data Processing,* provides the reader with a conceptual and theoretical orientation to the applications of language processing which follow.

Introduction

Harold Borko

Automated Language Processing is a somewhat ambiguous title which, in the course of the succeeding chapters, will be amplified so as to indicate more precisely the concern of the volume with digital computer processing of natural language. The range of tasks that can be undertaken when one engages in language processing, and more specifically in automated language processing, is broadly outlined in the introductory chapter. In addition, the purpose behind the research efforts for automating language processing is discussed.

1.1 LANGUAGE PROCESSING

A process is "a series of actions or operations definitely conducing to an end." * What, then, is the end or goal of language processing? Primarily, one uses language to communicate, and communication is the passing of information from one place or person to another place or person. The first stage in the communication process is the encoding of the information into a set of symbols that can be manipulated and transmitted from person to person or place to place. For the human being, these symbols are words and the encoding process is the translation of thoughts into words. Obviously, the receiver must have the ability to decode the words back into the original thoughts without introducing excessive noise or error into the system.

To transmit thoughts among people who are within sight and hearing of each other, the words are spoken. Speech is a complicated process and the mechanisms involved are tangential to this discussion. Here, it is sufficient to state that during speech the word (i.e., the encoded thought)

*Webster's New Collegiate Dictionary, 1961.

is itself encoded into complex pressure waves carried by air to the ear of the listener. The listener, through another complex process called hearing, decodes the pressure waves back into words. The brain must then decode the words into thoughts, and the communication cycle is complete (see Figure 1.1).

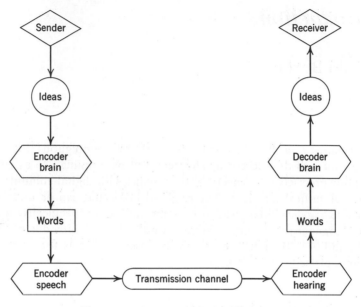

Figure 1.1. The communication process

In our discussion of language processing, we will not be concerned with the encoding and decoding of thoughts into language. This task we will leave to the psychologist [5]* and other specialists. Neither will we be concerned with the characteristics of the communication channel, for this is a problem for the communications engineer [6]. As information scientists specializing in language processing, we consider our task to begin with the encoded thought—that is, with the word—or, more properly, with the connected arrangement of words which constitute language. For communication to take place, the words must be subjected to additional coding procedures. Words can be spoken, printed, teletyped, and broadcast; words can be translated into foreign languages, stored in libraries, indexed, and abstracted. These are the tasks of language processing.

We consider the following an operational definition characterizing the usage in this text:

*Numbers in brackets refer to References at the end of each chapter.

Language processing is the manipulation, or coding, of language for specific purposes such as communication, translation, storage, and retrieval.

1.2 AUTOMATED LANGUAGE PROCESSING

The goal of automated language processing is to manipulate language by electromechanical means in order to facilitate the communication, translation, storage, and retrieval of information.

The process begins with the ideas already expressed in words, and the aim is to encode the words into a form more suitable for communication. For example, to be communicated by telegraph, the words must be translated into Morse code. To be communicated by teletype, the words would have to be converted into a teletype code. To be communicated as a written message to a blind person, the words would have to be printed in Braille. These very obvious applications are of no great theoretical importance. The departure from these commonplace examples to the present scientific interest in automated language processing is due largely to the remarkable capabilities of the high speed digital computer.

The computer was originally conceived as a device for performing mathematical calculations. After the analogous relationship between numbers as symbols and words as symbols was recognized, the modern digital computer as a symbol manipulator *par excellence* was obvious. Words are symbols; language is a string of symbols, and the task of the information scientist is to process these language symbols through the digital computer in order to perform some useful function.

The first problem faced by the information scientist is to specify the useful communication functions that he can reasonably expect to improve by automated techniques. The applications as they are presently conceived are

a. translating from one language into another,

b. improving the storage and retrieval of information, and

c. designing an "intelligent" automaton that would be able to answer questions.

All of these tasks involve the processing of language, but how does one go about translating languages or answering questions by computer? Translation of alphabetical characters into Morse code is a trivial problem and one that can be accomplished by a computer. In fact, as part of its normal functions, the computer can make such translations in the same manner as it translates decimal numbers to binary numbers and vice versa. Why is this translation trivial, whereas machine translation of Russian into English is complex? The answer lies in the fact that there is an invariant one-to-one relationship between the English alphabet and its Morse code equivalent. There is a similar invariant relationship between a decimal representation of a quantity and the binary notation.

In contrast, the rules that govern language usage are not precise and unambiguous. This is not to say that there are no rules, for we can characterize some sentences as being grammatically correct and others as being incorrect. However, formulation of a complete and precise mathematical model of language that will permit automatic evaluation and generation of correct and meaningful sentences has not yet been fully accomplished. The need for such models and the advantages and disadvantages of existing models are discussed in Chapter 3. The lack of a precise mathematical model of language makes unfeasible—in the words of Bar-Hillel—"full automation of many aspects of the information retrieval field, such as translation, abstraction, or indexing" [1].

Automatic language processing is not going to be perfect. Whether it could even be high quality or not is dependent on how high the standards are set. Most workers in the field consider as their standard the usefulness of the results. But even accepting utility as our standard, and recognizing that natural language is "unruly," what techniques are available for processing language?

At the present, automated language processing must rely on the use of statistical and syntactical techniques. Statistical techniques are based upon the distributional properties of the individual words or specified phrases in the languages. In its simplest form, statistical processing of language consists of counting the words in the text. The principle on which this procedure is based is that the meaning of the document is carried in the words in the text—that is, the vocabulary. Articles on different subjects use different vocabularies; therefore, if one knows the vocabulary, he should be able to determine the subject content. Statistical techniques have been used for automated indexing, classification, abstracting, and style analysis, as well as for machine translation. These topics are discussed in their respective chapters in this text.

The results of statistical processing of language data will not be perfect, although it is hoped that the outputs will be useful. The reason for this lack of perfection is that words have many meanings and that different ideas can be expressed with the same set of words. The same words in another order can be used to express different ideas. A classic example is the two sentences:

Man bites dog.
Dog bites man.

The words are identical, but the meanings are obviously different. Simple statistical counts of words will not enable us to discover these differences. The meaning of a string of words lies not only in the words themselves but in their arrangement—the syntactical structure of the sentence.

At this point in the discussion, the reader may well begin to question whether statistical processing of language can result in any meaningful or useful output. The question can be rephrased as an hypothesis, which can be tested experimentally. In fact, the studies described in Part II, *Statistical Analysis,* are designed to test this hypothesis. The aim of the researchers who are concentrating on statistical analysis of text is to provide quantitative data on the quality of their outputs. Once this base line has been established, it will be possible to show how much improvement results from the use of syntactical analysis.

Research in automated abstracting (Chapter 5) provides a very clear example of this step-by-step approach. The first automated extract was produced by H. P. Luhn [4]. He employed statistical techniques that enabled him to count and identify frequently used content words. Then he searched for sentences that contained a high density of these words. These sentences were selected to form the extract. Considering the simplicity of the technique, the results were surprisingly good. One was able to read the extracted sentences and deduce the content of the original article with a fair degree of success. To improve the selection of representative sentences, as is pointed out in the chapter by Wyllys, the value of other than statistical clues is now being studied. It is anticipated that, eventually, the use of highly sophisticated syntactical techniques will enable the computer program to select various phrases from the author-generated sentences and to combine them into a true machine-generated abstract.

Automating the syntactical analysis of natural language is a difficult but necessary task if we are to improve the quality of machine language processing. But even if these techniques were perfected, would we be able to achieve a truly high-quality output? Probably not, for there remain a number of *semantic* problems that would have to be solved. I recall seeing the machine translation of an engineering paper in which the word "water goat" kept reappearing, to the confusion of all concerned. Upon checking the original document, the source of the "error" quickly became apparent. What had been translated into "water goat" would have been more reasonable if translated into "hydraulic ram."

Can this and similar problems ever be solved by automation? No definitive answer can be given, but the problems must be identified before any attempt can be made to solve them. For example, in the case cited, it was suggested that the use of a specialized micro-thesaurus would avoid the problem of the "water goat" on the grounds that engineers do not use water goats but do use hydraulic rams. In all fairness, we should say that this may be an avoidance of the problem rather than a solution. What is needed is a method of analyzing the semantic contents of words and phrases. Simmons, in Chapter 8, discusses this problem.

1.3   THE IMPETUS FOR AUTOMATED LANGUAGE PROCESSING

The preceding sections have described language processing and the tasks the researcher in automated language processing is studying. The problems are difficult and numerous, and the possibility of achieving a high-quality output has been questioned. Why, then, do researchers persist in their efforts? In one sense this question is similar to asking why people struggle to climb mountains or to get to the moon. The mountain, or the moon, is a challenge, and science grows and makes new discoveries as it attempts to meet challenges. This is certainly true of the research efforts in automated language processing. Such efforts have led to increased knowledge in computer programming, linguistics, and library science. But this is knowledge for its own sake, and we live in a practical world. Are there any practical reasons for emphasizing research in automated language processing? The answer to this question is, "Yes, definitely yes." Unless we can develop more efficient means of communicating—sharing ideas from person to person and place to place—human progress will be inhibited.

Man's knowledge of himself and his environment has expanded exponentially, particularly during the last 100 years. There are many reasons for this increase: There are more scientists at work today than ever before; science is receiving strong financial support from both government and industry; the cold war has resulted in a competitive climate in which nations are striving for both military and scientific supremacy; etc. The horizons of science are expanding; new discoveries are being made. The communication sciences must not lag. Progress must be made on all fronts, for if it lags behind in any one area, especially communication, the rate of growth in other areas will necessarily slow down.

Senator Hubert Humphrey [3] claimed (as a result of an analysis, conducted by his subcommittee on government operations, of the handling of scientific and technical information by the Department of Defense)

... that the equivalent of 300,000 man years and a $1-to-$2 billion equivalent in funds are being wasted ... in needless, unintentional duplication of scientific research and development (owing to) poor communication which prevents exchange of ideas and information among scientists working in the same or related fields.

Why did communication break down? Surely the researchers and the research administrators recognize the need to document and exchange ideas. There are more science and technology societies in existence today than ever before, and the societies hold more conventions and publish more journals than ever before. The first two scientific journals appeared 300 years ago. Testimony given during the Senate Committee hearings relative to the Science and Technology Act of 1958 indicated that responsible technical journals then numbered approximately 50,000; some two million periodical articles were being published annually along with 60,000 technical books and 50,000 technical reports. And the rate of publication is increasing every year. The result of all this publication activity is that the individual scientist is drowning in a sea of documentation and is unable to keep his head up long enough to see the information he needs.

As Dr. B. Adkinson, head of the Office of Science Information Service of the National Science Foundation, put it,

...the volume of scientific information ... can no longer be published promptly and adequately managed within the framework of existing methods and organizations.
...effective solution of the scientific information problem...depends on improvement of present information services which use known and tested systems and techniques, and ... development of new and more powerful techniques, including mechanized systems, for coping with the rapidly expanding body of scientific and technical literature. [2]

The so-called "information explosion" has been discussed by others, and at great length. It is clear that a problem exists and that a solution must be found. Ways must be devised to help the scientist or engineer to keep up with the current literature in his field, to search the literature accumulated in the past, and to be made aware of literature relevant to his task so that he can forge ahead without unintentional and expensive duplication.

So far this discussion has been concerned only with the literature being produced in one country and one language. But no one country has a monopoly on science, a fact which was forcibly brought home to the citizens of the United States with the launching of Sputnik. How can the American scientist keep up with the unclassified developments taking place in Russia, Germany, France, Japan, etc.? Should we insist that our scientists be able to read one, two, or more foreign languages? Should we expend our resources in translating foreign documents, thus increasing the flood of literature? Neither solution seems practical or adequate.

Clearly, as Dr. Adkinson said, we need to develop "... new and more powerful techniques, including mechanized systems, for coping with the rapidly expanding body of scientific and technical literature."

These new techniques are the techniques of automated language processing. The immediate goal is not to build the perfect information retrieval system or to achieve high quality machine translation, but to build a system of communication that is more efficient than the one we have today. This is the task which the information scientist has set for himself. The results of his research are reported in the remainder of this book.

REFERENCES

1. Bar-Hillel, Y., Is information retrieval approaching a crisis?, *Amer. Doc.,* v. 14, no. 2, April 1963.

2. *Documentation, Indexing, and Retrieval of Scientific Information.* 86th Congress, 2nd Session, Senate Document No. 113. Washington: U.S. Government Printing Office, 1961.

3. Humphrey, H., *Congressional Record,* 17 April 1962.

4. Luhn, H. P., The automatic creation of literature abstracts, *IBM J. of Research and Development,* v. 2, no. 2, April 1958, pp. 159-317.

5. Miller, G. A., *Language and Communication.* New York: McGraw-Hill, 1951.

6. Shannon, C. E. and W. Weaver, *The Mathematical Theory of Communication.* Urbana, Ill.: U. of Illinois Press, 1949.

2

Language and the Computer

Louise Schultz

As a framework within which to examine the state of the art of automated language processing, this chapter summarizes the functions considered to be involved in the behavior we may characterize as "processing language," and among those, the functions that appear to be reasonably assignable to automatic processing systems.

Management of documented knowledge is a challenge described voluminously in the literature. Surveying the problem broadly is unproductive: Wringing one's hands does not make a roof more waterproof. If a problem exists, it impinges on individuals whose performance or intellectual satisfaction it impairs. What do individuals want of a system for managing documented knowledge? How much of what they want is technologically, economically, or theoretically attainable?

The ideal system would listen to the individual describe his information need, would interact with his statements to establish mutually the scope and depth of the need, and would without a delay of more than, say, five minutes deliver a brief aural essay—supplemented appropriately by visual displays of illustrations—that fills the need.

Such a description seems to be satisfied by a human being and a supply of documented knowledge. But, as the supply of documented knowledge increases, the delay between acceptance of the request for information and delivery of the response escalates. Interpreting the system description as specifying a human simply shifts the problem from an original requestor who needs the information to support some activity to an intermediary whose activity is wholly information management.

A system performing as described (where the individual posing the request is the one who interfaces with the system, regardless of whether he is an original requestor or an intermediary) must "listen," must "understand" well enough to "establish mutually the scope and depth of the need," and must deliver information in aural and visual forms. These functional requirements imply language and cognitive skills. How can such requirements be satisfied by automatic data processing equipment?

Originally, computing systems were developed for and were assigned to processing numerical data. The processes to be accomplished are not much more complex than those that are possible with a calculator. But, a computing system can be provided with a list of steps and can perform the processing without human intervention, in a fraction of the time needed for and more reliably than a human can operate a calculator.

As computing systems were put into wider service, their capabilities were expanded. In fact, in something like two decades, their ability to do arithmetic has become completely overshadowed by the implications of their ability to accept, obey, and even modify the instructions they execute. This latter ability hinges on the "logical" functions the system performs—functions that involve sequences of yes-no "decisions," and that include conjunction, selection, merging, collating, conditionality, sorting, etc. Clearly, functions such as these can be performed on alphabetic information as well as on numerical information. Thus, the "descendants" of a device designed to calculate ballistics tables are not computers so much as they are *symbol manipulators* and, therefore, potential language processors. In the next section, we will summarize the functions required in a system that may process language.

2.1 TO PROCESS AUTOMATICALLY

To assign to a machine the tasks of processing language requires enough knowledge of language to permit design of the processes and evaluation of the processing. Writing the preceding sentence has been easy; analyzing it to describe its structure and meaning in terms of the capabilities of automatic data processing equipment is presently impossible. The balance of this book reviews research being conducted by psychologists, linguists, logicians, and equipment designers to identify the necessary elements of this communication tool, which we use without conscious analysis.

As mentioned, language processing involves (1) acceptance of patterns of spoken or written symbols; (2) recognition of significance of symbols and patterns; (3) transformation of input elements and/or generation of reference labels or element identifications that are necessary for manipulating, storing, and subsequently relocating the input patterns; (4) synthesis of selected patterns; and (5) transformation of the result into a specified form for use.

2.2 SYMBOL RECOGNITION

Before any processing can be done, the processor must accept information in language form —either as speech or as writing or printing. "Recognition" may be considered to encompass awareness and mapping into a cognitive environment. Awareness, for a processing system, is a capability provided through mechanical design. The level of mapping involved in the recognition task can be considered to be controlled by a processing program. Its goal is to transform a mediating energy pattern in a form used by a human to a form usable by an automaton.

Speech pattern research remains in the area of fundamental research in acoustics, physiology, and linguistics. Some special equipment has been designed, for example, to separate the individual frequencies of a complex sound pattern and to measure the periods (fractions of a second) each frequency endures in the generation of certain speech sounds. Automated optical and magnetic character readers for particular reading problems are in operation and under development. For example, "controlled font" readers (capable of reading a prescribed type font) and magnetic ink character recognition equipment are in use. However, for multifont reading, text format and the measurable characteristics of each font constitute significant problems.

2.2.1 Recognizing Audible Language Symbols.   Researchers in speech analysis test their hypotheses by synthesizing speech patterns from analyzed elements. This work is moving toward providing a machine with the capability of reliably transforming patterns of comparatively different constituents into a generalized class of speech sound. The human apparently does something of this nature in recognizing a given word or word combination despite the obvious differences in the sounds created when the word is uttered by, for example, a child, a native adult male, an elderly female, a "first generation American" from a cultural and/or national extraction different from that of the listener, etc.

The Wiren-Stubbs machine, developed in 1956, attempts to recognize distinctive features (rather than the audible frequencies) of the elements of a language sound burst. Properties such as voiced versus unvoiced, turbulent versus nonturbulent, and the like, are distinguished in a sequence of dichotomous "choices" for each element. Vowels in short words were identified correctly in an average of 94 percent of all cases [14].

The Denes-Fry machine, developed in 1959, associates information about the probability that a given sound is followed by another (from a specified repertoire), as an aid to the output recognition function. The experiment involved four vowels and nine consonants. Such contextual information improved word recognition [14].

Subsequent research has increasingly recognized that abstract analysis of the acoustic characteristics of a language sound pattern is fruitless without associated linguistic data. The latter must include not only the phonetic characteristics but the discrimination of phonemic character-istics, the syntagmatic, and the syntactic characteristics of elements in a continuous speech event.

The mechanics of producing a particular speech pattern must be de-scribed in terms of an abstraction or class of patterns, each member of which may differ from all others—but not enough to be considered part of some other class. Assuming that these efforts are fruitful, they are only a first step toward automated processing. Speech is far less formal in structure than written language and, therefore, poses far more severe problems to automated processing.

Closer to application than are speech recognition devices are devices designed to recognize graphic symbols. Although direct speech input would make convenient a significant reduction in the amount of paper on which technical information is now documented, a major step in re-ducing the cost of automatically processing the present body of docu-mented knowledge could be achieved were a device available that could "read," without additional human processing, what is documented.

2.2.2 Recognizing Graphic Language Symbols. Humans now put information into computers through a keyboard—a laborious and expen-sive process. Intermediate steps between the keyboard and the computer include punched cards, perforated tape, and magnetic tape, all of which are buffer devices that accept information (initially) at the rate at which humans keyboard—fewer than 100 words per minute—and transmit it into computer storage at the rate of several hundred words per second, and that permit communication from more than one keyboard with the com-puter. Reading automata offer the promise of high-speed input without intermediate buffering between printed text and computer memory.

The individual who is not professionally involved in the graphic arts is seldom aware of the number of different type fonts encountered in his daily reading. Many qualitatively different patterns are used to represent the same alphabetic character. The most obvious examples are the upper and lower case letters. Using the letters E, G, g, a, t, e, and d; the presence of serifs; and other characteristics, Karch [11] has classified 1,500 type fonts. Commercial type fonts contain from 76 to 90 characters, includ-ing numerals and punctuation. Reading machine automata must also deal with differences that could be considered quantitative, such as character width, height, height/width ratio, and spacing. The quality of the type, printing, and paper present wide random variations that are as difficult to handle as differences in font.

To identify a character, the reading machine measures certain characteristics of the written or printed symbol, and emits a unique but corresponding computer language signal. Certain measurements, made in a particular order, are better than others for efficient, reliable identification. Deriving the smallest possible set of measurements that will yield the most certain identification is a challenging problem for the designers of reading machines [15 and 19].

The format problem—the second major problem—centers around distinguishing among the classes of text (captions, heads, tables, and photographs) that are to be read or ignored by the machine. Kirsch [12] contends that text in technical documents is a special case of graphic matter and that both have a syntactic structure "capable of being described to a machine and of being used for purposes of interpreting the information within a data processing system." Minimally, the reader must be able to accept body text and (in the order of desirability and technological difficulty) titles, heads, captions, foreign alphabets, and mathematical symbols and equations. Present reading automata that handle symbol strings bypass photographs, diagrams, etc., which are masked prior to input. Machines for reading the latter are also under development for map making and as experimental tools for developing the self-adaption capability in automatic processors [18]. Symbol readers sense the presence of printed lines and of margins, and can be instructed to read in certain areas or accept cues from the thickness or color of a line.

2.3 PATTERN PROCESSING

The development of reading machines for graphic symbols is highly promising; however, the product of that effort will do no more than transform symbols recognizable to humans into signals recognizable to automatic processors. Without a processing capability that uses such signals meaningfully, reading machines are unnecessary. The needed processing capability is a combination of what the processing system hardware, under control of the processing program, can do and of how effectively humans can exploit the processing system. The latter factor requires not only that humans understand the capabilities of the equipment but also that they can express (in terms recognizable to the system) the requirements of the process to be accomplished.

When the process is the manipulation of natural language, requirements are not so clearly specifiable as when the process is the manipulation (computation) of numbers.

2.3.1 Computability.   The theory of computability is developed from a generalization of a sequential processor, as described by Turing in a 1936 paper. The processor consists of a control element, a reading and writing head, and an infinitely long tape. The tape is considered to be a sequence of locations, each of which can contain any symbol from a finite set (an alphabet). Under direction of the control element, the read-write head can read a symbol from tape, the tape can be advanced or backspaced one location, or the read-write head can write a symbol on the tape. Combinations of these operations constitute the basis of operation of a sequential automatic digital computer. A process requiring operations other than those specified is "noncomputable."

Turing showed that if a process can be described in a finite number of symbols, the sequential machine performs the described process [22]. Thus, if we are to perform the task of processing natural language in a sequential machine, we must determine the portions of the task that are computable—and must describe the process in a finite number of symbols. Assuming the model of the sequential processor to be universally valid, the notion that automatic processing of natural language falls outside the scope of "computability" has many strong advocates. Chapter 9 discusses the impact of logical theories on mechanical translation, one of the earliest applications of automated language processing.

2.3.2 Natural Language Patterns.   The extension to natural language of the notion of computability is a simple analogy between the numerals as discrete symbols and alphabetic characters as discrete symbols. The expressions in which numerals convey any significance (aside from their own graphic form) are determinately few in comparison to the expressions in which alphabetic characters are combined to convey significance to humans. From a small set of elements, a limitless variety of meaningful alphabetic combinations is possible. How the combinations are formed is central to equipping an automatic processor to analyze a given combination.

The approaches taken in determining and characterizing linguistic patterns may be classified as "rationalistic," "empirical," "pragmatic," and "probabilistic" [20]. Logicians, in designing formal languages as the tool for hypothesizing the structure of natural language, may be considered rationalistic. Some of the languages developed for retrieval systems are discussed in Chapter 10. A few remarks about languages developed for, primarily, communication and automatic processing are provided later in this chapter. The rationalistic approach is also taken by the theoretic linguist, * as discussed in Chapter 7.

> ...Within the last quarter century, interest in the study of language has been aroused to an unprecedented level among an unexpected range of scholars. However, almost uninterruptedly since five centuries B.C., occidental philosophers have argued the subject of "universals": What is the basis for notions (and names) for classes of things? Such speculation has not considered the linguistic systems in which the names of universals are embedded. Logicians have framed arguments in language forms, to derive other language forms, without defining the system in which the forms are meaningful. Increasing interest in the performance of the human mind, buttressed by collection of physical, physiological, and sociological data, focused attention on language beginning in the 17th century.
>
> Growing out of the philosopher logician's approach to language study are contemporary systems of formal logic, the tool of logical modeling, and emphasis on synthesis or design as the hypothesis of natural language structure.
>
> In contrast to this emphasis by logicians on design of increasingly complex formal systems (that is, formal systems increasingly closer to natural language in the capabilities for expression) is the empirical, analytic approach of contemporary structural, or descriptive, and statistical linguistics. Based on the identification of linguistic units and observation of the occurrence of these units, descriptive linguistics describes the structure of a language, inferring from sample occurrences the combinatory rules to which each unit is subject.
>
> The approach of behavioral scientists to the study of language can be characterized as pragmatic, both in the sense of using the study as a tool for probing and for interpreting observations of other human behavior, and in the sense of centering their interest in the relationships between language and its users. Recent work, labeled psycholinguistics, combines the ... phenomenological aspects (of psychology) and the abstract aspects of language (as studied by linguists).
>
> Technology, in contrast, neither cuts off specimen heads from the Hydra of language nor introspects on the effects of its behavior—it counts the "heads" it observes; analyzes probabilities that anything nine-headed will grow two new heads for each one cut off; and, resigned to coping with the beast, determines how to spend the least on its upkeep.
>
> The logician *establishes* what the elements of the language in which he is interested "mean." The linguist *avoids* what they "mean" as long as he confirms that they are "meaningful." The behaviorist attempts to *unmask* their "meaning" to a particular user. The statistician *infers* "meaning" from frequency of patterns of occurrence. From the same data, the engineer determines how to transfer the element from source to user. [20, pp. 6-7]

The automatic processor, under program control, can handle natural

---

*Bar-Hillel and others discuss the convergence of the logician's and linguist's approach [1].

language inputs in two ways:* (1) as strings of discrete elements (words) each of which is tagged with some kind of identification that facilitates retrieval, or (2) as strings of elements whose interrelationships are analyzed to retrieve full or partial strings. The assumption underlying the first technique is that an individual word constitutes a strong clue to the meaning of the string (and of the text from which the string was taken). The assumptions underlying the second technique are that meaning is a matter of context and that contextual associations reveal meaning.

Notice that, as long as the processor deals with words as discrete units, a finite vocabulary is analogous to the finite alphabet "computable" on the Turing machine. For the processor to analyze relationships between words, the process of analysis must be described.

Every school child is required to perform the exercise of analyzing natural language sentences to describe relationships between constituent words in terms of grammar labels. As described in Chapter 7 and in Reference 8, versions of that process are being performed by automatic processors. The vocabulary of grammar labels describes a process the processor is to simulate. Intuitively, we consider the vocabulary finite despite the large number—more than 5,000 expressible rules—of elements. Although such elements are part of the object vocabulary being analyzed, they express ideas *about* that vocabulary.

2.3.3 Languages About Language. Before examining further the two types of approach of which an automatic processor is capable, we should consider the languages the processor uses. Although the goal in designing processors (that is, the combination of equipment and instructions) is to allow humans to communicate with the processor in natural language, the processor must transform natural language (or some formal subset of natural language) into an electronic control signal pattern bearing very little resemblance to natural language. The transformation involves at least three major steps: compilation, assembly, and execution.

Compilation is the process in which the processor (1) accepts an electronic pulse pattern representing a string of graphic symbols allowable in the vocabulary of the compiler language—a formal "procedural" language, and (2) generates from each string one or more strings. Each of the generated strings represents a single step which the processor must perform in a processing procedure. The compilation process is an anal-

*Whether the human mind handles natural language in either or both of these ways is outside the scope of this book. However, some researchers believe that to the extent that an automatic processor behaves like a human (so that a person cannot discern from *responses* whether another human or an automatic processor is his partner in a dialog), its operational pattern constitutes an hypothesis of human cognitive functions.

ysis and its output is the input to the assembly process. Assembly consists of transforming signals representing individual steps into signals that actually set the states of each affected circuit in the processor. The list of statesetting signals is the program which, when supplied with data (numeric or linguistic) on which to operate, controls execution.

The "vocabulary" of a processor consists of a set of pulse patterns, each element of which controls the *state* ("on" or "off") of one circuit. A "word" in "machine language" means "set circuit(s) (specified) to state(s) (specified)." Communicating with a processor directly requires that a human use machine language, specifying the state of each circuit for every state involved in the processing task.

To avoid that source of communication error, the processor is equipped with a tool, such as a conversion table, allowing the input vocabulary to be expressed in "assembly language" and to consist of "words"—alphabetic characters and digits that are comparatively meaningful to the human, such as "READ"—describing an *action* to be taken by the processor. The processor determines to which state its circuits are to be set by comparing the input word with entries in the conversion table. The processor cannot be considered to be interpreting the input as an order, in this case, to read. Rather, it is using the input word as the control for determining the state in which its circuits are to be set for some specified period.

The string "READ" may also be an acceptable word in the vocabulary of what are called "higher order," "compiler," or "procedural" languages. A processor equipped to accept a procedural language compares an input word with entries in a table. However, it does not find there a simple one-to-one conversion from input word to machine word. Instead, it finds a *sequence* of assembly or else machine language words. The compiler language word summarizes or represents a sequence of actions, or modifies the actions specified by some other word in a compiler language expression.

A compiler language consists of a limited vocabulary and determinate combinatory rules. Nevertheless, even though the precedence of its operators is known, a phrase structure grammar cannot be synthesized for a programming language.

> For a given language, it is not known how to synthesize a grammar which best displays the structure of its sentences, best accommodates a particular method of syntactic analysis, or best accounts for the structure of sentences containing slight syntactic errors. [7, p. 351]

Compiler languages are designed to facilitate communication by a human to a processor of the procedures leading to accomplishment by that processor of some task. Thus, a compiler language for processing natural language consists of words convenient for expressing the actions considered to be involved in language analysis.

In the next section, some of the hardware* capabilities for language processing are outlined. The compiler languages best expressing the procedures that a sequential machine can accomplish to process natural language are a class called "list processors." Four of the most frequently used list processing languages (COMIT, IPL, LISP, and SLIP) are summarized by Bobrow and Raphael [2].

Common features of list processing languages are:

a. Data consist of natural language strings or lists;

b. Memory allocation is dynamic—storage into a particular location is based on an availability list to which the processor refers;

c. Memory is used in "stacks"—data entered at the top of a stack "push down" data already in the stack, in respect to accessibility; and

d. Subroutines may include a call for themselves, making necessary temporary storage of all present values of the argument while the subroutine is executed for other variables.

Bobrow and Raphael evaluate the basis for choosing any of the four they discuss as follows:

> If the data is in the form of strings of alphanumeric characters—e.g. natural language text and the operations to be performed on this data are string manipulations, such as substitution, rearrangement and duplication, then COMIT is a natural choice of a programming language. If extensive arithmetic or statistical operations are also to be performed, then COMIT's awkward arithmetic facilities would be a hindrance, and if these operations constitute the bulk of the task, then perhaps the superior FORTRAN arithmetic in SLIP would make it worthwhile to use SLIP, even for the string manipulations. (However, we understand that COMIT II, soon to be available for the 7090, will have facility for incorporating FORTRAN-compiled functions.)
>
> If some string manipulation is to be done, but processing of complex list structures is also needed, LISP is probably a good language to use. There is documented and available a LISP function, 'METEOR,' ... which performs COMIT-type string manipulations and allows full use of other LISP facilities.
>
> Highly recursive processes are most easily expressed in the LISP formalism, and programmers with mathematical training will probably find it the most natural. ...

*I cannot emphasize too strongly the interdependence of hardware and software (the statements of procedures, implementation of which in a given equipment configuration constitutes the processing capability). While this statement would remain unchallenged by those engaged in automated language processing research, an analogous statement about human language processing is probably vacuous. The human physiologically cannot be modeled as a sequential machine in Turing's terms. Nevertheless, all research into automated language processing is based on the premise that a sequential machine can be equipped with a program enabling it to model the human language processing capability.

Programs working with complex list structures and needing auxiliary storage to handle large amounts of data should probably be written in IPL or SLIP. It is difficult to choose between these two languages, except that much more background information and documentation is available for IPL than for the newcomer, SLIP. For ease of insertion of an LP language into a monitor system and for programmers brought up on a FORTRAN diet, SLIP is an excellent starting language. The principal disadvantage of SLIP is that very little experience has been accrued with it, and further, some care must be taken to fool a too clever FORTRAN compiler.

To reiterate, no one of these LP languages is distinctly superior over the entire range of problems for which LP techniques are needed. They all provide a sufficient number of built-in operations so that a programmer may directly express and deal with his own problem in the formalism of the chosen language without having to prepare many basic utility routines. [2, p. 240]

Using a procedural language and compiler compatible with natural language processing requirements, what can be done?

2.3.4 Tagging Discrete Elements — References, then Statistics, then Syntax, then Answers. The automatic processor can tag each input word on the basis of its appearance in some sequence, just as a person tags a term with a page number, for retrieval. Such tagging amounts to assigning to a term an address in storage, and recording the term out of context with the tag(s) for all locations in which it is stored. The secondary record is an index to the primary storage.

When primary storage is large, as the volume of scientific and technical knowledge, the index is large. Retrieval using an index such as that just described requires search through some portion of the text at each location the index specifies as containing a reference to a term of interest. For some terms in a store, the number of references may be so high that some additional discrimination among possible portions of text is imperative.

Using the same level of secondary data, an automatic processor can produce statistics relative to the frequency and distribution of occurrence of a term and to its occurrence in combination with one or more other terms. The application of these techniques is discussed in Part II *Statistical Analysis*. To perform the tagging function and generate statistics, the processor needs elementary arithmetic capabilities and a large enough store, each location of which is identified by an "address." Processing is sequential and single level. In terms of a Turing machine, no change in state is produced by and, therefore, no relevant information is generated by reversal of the tape bearing input signals (that is, the processing program gains no additional data relative to the identification of an input signal).

Elaboration of the discrete-element tagging policy arises from practical limitations of the processing system and from user expectations in regard to (1) processing time and (2) the degree and accuracy of discrimination provided. Among the limitations of the processing system are size, and speed of access to any portion, of storage. The latter is influenced by the organization of contents and the effectiveness of the processor in searching. At this point, then, we should consider briefly the capabilities built into storage hardware.

Consider the analogy of a bookshelf large enough and strong enough to support 200 books. The time needed to locate any one of a collection of 200 or fewer depends on the number of books and the correspondence between the shelving scheme and the search scheme. If the books were in closed (but labeled) boxes of 10 each, organization increases in importance; and if the information is stored in a different language, in units of one letter each, organization is a critical problem.

Storage in an automatic data processing system is provided by the state in which each of thousands of circuits is set by the processor accepting information. Determining what state any combination of circuits is in (and therefore what information the combination holds) requires that the combination be identified. Such identification is called the "address." Correspondence between an address specified and the identification implicit in the wiring of the circuits is the basis for access to the "contents" of the specified address.

In the traditional data processing analogy of the post office pigeonholes, addresses may be numeric. In certain data processing systems, numeric references are not useful because the compiler has control of the location in which it may store what it has accepted. For the user of such a system, numeric addresses are replaced by address "names." That is, rather than seeking "1492 Main Street," the searcher specifies "the Jones' house."

During the last few years, processors have been developed that (in effect) allow the searcher to specify a characteristic of the stored information, rather than either the number or name of its address [13]. This capability is analogous to needle-sorting a deck of edgenotched cards. Because the needle passes through the full deck, all cards are interrogated simultaneously.

> Memory systems which retrieve information on the basis of a given characteristic rather than by physical location...are called "content-addressed," "catalog," or "associative." In these types of memory systems,

an interrogation word...is presented to the memory and a parallel search of all words within the memory is conducted. Those stored words which have a prescribed relationship (e.g., equal to, nearest to, greater than, etc.) to the interrogation word are tagged. Subsequently, the multiple tagged words or responses are retrieved by some interrogation routine. [17, p. 614]

Experimentation with processors and compiler languages designed to facilitate communication of the "association" specifications that provide content addressability is in part hampered by the physical characteristics of memories. The storage of appropriate characteristics tags takes memory space and/or control circuitry. Hence, for a system of a given memory size, less direct content can be stored when it must be accompanied by "indirect" content—that is, the book containing the index to a set of books occupies shelf space otherwise occupiable by some other book.

Development of memories consisting of arrays of photoetched circuits, for compact size and high switching and accessing speeds, is promising to increase the capacity of a storage element to a density of some 10,000 circuits per square inch [24]. Nevertheless, "a large memory...will have a retrieval time in milliseconds* unless a solution can be found for the interplane connections of the ladder network" [24, p. 335].

Photochromic memories are also under investigation and in experimental use for machine translation. The property of certain glass to change color and density may be exploited for computer system storage. Exposure of microscopic segments of the glass plane to ultraviolet light can produce the change of state interpretable as binary information. Information storage density in such a device is extremely high.

The previous discussion of content-addressable memories amplified on the capability appropriate to tagging linguistic units (words or word fragments) with a characteristic such as membership in the same class— by virtue of appearing in the same document or in the same string. As is pointed out in Chapter 4, such techniques are well known and were, for example, used to develop the index to this text. Research involving automatic indexing is concerned with derivation of principles of (1) occurrence of linguistic units, (2) structure of linguistic strings, and (3) display of units for human use. In the first of these three areas falls the work in stylistic analysis, described in Chapter 6. Syntax analyzing systems (Chapter 7) and question answering systems (Chapter 8) fall into the second category. The third category of research is only briefly mentioned, in Chapter 4, and is exemplified by the association map [4 and 5].

The notion of tagging discrete elements to research the principles of the structure of language strings involves assignment of structural class

*This is comparatively slow in terms of conventional sequential machine technology, in which access to any one circuit can be made in a few billionths of a second.

tags, rather than occurrence tags. The processor making such assignments must be equipped with identification information—for instance, in a table of word stems and form classes—or with a set of procedures (algorithmic or heuristic). Except for requirements for large, rapid-access memory and convenient, low-cost input, the research task imposes no new demands on the equipment portions of the automatic processing system. The third category of research does make significant additional demands, as implied by the next few paragraphs.

2.4 TRANSMISSION AND DISPLAY

The automatic processing system capable of recognizing symbols sensible to a human and of processing what it has accepted must perform one last group of functions: delivering a desired product to a user. In the late 1940's, Shannon developed formal mathematical expressions representing the relationships between signal phenomena and the capabilities of the system by which they are transferred from transmitter to receiver [23]. These expressions aid in designing and in evaluating the limitations of automatic processing systems, and have been considered broad enough to bear extension into less quantifiable information transfer events (see Figure 1-1 for example).

2.4.1 A Transfer Model. His concern being centered on the equipment systems interposed as the medium of signal transfer, Shannon considered the *source* to be the producer of *messages* such as a sequence of letters or as an electromagnetic and time-dependent transformation of linguistic or optical phenomena—that is, radio, telephony, and television. The *transmitter* he defines as performing an encoding function (for signal transmission). The medium of transmission is the channel, which is subject to *noise*. The *receiver* he defines as performing a decoding function that reconstructs the message from the signal. The *destination* is the information user.

For this approach to language study, we consider the information source as a finite set of messages, each of which has a certain probability of being "produced" or selected for transfer. As long as all are meaningful, we can say (intuitively) that a message with a high probability of occurrence (e.g., "hello") carries little information—in the sense of "news," rather than the sense of "meaning." A transmitter, transfer channel, or receiver handling such a message in a given unit of time may be said to exhibit a low information rate. By contrast, a message with a low probability of occurrence (e.g., "snow covers Miami") carries proportionately more information. The source producing the message and the system transferring it in a given period of time exhibit a high information rate.

From the viewpoint of the destination, uncertainty about the message is highest if all messages in a large repertoire or set are equally probable, and lowest if only one message is probable. That is, if only one message can be generated, its transmission carries no information; its reception effects no reduction in an uncertainty that is already zero. The mathematical statement satisfying these verbal conditions and quantifying the information content of a message from a finite set is:

$$H = -K \sum_{i=1}^{n} p_i \log p_i$$

where H is the statistical measure of information (from a source, in a signal or message string, available for decoding, etc.); K is a positive constant providing the measurement unit corresponding to the logarithm base; and p_i is the probability of occurrence of the ith choice, event, message, signal, etc. (i.e., of one from some total set). The minus sign produces a positive measure from the summation of negative products arising from the logarithms of fractions. The form of H is that of entropy, a measure of randomness in a thermodynamic system. The term "entropy" is used by Shannon. As the generality of the theory became apparent and its theorems exploited in applications hard-pressed to be considered related to thermodynamics, other terms have been used. Here, the measure will be called "uncertainty," "randomness," "choice," and "information." Notice that information is not an intrinsic property of some arbitrary string of symbols *except in relation to the probability of occurrence of that string as one of a set of probable strings.*

Because engineering parameters tend to vary linearly with the logarithm of the number of possibilities and for other reasons related to expressing empirical conditions in mathematical notation, the measure is logarithmic. Similarly, for convenience in design and analysis of systems of two-stated devices such as switching circuits, the logarithmic base is 2; the unit of information is the binary digit or *bit*; uncertainty or information is quantified in bits per choice; and the channel capacity or information rate is expressed in bits per second.

When all choices are not equally probable, the measure of H is less than maximum. The ratio of measure of information for such a set to that (maximum) of an equally probable set is called *relative entropy* or the measure of the maximum compression that could be achieved by recoding the message optimally. *Redundancy* is the arithmetic difference between unity and the compression factor. Herdan computed the redundancy of English as between 40 and 67 percent; German, approximately 30 percent; and Russian, between 22 and 29 percent [10]. On the average, half of any sequence of English is freely chosen while the other half is determined by the structure of the language.

The probabilities of occurrence of individual alphabetic characters in English text provide that the information measure of individual letters is 4.03 bits, the maximum possible being 4.76 (for a 27-symbol set of equally probable choices), and the redundancy is 15.34 percent. Adding digrams to the population reduces uncertainty to 3.32 bits per letter; trigrams, to 3.1 bits per letter [9].

For maximum transmission efficiency, redundancy should be minimized, by recoding. But redundancy cannot so curtly be "coded out," for not only do we seek efficient use of the channel capacity, we also require reliable transfer—in a real situation. The source of unreliability is conceived as noise on the channel—using some of the channel capacity needed for accurate signal transfer. To combat the effects of noise, we can recode and we can increase channel capacity—either directly or effectively, through introduction of a correction channel. In effect, we are increasing the redundancy in the transferred signal(s) and thus, for recovery of a given message, increasing the time required for coding, transmitting, and decoding. The resulting effective information rate is formulated as the arithmetic difference between the measure of uncertainty of the source and a factor called *equivocation,* which is the average amount of additional information needed by the receiver to correct the received signal. Data sent over a correction channel whose capacity equals the equivocation measure can be coded to correct all but an arbitrarily small fraction of error in the signal delivered to the receiver from the combination of the principal channel and the correction channel.

Weaver discusses the generalization of Shannon's theory as a measure of the relationships of semiotics (syntactical, semantic, and pragmatic). He suggests considering that the separation between "information source" and "transmitter" is a channel, subject to "semantic" noise, and that a semantic "receiver" or decoder is also needed between the "receiver" and the "destination" [23].* Borko suggests in Chapter 1 an elaboration of the system diagram to include recognized and inferred coding and

*From the standpoint that a channel is a system of constraints, the channel between source and transmitter is more likely the grammar or combinatory rules under which the linguistic expression can occur. Just as the "noise" on a signal transmission channel may, in fact, be a meaningful but undesirable signal, the "noise" on the grammar channel may be considered "syntactic." Semantic noise would be introduced on some channel between the source and the system by which he encodes experiences into language representation. (See also Reference 21.)

decoding elements in human communication such as are summarized by Cherry [3].

Given a message set small enough to permit determination of occurrence (including transition) probabilities and large enough to make design of a coding system interesting and necessary, the Shannon model is the foundation for a family of mathematical design techniques.

2.4.2 From Call Number to Man-Machine Interface. The field of automated language processing boasts few such precise theories as Shannon's and, having touched lightly on what appears to be an increasingly applicable tool, we return to the empirical. For, in an automated language processing system, the messages transferred become available for the decoding function at a mechanism whose output is intended for use by a human.

An automatic processor is commonly equipped with a high-speed printer on which the data required by a user is printed. The printout may be selected portions of stored data or summary data such as tabular postings of reference identifications. Less conventional output is presented to a user on the face of a cathode ray tube. Doyle's association map technique was suggested for such a man-machine communication tool.

> In a retrieval system, the part played by an association map would be as a point of departure for more detailed searching. As a searcher scans such a map, his eye should soon come to rest in a cluster of words which equate semantically to the topic in which he is searching. There is a reasonable guarantee that this will happen because...the very cognitive processes which lead to the generation of pairs and clusters of co-occurring words should lead to the recognition of the pairs and clusters as represented on a map. When this recognition occurs, the next step in the operation of the system is to give the searcher more information about those documents which have "caused" a particular cluster of words. ...
>
> The primary map is a view of the entire library at a distance. Subsequent operations can be visualized as focusing on smaller and smaller portions of the library, with "microscopes" of successively higher power, bringing out more and more detail about each remaining potentially relevant document. ...
>
> In the long run we hope for more organic, highly automated systems which can carry out smoothly the process of focusing on successively smaller portions of the library, as described above. At this point two modes of operation of such systems are distinguishable: an off-line and an on-line mode. The off-line mode would make use of a book or file of association map printouts and the on-line mode, which would be both more flexible and more costly, would represent association maps on display scopes. In the off-line mode, the searching pathways used in going from large to small portions of the library would have to be standard or fixed for all searchers. In the on-line mode, the various stages of the search

process would be under individual control of the searcher at the display console, and therefore more adaptable to his momentary needs. [5, pp. 11-13]

The first drastic change in the map idea came...when it was realized that word-hierarchies could be generated through the prohibition of co-occurrence computations for pairs of words roughly equal to each other in frequency. When only unequally frequent words are permitted to be linked on a map, a hierarchical relationship necessarily results, in which frequent words become categories and words of lesser frequency become subcategories; the number of levels in such a hierarchy would increase with the size of the document collection, because a greater range of frequencies *would* be available. [4, p. 13]

Despite the shift in emphasis of use of the association map, the suggestion that the user might negotiate on-line with a computer-based system processing natural language has been implemented as the BOLD system at SDC and in Project MAC [6].

The main problem of modern computation theory and methodology arises from the fact that conventional digital computers, developed following the classical ideas of Alan Turing and Jan von Neumann, fail to meet many requirements as components or terminals of complex man-computer systems. Their main limitation in such context is their exceedingly high needs regarding the specificity of both the algorithms that they can accept for execution and their data, which makes them not primarily suitable as organs for incremental data assimilation through adaptively growing and incrementally modifiable algorithms and machines.

Accordingly, a radically new, very simple design logic, yielding processors (called "incremental" or "open-ended" computers) which can meaningfully utilize both algorithms and data supplied in successive fractions, and issue indicative requests for new pertinent information, has been defined. Such philosophy yields processors where open-endedness is radicated in the very foundations, that is, implicit in the primitive functions. Such processors, in addition to preserving the usual performance of classical computers in conventional mathematical and business processes, open new possibilities of fruitful collaboration among separate independent computers, and between these and humans, in future business and military information system textures. ...A new unified philosophy of designing both computers and languages chiefly (aims) to provide them with the following features:

(1) Ability of meaningfully applying algorithms which are defined incompletely, by performing just as much computation as possible with the available information, and leaving the result open to further computation upon presentation of further increments of the definition of the algorithm.

(2) Capability of meaningfully applying algorithms to fractions of their set of argument values, issuing as results functions of the missing argument values, that is, new algorithms which can accept addi-

tional increments of argument values; it is well understood that argument values can in turn be algorithms.

(3) Whenever either an algorithm (Case 1) or its argument values (Case 2) are incompletely defined, the computer should indicate which further increments of information could be profitably presented for assimilation.

(4) The thoroughness of the execution of algorithms is controlled by the context of both argument values and library algorithms provided within any given computer. The result of such execution should be again an algorithm which, in a different context (that is, confronted with further data and library increments) can be meaningfully further executed. Thus, the computation philosophy consists of submitting an algorithm successively to different computers and to different persons, from which it would drain, select, absorb, distill, reduce, and utilize all pertinent information. Unlike what happens in conventional computers, here all information processes or computations are open-ended.

...The incremental computer has exactly the same scope and limitations of operations as the conventional ones, that is, it can compute no more and no less functions. ...The point is not which computations a machine can potentially execute in abstract, but rather the way the computer selects by interacting with its environment the computations that it will actually execute, and when (in time), where (i.e., in which information context), under what stimuli, in what mode, and to what extent it will execute them. So it is not in the isolated computer itself, but rather in its interface with the variable environment, that the new design yields a drastic difference of behavior. [16, pp. 2-4]

This goal of man-machine interplay is also offered by a system introduced in late 1964 by IBM. Sitting at a display console on which the image from a microfilm frame has been "written" by the electron beam, a user can erase from or add to the image, using a light gun (electronic pen) or a keyboard. The modified image can then be microfilmed and reviewed on a projection screen.

The RAND Corporation has developed a similar communication tool in which reference to a desired portion of the displayed image is made indirectly through a stylus and electronic tablet. Users are said to adapt rapidly to using the stylus and to controlling the effect produced on the displayed image by their actions.

2.5 CONCLUSION

The somewhat "blue-sky" sounding description of an ideal system for managing documented knowledge based on automated language processing proves to be both nearer and more distant after a survey of the increasing capabilities being provided in data processing equipment and in languages with which humans can communicate with data processing systems. Still minimally implemented are input devices that could accept, as is, what is already documented. Equipment limitations relative to storing in the form it can use the documented symbols also remain. "Exotic" communication devices such as cathode ray tube displays and direct negotiation between user and system, for instance, by means of a light gun are operational. Processing systems adapting their performance to the individual user's needs are also operational.

The computer will never learn to use human language: It is rapidly being equipped to cope with it.

REFERENCES

1. Bar-Hillel, Y., C. Gaifman, and E. Shamir, On categorial and phrase-structure grammars, *Bull. Res. Council Israel,* v. 9F, no. 1, June 1960.

2. Bobrow, D. G., and B. Raphael, A comparison of list-processing computer languages, *Comm. of the ACM,* v. 7, no. 4, April 1964, pp. 231-40.

3. Cherry, C., *On Human Communication.* New York: John Wiley and Sons, 1957.

4. Doyle, L. B., Is automatic classification a reasonable application of statistical analysis of text?, *SP-1753.* Santa Monica, Calif.: System Development Corp., 31 August 1964.

5. Doyle, L. B., Indexing and abstracting by association, Part 1, *SP-718/001/00.* Santa Monica, Calif.: System Development Corp., 9 April 1962.

6. Fano, R. M., The MAC system: the computer utility approach, *IEEE Spectrum,* v. 2, no. 1, January 1965, pp. 56-64.

7. Floyd, R. W., The syntax of programming languages—a survey, *IEEE Transactions on Electronic Computers,* v. EC-13, no. 4, August 1964, pp. 346-53.

8. Greibach, S. A., Formal parsing systems, *Comm. of the ACM,* v. 7, no. 8, August 1964, pp. 499-504.

9. Herdan, G., *Type-Token Mathematics.* 'S-Gravenhage: Mouton, 1960.

10. Herdan, G., *Language as Choice and Chance.* Gron'ngen, Holland: Noordhoff, 1956.

11. Karch, R. R., *How to Recognize Type Faces.* Bloomington, Ill.: McKnight and McKnight Publishing Co., 1952.

12. Kirsch, R. A., Computer interpretation of English text and picture patterns, *IEEE Trans. on Electronic Computers,* v. EC-13, no. 4, August 1964, pp. 363-76.

13. Landauer, W. I., The balanced tree and its utilization in information retrieval, *IEEE Trans. on Electronic Computers,* v. EC-12, no. 6, December 1963, pp. 863-71.

14. Lindgren, N., Machine recognition of human language, Part I—Automatic speech recognition, *IEEE Spectrum,* v. 2, no. 3, March 1965, pp. 114-36.

15. Liu, C. N., A programmed algorithm for designing multifont character recognition logics, *IEEE Trans. on Electronic Computers,* v. EC-13, no. 5, October 1964, pp. 586-93.

16. Lombardi, L. A., Incremental data assimilation in open-ended man-computer systems, *Research Summary MAC-M-104 (S63),* 1 October 1963.

17. Miller, H. S., Resolving multiple responses in an associative memory, *IEEE Trans. on Electronic Computers,* v. EC-13, no. 5, October 1964, pp. 614-16.

18. Narasimhan, R., and J. P. Fornango, Some further experiments in the parallel processing of pictures, *IEEE Trans. on Electronic Computers,* v. EC-13, no. 6, December 1964, pp. 748-50.

19. Perotto, P. G., A new method for automatic character recognition, *IEEE Trans. on Electronic Computers,* v. EC-12, no. 5, October 1963, pp. 521-26.

20. Schultz, L., Language, an overview of a range of viewpoints, *SP-1732.* Santa Monica, Calif.: System Development Corp., 30 November 1964.

21. Schultz, L., Toward a system model of human communication, *SP-1763.* Santa Monica, Calif.: System Development Corp., 3 October 1964.

22. Shannon, C. E., and J. McCarthy, eds., *Automata Studies.* Princeton, N. J.: Princeton U. Press, 1956.

23. Shannon, C. E., and W. Weaver, *The Mathematical Theory of Communication.* Urbana, Ill.: U. of Illinois Press, 1949.

24. Slade, A. E., A discussion of associative memories from a device point of view, *Proc. of the Amer. Doc. Institute,* v. 1, Philadelphia, 5-8 October 1964, pp. 331-35.

3

Mathematical Models in Linguistics and Language Processing

H. P. Edmundson

In a book on automated language processing there must be, in addition to examples and applications of such processes, a description of the theoretical foundations. This chapter examines these foundations by describing mathematical models that have been used in research on linguistics and language processing. The purpose of this chapter is to present in sufficient detail a variety of models so that the reader can learn what has been attempted with respect to the linguistic objects or processes being modeled and the theories on which the models have been based.

Instead of presenting various models for each of the linguistic objects or language processes in turn, the method of presentation here is to examine successively various mathematical theories and to give examples of various objects that have been modeled by them. This method of presentation is intended to emphasize the scope of the mathematical theory.

It is clear that a chapter as short as this can scarcely do justice to a topic of this magnitude. Thus, it will be impossible to describe all the theories and models that have been proposed and studied. Moreover, even for those included here, the discussions are necessarily condensed. The models selected for description undoubtedly reflect the interest of the author.

3.1 MATHEMATICS

3.1.1 Definition of Mathematics. Unfortunately, the layman often holds a mistaken view of mathematics. A mathematician is usually considered to be interested solely in numbers, when in fact he is concerned with the structure of abstract objects, particularly as to their deductive consequences, rather than with arithmetic relations. *Mathematics* is the study of abstract objects and their abstract properties and relations. It requires the development of a formal language to give precision to intuitive thinking.

It must be noted especially that mathematics is not a science since it is not directly concerned with physical data or experiments; instead it is concerned with the deduction of necessary consequences from hypotheses. Exactly for this reason mathematics plays a key role in the scientific method as the deductive step that occurs after the hypothesis step and before the testing step.

3.1.2 Branches of Mathematics. The different branches of mathematics arise due to different kinds of mathematical objects. The traditional branches of mathematics of particular interest in the study of mathematical linguistics are logic, analysis, algebra, geometry, probability, and statistics. These branches and their subbranches can be schematized by means of the following diagram where the words in parentheses denote the principal object of study of that branch:

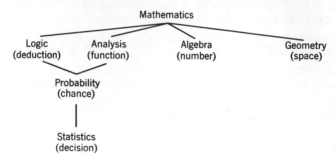

Although there are other branches such as number theory and numerical analysis and more interconnections between branches, the above diagram is sufficient for our present purposes.

In later sections we will explore the above branches in more detail. Of the many logics, we will consider propositional logic, predicate logic, set logic, and relational logic. In analysis we will treat point functions, algebraic equations, differential equations, measure functions, and transformations. For algebra we will consider associative syntactic calculus, semigroup algebra, semi-Thue systems, automata theory, vector algebra, matrix algebra, and Boolean algebra. Under geometry, we will examine metric geometry, projective geometry, topology, graphs and trees, and semilattices and lattices. For probability we will consider mathematical probability, distribution theory, stochastic processes, information theory, and logical probability. In statistics we will treat sampling theory, estimation of parameters, and testing of hypotheses.

3.2   MATHEMATICAL MODELS

The two important uses of mathematics in any science are the formulation of problems and the solution of problems. By training, a mathematician is very effective in formulating a problem in mathematical terms: precisely, abstractly, and with generality. The ability to formulate is just as important as the ability to solve problems by mathematical methods. The use of models by mathematicians permits the careful formulation of problems found in the real world (see Braithwaite, Putnam, Suppes) [22].

Unfortunately, some confusion exists because there are two inversely related concepts of what a mathematical model is. The first concept of a mathematical model is used in pure mathematics when formal axiom systems are being considered. Here, a *model of an axiom system* is a realization that is used to represent the system in a more concrete way. An axiom system can have several models that are isomorphic to one another in the sense that they are formally equivalent. For example, the axioms of Boolean algebra have, as isomorphic models, the logic of propositions and the logic of sets. This concept of a model is a concretization of something more abstract.

The second concept of a mathematical model is used in applied mathematics when physical entities are being considered. Here, a *model of a physical entity* is an abstraction that is used to represent the entity as it is theoretically conceived. For example, Bohr's theory of the atom is a model of physical atoms. This concept of a model is an abstraction of something more concrete.

In this chapter we will be concerned only with the latter concept of model since the objects being modeled are linguistic entities. For example, we will examine several different models of natural grammars and natural languages. Mathematical models provide one of our most powerful tools in the application of mathematics to linguistics since we gain manipulative and deductive power even though we lose some reality.

In a later section we will give a more precise definition of mathematical model.

3.2.1   Types of Physical Entities.   Before defining models of physical entities we must examine the various kinds of physical entities that can be modeled. For this purpose it is helpful to classify physical entities.

An entity is called *static* if its nature is independent of time; otherwise it is called *dynamic*. A single static entity will be called an *object* and a set of static entities will be called a *structure*. A single dynamic entity will be called an *event* and a set of dynamic entities will be called a *process*. For our purposes a *state* will be regarded as an event, while a *system* will be regarded as a process.

A phenomenon may be regarded either as a single physical event occurring in the real world or as a closely related set of such events. If the closely related events are regarded as being principally ordered by time, then the term "process" is preferred. However, another interpretation is often used to define a process by regarding it as a physical system that "causes" an event or a set of events. For example, in linguistics we assume that man has some mental process by which he produces linguistic utterances as output. The linguist F. de Saussure named the process "la langue" and called the set of utterances "la parole".

3.2.2   Types of Models.   A model of an entity is a representation that mirrors certain chosen properties. Hence, a model may serve as a replica, substitute, or simulation of the entity being represented. A model is always an approximation, usually a simplification, and hopefully an aid to insight. An abstract model is said to be *formal* or *symbolic* if the representation is by means of a formal language.

A formal model is said to be *mathematical* if the representation is by means of a set of mathematical expressions (axioms, definitions, or theorems). Mathematical models usually take the form of equations or inequalities. There are two broad classes of mathematical models: deterministic and stochastic. A mathematical model is said to be *deterministic* if it does not involve the concept of probability; otherwise it is said to be *stochastic*. A deterministic model is said to be *logical, analytic, algebraic,* or *geometric*, if its representation is from the theories of logic, analysis, algebra, or geometry, respectively. A stochastic model is said to be *probabilistic* or *statistical,* if its representation is from the theories of probability or statistics, respectively. In practice most mathematical models of physical entities are mixed, rather than pure, in that their representation is from more than one of the above six theories of mathematics. This is particularly true within the class of deterministic models. However, any deterministic model can be made stochastic (but not conversely) by the choice of causal distribution functions. The types of mathematical models are shown in the following diagram:

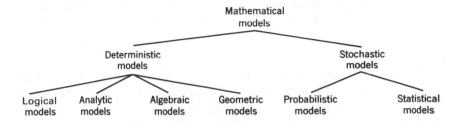

3.2.3 Definition of Mathematical Model. To make the concept of mathematical model clearer, we will introduce some definitions and notations. The three basic concepts will be entity, theory, and model. An *entity E* is defined as a physical entity of the real world. A (mathematical) *theory T* is defined as a mathematical system of uninterpreted symbols $s_1, \ldots, s_n$ (that is, terms and relations on them). A *mathematical model M of entity E using theory T* is defined as a system of E-interpreted symbols $s'_1, \ldots, s'_n$ of T. Here, E-interpretation means that the symbols (terms and relations) $s_1, \ldots, s_n$ of theory T are given in terms of the entity E. The process of interpretation can be pictured in a table of correspondences as follows:

Model M

Symbols of Theory T	E-Interpreted Symbols of Theory T
s_1	s'_1
s_2	s'_2
.	.
.	.
.	.
s_n	s'_n

Note that the concept that M is a model of entity E must be replaced by the concept that M is a T-model of entity E. For example, Shannon's information theory is a probabilistic model of the communication process.

Notice, also, that a model of an entity is not unique since it is a function of the theory selected. For example, as we shall see, sentence structure may be modeled using either the theory of trees or of automata. Moreover, a single theory may serve as the basis for the modeling of different entities. For example, the theory of trees provides models for both sentence structure and communication systems.

The modeling problem may be stated as follows: given an entity E and a set $\{T_i\}$ of theories, find a theory T_i and a model M_j so that E is modeled by $M_j(T_i)$.

3.2.4 Choice of Models. From the definition of a model of an entity, it follows that every entity E has infinitely many different models $M(E)$. That is, there are infinitely many representations $M(E)$ of E. For example, suppose that E has two models $M_1(E)$ and $M_2(E)$:

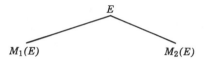

Now, the question is not whether $M_1(E)$ or $M_2(E)$ is the "true" model since models do not have the property of being true or false. However, it is proper to ask the question: Which is the "better" model? The answer to this question will be discussed in a later section. Also, it is important to realize that it is foolish to claim the "best" model since there is none. The ways in which models may differ as to their intended role are discussed next.

3.2.5 Roles of Models. A model may play one or more of the following roles: descriptive, explanatory, or predictive. A model may be *descriptive* in that it describes (tells what) the observed behavior of a physical entity. For example, the Copernican model described the solar system. A model may be *explanatory* in that it explains (tells why) the observed behavior of a physical entity. For example, Newtonian mechanics explained motions in terms of forces. A model may be *predictive* in that it predicts (tells if . . ., then . . .) the unobserved behavior of a physical entity For example, Einstein's theory of gravitation predicted the amount of bending of starlight by the sun. These three roles are not disjoint; in fact, a predictive model is usually descriptive and explanatory. Which role a model plays is relative to its "age"—that is, yesterday's predictive model may be regarded as explanatory today, and descriptive tomorrow.

3.2.6 Properties of Models. Since a model is neither true nor false, we must consider other properties of models. It is important to differentiate two kinds of properties: intrinsic and extrinsic. Properties are called *intrinsic* if they refer to the model itself and *extrinsic* if they refer to physical entities or mathematical deductions. The ultimate intrinsic property of a model is its *consistency*—that is, whether the model is self-consistent or, at least, is relatively consistent with respect to a larger theory. The ultimate extrinsic property of a model is its *adequacy*—that is, how successfully the model explains or predicts.

Many properties of a model can be partially specified. However, the absolute concept of "goodness" of a model must be replaced with the relative concept of "better than". A model is said to be *better than* another if it is better with respect to at least one property, while not worse with respect to all others.

3.3 MODELING

3.3.1 Modeling and Remodeling.   The construction of a model, as a scientific procedure, is founded on the belief that there can be order and reason in the mind, if not in the real world. The construction of a model is closely related to the steps used in the scientific method. To explain these ideas, we will consider three worlds that may be likened to levels of language; real world, deductive world, and inductive world. The real world is regarded as consisting of physical entities. The deductive world is regarded as consisting of symbols and symbol manipulation. The inductive world is regarded as consisting of statements about physical entities, symbols, and symbol manipulation. The construction of an initial model in terms of these worlds is indicated in the following diagram, which is a modification of one due to Bross [3]:

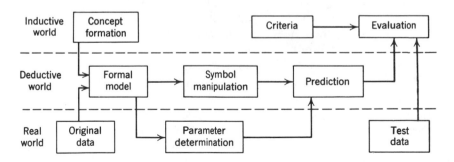

An example of modeling is given by a model of a natural language in which the set of original data is a suitably large corpus, the formal model is a set of grammar rules, the parameter determination is an assignment of grammatical classes to words, the symbol manipulation is

the derivation of strings, the prediction is an infinite set of derived terminal strings, the set of test data is a fresh corpus, and the evaluation is an
informal measure of the adequacy of the grammar.

Just as the construction of an initial model is related to the steps of the
scientific method, so is the improvement of a model by an iterative process of remodeling as indicated in the following diagram:

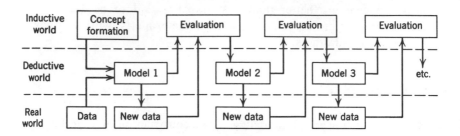

A good linguistic example of the above process is the modeling of a
natural language, first by a finite-state grammar, then by a phrase-structure
grammar, and finally by a transformational grammar. These will be discussed later in this chapter.

3.3.2   Advantages of Modeling.   Now that we have discussed the
definition, properties, and construction of mathematical models, we will
examine in turn their advantages and disadvantages. These topics concern the use and misuse of models rather than their structure.

As we shall see, a mathematical model often better describes a physical entity (or at least some aspects of it) than does a verbal description. Setting concepts into a precise, abstract, and general mathematical
form and stating their interrelations mathematically greatly contribute
to a clearer understanding of these concepts, and also to the comprehension of their quantitative interrelations.

Mathematical modeling of a physical entity can be seen to have the
following general advantages over the use of an informal model: precision, abstractness, generality, compactness, manipulability.

The following specific advantages of mathematical modeling are
some of the criteria that help to decide whether or not it should be used.
Every mathematical model:

a. Indicates the various types of data that should be collected and
   measured.

b. Permits the consideration of the entity as a whole—that is, all of the
   chosen aspects of the entity simultaneously.

c. Permits the determination of the effect of a change of one of the variables on the other variables.

d. Permits known mathematical theories to be used effectively.

e. Is casily integrated with other mathematical models because of their common language.

f. Guides the search for appropriate theoretical tools.

g. Provides a logical and systematic research approach, reference frame, and tools.

h. Prepares the groundwork for the use of electronic data processing techniques.

i. Provides a precise medium for communicating assumptions and consequences.

Some of the possible benefits that may be realized once a mathematical model has been constructed are the following:

a. May make it possible to use mathematical theories that otherwise might appear to have no applicability to the problem.

b. May be enlarged step-by-step to include aspects that were neglected.

c. May uncover new relations between aspects of the physical entity that are not apparent in a verbal description.

d. May suggest informational gaps that otherwise might be overlooked.

e. May reveal the scope and limitations of the theory being used.

f. May indicate the scope and limitations of possible simulation.

g. May permit improvement in future modeling efforts.

h. May suggest more quantitative measures of adequacy.

i. May be the cheapest and fastest way to predict.

3.3.3 Disadvantages of Modeling. The following specific disadvantages of mathematical modeling are more of the criteria that help to decide whether or not it should be used. Every mathematical model:

a. Requires an existing mathematical theory.

b. Requires or produces an over-simplification.

c. Does not guarantee satisfactory predictions.

d. Has no intrinsic scheme for evaluation.

e. Requires a moderate degree of mathematical knowledge and sophistication.

Some of the possible errors that may be made in the construction or use of a mathematical model are the following:

a. May contain nonrelevant variables — that is, variables that do not represent properties of the entity being modeled.
b. May omit critical variables — that is, variables corresponding to important physical properties.
c. May have functions and relations that relate the variables incorrectly or inappropriately.
d. May have wrong or imprecise numerical values assigned to the parameters.
e. May be defined in such a way that it is practically impossible to devise either a direct or indirect test of it.
f. May contain a hidden internal inconsistency.
g. May be unnecessarily detailed and hence unnecessarily complex or large.
h. May be too inflexible — that is, must be abandoned as a whole rather than modified by minor amendments to improve its predictive power.
i. May be based on a theory that has a poorly developed calculus.
j. May be mistakenly identified with, or equated to, the real world.
k. May become a cult, dogma, or fad.

From the above discussion we must conclude that the decision to use a mathematical model to describe or explain an entity is influenced by many factors, some of which are under our control, while some are not, and by many other factors that are matters of personal preference. In the next section we will examine the general nature of models and linguistic processes and their interrelations with language data processing.

3.4   MODELS OF LINGUISTIC ENTITIES

Mathematical models have been applied to some linguistic concepts and problems with partial success. The application of mathematical models to linguistics has necessarily occurred in terms of formulation rather than solution since, until a linguistic problem is mathematically formulated, there is no point to attempt its mathematical solution (see Bar-Hillel, Chao, Chomsky, Householder, Whitfield) [22].

3.4.1   Definition.   A *mathematical model* of a *linguistic entity* is defined as an abstract representation of a natural-language object or process. The level of abstraction can vary from a simple formula to a formal axiomatic system. Whatever the level of abstraction, all models of linguistic entities have at least one of three roles: description, explanation, or prediction. A descriptive model attempts to describe the features of the object or the steps of the process, for example, B. Bloch's immediate-constituent grammar. An explanatory model attempts to explain the object or process, for example, S. Lamb's stratificational grammar. A predictive model attempts to predict future behavior in the form of either new phenomena or new combinations of old ones, for example, N. Chomsky's transformational grammar and V. Yngve's depth hypothesis.

3.4.2 Examples of Models. A linguistic entity may have several models depending on which aspects of the entity the model is intended to stress. For example, let E denote the English language. In one model $M_1(E)$, E is represented by means of geometrical figures denoting parsing trees. In a second model $M_2(E)$, E is represented by means of computer programs that either generate or recognize grammatical strings. In a third model $M_3(E)$, E is represented by means of mathematical expressions that denote the formal rules of the grammar. The following table gives some examples of various modes of representation that have been used in modeling linguistic entities:

Representation	Model
Diagram, flowchart	Sentence parsing, Stratificational grammar
Computer program	Phrase-structure grammar, Dependency grammar
Mathematical formulas	Rank hypothesis, Associative retrieval

Some models of linguistic entities are deterministic, that is, no concept of chance is involved. For example, the depth hypothesis proposed by Yngve is a deterministic model since the fundamental concepts are taken from algebra and geometry. In this model a string of words is regarded as being generated by a finite automaton and each string has its syntactic structure represented by a labeled oriented tree (see [1], [4], [27]).

On the other hand, some models of linguistic entities are stochastic, that is, the concept of chance is crucial. The defining statements of stochastic models are in terms of probabilities, random variables, or distribution functions. For example, the theory of information developed by Shannon is a stochastic model since the fundamental concepts are taken from probability theory. In this model a string of words is regarded as being generated by letters emanating from a source according to given probabilistic laws so that certain features of its statistical behavior can be predicted.

3.4.3 Interrelations. Mathematics can aid in the *analysis* of a corpus of natural-language text by means of computer programs, to produce the data necessary for the formulation of a mathematical model such as those of Chomsky, Zipf, Shannon, Markov, Carnap, and Yngve. Also, mathematics can aid in the *synthesis*, from natural-language text by means of computer programs, of mathematical models of language processes such as automatic translating, indexing, classifying, abstracting, parsing, generating, retrieving, querying, and editing. These interrelations of models and processes are shown in the following figure [see 8]:

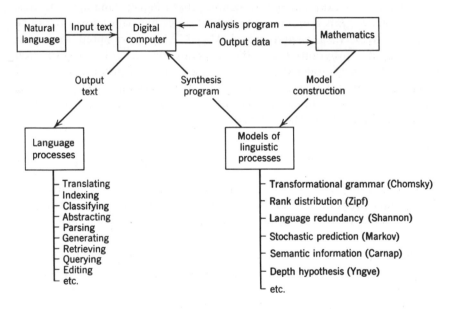

In the following sections we will examine, first, deterministic models, and then stochastic models, of natural-language processes.

3.5 LOGIC

In this section we will consider models of linguistic processes that are based on theories of logic. As we will see, some of these logics lend themselves naturally to the modeling of languages since they themselves were originally constructed out of linguistic considerations concerning the properties of natural languages. Hence, the logics are artificial languages whose properties roughly parallel some properties of natural language. We will confine our attention to models based on the logic of propositions, logic of predicates, logic of sets, and logic of relations.

3.5.1 Logic of Propositions. The *logic of propositions* is also called *propositional logic, propositional calculus,* or *sentential calculus.* This logic concerns propositions, which are denoted by $p, q, r, \ldots$ and assigns to each of them one of two truth values: true (T) or false (F). Only the truth value of a proposition is considered relevant; its meaning plays no role. *Elementary* or *atomic* propositions are defined as those that cannot be decomposed into more basic ones. *Connectives* are logical operations that operate on one or two propositions at a time. The connectives are used to combine given propositions to form *compound propositions* whose truth values may be computed from those of the given ones. The *negation* $\bar{p}$ of p is defined to be true when p is false and false when p is true. The *disjunction* $p \vee q$ of p and q is defined to be true except when both p and q are false. The *conjunction* $p \wedge q$ of p and q is defined to be true only when both p and q are true. The *implication* $p \Rightarrow q$ is defined to be false only when p is true and q is false. A compound proposition is called a *tautology* t or a *contradiction* u if it is true or false, respectively, for all truth values of its elementary propositions.

The logic of propositions has been proposed to model sentences as follows (see Bar-Hillel [1]; Quine [see 16]):

Logic of Propositions	Sentences
proposition p	declarative sentence p
truth value T	true
truth value F	false
tautology t	always-true sentence t
contradiction u	always-false sentence u
logical connectives: $^{-}$, $\vee$, $\wedge$, $\Rightarrow$	function words: "not", "or", "and", "if ..., then ..."
$\bar{p}$	sentence: not p

(Continued)

Logic of Propositions	Sentences
$p \lor q$	sentence: p or q
$p \land q$	sentence: p and q
$p \Rightarrow q$	sentence: if p, then q

3.5.2 Logic of Predicates. The *logic of predicates* is also called *predicate calculus,* the *logic of functions,* or *functional calculus.* This logic concerns the truth value of a proposition by examining those parts that involve individuals and their properties. It treats the subject-predicate features of whole propositions and assigns to every proposition one of the truth values: true or false. Again, only the truth value of a proposition is considered relevant. As a matter of convention, *individuals* are customarily denoted by the symbols $x, y, z, \ldots$, while *predicates* are denoted by the symbols $f, g, h, \ldots$.

A more detailed analysis of a proposition is permitted in this logic by explicitly allowing an individual x to have a *property f*. When x has the property f we have the *propositional function $f(x)$* which is read *"x is f"*. For example, "x is a father". Since the logic of predicates concerns properties of individuals, it is necessary to introduce two new logical constants called *quantifiers* that operate on propositional functions to produce propositions. The *existential* quantifier $\exists$ appears in the expression $(\exists x)$ which means "for some x" or "there exists an x". The *universal* quantifier $\forall$ appears in the expression $(\forall x)$ which means "for all x" or "for every x".

The logic of predicates has been proposed to model sentences by letting properties correspond to the *intensions* of one-place predicates as follows (see Bar-Hillel [1]; Quine [see 16]):

Logic of Predicates	Sentences
individual x	subject (proper name, common noun, or pronoun) x
predicate f	predicate (verb phrase) f
propositional function $f(x)$	x is f
truth value T or F	truth or falsity
tautology $f(x) \lor \overline{f(x)}$	x is f or not f
contradiction $f(x) \land \overline{f(x)}$	x is f and not f
$\overline{f(x)}$	x is not f
$f(x) \lor g(x)$	x is f or g

(Continued)

Logic of Predicates	Sentences
$f(x) \wedge g(x)$	x is f and g
$f(x) \Rightarrow g(x)$	if x is f, then x is g
$(\exists x)f(x)$	some x is f
$(\forall x)f(x)$	all x are f

3.5.3 Logic of Sets. The *logic of sets* is also called the *theory of sets, set theory,* or the *calculus of classes.* This logic concerns operations on and relations between collections of individuals; the collections are called *sets* or *classes* and the individuals are called *points* or *elements.*

The *membership* of the point x in the set A is denoted by $x \in A$. For example, x belongs to the set A of all fathers. Set A is said to be a *subset* of set B $(A \subseteq B)$ provided every point of A is also a point of B. Set A is said to be *equal* to set B $(A = B)$ provided A is a subset of B and B is a subset of A. The *complement* $\overline{A}$ of set A is defined as the set of all points (of the universal set S) that are not in A. The *union* $A \cup B$ of sets A and B is defined as the set of all points that are in at least one of them. The *intersection* $A \cap B$ of sets A and B is defined as the set of all points that are in both of them. The *null* set $\emptyset$ is defined as the complement of the *universal* set S. Sets A and B are called *disjoint* if they have no points in common—that is, $A \cap B = \emptyset$.

The logic of sets has been proposed to model sentences by letting sets correspond to the *extensions* of one-place predicates as follows (see Mooers [21]; Hillman [14]; Fairthorne [9]):

Logic of Sets	Sentences
point x	subject x
set A	predicate a
universal set S	tautologous predicate
null set $\emptyset$	contradictory predicate
$x \in A$	x is a
$A \subseteq B$	predicate a implies predicate b
$\overline{A}$	predicate not-a
$A \cup B$	predicate a or b
$A \cap B$	predicate a and b
$A \cap B = \emptyset$	predicates a and b are contradictory

3.5.4 Logic of Relations. The *logic of relations* is also called the *theory of relations,* the *calculus of relations, relational calculus,* or *rela-*

tional logic. This logic concerns the relations that may or may not exist between two or more individuals. If the relations concern pairs of individuals, then they are called *binary.* We will limit our attention to these. Although a theory of ternary relations (that is, three-place predicates) has been developed, it reduces to the theory of binary relations (that is, two-place predicates).

The foundation of the logic of binary relations is the theory of sets in which a *relation* is defined as a set of ordered pairs (x, y) of elements x and y. Relations will be denoted by the symbols R, S, T, ... The expression xRy denotes that element x stands in the relation R to element y. For example, x is the father of y. The *inverse* relation R^{-1} of R is defined to be the one that holds between y and x when xRy—that is, $yR^{-1}x$ if, and only if, xRy. Relation R is said to be a *subrelation* of S provided R is a subset of S—that is, $R \subseteq S$. Relation R is said to be *equal* to relation S provided R is a subrelation of S and S is a subrelation of R — that is, $R = S$. The *complement* relation $\bar{R}$ of R is defined as the set of ordered pairs for which R does not hold. The *union* $R \cup S$ of R and S is defined as the set of ordered pairs for which either R or S holds. The *intersection* $R \cap S$ of R and S is defined as the set of ordered pairs for which both R and S hold.

The logic of relations has been proposed to model sentences by letting relations correspond to the *extensions* of two-place predicates as follows (see Abernathy, Curry [16]; Edmundson [7]).

Logic of Relations	Sentences
element x	subject x
relation R	subject-subject predicate r
universal relation U	tautologous predicate
null relation $\emptyset$	contradictory predicate
xRy	x is r of y
$xR^{-1}y$	y is r of x
$R \subseteq S$	predicate r implies predicate s
$\bar{R}$	predicate not-r
$R \cap S$	predicate r and s
$R \cup S$	predicate r or s

3.5.5   Summary of Logical Models. From the foregoing survey of logical models we have seen that the logic of propositions concerns only the truth values of a sentence when regarded as a whole, while the logic of predicates analyzes only the subject-predicate structure of a sentence in terms of individuals and their properties. The logic of sets parallels the logic of one-place predicates by analyzing the structure of sentences only in terms of individuals and their membership in sets. The logic of binary relations is a special case of the logic of sets in the sense that relations are sets of ordered pairs of elements. It appears that the logic of propositions is far too primitive to provide interesting models of sentences. On the other hand, the logic of relations seems most appropriate so long as we are content to ignore the concepts of necessity and possibility which are treated only in modal logics.

In the next section we will examine the branch of mathematics called analysis.

3.6 ANALYSIS

In the nontechnical sense analysis refers to the process of analyzing or investigating, and hence, can be applied in all branches of mathematics. However, in the following discussion we will be concerned with the technical meaning of analysis and examine models based on the theories of functions, equations, and transformations.

3.6.1 Functions. The fundamental concept in analysis is that of function. Let f be a relation between the elements x of set A and the elements y of set B. The relation f is said to be a *function* from A onto B ($f:A \rightarrow B$) provided there exists exactly one y corresponding to each x. The functional relation is expressed by xfy if f is the name of the function. Notice that this modern definition refuses to specify which element is dependent and which is independent. The *graph* of the function f is defined as the set of all ordered pairs (x, y) such that xfy. If f is a function and xfy then, in the sense of the correspondence mentioned above, we customarily write $y = f(x)$ and call x the *argument* of the function f and call y the *value* of the function f for the argument x. The *domain* of f is the set A of all arguments x of f and the *range* of f is the set B of all values y of f.

3.6.2 Point Functions. A *point function* is defined as one whose domain has points as elements. It is customarily denoted by the letters $f, g, h, \ldots$ as in the study of differential and integral calculus. For example, particular point functions are ordinate, slope, and curvature.

Perhaps the simplest model based on a point function of one argument concerns the frequency of occurrence of words in a corpus of text. The frequency function is a function of one argument, namely, the distinct words of the text; and the values of the function are nonnegative integers. The resulting function model of frequency of occurrence is:

Point Functions	Word Frequency
argument i	word i
function f	number of occurrences of a word
value $f(i)$	number of occurrences of word i
domain of f	set of all words in text
range of f	subset of nonnegative integers
graph of f	plot of number of occurrences versus words

A model based on a point function of two arguments concerns indexing and relevance. The conventional model of indexing is simply a way of expressing a yes or no decision. For a given document D and index term I, either I applies to D or it does not apply. Thus, the deterministic notion of the relevance $r(D, I)$ of document D to index term I can be quantized by means of the function

$$r(D, I) \; = \; \left\{ \begin{array}{ll} 1 & \text{if } I \text{ applies to } D \\ 0 & \text{if } I \text{ does not apply to } D \end{array} \right.$$

Such quantification of qualitative concepts is usually, although not necessarily, performed in modeling. The following function model of relevance results:

Point Functions	Document Relevance
argument D	document D
argument I	index term I
function r	relevance of document to index term
value $r(D, I)$	0 or 1
domain of r	set of all ordered pairs of documents and index terms
range of r	set $\{0, 1\}$
graph of r	plot of relevances versus ordered pairs of documents and index terms

3.6.3   Algebraic Equations.   In many cases a model of a process is best expressed in terms of the functional relations that hold between the assumed variables of the model. The simplest such case expresses the interrelations of these variables by means of a set of one or more algebraic equations. Since, in a mathematical sense, the solution of these equations is implicitly contained in them, the model may also be represented by the solution itself. Despite the fact that the solution represents the functional relation in a highly succinct way, it is often preferable to state the model in terms of the original equations since it is there that the assumptions are laid bare.

V. Giuliano and P. Jones [10] have modeled information retrieval by means of a system of algebraic equations. Since the equations are linear, the technique is called linear associative retrieval. For a collection of d documents and t index terms the following assumptions were made:

a. The relevance r_i of document i to a question is a linear function of the weights w_j of the index terms, that is:

$$r_1 = a_{11}w_1 + \cdots + a_{1t}w_t$$

$$\vdots$$

$$r_d = a_{d1}w_1 + \cdots + a_{dt}w_t$$

b. The weight w_j of an index term is the original weight q_j assigned by the question plus a linear function of the relevance r_j of the documents containing it, that is

$$w_1 = b_{11}r_1 + \cdots + b_{1d}r_d + q_1$$

$$\vdots$$

$$w_t = b_{t1}r_1 + \cdots + b_{td}r_d + q_t$$

The relevances r_i can be expressed in terms of the given quantities a_{ij}, b_{ji}, and q_j by eliminating the weights w_j. The following table summarizes the linear model of associative retrieval:

Linear Algebraic Equations	Linear Associative Retrieval
argument i	document i
argument j	index term j
value r_i	relevance of document i to question
value w_j	weight of index term j
value q_j	original weight of index term j for question
parameter a_{ij}	relevance factor
product $a_{ij}w_j$	relevance of index term j for document i
$r_i = a_{i1}w_1 + \cdots + a_{it}w_t$	relevance assumption

(Continued)

Linear Algebraic Equations	Linear Associative Retrieval
parameter b_{ji}	weight factor
product $b_{ji}r_i$	weight of index term j for document i
$w_j = b_{j1}r_1 + \cdots + b_{jd}r_d + q_j$	weight assumption

Another model using algebraic equations has been proposed by
H. P. Edmundson to select sentences for an abstract by means of various
linguistic factors, and combine them to form a single factor. Suppose that each
s_i denotes a factor such as semantic, syntactic, locational or editorial. To
each s_i associate a weight w_i and form the *linear combination* $t = \Sigma_i w_i s_i$ of
the s_i. The parameters w_i then can be adjusted to reflect the relative importance of the factors s_i. It is convenient, but not necessary, to select
the values of the parameters to form a *convex linear combination* $t = \Sigma_i w_i s_i$
where the w_i are nonnegative and sum to 1. The linear model of sentence
significance is summarized by:

Linear Algebraic Equations	Sentence Significance
integer i	linguistic factor i
value s_i	significance value of factor i for sentence
value w_i	weight of factor i
product $w_i s_i$	weighted significance of sentence for factor i
sum $w_1 s_1 + \cdots + w_n s_n$	weighted significance value of sentence

3.6.4 Differential Equations. In addition to algebraic equations, a
second important source for models is the theory of differential equations. This theory provides a natural setting for many physical processes
that are inherently concerned with the rate of change of one quantity
as a function of change of another quantity. The theory of differential
equations uses the concepts and results of differential and integral calculus,
which will not be described here. Models that rely upon the theory of
differential equations typically take the form of a set of one or more equations that express the functional relations of several variables in terms of
their *derivatives*. These models may also be represented by the functions
that form the solutions to the original differential equations and that are
obtained by the methods of *integration*.

For example, the bilogarithmic type-token ratio has been proposed to
model the quantification of writing style since it remains relatively constant for different sample sizes from a given literary corpus. Instead of
conjecturing the bilogarithmic relation from empirical evidence, G.
Herdan [13] derived it from more basic linguistic assumptions. This

derivation is similar to those of the exponential law of growth encountered in biostatistics, in which the rate of growth of a system, growing
uniformly, is at any moment proportional to the size of the system, decreases with increasing age (size), and is affected by external environment. Herdan assumed that the growth rate of the vocabulary is simultaneously proportional to (1) a vocabulary constant, (2) the size of the
present vocabulary, and (3) certain environmental conditions such as
style and content. Similarly, he assumed that the growth rate of the text
length is simultaneously proportional to (1) a length constant, (2) the
length of the present text, and (3) the environmental conditions such
as style and content. These assumptions were translated into mathematical expressions involving continuous functions for simplicity. Let
$v(t)$ denote the vocabulary size at time t and let $n(t)$ denote the text
length at time t. Moreover, let k_v and k_n denote the constants for
vocabulary and text length, respectively. Finally, let $g(t)$ denote all the
environmental factors of growth of a linguistic system as influenced by
the style of the writer and the content of the text.

The above two sets of three conditions concerning the rates of growth
are expressed by the following set of simultaneous differential equations

$$\frac{d\,v(t)}{dt} = k_v v(t)g(t)$$

$$\frac{dn(t)}{dt} = k_n n(t)g(t)$$

whose solution is

$$\frac{\log v(t)}{\log n(t)} = c \qquad\qquad c = k_v/k_n$$

which is the desired relation for the constancy of the bilogarithmic type-
token ratio. Herdan's differential-equation model of the type-token relation may be summarized as follows:

Differential Equations	Type-Token Relation
variable t	time
function value $v(t)$	vocabulary size (number of types) at time t
function value $n(t)$	text size (number of tokens) at time t
derivative $d\,v(t)/dt$	rate of vocabulary growth
derivative $d\,n(t)/dt$	rate of text growth
diff. eq. $f(v,n,dv/dt,dn/dt)=0$	fundamental type-token relation

3.6.5 Measure Functions. An important subclass of set functions consists of measure functions. A *measure function* is defined as a function, from sets into the real numbers, that is nonnegative and additive. The condition of nonnegativity assures that the measure of any set is a nonnegative real number. The condition of additivity assures that the measure of the union of two disjoint sets is equal to the sum of their measures, and that the measure of the empty set is zero. For example, particular measure functions for sets are cardinality, length, area, volume, and probability.

In the logic of sets we examined the notion of a set and a variety of relations between sets. We will now consider the notion of the number of points in a set. If we were dealing only with finite sets (sets having a finite number of points), we would encounter little difficulty. However, we also must consider infinite sets, that is, sets having infinitely many points. The *cardinality $N(A)$* of the set A is (roughly) the number of points in A. The cardinality of A is said to be *equal* to the cardinality of B provided their points are in a one-to-one correspondence.

As a measure function, cardinality has been proposed by G. Salton, T. Tanimoto, and others [see 2, 8] to model the similarity of index terms with respect to a set of documents. In general, the similarity of two sets A and B may be defined as the following ratio:

$$\frac{N(A \cap B)}{N(A \cup B)}$$

The following table summarizes this cardinality model of index-term similarity:

Set Theory	Index-Term Similarity
A	set of documents indexed by term A
$A \cap B$	set of documents indexed by terms A and B
$A \cup B$	set of documents indexed by term A or B
$N(A \cap B)$	number of documents indexed by terms A and B
$N(A \cup B)$	number of documents indexed by term A or B
$N(A \cap B)/N(A \cup B)$	similarity of index terms A and B

3.6.6 Transformations. Another important subclass of set functions consists of transformations. A function is called an *operator* or *transfor-*

mation on a set A provided the domain and range are the same set A — that is,

$$f: A \rightarrow A$$

This means that each element is mapped into a unique element that is also in A. The *product* $g * f$ of the transformations f and g is defined as the application first of the transformation f and second of the transformation g. In general, the product of transformations is not *commutative* — that is, $g * f \neq f * g$. However, transformations are *associative* — that is, $f * (g * h) = (f * g) * h = f * g * h$.

N. Chomsky [6] has used the notion of transformation in modeling the grammar of a natural language. His grammatical transformations are applied to elements called *phrase-markers*, which give structural descriptions of sentences. A phrase-marker $s(x)$ is modeled either by a labeled tree or a labeled bracketing of the immediate-constituent structure of the sentence x. For example, the sentence $x = abc$ may have the phrase-marker $s(x)$:

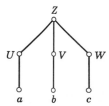

A *transformational rule* (T-rule) is defined as one of the form

$$T: s(x) \rightarrow s(y)$$

where $s(x)$ and $s(y)$ denote phrase-markers. Thus, a grammatical transformation T is a rule that maps a phrase-marker (sentence x with a given structure $s(x)$) into a new derived phrase-marker (sentence y with a new structure $s(y)$). For example, if the transformation is the permutation rule $T: UVW \rightarrow WVU$, then the above phrase-marker $s(x)$ with $x = abc$ is transformed into the new phrase-marker $s(y)$ with $y = cba$:

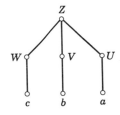

Transformational grammars provide a more adequate model of a language than do phrase-structure grammars because they account for relations between sentences. The following table summarizes N. Chomsky's transformational model of grammar:

Transformation Theory	Transformational Grammar
terminal node a	word a
terminal string x	sentence x
nonterminal node W	grammatical class W
branch ZW	relation of immediate constituency of W to Z
labeled tree $s(x)$	structural description (phrase-marker) of sentence x
transformation T	rule of structural change

3.6.7 Summary of Analytic Models. From the above survey of analytic models we have seen that, in some cases, the concept of a function is used in the sense of a point function to describe the variables of the model, while in other cases it appears in the form of a set function. Most models of linguistic processes involve analytic concepts in one way or another and the fundamental relations between the variables take the form of algebraic or differential equations. In both cases the complexity of the model depends upon the number and type of the equations. The solution or solutions to the set of equations is also said to represent the model.

3.7 ALGEBRA

In the nontechnical sense, algebra refers to the process of reckoning or calculating. However, in the following discussion we will be concerned with the technical meaning of algebra and examine models based on the theories of discrete quantities such as numbers, vectors, and matrices and the operations performed on them such as addition and multiplication. In fact, there are algebras for each of these quantities, and for many other discrete systems of generalized numbers.

3.7.1 Associative Syntactic Calculus. In this section we will consider associative syntactic calculi that were developed initially by S.

Lesniewski and K. Ajdukiewicz as a formal decision procedure in logic for determining whether a string of symbols is a well-formed formula or not. This was accomplished by establishing a system of categories and a system of rules that operate on the categories.

First, we assume a finite set C of *primitive categories* c_1, c_2, . . . , c_n and second, from the primitive categories we form the set C' of *derived categories* c_1', c_2', . . . by the following recursive definition: if a and b are categories, then ab, a/b, and $a\backslash b$ are categories where a/b is read *"a super b"* or *"a over b"* and $a\backslash b$ is read *"a sub b"* or *"a under b"*. The meaning of this notation can be made clearer by the following definitions. *Product:* string xy is said to belong to category ab provided string x belongs to category a and string y belongs to category b. *Right-diagonalization:* string x is said to belong to category a/b provided string xy belongs to category a for all strings y belonging to category b. *Left-diagonalization:* string y is said to belong to category $a\backslash b$ provided string xy belongs to category b for all strings x belonging to category a. *Rewrite* or *convert:* $a \rightarrow b$ denotes that every string x that belongs to category a also belongs to category b. Each member v of the given vocabulary V is assigned one or more categories a_i according to an *assignment function* $A(v)$. The following two rules of *cancellation* or *resolution* permit the simplification of a sequence of two categories to one category:

$$(1) \ (a/b)b \rightarrow a$$
$$(2) \ b(b\backslash a) \rightarrow a$$

where (1) means the category a/b when followed by category b is rewritten as category a and (2) means that category $b\backslash a$ when preceded by category b is rewritten as category a. The connectives of left and right diagonalization were chosen by analogy with the division sign in arithmetic. Hence, the above rules are called cancellation rules since in both cases the "multiplier" simplifies the "fraction" to its "numerator".

Although the concept of various categories for sentences, phrases, words, and so on is an old one, Y. Bar-Hillel [1], J. Lambek [18], and others have developed a theory of categorial grammars to model natural grammars. Words and phrases are assigned a very limited number of possible categories. The categories are given an arithmetic or algebraic representation so that the decision procedure is an algorithm that operates on these categories in a mechanistic way to recognize sentences from nonsentences. The following table summarizes the modeling of a grammar by an associative syntactic calculus:

Associative Syntactic Calculus	Categorial Grammar
vocabulary symbol v	word v
assignment function $A(v) = a$	word v has grammatical class a
string x	phrase x
primitive category s	sentence class
primitive category n	noun class
right diagonalization /	premodifier
left diagonalization \	postmodifier
derived category n/n	adjective class
derived category $(n/n)/(n/n)$	adverb class
derived category $n\backslash s$	intransitive verb class
derived category $(n\backslash s)/n$	transitive verb class
derived category $(s\backslash s)/n$	preposition class
derived category $(s\backslash s)/s$	conjunction class
$a \rightarrow b$	if phrase x belongs to class a, then it belongs to class b
cancellation rules	rules for simplifying grammatical classes

3.7.2 Semigroup Algebra. The algebra of semigroups and monoids has received increasing attention in mathematical linguistics. A *semigroup* is defined as an algebraic system $(A, *)$ in which A is a set of elements and $*$ is a binary operation that is *closed* ($x, y \in A$ imply $x * y \in A$) and *associative* ($x * (y * z) = (x * y) * z$) with respect to these elements. A *monoid* is defined as an algebraic system $(A, *)$ in which A is a set of elements and $*$ is a binary operation that is closed, associative with respect to these elements, and the set A has an *identity* element e ($x * e = e * x = x$). Thus, a monoid is a semigroup with an identity element.

The theory of semigroups and monoids has been applied to the study of formal grammars and languages by N. Chomsky and P. Schützenberger [see 1, 5, 6]. Let A denote a finite *alphabet* or *vocabulary* of symbols a_i. A *string* x is defined as any finite sequence (under concatenation) of symbols from A — that is,

$$x = a_{i_1} \cdots a_{i_n} \qquad\qquad n = 0,1,\ldots$$

The *concatenate* xy of the strings $x = a_{i_1} \cdots a_{i_n}$ and $y = a_{i_{n+1}} \cdots a_{i_m}$ is defined as the string

$$xy = a_{i_1} \cdots a_{i_n} a_{i_{n+1}} \cdots a_{i_m}$$

The *identity element* e is the empty string—that is, the string of length zero. Now, it can be shown that the set of all nonempty strings of elements of A under the operation of concatenation is a semigroup, called the *free semigroup generated by* A. Note, however, that the set of all words of a natural language under the operation of concatenation is not a free semigroup since the set is not closed. Also, it can be shown that the set A^* of all (empty or nonempty) strings of elements of A under the operation of concatenation is a monoid, called the *free monoid generated by* A, where the empty string is the identity element e for A^*.

The following table summarizes the free-monoid model of language proposed by Chomsky and Schützenberger:

Free Monoid	Language
element a_i	symbol (letter, space, punctuation, word, etc.)
set A	alphabet or vocabulary
identity element e	empty string e
binary operation $*$	concatenation of strings
finite sequence x of elements	string x of symbols
free monoid A^*	set of all strings (grammatical and ungrammatical)

3.7.3 Semi-Thue System or Associative Calculus. In this section we will examine some models of grammar that are based upon the theory of semi-Thue systems or associative calculi developed by A. Markov, E. Post, and others [see 1]. These theories are of recent origin and represent a distinct break with the past since they were proposed as models of the competence of a native speaker of a language rather than of his performance. For this reason these formal grammars are called *generative* instead of taxonomic or descriptive [see 4,6].

The *vocabulary* V is defined as a finite set of elements called *symbols* and is partitioned into two exhaustive and exclusive subsets called the *terminal vocabulary* T and the *nonterminal, intermediate,* or *auxiliary vocabulary* V-T. The terminal vocabulary T is defined as a nonempty finite subset of *terminal symbols* $a, b, c, \ldots$. T is sometimes considered to contain the identity element e and the boundary element $\#$. The nonterminal vocabulary V-T is defined as a nonempty finite subset of *nonterminal symbols* $A, B, C, \ldots$ and contains a distinguished element called the *initial symbol* S. A *string* over V is defined as a finite sequence of symbols of V. The *set of all strings over* V is denoted by V^*. The *empty* *string e* is a member of V^* such that $ex = xe = x$ for all strings x over V. The string x is called a *terminal string* provided x is a string over the terminal vocabulary T.

We will now see how an associative calculus was used by N. Chomsky [6] to model grammar and language. A *grammar* is defined as an ordered quadruple $G = \{V,T,S,P\}$ where the vocabulary V is a nonempty finite set of symbols, the terminal vocabulary T is a nonempty subset of V, the initial symbol S is a distinguished element of the nonterminal vocabulary V-T, and the set P of *productions* is a nonempty finite set of rewriting rules of the form

$$x \rightarrow y \qquad\qquad\qquad x,y \in V^*$$

where $\rightarrow$ is a binary relation defined on certain strings over V and is interpreted as "is rewritten as". Chomsky [5] has defined four important classes of grammars called *finite-state, context-free, context-sensitive,* and *unrestricted grammars* and proved that each class is a proper subset of the next. The string x is said to be *generated by G* provided x is generated from the initial symbol S. The string x is said to be a *sentence* of G provided x is a terminal string generated by G. The *language L = L(G) generated by the grammar G* over the vocabulary V is defined as the set (finite or denumerable) of all sentences x of G. Similarly, Chomsky defined four corresponding classes of languages called *finite-state, context-free, context-sensitive,* and *unrestricted languages* and proved that each class is a proper subset of the next.

The following table summarizes Chomsky's [4, 5, 6] model of a generative grammar for a natural language:

Associative Calculus	Grammar and Language
terminal symbol	word
set T of terminal symbols	vocabulary of language
set V-T of nonterminal symbols	grammatical classes (parts of speech)
initial symbol S	sentence class S
string x of symbols	phrase x
empty string e	phrase e of length zero
production $x \rightarrow y$	grammar rule
set P of all productions	set P of grammar rules
ordered quadruple $G = \{V,T,S,P\}$	grammar G

(Continued)

Associative Calculus	Grammar and Language
terminal string generated from initial symbol	grammatical sentence
set L of all terminal strings generated from initial symbol	language L

The above formal grammars and languages represent an important class of models since they are mathematically simple. In addition they have the important property of being related in a definite way to the various automata discussed next. However, despite these virtues, it would be premature to claim that the problem of modeling of natural languages by means of formal grammars has been solved. What can be claimed is that totally new insights have resulted and new tools have been fashioned.

3.7.4 Automata Theory. As may be guessed, the automata of A. Turing, E. Moore, M. Rabin and D. Scott, and others have provided models of great linguistic interest [see 1]. This is due to several reasons. First, automata seem to be natural or appropriate since they involve concepts similar to those of word, string, input, and output. Second, automata have enough complexity to match that of natural grammars and languages.

An *automaton* is defined as an abstract machine of finite size at any time with certain parts specified as inputs and outputs such that what happens at the outputs at any time is determined (either exactly or probabilistically) by what happened at the inputs. The purpose of an automaton is to transform information. However, an automaton must be distinguished from a computer since the former is abstract while the latter is concrete.

An automaton is composed from three kinds of idealized units: one or more tapes, one head for each tape, and one control. A *tape* is conceived as a strip that extends finitely (but unboundedly) far to the left and right, may move either one or two ways, and is divided into discrete segments called *cells* or *squares*. A *head* is conceived as a device that scans a tape, one cell at a time, and performs one or more of three operations: read, write, or erase a symbol. The *control* is conceived as having several internal parts that are arrangeable in a variety of distinct ways. Each of the possible arrangements of the internal parts of the control is called a *state* s_i of the automaton. The set of states may be finite or infinite and contains a distinguished state s_0 called the *initial state* and a distinguished proper subset F of states called the set of *final states*. The number of states is an indication of the amount of memory of an automaton. An automaton is in a particular state at a particular time and switches from one state to another according to a set of *instructions*.

Many different types of automata have been defined, such as a *finite automaton* (fa) which has a one-way tape and a write head, a *pushdown-storage automaton* (pda) which has a one-way tape with a read head and a two-way tape with a read-write-erase head, a *linear-bounded automaton* (lba) which has a two-way tape and read-write head, a *finite transducer* (ft) which has a one-way tape with a read head and a one-way tape with a write head, a *Turing machine* (tm) which has a two-way tape with a read-write head, and a *universal Turing machine* (utm) which simulates an arbitrary Turing machine.

The following table summarizes automata models of a generative grammar for a natural language [see 1, 5]:

Automaton	Grammar and Language
alphabet A	vocabulary A
symbol a_i	word a_i
tape x	phrase x
empty tape e	phrase e of length zero
instruction	grammar rule
set of instructions	set of grammar rules
initial set S of states	grammatical class s_i
initial state s_0	sentence class s_0
set of all states	set of all grammatical classes
number of states	number of grammatical classes
automaton	generative grammar
generated tape	sentence (grammatical)
set of generated tapes	language generated by grammar
equivalence of two automata	equivalence of two grammars

Using a variant of the above concept of automaton, V. Yngve [27] proposed a model of a generative grammar for natural language that predicted certain syntactic properties of sentences involving what he called *depth*. The following table summarizes this automaton model:

Pushdown Automaton	Grammar and Language
symbol	word or grammatical class
state	present word or class, plus next class

(Continued)

Pushdown Automaton	Grammar and Language
contents of permanent store	vocabulary and grammar
instruction	grammar rule
two-way temporary storage tape	temporary memory
length of temporary storage tape	maximum depth of sentences
contents of computing register	present word or grammatical class
one-way output tape	sentence

3.7.5   Vector Algebra.   In classical mathematics, the only algebra developed was the algebra of real numbers. Such numbers are called *scalars* since their principal attribute is that of magnitude: for example, the integers, rational numbers, and real numbers such as -1, 0, 1, 3/2, π, and e. The notion of scalars was generalized to that of vectors.

Informally, a (finite) vector is an ordered set (linear array) of scalars —that is, the *vector a* is an n-tuple $(a_1, \ldots, a_n)$ whose *components* or *elements* are the scalars a_i where $i = 1, \ldots, n$. The *zero* or *null* vector o is one whose components are all zero—that is, $a_i = 0$. The *scalar product* ka of a vector a by the scalar k is the vector b defined by $b_i = ka_i$. The *sum* $a + b$ of the vectors $a = (a_1, \ldots, a_n)$ and $b = (b_1, \ldots, b_n)$ is the vector c defined by $c_i = a_i + b_i$. The *inner* or *dot product* $a \cdot b$ of the vectors $a = (a_1, \ldots, a_n)$ and $b = (b_1, \ldots, b_n)$ is the scalar defined by

$$a \cdot b = \sum_{i=1}^{n} a_i b_i = a_1 b_1 + \cdots + a_n b_n$$

To complement the algebraic nature of vectors it is instructive to establish a geometric representation for them as follows. In general, a (finite) vector corresponds to a point in an n-dimensional space. An *n-dimensional vector space* is one whose base vectors are n-tuples, the *dimension* being the number of components in every base vector in the vector space. Vectors conveniently allow us to describe algebraically a high-dimensional space that cannot be easily pictured geometrically.

Some linguistic applications of vectors will now be given. Vectors have been used to model a process in information storage and retrieval known as *coordinate indexing*. This model is summarized in the following table:

Vector	Document Indexing
integer i	index term i
coordinate a_i	weight of index term i for document a
vector a	indexing representation of document a

(Continued)

Vector	Coordinate Indexing
dimension n	maximum indexing depth
inner product $a \cdot b$	similarity of documents a and b

As another example, vectors can be used to model the Jakobson-Fant-Halle [15] distinctive-feature table for phonemes. The following table summarizes this model:

Vector	Distinctive Features of Phonemes
integer i	distinctive feature i
coordinate a_i	presence or absence of distinctive feature i in phoneme a
vector a	distinctive features of phoneme a
dimension n	number of distinctive features

3.7.6 Matrix Algebra. Just as scalars may be generalized to vectors, so may vectors be generalized to algebraic quantities called matrices. Informally, a matrix is a doubly ordered set (rectangular array) of scalars. Formally, the *matrix A* is an ordered m-tuple of n-tuples whose elements are a_{ij} where $i = 1, \ldots, m$ and $j = 1, \ldots, n$. Thus, the matrix A is a rectangular array of elements a_{ij} having m rows and n columns, and is denoted in any of the following ways:

$$A = \underset{m \times n}{A} = \begin{bmatrix} a_{11} & a_{12} & \cdots & a_{1n} \\ a_{21} & a_{22} & \cdots & a_{2n} \\ \cdot & \cdot & & \cdot \\ \cdot & \cdot & & \cdot \\ \cdot & \cdot & & \cdot \\ a_{m1} & a_{m2} & \cdots & a_{mn} \end{bmatrix} = (a_{ij})$$

If $m = n$, the matrix is called *square*. The *zero* or *null* matrix is one whose elements are all zero—that is, $a_{ij} = 0$ for $i = 1, \ldots, m$ and $j = 1, \ldots, n$. The *scalar product* kA of a matrix A by the scalar k is the matrix B defined by $b_{ij} = ka_{ij}$. The *sum* $A + B$ of matrices $\underset{m \times n}{A} = (a_{ij})$ and $\underset{m \times n}{B} = (b_{ij})$ is the matrix C defined by $c_{ij} = a_{ij} + b_{ij}$. The *product* AB of matrices $\underset{m \times r}{A} = (a_{ij})$ and $\underset{r \times n}{B} = (b_{ij})$ is the matrix $\underset{m \times n}{C}$ defined by $c_{ij} = \Sigma a_{ik}b_{kj} = a_{i1}b_{1j} + \cdots + a_{in}b_{nj}$. The *transpose* A' of matrix A is the matrix C defined by $a_{ij}^{t} = a_{ji}$—that is, a matrix whose rows and columns are, respectively, the columns and rows of A.

We will now consider several matrix models of linguistic entities. First, suppose a corpus of documents is indexed by a set of index terms. Let the

rows of a matrix A correspond to the index term and the columns correspond to the documents. Matrix A is called an *incidence* matrix if a_{ij} equals
1 or 0 according to whether or not index term i is relevant to document j.
Then it can be shown that the products AA' and $A'A$ correspond to two
frequency matrices, for documents and index terms, respectively. The
following table summarizes this matrix model of document indexing:

Matrix Algebra	Document Indexing
row i	index term i
column j	document j
element a_{ij}	1 if index term i is relevant to document j ; 0 if otherwise
incidence matrix $A = (a_{ij})$	relevance of terms to documents
$i_1 i_2$-th element of frequency matrix AA'	number of documents common to terms i_1 and i_2
$j_1 j_2$-th element of frequency matrix $A'A$	number of terms common to documents j_1 and j_2

As a second example, C. Osgood [23] has proposed a matrix model for
a concept in semantics that he calls the *semantic differential*. By psy-
chologically testing the similarity of word pairs, he sought to isolate a
small number of semantic factors using the statistical method of factor
analysis. The purely matrix aspects of the model are summarized below:

Matrix	Semantic Differential
row i	semantic factor i
column j	word j
element a_{ij}	weight of factor i for word j
j-th column A_j of A	set of weights for word j
$\bar{a}_j = \frac{1}{n} A_j \cdot A_j \ (1 \cdots 1)$	mean weight for word j
$A_j \cdot A_k - n\,\bar{a}_j \bar{a}_k$	semantic similarity of words j and k

3.7.7 Boolean Algebra. The algebraic system, called Boolean algebra in honor of the English mathematician G. Boole, was originally developed as the algebra of sets but subsequently has assumed importance
as an abstract algebra whose applications extend beyond logic into the
theory of partially ordered systems such as lattices.

A *Boolean algebra* is defined as a system $(S, \cdot, *, ', 0, 1)$ for which the
following axioms hold:

Axiom 1: The binary operations $\cdot$ and $*$ are commutative.

Axiom 2: Each binary operation is distributive over the other.

Axiom 3: There exist in the set S two distinct identity elements 0 and 1 relative to the binary operations $\cdot$ and $*$, respectively.

Axiom 4: The unary operation $'$ is such that for every element a in set S there exists an element a' in S such that $a \cdot a' = 1$ and $a * a' = 0$.

Two important examples are the following:

a. The algebra $(\{A\}, \cup, \cap, {}^-, \emptyset, V)$ of subsets A of a set V is a Boolean algebra.

b. The algebra $(\{p\}, \vee, \wedge, {}^-, u, t)$ of propositions p is a Boolean algebra.

It is not necessary that the set S be infinite. In fact, the set S consisting of the elements 0 and 1, together with the operations defined by the following tables, is a Boolean algebra.

$'$				$\cdot$	0	1		$*$	0	1
0	1			0	0	1		0	0	0
1	0			1	1	1		1	0	1

The use of Boolean algebras to model the storage and retrieval of information was proposed by M. Taube and others. The following table summarizes this Boolean-algebra model of document indexing [see 2, 14]:

Boolean Algebra	Document Indexing
element a	set of all documents indexed under term a
0	set of no documents
1	set of all documents
a'	set of all documents not indexed under term a
$a * b$	set of all documents indexed under terms a and b
$a \cdot b$	set of all documents indexed under term a or b

This model has largely been accepted on faith by many workers in the field. However, the inadequacies of this model have been pointed out by C. Mooers [21] and D. Hillman [14] who correctly observe that Boolean algebra has been confused with *Boolean polynomial* or *function* (one whose domain and range is the set $\{0, 1\}$) which is appropriate.

3.7.8 Summary of Algebraic Models. In the above survey of algebraic models we have seen that such models are appropriate if the fundamental objects of the linguistic process are intrinsically discrete in nature. Associative syntactic calculi offer a theoretical basis in those cases where all the objects may be placed in a small number of distinct categories. Semigroup algebras are appropriate when the objects of the system may be concatenated to form longer strings of objects, and semi-Thue systems or associative calculi may be used when the system involves substitution algorithms for the rewriting of strings of objects. Automata theory provides an appropriate model when the linguistic system involves either the generation, acceptance, or transduction of strings of objects. Vector algebra is appropriate when the linguistic entities may be regarded as having a fixed number of more elementary components, while matrix algebra yields an appropriate model when the entities may be classified simultaneously with respect to two distinct sets of components—that is, rows and columns. Boolean algebra may be used particularly when the linguistic entities inherently involve a unary operator and two binary operators in a way completely analogous to the logic of propositions or the logic of sets.

3.8 GEOMETRY

In this section we will discuss several geometric models of linguistic entities. As we will see, the geometric theories are related to certain analytic and algebraic theories. For example, the concept of a metric space depends on the concept of a distance function and is related to that of a vector space.

First, we will treat models based upon both metric and nonmetric geometries. Of metric geometries we will consider Euclidean spaces, while in nonmetric geometry we will examine a particular projective geometry called barycentric, as well as several topological spaces. Last, because it is intuitively proper in a discussion of geometries, we will examine the theory of certain partially ordered sets called graphs, trees, semilattices, and lattices.

3.8.1 Metric Geometry.   Consider a set S of elements x (of any nature whatever) and a function d mapping pairs (x,y) of elements into the set R of real numbers. The space (S,d) is called a *metric space* provided the function d is nonnegative, symmetric, equals zero if and only if $x = y$, and satisfies $d(x,z) \le d(x,y) + d(y,z)$; otherwise it is called *nonmetric*. We also say that S is a metric space with *metric d*. The value $d(x,y)$ is called the *distance* between x and y. The last condition above is called the "triangle inequality" since it generalizes the statement from plane geometry that the length of any side of a triangle is less than or equal to the sum of the lengths of the other two sides.

An *n-dimensional Euclidean space* E_n is defined as the set of all *n*-tuples of real numbers $(x_1, x_2, \ldots, x_n)$ where the *Euclidean distance* in E_n between the two points $x = (x_1, x_2, \ldots, x_n)$ and $y = (y_1, y_2, \ldots, y_n)$ is defined by

$$d(x,y) = \left\{ (x_1 - y_1)^2 + \cdots + (x_n - y_n)^2 \right\}^{1/2} = \left\{ \sum_{i=1}^{n} (x_i - y_i)^2 \right\}^{1/2}$$

In the *n*-dimensional case we have *n* straight lines called the $x_1, x_2, \ldots, x_n$ *axes* which are perpendicular to one another and intersect at a point called the *origin*. A *point P* in E_n is defined by the *n*-tuple $(x_1, x_2, \ldots, x_n)$ of real numbers where the *coordinates* $x_1, x_2, \ldots, x_n$ are measured from the origin $(0, 0, \ldots, 0)$ along the corresponding axes. Thus, a point $(x_1, \ldots, x_n)$ is seen to be a vector by our previous algebraic definition since an *n*-dimensional vector is simply an *n*-tuple. Because it is difficult to represent geometrically more than three dimensions on a two-dimensional surface such as paper or blackboard, we rely on these algebraic expressions.

Euclidean spaces have been proposed to model what linguists call a *semantic space* in which points correspond to words and distance corresponds to their semantic similarity [see 8, 23]. The simpler aspects of this model are summarized in the following table:

Euclidean Space	Semantic Distance
coordinate or axis x_i	semantic property or sense x_i
origin	neutral or null sense
point x	word x
region	set of words
space S	set of all words
distance $d(x,y)$	semantic similarity of words x and y

However, the difficulty with these suggestions is that there is no basis for selecting either the type or number of the semantic properties. Moreover, the choice of a Euclidean metric is linguistically unsupported.

Euclidean space has also been suggested to model the relevance of an index term to a document. One of the more interesting models was proposed by R. Hayes [2] to account for the similarity of two documents with respect to an indexer. This model depends on the geometric fact that in a Euclidean space the distance between two points x and y is related to the angle $a(x,y)$ formed by the lines from each of the points to the origin, which is given by

$$\cos a(x,y) = \frac{x \cdot y}{(x \cdot x)^{1/2}(y \cdot y)^{1/2}} = \frac{x \cdot y}{d(o,x)\,d(o,y)}$$

The following table summarizes the interpretations in this model:

Euclidean Space	Document Similarity
coordinate x_i	relevance of index term i to document x
point x	index representation of document x
origin o	indexer or indexing protocol
distance $d(o,x)$	importance of document to indexer
angle $a(x,y)$	similarity of documents x and y with respect to indexer

Another aspect of automatic indexing concerns the dual notions of index space (the set of all index terms) and document space (the set of all documents). A point in the index space corresponds to a unique index term; a point in the document space corresponds to a unique document. Since the problem of classifying documents with respect to the set of index terms is the same, mathematically, as that of classifying index terms with respect to the set of documents, one problem is called the *dual* of the other. The distance between two points in index space is a measure of the "closeness" of the corresponding index terms.

3.8.2 Projective Geometry.   In this and the next section we will consider nonmetric geometry. The first geometry to be discussed is a representation of plane projective geometry by means of barycentric coordinates. This theory affords a model of the representation of documents by means of index terms and with the measurement of relevance of documents to information requests.

To establish a coordinate system in the projective plane, we assume four points P_1, P_2, P_3, and D, no three collinear. The triangle $P_1P_2P_3$ is called the *triangle of reference*. Then it can be shown that the projective coordinates of a finite point P, interpreted metrically, are proportional to multiples of the directed distances from the sides of the triangle of reference to P: the multipliers are the reciprocals of the corresponding directed distances from the sides to the unit point. One such metric interpretation of projective coordinates is given by barycentric coordinates. As *barycentric coordinates* for the point P we use three masses m_1, m_2, m_3, which are placed at the vertices P_1, P_2, P_3 of the triangle of reference so that P becomes the center of gravity of the triangle. It can be shown that the masses m_1, m_2, m_3 are proportional to the distances z_1, z_2, z_3 of the point P from each of the sides of the triangle as shown below. The point D, obtained by taking the intersections of the medians, is called the *unit point* of the projective coordinate system since $(1, 1, 1)$ is a simple set of barycentric coordinates for it.

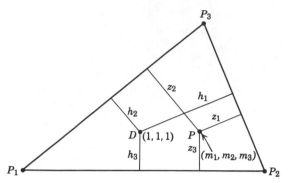

Thus, every point P is described by infinitely many projective coordinates (m_1, m_2, m_3), each with different masses but the same relative proportions. The above concept of barycentric coordinates for the plane can be extended to projective spaces of higher dimensions.

R. Hayes [2] has proposed to model the indexing of documents by means of barycentric coordinates. In this model the vertices of the triangle of reference are interpreted as a set of index terms and the mass at each vertex is interpreted as the weight assigned to the corresponding index term. The point P is interpreted as a document whose barycentric coordinates m_i are the weights of the document with respect to each of the index terms so that the mass $m = \Sigma_i\, m_i$ of point P is the value of the document in the library. The barycentric model of document indexing is summarized as follows:

Projective Geometry	Document Indexing
barycentric vertex P_i	index term i
mass m_i at vertex P_i	weight m_i assigned to index term i
unit point D	center of interest in library
point P	document P
barycentric coordinates $(m_1, \ldots, m_n)$ of P	weights of document with respect to each index term
mass $m = \Sigma_i\, m_i$ of point P	total value of document in library

Although the above model is theoretically interesting, no serious attempts have been made to implement or test it even on a small scale.

We will now examine another nonmetric geometry that is topological rather than projective.

3.8.3 Topology. A *topological property* of a geometrical figure is one that remains invariant under a topological (that is, bicontinuous) transformation. *Point-set topology* is the study of the topological prop-·erties (for example, open, closed, compact, connected) of sets. A set can be assigned a *topology* by specifying a family of subsets with the property that certain operations, when applied to members of the family, produce sets that are also members of the family.

A set S is said to have a *neighborhood topology* if there exist subsets called *neighborhoods* N_x of points x such that (1) every point x has a neighborhood N_x containing it, (2) the intersection of two neighborhoods of a point x contains a third neighborhood of x, and (3) every point y in a neighborhood N_x of x has its own neighborhood N_y contained in N_x. These axioms can be pictured informally by the following Euler diagrams:

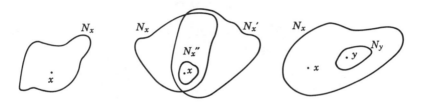

A set S is said to have a *closure topology* if there exists a unary opera-ation ~ called the *closure* on its subsets E such that (1) the closure of the null set is null, (2) every set is contained in its closure, (3) the closure of a set contains the closure of its closure, and (4) the closure of the union of two sets equals the union of their closures.

Two topological models have been proposed by H. P. Edmundson to model the synonymy of words. Assume that synonymy is a ternary relation among words. Let yS_ix denote that word y is synonymous in sense i with word x. The synonymy relation S_i is assumed to be reflexive, symmetric, and transitive. The i-synonym class of a word x is defined by

$$s_i(x) = \{y : yS_ix\}$$

This definition may be extended to an arbitrary set E of words by

$$s_i(E) = \{y : (\exists x)(x \epsilon E \wedge yS_ix)\}$$

First, define the i-neighborhood $N_i(x)$ of a word x as any subset of the synonym class of x that also contains x,

$$x \epsilon N_i(x) \subseteq s_i(x)$$

Then it follows that the above neighborhood axioms are satisfied. The following table summarizes the modeling of synonymy by a neighborhood topology:

Neighborhood Topology	Synonymy
point x	word x
set E	class E of words
$E \cap F$	class of words in E and F
$E \subseteq F$	every word in E is in F
space S	vocabulary
neighborhood N_x of point x	synonym class $N_i(x)$ of word x for sense i

Second, define the closure of a set E of words as the synonym class of E,

$$\tilde{E} = s_i(E)$$

Then it follows that the above closure axioms are satisfied. The following table summarizes the modeling of synonymy by a closure topology:

Closure Topology	Synonymy
point x	word x
set E	class E of words
$E \cup F$	class of words in E or F
$E \subseteq F$	every word in E is in F
null set $\emptyset$	class of no words
space S	vocabulary
closure $\tilde{E}$ of set E	synonym class $s_i(E)$ of word class E for sense i

The adequacy of these models remains unexplored.

3.8.4 Graphs and Trees.   In this section we will examine the theory of graphs and trees and indicate how this theory can be used to model certain linguistic entities. Before doing so, however, it is necessary to discuss the binary relation of partial order.

The relation of partial order is a generalization or relaxation of linear order. The relation R is said to be a *partial order* on a set S provided R is

a. *Reflexive:* for all x in S, x stands in relation R to itself.

b. *Antisymmetric:* for all x and y in S, if x stands in relation R to y and y stands in relation R to x, then x is identical to y.

c. *Transitive:* for all *x, y,* and *z* in *S,* if *x* stands in relation *R* to *y* and *y* stands in relation *R* to *z,* then *x* stands in relation *R* to *z.*

A *partially ordered set* or *system (S,R)* is defined as a set *S* with a binary relation *R* that is reflexive, antisymmetric, and transitive. As we shall see, the graph of a partially ordered set is a directed graph.

As a foundation for the study of trees, we will begin with the study of graphs. In nonmetric geometry a graph is a set of points together with a set of lines joining the points subject to several rules. A *linear graph* is defined as a set of *n* points and the lines joining them in pairs so that each pair is either connected by just one line (that is, no *parallels*) or not connected, and no line joins a point to itself (that is, no *loops*). In a graph the points and lines are often called *nodes* and *branches*, respectively. A *subgraph* of a graph is defined as a graph consisting of some of the points and some of the lines of the original graph. A *path* is defined as a subgraph of the form $p_1p_2, p_2p_3, \ldots, p_{k-1}p_k$ with no point p_i repeated. A *cycle* is defined as a subgraph of the form $p_1p_2, p_2p_3, \ldots, p_kp_1$ where the points p_i are distinct except for the initial and terminal point p_1. A graph is said to be *labeled* if its points are not regarded as alike and the distinct points are kept distinct by labels. A graph is said to be *directed* or *oriented* if each of its lines is assigned one of the two possible directions, which is usually indicated by an arrowhead. A graph is said to be *connected* if every pair of points is joined by a path. A *tree* is defined as a connected linear graph without cycles. A *rooted tree* is defined as a tree with one point called the *root* distinguished from all other points by this very fact.

Graphs have been used by G. Salton, L. Doyle, and others to model the associations between pairs of words, documents, or categories [see 10]. If the points are interpreted as words, then a line connecting two points is interpreted as the co-occurrence of the two words in a given document or set of documents. Hence, the total graph is interpreted as the set of all associations among the words of the corpus. This graph model is summarized in the following table:

Graph	Word Association
node	word
branch	co-occurrence of two words in one document
graph	set of all word associations
length of path	degree of association between two words

Also, the syntactic structure of sentences has been modeled by labeled oriented trees—not just trees [see 6]. Abbreviations are customarily used to label the nodes of the trees and the orientation of the tree is given by the partial ordering of the nodes starting at the root of the tree. We will now give two tree models of syntactic structure. First, consider immediate-constituent or phrase-structure analysis as developed by R. Wells, C. Hockett, and others. A sequence of words is said to be a *constituent of type A* if one can trace the sequence back to the single node labeled *A*. The *immediate constituents* of any construction (node) are the nodes that immediately branch from that node. For example, the immediate-constituent analysis of the sentence "Little girls like dolls." is:

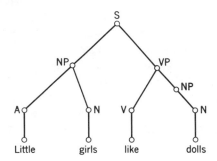

Notice that the constituents are *immediate* in terms of the level of branching of nodes in the structural tree, not in the sense of immediately contiguous locations in the sentence—that is, above and below in the tree, not left and right in the sentence. The tree model of immediate-constituent analysis is summarized as follows [see 4, 27]:

Tree	Immediate-Constituent Analysis
node	construction or constituent
node label	word or grammatical class
branch	immediate-constituent relation
branch label	grammatical relation
root	sentence
leaf	word
tree	phrase structure of sentence

Second, consider dependency analysis as developed by L. Tesnière, Y. Lecerf, D. Hays, and others. Exactly one word token (say, main verb) in a sentence is assumed to be independent and is called the *origin*. Every other word token in the sentence is assumed to depend on exactly one other word token. Hence, every word token, except the origin, depends either directly or indirectly on the origin. The *dependency* relation is regarded as the inverse of the *government* relation. The dependents of any word (node) are the nodes that branch from it. For example, the dependency analysis of the above sentence is:

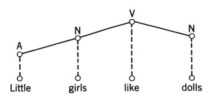

The tree model of dependency analysis is summarized as follows [see 12]:

Tree	Dependency Analysis
node	word
node label	word or grammatical class
branch	dependency relation
branch label	grammatical relation
root	independent word (grammatical class)
leaf	word
tree	dependency structure of sentence

A third model based on categorial analysis also has been studied [see 1, 18].

3.8.5 Semilattices and Lattices.   We will now see how the theory of semilattices and lattices can be used to model linguistic entities. First, however, we must introduce some definitions concerning the mathematical concept of bounds.

As before, consider a partially ordered set *(S,R)*. It will be convenient to read the expression xRy as "y includes x", "y contains x", "x is included in y", or "x is contained in y". Using the notion of partial order of the elements of S we can define bounds for elements of S. An *upper bound* of two elements is defined as an element of S that contains both. The *join* or *least upper bound* $x \cup y$ of two elements x and y is defined as an upper bound that is contained in every other upper bound. A *lower bound* of two elements is defined as an element of S that is contained in both. The *meet* or *greatest lower bound* $x \cap y$ of two elements x and y is defined as a lower bound that contains every other lower bound. By definition, every join and meet are unique, if they exist.

A *(lower) semilattice* is defined as a partially ordered system (S,R) in which every pair of elements x and y has a meet $x \cap y$. Every semilattice can be represented geometrically by a directed graph. Each element of the system is represented by a node so placed that the node for y is above that for x if xRy. A descending line is drawn from y to x provided y contains x and no other element is contained in y and contains x. The relation xRy can be reconstructed from the graph provided it is possible to climb from x to y along an ascending branch in the graph. An *(upper) semilattice* is defined in terms of the *dual* operation of join.

The theory of semilattices has been proposed by D. Hillman and others to model the indexing of documents [see 9].

Semilattice	Document Indexing
element x	index term x
partial order relation R	relation "more specific than"
meet $x \cap y$	least specific term that is more specific than both x and y

A *lattice* is defined as a partially ordered system (S,R) in which every pair of elements x and y has a meet $x \cap y$ and a join $x \cup y$. Every lattice can be represented geometrically by a directed graph. Each element of the system is represented by a node so placed that the node for y is above that for x if xRy. A descending line is drawn from y to x in case y contains x and no other element is contained in y and contains x. The relation xRy can be reconstructed from the graph provided it is possible to climb from x to y along an ascending branch in the graph. According to the above definition, every Boolean algebra is a lattice, but not conversely.

Lattices have been proposed by R. Fairthorne [9] to model some of the semantic aspects of a thesaurus. Thus, when the elements $x, y, \ldots$ are interpreted as thesaurus heads and the partial order relation is interpreted as "less general than", hierarchical relationships may be expressed and studied as lattice properties.

Lattice	Thesaurus
element x	thesaurus head x
partial order relation R	relation "less general than"
join $x \cup y$	least general head that is more general than either x or y
meet $x \cap y$	most general head that is less general than both x and y

As another example, R. Hayes [2] has proposed the following lattice model. Consider a dictionary of terms in which the entry for each term consists of two lists containing terms that are more general than and more specific than the given term, respectively. The relations of "more general" and "more specific" suggest that the dictionary terms be modeled by a partially ordered system in which the set S is the collection of basic terms and the binary relation R is "more general". This model is given by a lattice in which the most general terms correspond to the nodes immediately covered by the universal element 1 and the most specific terms correspond to the nodes that immediately cover the null element 0.

3.8.6 Summary of Geometric Models. From the above survey of geometry we have seen that geometric models are appropriate if the fundamental linguistic entities can be conceived in terms of spaces, distances, intersections, projections, and so on. Metric spaces apply only when a concept of distance makes sense for the fundamental variables of the linguistic process. Euclidean spaces may be used only if the Euclidean metric is a reasonable one. Nonmetric geometries are appropriate provided it is unrealistic to assume a distance function. Projective geometries apply when it is important to regard that points and lines are duals of one another in the sense that two points determine a unique line and two lines determine a unique point. Topological spaces are appropriate when the dominant concepts are those of invariance of geometric figures under continuous stretchings or deformations. Partially ordered sets are applicable whenever some of the elements are incomparable in terms of linear order. Graphs and trees can be used when the elements are discrete and every element is related to at least one other element to form chains of related elements. Semilattices are appropriate if, in addition to the above requirement, every pair of elements has either a least upper bound or a greatest lower bound; lattices apply when every pair of elements has both.

3.9   PROBABILITY

In the following sections we will treat models based upon mathematical and logical probability. In the case of mathematical probability we will examine the theory of A. N. Kolmogorov, while in logical probability we will examine the theory created by R. Carnap.

3.9.1 Mathematical Probability. Probability, and hence, statistics, deals with repetitive events where an *event A* is a type of outcome of an experiment or trial. The set of all logically possible outcomes is called the *event space S*. It is important to note that probability is defined only for events (that is, subsets A of the set S), and that it is meaningless to talk about probabilities unless there is a well-defined set of events. In the classical relative-frequency theory of probability, the *probability* of an event A in a space S of events was defined as the limit of the relative frequency of occurrence

$$P(A) = \lim_{n \to \infty} \frac{m}{n}$$

where m is the number of occurrences of A in n trials. For technical reasons this theory is inadequate to treat some important event spaces S, so the modern axiomatic theory of Kolmogorov is used instead. This theory accounts for a very large class of events by means of an implicit definition of probability. The *probability function P* is defined as a real-valued set function whose domain consists of subsets A of a space S such that P is nonnegative, normed, and additive — that is,

Axiom 1 (Nonnegative): $P(A) \geq 0$
Axiom 2 (Normed): $P(S) = 1$
Axiom 3 (Additive): $P(A \cup B) = P(A) + P(B)$ for $A \cap B = \emptyset$

Events are defined as subsets of the space S, which is also called the *probability space,* and the notions of set theory are made to correspond to the notions of events as follows. Event A is said to be probabilistically *impossible* provided $P(A) = 0$, even though A may be logically possible. Event A is said to be probabilistically *certain* or *sure* provided $P(A) = 1$; even though A may not be logically certain. In addition to the absolute probability $P(A)$, we require another type of probability. The above definition of absolute probability is used to define the *conditional probability* $P(A \mid B)$ that A occurs, given that B has occurred, by setting

$$P(A \mid B) = P(A \cap B)/P(B) \qquad\qquad P(B) \neq 0$$

The most important notion in probability theory is that of independent events. Two events A and B are said to be (probabilistically or stochastically) *independent,* provided

$$P(A \cap B) = P(A)P(B)$$

M. Maron and J. Kuhns [20] proposed a probabilistic model of literature indexing and searching in a mechanized library system. A concept of relevance was developed from probability theory, which, given an index term I_j, allows the making of a statistical inference and the derivation of a relevance number $r(D_k, I_j)$ for each document D_k. This is done by defining the *relevance* $r(D_k, I_j)$ to be the conditional probability $P(D_k \mid I_j)$ that the document D_k satisfies the user, given that the request used index term I_j. Document D_1 is said to be *more relevant* to index term I_j than document D_2 if its relevance is greater — that is, $r(D_1, I_j) > r(D_2, I_j)$. The result of a search is an ordered list of the documents that satisfy the request, ranked according to their relevance to the request. In practice, $P(D_k \mid I_j)$ can be calculated from Bayes' theorem

$$P(D_k \mid I_j) = \frac{P(D_k)\, P(I_j \mid D_k)}{P(I_j)}$$

where $P(D_k)$ is the prior probability that D_k will satisfy the request, $P(I_j)$ is the prior probability of choosing index term I_j, and $P(I_j \mid D_k)$ is the conditional probability that the user will formulate a request by using index term I_j, given that he wants information contained in D_k. The probability $P(I_j \mid D_k)$, which corresponds to the degree to which term I_j applies to document D_k, is estimated by the indexer. The following table summarizes this probabilistic model of document indexing:

Probability Theory	Document Indexing
event I_j	index term I_j
event D_k	document D_k
absolute probability $P(D_k)$	likelihood that document D_k satisfies request
absolute probability $P(I_j)$	likelihood of choosing index term I_j
conditional probability $P(D_k \mid I_j)$	relevance of document D_k to request given that index term I_j was used
conditional probability $P(I_j \mid D_k)$	weight of index term I_j for document D_k

We will now give another example of a simple probability model that has been proposed in the field of comparative linguistics. Despite the fact that the term *index* is involved, the reader should be warned that its use here has no relation to that in the preceding model. J. Greenberg [11] sought to define a quantitative objective measure of linguistic diversity to replace qualitative subjective opinion. In the simplest case, consider a region with two languages. As a measure of linguistic uniformity, he used the probability p that two individuals selected at random speak the same language and, as a measure of linguistic diversity, he used $1-p$. Hence, the minimal diversity corresponds to 0 and the maximal diversity corresponds to 1. In the general case, consider a region comprising speakers of r languages in which the proportion of speakers of language j is p_j, where $j = 1, \ldots, r$. Then the probability $p_1^2 + \cdots + p_r^2$ that two speakers selected at random speak the same language serves as an index of linguistic uniformity. Hence, the *index of linguistic diversity* is

$$A = 1 - \sum_{j=1}^{r} p_j^2 \qquad \text{where } \sum_{j=1}^{r} p_j = 1$$

The following table summarizes Greenberg's probabilistic model of linguistic diversity:

Probability Theory	Linguistic Diversity
integer r	number of languages
integer j	language j
probability p_j	proportion of speakers of language j
$1 - \sum_{j=1}^{r} p_j^2$	index of linguistic diversity

3.9.2 Distribution Theory. Distribution theory is used in statistics but is founded on probability concepts. If we consider an event space S of events A, then any function defined on S is called a *random* or *stochastic variable* and is customarily denoted by a capital letter, say X. It is customary to denote the value that a random variable can assume by the lower case of the capital letter that denotes the random variable, for example, X assumes value x. Thus, the random variable X is simply a way of describing the distribution of the total probability mass or weight of 1 over the points or sets of points of S. A random variable is said to be *discrete* if it can assume only discrete values (for example, the length or the number of words); a random variable is said to be *continuous* if it can assume a continuous interval of values (for example, the amplitude or the pitch of speech). The *probability mass function* of a discrete random variable X is defined by the function

$$f(x) = P(X = x)$$

The *probability density function* of a continuous random variable X is defined by the derivative

$$f(x) = \frac{d}{dx} P(X \le x)$$

Every random variable X has a *distribution* representable by its graph $y = f(x)$. A distribution is called *discrete* or *continuous,* depending on whether its random variable is discrete or continuous. For a discrete distribution the graph is a step-like function and for a continuous distribution the graph is a smooth curve. In general the distribution for a population is a function of several population *parameters* $\Theta_1, \ldots, \Theta_k$ so that $f(x)$ should be written $f(x; \Theta_1, \ldots, \Theta_k)$. By specifying the parameters we specify a particular curve of a family of curves.

   To illustrate a probability model that concerns a distribution function we will next present two examples. In the first, the lognormal distribution will be used to model the distribution of word and sentence length, while in the second the geometric distribution will be used to model the distribution of gaps between word repetitions.

   First, we will consider the distribution of word length. Word length can be measured in terms of the number of letters, syllables, or phonemes. Empirical evidence shows that word length, and hence sentence length, has a distribution that is skewed to the right, that is, the distribution has its long tail to the right. In statistical linguistics we often encounter distributions that are skewed, rather than symmetrical. One class of these distributions that are skewed to the right (called positive skewness) can be transformed into the class of normal distributions that are symmetric by taking the logarithm of the random variable. A random variable X is said to have a *lognormal distribution* if the random variable log X has a normal distribution—that is,

$$f(x) = \frac{1}{\sigma x \sqrt{2\pi}} e^{-(\log x - \mu)^2/2\sigma^2} \qquad x > 0$$

G. Yule [28], C. Williams [25], and G. Herdan [13] have studied the distribution of word length in terms of both number of letters and number of phonemes in large samples of English text and have concluded that the distribution of word length is adequately modeled by the lognormal distribution. This probability model of word-length distribution can be summarized as follows:

Distribution Theory	Word-Length Distribution
random variable X	theoretical word length
value x	actual word length
real number $e^{\mu + \sigma^2/2}$	theoretical mean of word length
real number $e^{2\mu + 2\sigma^2} - e^{2\mu + \sigma^2}$	theoretical variance of word length
lognormal distribution $f(x)$	distribution of word length

Second, we will consider the distribution of repetitions of a word type. The *gap* or *interval* between repetitions of a word type is defined as the number of word tokens between, but excluding, the tokens in question. For example, if two successive tokens are the same word type, then the gap or interval is zero; if they are separated by one token, then the interval is one, and so on. Let x denote the length of the interval between repetitions of word type i, p_i denote the probability of word type i, and $q_{ii}^{(x)}$ denote the probability of an interval of length x between words of type i. In general the probability $q_{ii}^{(x)}$ that word type i is followed x times by words of other types and then repeated at the $(x + 1)$-st position is given by the geometric density function

$$q_{ii}^{(x)} = (1 - p_i)^x p_i \qquad\qquad x = 0, 1, \ldots$$

Thus, the probability of intervals of length x decreases asymptotically to 0 as x increases. Since long intervals are rare, the Poisson distribution, which has been extensively tabulated, can be used to approximate the probability of long intervals. The following table summarizes this probability model of gaps:

Distribution Theory	Gap Distribution
variable i	word type i
value x of random variable X	length x of interval or gap between occurrences of a word type
probability p_i	likelihood of word type i
geometric density function $q_{ii}^{(x)}$	distribution of gap length for word type i

V. Yngve [26] analyzed gaps as a method of investigating the structure of sentences. He hoped that deviations of the observed number from the expected number would reveal the structural constraints between word types in a language. The frequency of gaps of various lengths between occurrences of two specified word types was counted. The results were then compared with what would be theoretically expected under the hypothesis that the two word types were statistically independent, and the hypothesis was rejected.

3.9.3 Stochastic Processes.

We will now turn our attention to a particular branch of modern probability theory called stochastic processes. Their study is important in mathematical linguistics because they provide models of certain random phenomena that are interesting to the linguist. For example, a knowledge of stochastic processes permits a clearer view of several linguistically important topics such as Zipf's rank hypothesis, Shannon's information theory, and Chomsky's finite-state grammars (see Herdan [13] and Edmundson [8].

Informally, a stochastic process is defined as a probabilistic model of a physical process whose evolution is a function of time. This concept can be made precise by representing the outcomes of the dependent trials as a random variable $X(t)$ that is a function of a real variable t which denotes time. Hence, formally, a *stochastic process* is defined as a set $\{X(t)\}$ of time-dependent random variables. When t takes on a specified value t_1, then $X(t_1)$ is simply a random variable as defined previously. For our purposes the stochastic processes called simple finite Markov chains are important. A *simple finite Markov chain* is a sequence $\{X_n: n = 1, 2, \ldots\}$ of random variables X_n that can assume only a finite number of values called *states* $i = 1, \ldots, r$ and the present state i_n depends probabilistically only on the preceding state i_{n-1} —that is,

$$P(X_n = i_n \mid X_1 = i_1 \wedge X_2 = i_2 \wedge \ldots \wedge X_{n-1} = i_{n-1})$$
$$= P(X_n = i_n \mid X_{n-1} = i_{n-1})$$

The system is said to be in state i at time n if $X_n = i$. A simple finite Markov chain is completely determined by two probabilistic quantities: a vector of initial probabilities and a matrix of transition probabilities. The *initial probability vector* $a^{(0)}$ describes the initial probability distribution of the system at time $n = 0$,

$$a^{(0)} = (a_1^{(0)}, \ldots, a_r^{(0)})$$

where $a_i^{(0)} = P(X_0 = i)$. The *transition probability matrix* P describes the one-step transition probabilities from state to state,

$$P = (p_{ik}) \qquad\qquad i,k = 1, \ldots, r$$

where $p_{ik} = P(X_{n+1} = k \mid X_n = i)$. Roughly speaking, the initial vector starts the process and the transition matrix keeps it stepping. Hence, a Markov chain is a stochastic process with some amnesia present, in the sense that the probability that state k occurs next, given that state i occurs now, is stochastically independent of what states occurred before. Thus, a Markov chain is the first possible generalization beyond a completely independent sequence of trials. Finite Markov chains of general *order m* can be defined by replacing the above conditional probability statement for simple chains by

$$P(X_n = i_n \mid X_1 = i_1 \wedge X_2 = i_2 \wedge \ldots \wedge X_{n-1} = i_{n-1})$$
$$= P(X_n = i_n \mid X_{n-m} = i_{n-m} \wedge \ldots \wedge X_{n-1} = i_{n-1})$$

Therefore, in an *m*-th order Markov chain the present state depends probabilistically only on the preceding *m* states.

We will now consider a stochastic model of language proposed by C. Hockett [see 16] and others that is based on the theory of Markov chains and is more general than Chomsky's finite-state model. Suppose we have an alphabet of *r* symbols or states—the symbols could be letters, letters plus a word space, entire words, phrases, or parts of speech. Let $a_i^{(0)}$ be the absolute probability that the text begins with symbol *i*. Let p_{ik} be the conditional probability that symbol *k* occurs next, given that symbol *i* has just occurred. A string of symbols is generated by this Markov process. Given the transition probabilities, we can compute the conditional probability that in *n* steps we move from symbol *i* to symbol *k*. The Markov-chain model of text generation can be summarized as follows [see 8, 5, 24]:

Markov Chain	Probabilistic Finite-State Language
step *n*	position in text
state *i*	symbol: letter, space, punctuation, word, etc.
number *r* of states	size of vocabulary
initial probability $a_i^{(0)}$	likelihood of starting with symbol *i*
n-step absolute probability $a_i^{(n)}$	likelihood that *n*-th symbol is *i*
1-step transition probability p_{ik}	likelihood that symbol *i* is succeeded by symbol *k*
n-step transition probability $p_{ik}^{(n)}$	likelihood that *n*-th symbol after symbol *i* is *k*

However, the basic limitation of the theory of simple Markov processes makes them inadequate as models of natural languages. By definition, simple Markov processes are stochastic processes for which the state of the system at time *n* depends only upon its state at time *n* − *1,* and not at all upon its state at time *n* − *m* for *m* > *1.* Sentences contain constraints operating over much greater time (space) ranges than this. The higher the order of the Markov chain, the closer the model approximates the generation of English words. However, the estimation of the higher-order transition probabilities becomes correspondingly more difficult and, beyond a certain order, does not result in a significantly better model of English.

3.9.4 Information Theory.   In this section we will see how stochastic processes were used as the theoretical foundation to model a communication system.

The theory of information created by C. Shannon [24] concerns the amount of information communicated by a source that generates messages. This theory does not treat the meaning of a single message, but is concerned with the statistical rarity of logically possible messages. The transmission of information may be initiated by a source. Every source that generates *messages* composed from a finite alphabet of r discrete *symbols* can be represented by a discrete random variable X defined over the symbols $x = 1, \ldots, r$, with $p_x = P(X = x)$. The simplest possible alphabet consists of just two symbols, say the binary digits 0 and 1, and its messages are called *binary sequences.* This provides the basic unit of information called the *bit* (a contraction of the words *binary unit*), which is defined as the amount of information contained in the choice of one out of two equiprobable symbols (for example, 0 or 1, yes or no). Every message whose alphabet has r symbols may be *coded* into such a binary sequence. In general, each symbol of an r-symbol alphabet contains $\log_2 r$ bits, since that is the number of binary digits required to transmit each symbol. For example, a decimal digit represents $\log_2 10 = 3.32$ bits, a Roman letter represents $\log_2 26 = 4.68$ bits, and a Cyrillic letter represents $\log_2 32 = 5.00$ bits. For the discrete source X, Shannon defined a measure of uncertainty

$$H(X) = H(p_1, \ldots, p_r) = - \sum_{x=1}^{r} p_x \log_2 p_x$$

measured in bits per symbol, called the *entropy* of the source. The minus sign in the above expression makes $H(X) \geq 0$ since logarithms of the p_x are negative. For a general r it can be shown that the minimum value of $H(p_1, \ldots, p_r)$ is 0 bits per symbol and this occurs when exactly one symbol is certain; and that the maximum value of $H(p_1, \ldots, p_r)$ is $\log_2 r$ bits per symbol and this occurs when all symbols are equiprobable. Because of this, the ratio $H(X)/\log_2 r$ is called the *relative entropy* and the difference

$$1 - \frac{H(X)}{\log_2 r}$$

is called the *redundancy* or *inefficiency* of the source. The redundancy gives the factor by which the average lengths of messages are increased due to intersymbol statistical behavior beyond the theoretical minimum length necessary to transmit the desired message.

Shannon [24] developed an information-theoretic model of a communication system that applies to natural language. The discrete message *source* is defined as a discrete random variable X and the *transmitted messages* are defined as finite sequences of symbols x. The *receiver* is defined by another random variable Y and the *received messages* are defined as corresponding finite sequences of symbols y. The transmitted message becomes a received message after being carried through a *channel* defined by the pair (X,Y) of random variables. The conditional probabilities $P(X = x \mid Y = y)$ and $P(Y = y \mid X = x)$, rather than the absolute probabilities $P(X = x)$ and $P(Y = y)$, characterize the channel. The statistical difference between the set of transmitted messages and the set of received messages is used to define the information *capacity* of the channel, that is, the maximum information carried by the channel. Loss of communicated information is said to be due to another random variable Z called the *noise* in the channel. In the case of a noiseless channel, the capacity reduces to max $H(X)$. The following table summarizes Shannon's information-theoretic model of a noiseless verbal communication system:

Information Theory	Verbal Communication System
source X	speaker
transmitted message $x_{i_1} \cdots x_{i_n}$	spoken utterance
coder	brain-voice
channel (X,Y)	air
decoder	brain-ear
receiver Y	hearer
received message $y_{j_1} \cdots y_{j_m}$	heard utterance
entropy $H(X)$	uncertainty of next utterance
capacity max $H(X)$	maximum communication flow
redundancy $1 - H(X)/\max H(X)$	inefficiency of language

3.9.5 Logical Probability.   In this section we will see how the theory of logical probability, which differs from mathematical probability, was used by R. Carnap and Y. Bar-Hillel [1] as the theoretical foundation for a theory of semantic information. This theory of semantic information should not be confused with Shannon's theory of information since it has different goals and methods despite certain formal similarities.

The theory of semantic information developed by Carnap and Bar-Hillel is based upon a formal axiomatic system that implicitly defines a concept of logical probability of a sentence. The *logical probability* $M(x)$ of sentence x is a measure function satisfying nine axioms [see 1]. We will not concern ourselves here with the details of why these axioms were selected by Carnap and Bar-Hillel but will simply note that the ideas contained in them are found to be necessary for the proper development of the theory. Two sentences are said to be *logically* or *inductively independent* if the logical probability of their conjunction is equal to the product of their logical probabilities, that is,

$$M(x \wedge y) = M(x)\, M(y)$$

The *degree of confirmation* $M(x|y)$ of sentence x based on sentence y is defined as the conditional logical probability

$$M(x|y) = M(x \wedge y)/M(y) \qquad\qquad M(y) \neq 0$$

Carnap and Bar-Hillel sought to approximate natural language by considering an artificial language constructed from

n individuals $a_1, \ldots, a_n$
m properties $F_1, \ldots, F_m$
Five logical connectives: $-$ (not), $\vee$ (or), $\wedge$ (and), $\Rightarrow$ (implies),
  $\Leftrightarrow$ (equivalent)

where the properties do not overlap in meaning and no property says anything about the use or nonuse of any other property. An *atomic sentence* is of the form $F_j(a_i)$, that is, individual a_i has property F_j. A *basic sentence b* is an atomic sentence or its negation. A *state description s* is a conjunction of nm basic sentences containing each of the n individuals with each of the m properties or their negations, but not both. A *molecular sentence x* is a disjunction of state descriptions. A sentence is called a *tautology t* if it is logically true, a *contradiction u* if it is logically false, and a *factual* sentence i if it is logically indeterminate. The fundamental assumption is the following:

> The semantic information or content of a sentence is an increasing function of the number of basic sentences implied by it.

The following definitions stem from notions in inductive logic and its statistical nature. The *semantic content* of sentence x is

$$C(x) = 1 - M(x)$$

and the *semantic information* in sentence x is

$$I(x) = -\log_2 M(x)$$

The following table summarizes the model of semantic information based on logical probability:

Logical Probability	Semantic Information
argument a_i	individual a_i
function F_j	property F_j
$-$, $\vee$, $\wedge$, $\Rightarrow$, $\Leftrightarrow$	"not", "or", "and", "implies", "equivalent"
atomic sentence $F_j(a_i)$	individual a_i has property F_j
basic sentence b	atomic sentence or its negation
state description s	statement of which individuals have each property
molecular sentence x	disjunction of state descriptions
absolute logical probability $M(x)$	degree of belief in sentence x in the face of no evidence
conditional logical probability $M(x\mid y)$	degree of confirmation of sentence x by sentence y
$1 - M(x)$	semantic content of sentence x
$-\log_2 M(x)$	semantic information in sentence x

3.9.6 Summary of Probabilistic Models. From the above survey of probability theory we have seen that such models are appropriate if the fundamental variables of the linguistic entities are intrinsically of a chance nature. Mathematical probability forms a good theoretical basis in those cases where the fundamental events are repeatable, at least in principle. The theory of stochastic processes is appropriate when the linguistic process being modeled evolves as a function of time. As a particular case, the theory of Markov chains applies when the probability of future events is a function of the current state—not the entire past history of the process. Logical probability can be used when the events are intrinsically unrepeatable and involve subjective concepts such as degree of belief.

In the next section we will see how the theory of statistics forms a foundation for modeling linguistic entities.

3.10 STATISTICS

The theory of statistics differs from the theory of mathematical probability in several respects. First, it is founded on, rather than parallel to, the theory of mathematical probability. Second, it is concerned with decision making, while probability is concerned with prediction. Third, it is concerned with empirical observations, while probability is concerned with theoretical deductions. The models of interest here are based on sampling-distribution theory and inference theory.

3.10.1 Sampling-Distribution Theory.   In this section we will examine the theory of sampling distributions and indicate how this theory has been used to model certain linguistic entities. But first it is necessary to present some definitions.

The fundamental concepts in statistics are population, sample, and statistic. A *population* is the total set of objects under consideration or, more precisely, the set of possible measurements of some particular attribute of these objects. For example, the set of word lengths of a given corpus is a population. Thus, a population is a theoretical abstraction or mental construct of the physical world and is said to be finite if the set involved is finite, or infinite if the set is infinite. A *sample* of the population is a finite set of observations taken on the corresponding finite subset of the population. A *random sample* is defined as one in which the trials $X_1, X_2, \ldots, X_n$ are mutually independent and identically distributed, that is,

$$f(x_1, \ldots, x_n) = f(x_1) \cdots f(x_n) \text{ and } f(x_1) = \cdots = f(x_n) = f(x)$$

since the observations are independent and from the same population. A *statistic* is a function of the observations in a sample. Thus, a statistic is not only a function of the sample size n but also a function of the particular random sample. This implies that the value of the function changes from sample to sample for a fixed n. Since the sample was selected at random, the value of the function has a random behavior. Thus, a statistic is a random variable, and so, by definition, has a distribution function called its *sampling distribution*.

The theory of sampling distribution has been used by G. Zipf, M. Joos, and B. Mandelbrot to model the interrelation between the rank and probability of linguistic types. It was noted separately by J. Estoup, E. Condon, and G. Zipf, while examining large samples of text, that the rank r of a word type and its (relative) frequency f_r were inversely related according to a mathematical approximation of the form $f_r r = c$ involving a single parameter c that Zipf [29] estimated as 0.1 for English. Zipf's model is

$$p_r = cr^{-1} \qquad\qquad c = 0.1$$

where p_r denotes the probability of rank r. This soon became known as Zipf's law, but it is better to regard it as a hypothesis. However, the data did not support Zipf's rank hypothesis and it was suggested that these discrepancies were due to too small a sample, sampling variation, and so on. M. Joos [17] believed that Zipf's model was inadequate and so conjectured another model of the form

$$p_r = cr^{-b} \qquad\qquad c > 0, b \geq 1$$

involving a second parameter b which he estimated as $b \geq 1$ for English. This model was tested by a comparison of the predictions with actual behavior with similarly disappointing discrepancies [see Edmundson, 8]. The above models are inadequate since if v is the total number of word types in the vocabulary, then

$$1 = \sum_{r=1}^{v} p_r = \sum_{r=1}^{v} \frac{1}{10r^b} = \frac{1}{10} \sum_{r=1}^{v} \frac{1}{r^b} = \frac{1}{10}(1 + \frac{1}{2^b} + \frac{1}{3^b} + \cdots + \frac{1}{v^b})$$

This implies that v and b are functionally related; in fact, it follows that if $b = 1.000$, then $v = 12,370$, and if $b = 1.106$, then $v = \infty$. These mathematical conclusions are linguistically untenable. Mandelbrot [19] proposed a third model for the rank distribution by assuming that text is generated by a sequence of letters and spaces selected randomly but subject to cost constraints. From this assumption he showed that the probability of a word type of rank r is of the form

$$p_r = c(r + a)^{-b} \qquad c > 0, b > 1, 0 \leq a \leq 1$$

where a, b, and c are such that

$$\sum_{r=1}^{v} p_r = 1$$

This model includes Joos' model, and hence Zipf's, as a special case, and fits the data more closely than either of them. Mandelbrot's probability model of the rank distribution is summarized below:

Distribution Theory	Rank Distribution
constant v	number of word types in vocabulary
integer r	rank of word type
probability p_r	likelihood of word type of rank r
parameter b	function inversely proportional to the number of very likely word types
parameter a	function of number of letters in alphabet
parameter c	likelihood of most likely word type
equation $p_r = c(r + a)^{-b}$	rank distribution

Presently the question is still open concerning the adequacy of this last model as a predictor of word behavior with respect to rank and frequency.

3.10.2   Parameter Estimation.   We will now see how the theory of parameter estimation has been used in modeling linguistic entities. First, however, we must introduce some terminology.

Parameter estimation is the study of methods of inferring the numerical values of parameters of the population by means of sample statistics. A *parameter* of the population is a quantity that partially characterizes its distribution. For example, the theoretical mean and variance are parameters of a normal distribution. Often we do not know their values and are therefore confronted with the problem of estimating them. We do so by taking a sample, devising statistics whose values are computed from the sample, and then using these statistics as *estimators* of the unknown parameters. To estimate the unknown parameter θ in a population whose distribution is given by $f(x;\theta)$, we must first choose an estimator $\hat{\theta}$ of θ. Of course, the estimator $\hat{\theta}$ is a statistic since it is a function of the observed sample values $x_1, \ldots, x_n$ of the random variable X. For example, the sample mean

$$m = \frac{1}{n} \sum_{i=1}^{n} x_i$$

and the sample variance

$$s^2 = \frac{1}{n} \sum_{i=1}^{n} (x_i - m)^2$$

are common estimators of the population mean and variance, respectively. Some of the parameters most commonly estimated in statistics are the theoretical mean, variance, standard deviation, median, percentage, probability, and range.

Parameter estimation has been used by J. Chotlos, P. Guiraud, and G. Herdan to quantify literary style. There are two main kinds of style: the style of an author (for example, Shakespeare versus Bacon) and the style of a discipline (for example, literature versus science). Moreover, it is thought that an author's style is a product of unconscious or subconscious linguistic habits rather than conscious and deliberate ones. Since the conscious features of style can be imitated, an analysis of style, and hence a test of authorship, must be based on the unconscious and subconscious features that cannot be imitated. One of the linguistic features that has been proposed as an index of style is the type-token ratio. The *type-token* ratio for a corpus is defined as the number of word types divided by the number of word tokens. Although the number of word types in the sample increases to the vocabulary size as the sample size increases, the type-token ratio decreases asymptotically to zero as the sample size increases. Hence, the type-token ratio cannot serve as a stylostatistical parameter since it is dependent on the sample size. Therefore, Herdan [13] proposed the bilogarithmic type-token ratio to measure style. In particular, he estimated the constancy parameter of the bilogarithmic type-token ratio for the Pauline Epistles of New Testament Greek. The following table summarizes Herdan's statistical model for estimating the parameter in the bilogarithmic type-token ratio:

Parameter Estimation	Style Index
parameter v	size of vocabulary
sample size n	number of word tokens
$\log v / \log n = c$	theoretical bilogarithmic type-token ratio
parameter c	style parameter
statistic $\hat{v}$	number of distinct word types in sample
$\hat{c} = \log \hat{v} / \log n$	estimator of style parameter

3.10.3 Hypothesis Testing. Finally, we will see how the theory of hypothesis testing has been used in modeling linguistic questions.

Hypothesis testing is the study of methods of deciding whether to accept or reject assumptions made about the population after examining the evidence in the sample. A *statistical hypothesis H* is an assumption about the distribution of a random variable. It often takes the form of a statement about the value of a parameter of the population, for example, $H: \theta = 5$. A *test* of a hypothesis is a decision method for accepting either hypothesis H or an alternative hypothesis $\bar{H}$. For example, let θ be a location parameter, so that $f(x;\theta)$ denotes that the distribution of the random variable X is centered over the point θ, and the hypothesis and its alternative hypothesis be

$$H: f(x;\theta) = f(x;\theta_1) \text{ versus } \bar{H}: f(x;\theta) = f(x;\theta_2)$$

In deciding from a sample whether to accept H or $\bar{H}$ there are two types of error: (1) reject a true hypothesis H and (2) accept a false hypothesis H. The probability of a *type 1 error* is the conditional probability $P(\bar{H}|H)$ of rejecting H (that is, accepting $\bar{H}$) when H is true. Similarly, the probability of a *type 2 error* is $P(H|\bar{H})$. Since, for a given fixed sample size, both types of error cannot be simultaneously minimized, statisticians have elected to minimize the probability $P(H|\bar{H})$ of the type 2 error while holding the probability $P(\bar{H}|H)$ of the type 1 error fixed at some pre-selected *significance level*, say $p = .05$ or $p = .01$. The set of all possible values of the parameter θ is called the *parameter space,* which consists of two regions called the *acceptance region A* and the *rejection region R* for hypothesis H. If the statistic $\hat{\theta} = w(x_1, \ldots, x_n)$ falls in A, then H is accepted at the preselected significance level; if $\hat{\theta}$ falls in R, then H is rejected at that level of significance. Some of the hypotheses most commonly tested in statistics are goodness-of-fit, independence, randomness, homogeneity, equality of means, and equality of variance.

Hypothesis testing has been used by A. Ellegård, F. Mosteller and D. Wallace, C. Brinegar, and others to test the authorship of literary works. For example, Brinegar became interested in whether Mark Twain was the author of the Quintus Curtius Snodgrass letters that appeared in 1861. He selected word-length distribution as his criterion since he felt that the distribution of word length, as measured by the number of letters, was sufficiently stable, and concluded that Mark Twain was not the author. The following table summarizes Brinegar's statistical model for testing the authorship of the Snodgrass letters.

Hypothesis Testing	Authorship Test
null population distribution $f_2(x)$	distribution of word length in writings of Mark Twain
alternate population distribution $f_1(x)$	distribution of word length in writings of Q. C. Snodgrass
test statistic χ^2	chi-square goodness-of-fit criterion
significance level	risk tolerated in rejecting hypothesis that Mark Twain is Q. C. Snodgrass, when true
null hypothesis $H : f_1(x) = f_2(x)$	Mark Twain is Q. C. Snodgrass
decision	accept or reject that Mark Twain is Q. C. Snodgrass

3.10.4 Summary of Statistical Models. In the preceding survey of statistical theory we have seen that such models are appropriate when the fundamental problem involving the linguistic entities is one of inference or decision making. Statistics provides the linguist with a theoretical basis for drawing inferences about a population from the evidence afforded by a sample. The theory of parameter estimation is appropriate when the functional form of the population distribution is known or assumed, while the theory of hypothesis testing applies when both a hypothesis and its alternatives can be specified. In both cases of inference the theory of sampling distributions helps us select and use an appropriate statistic.

3.11   SUMMARY

In the preceding sections we have surveyed mathematical models of linguistic entities that have been based on logic, analysis, algebra, geometry, probability, and statistics. These theories were sketched and examples of models were given for each.

The following table summarizes the foregoing mathematical models of linguistic entities and language processes.

Linguistic Entity or Language Process	Model					
	Logic	Analysis	Algebra	Geometry	Prob.	Stat.
Sentences	x					
Word frequency		x			x	x
Document relevance		x				
Linear associative retrieval		x	x			
Sentence significance		x	x			
Type-token relation		x				
Index-term similarity		x		x		
Transformational grammar			x	x		
Categorial grammar	x		x	x		
Grammar and language			x			
Distinctive features			x			
Document indexing			x	x	x	
Semantic differential			x			
Semantic distance				x		
Synonomy				x		
Word association				x		
Immediate-constituent analysis				x		
Dependency analysis				x		
Thesaurus				x		
Linguistic diversity					x	
Word-length distribution					x	x
Gap distribution					x	x
Finite-state language			x		x	
Communication system		x	x		x	
Semantic information	x	x			x	
Rank distribution		x			x	x
Style index					x	x
Authorship test					x	x

Earlier, in the sections on models and modeling, some cautions were expressed with regard to both their use and misuse. It is now appropriate to say more about this. The use of mathematical models is somewhat controversial. Some researchers regard them as unnecessary or unproductive, while others treat them far too seriously as ultimate answers. However, this situation is not peculiar to linguists and linguistics since it also appears in other sciences such as biology, psychology, and economics. Moreover, it will appear again in other newly emerging fields and hence should be regarded in the proper perspective. Mathematical models can be helpful if their advantages are balanced against their disadvantages.

REFERENCES

1. Bar-Hillel, Y., *Language and Information*. Reading, Mass: Addison-Wesley, 1964.
2. Becker, J., and R. Hayes, *Information Storage and Retrieval: Tools, Elements, Theories*. New York: John Wiley & Sons, 1963.
3. Bross, I., *Design for Decision*. New York: Macmillan, 1953.
4. Chomsky, N., On the notion 'rule of grammar', *Structure of Language and its Mathematical Aspects*. R. Jakobson (ed.), Providence, R.I.: American Mathematical Society, 1961, pp. 6-24.
5. Chomsky, N., Formal properties of grammars, *Handbook of Mathematical Psychology*. v. II, R. Luce, R. Bush, and E. Galanter (eds.), New York: John Wiley and Sons, 1963, pp. 323-418.
6. Chomsky, N. and G. A. Miller, Introduction to the formal analysis of natural languages, *Handbook of Mathematical Psychology*. v. II, R. Luce, R. Bush, and E. Galanter (eds.), New York: John Wiley and Sons, 1963, pp. 269-231.
7. Edmundson, H. P., Linguistic analysis in machine translation research, *Modern Trends in Documentation*. M. Boaz (ed.), New York: Pergamon Press, 1959, pp. 31-37.
8. Edmundson, H. P., A statistician's view of linguistic models and language data processing, *Natural Language and the Computer*. P. Garvin (ed.), New York: McGraw-Hill, 1963, pp. 151-179.
9. Fairthorne, R., *Toward Information Retrieval*. London: Butterworths, 1965.
10. Giuliano, V. and P. Jones, Linear associative information retrieval, *Vistas in Information Handling*. P. Howerton and D. Weeks (eds.), Washington: Spartan, 1963, pp. 30-46.
11. Greenberg, J., The measurement of linguistic diversity, *Language*. v. 32, 1956, pp. 109-115.
12. Hays, D. G., Automatic language-data processing, *Computer Applications in the Behavioral Sciences*, H. Borko (ed.), Englewood Cliffs, N. J.: Prentice-Hall, 1962, pp. 395-423.
13. Herdan, G., *The Calculus of Linguistic Observations*. The Hague: Mouton & Co., 1962.
14. Hillman, D., Two models for retrieval system design, *American Documentation*. v. 15, no. 3, July 1964, pp. 217-225.
15. Jakobson, R., G. M. Fant, and M. Halle, *Preliminaries to Speech Analysis: The Distinctive Features and their Correlates*. Third printing, Cambridge, Mass.: M.I.T. Press, 1955.
16. Jakobson, R. (ed.), *Structure of Language and its Mathematical Aspects, Proceedings of Symposia in Applied Mathematics*. v. XII, Providence, R.I.: American Mathematical Society, 1961.

17. Joos, M., Review of Zipf's 'The psycho-biology of language', *Language.* v. 12, 1936, pp. 196-210.

18. Lambek, J., On the calculus of syntactic types, *Structure of Language and its Mathematical Aspects.* R. Jakobson (ed.), Providence, R. I.: American Mathematical Society, 1961, pp. 166-178.

19. Mandelbrot, B., An informational theory of the structure of language based upon the theory of the statistical matching of messages and coding, *Proceedings of a Symposium on Applications of Communication Theory.* W. Jackson (ed.), London: Butterworths, 1953, pp. 486-502.

20. Maron, M. E. and J. L. Kuhns, On relevance, probabilistic indexing, and information retrieval, *Journal of the Association for Computing Machinery.* v. 7, no. 3, 1960, pp. 216-244.

21. Mooers, C., A mathematical theory of language symbols in retrieval, *Proceedings of the International Conference on Scientific Information.* v. II, Washington: National Academy of Sciences, National Research Council, 1959, pp. 1327-1364.

22. Nagel, E., P. Suppes, and A. Tarski (eds.), *Logic, Methodology, and Philosophy of Science: Proceedings of the 1960 International Congress.* Palo Alto: Stanford University Press, 1962.

23. Osgood, C., G. Suci, and P. Tannenbaum, *The Measurement of Meaning.* Urbana: University of Illinois Press, 1957.

24. Shannon, C. and W. Weaver, *The Mathematical Theory of Communication.* Urbana: University of Illinois Press, 1949.

25. Williams, C., A note on the statistical analysis of sentence length as a criterion of literary style, *Biometrika.* v. 31, 1940, pp. 356-361.

26. Yngve, V., Gap analysis and syntax, *IRE Transactions on Information Theory.* v. IT-2, 1956, pp. 106-112.

27. Yngve, V., A model and an hypothesis for language structure, *Proceedings of the American Philosophical Society.* v. 104, no. 5, 1960, pp. 444-466.

28. Yule, G. U., *The Statistical Study of Literary Vocabulary.* London: Cambridge University Press, 1944.

29. Zipf, G. K., *Human Behavior and the Principle of Least Effort.* Cambridge, Mass.: Addison-Wesley, 1949.

Part II

STATISTICAL ANALYSIS

Information scientists have had as one of their objectives to automate the process of indexing, classifying, and abstracting documents. Having set these goals, we have had to devise methods for achieving them. The most basic method of analysis is that of statistical computation, for the computer is basically a counting device. The application of statistical procedures is the first stage in the processing of language.

The statistical techniques used to index, classify, or abstract the meaning of reports are surveyed and described in this section. Chapter 4 is concerned with automatic methods of indexing and classification. Chapter 5 extends the use of word count procedures to condensing documents while preserving content, and Chapter 6 describes the application of statistical techniques to the analysis of the author's style of writing so as to be able to distinguish between different authors.

In essence, statistical analysis of text is based upon counting and correlating various characteristics of written language. Letters, punctuation marks, words, or sentences can be counted. The smallest independent linguistic unit that carries meaning—some meaning, but not all of it—is the word. Use of the sentence as the basic unit would involve the arrangement of the words or the syntax of the sentence. The application of syntactical analysis will be discussed in the next section; in this section, the emphasis is on the statistical analysis of language.

For computational purposes, a word is defined as a sequence of characters, either alphabetic, numerical, or special—such as periods, equal signs, dashes, etc.—separated by blank spaces on either side. Assuming that the words are in machine readable code, the computer can be programmed to count them in a variety of ways. One can count the number of words in the document; the average number of words in a sentence; the number of times the word "analysis" is preceded by the word "statistical," etc. An almost unlimited number of different kinds of word counts can be made. The difficulty is to determine the word counts that prove useful in automating the assignment of index terms or in determining the content or style of a document. Researchers have applied a great deal of ingenuity to make this determination, as the studies recorded in the following chapters indicate.

4

Indexing and Classification

H. Borko

Ever since man began recording information—and it makes little difference whether this information was baked in clay tablets, written on papy-
rus scrolls, or printed in books—he was faced with the problems of storing
the records so they could be located when needed. Basic to the organization
of a store of information is the need to index and classify the literature.
Many systems of indexing and classification have been devised. Among
the important recent innovations are the use of descriptors and uniterms,
and techniques of coordinate indexing.

Early in 1951, Mooers [31] published a description of the Zator
Selector and a method of superimposed coding. The report contained
one of the earliest presentations of procedures for indexing information
by means of separate descriptor terms and for retrieving information by
searching for a combination of descriptors. In the following year, Taube
and his associates [44] made the first public announcement of the uniterm system of coordinate indexing. This innovation led to a revival of
interest in documentation and to many applications. The initial paper
described the development of a uniterm vocabulary (by breaking up standard subject headings) and procedures for coordinating and posting the
terms. Coordinate indexing is now widely used [21] for mechanical and
automatic indexes.

Manual methods of indexing and classification are time consuming
tasks requiring skilled personnel. Although uniterm indexing is a more
routinized procedure than traditional subject heading indexing, it is still
manual. The challenge to automation is to develop ways of applying computer technology to the analysis of natural language text in order to derive automated procedures for indexing and classifying documents.

In designing automated indexing and classification systems, the goal
may be production of an index that is similar to one made by humans:

Do the same thing that is now being done, but do it mechanically. Since the capabilities of the data processing system are not equivalent to those of the human, this is not a fruitful approach. Alternatively, the goal may be production of an index or classification system that, though different from the traditional types, has its own advantages. If this latter approach is adopted, then it must be recognized that the machine output cannot be compared directly with the human output (they are not the same) and each must be evaluated on its own merits. The various machine methods for indexing the documents described in the following paragraphs are, for the most part, nonconventional, but they do facilitate retrieval of relevant information.

In the sections on mechanized document classification, two approaches are discussed. One group of studies aims at automating the work of the classificationist in that they attempt to derive a set of classification categories by mathematical procedures. The other group of experiments applies computer technology to the task of the classifier by automating the procedure for placing documents into their proper categories. The methods used for automating indexing and classification are statistical language processing techniques, and the results are both promising and ingenius.

4.1   AUTOMATIC METHODS OF INDEXING

Indexing is the assignment to a document of a set of tags, keywords, uniterms, or descriptors, to provide an indication of the contents of a document and a means of retrieval. Normally, a document is indexed by a trained librarian or a subject specialist. This is a costly and time consuming task. Moreover, the number of documents to be indexed is increasing and the number of available librarians is not keeping pace. In response to this imbalance, the information scientist, using automated language processing techniques, is studying ways of analyzing documents and automatically assigning index terms. The techniques being investigated have already led to the development of statistical indexing, permutation indexing, citation indexing, and association indexing.

4.1.1   Statistical Indexing.   The basic assumption underlying statistical methods of indexing is that the more frequently a word is used in a document, the more likely it is that the word is a significant indicator of the subject matter. As a first step in machine processing, the document is transliterated into machine readable code. A computer program develops a machine listing of all words in the document, arranged by frequency of occurrence and alphabetically within frequency. Function words, such as articles, conjunctions, prepositions, etc., are excluded. Depending upon the degree of sophistication desired, words that have the same stem but different inflections can be counted either as repetitions of the stem or as separate words. Statistical processing of the document produces a list of words arranged by frequency of occurrence, from which index terms can be selected automatically according to prespecified rules such as minimum frequency of occurrence.

It is simple to write a program that will cause the computer to select as index terms all words of a given minimum frequency (less specified exceptions). However, the application of this rule will invariably result in the selection of large numbers of index terms, many of which will have very little retrieval value. To make statistical indexing effective, it is necessary to limit the number of index terms per document by eliminating nondescriptive terms, and to insure that the selected terms enable relevant documents to be retrieved in response to a request. Much research effort is being devoted to this difficult task.

In February 1961, the American University [29] sponsored its Third Institute on Information Storage and Retrieval and addressed itself to the problem of machine indexing. The published papers presented the state of the art at that time and provided a useful overview of the research in the area. In 1963 Artandi [1] prepared a bibliographic survey of the research that has been done on automatic indexing of natural language texts. The most recent state of the art report on this field was prepared by Stevens [41] and contains a 662-item bibliography.

A number of procedures exist for automatically indexing a document. Luhn's early work is based upon the concept that uncommon words which appear frequently in a document are suitable index terms [26]. He also demonstrated the application of the statistical approach to the automatic extracting of sentences [27]. O'Connor [34] studied the problem of the adequacy of mechanized indexing and tried to develop rules for deciding how many times a term must appear in a text before it should be selected as an index term. His results were inconclusive.

Stiles [42] recognized that automatic indexing of a document by listing the content words in that document would result in a large number of index terms. Some of these words, while not function words, are also not the type of word used in a retrieval request. For example, if the first sentences in this paragraph were indexed by all content words, the index listing would have included such terms as "recognized," "listing," "result," "large," and "number." It is highly unlikely that these words would be used in a search request. They are, therefore, useless as index terms but also difficult to eliminate by a rule applied logically but mechanically by an automatic data processing system. Human post-editing corrects the deficiency.

Of greater concern is the fact that, since the computer retrieves on the basis of an *exact* match between the index terms and the request terms, many relevant documents can be missed in an automated search. The first sentence in the last paragraph would have been indexed under "automatic indexing," but it would have been missed if the searcher requested documents on "statistical indexing." Stiles solved this problem by using an association factor—a statistical formula with which the computer calculates the degree of association between index terms. In this manner, one would find that language processing, automatic indexing, and statistical indexing are related concepts with a high index of association. A request containing only one of these terms would probably be extended by Stiles to include all three on the grounds that the requester is probably interested in all three. Thus, the use of the association factor solves the problem of nonretrieval of relevant documents and improves the efficiency of automatic indexing and retrieval.

Somewhat similar associative techniques are being investigated by Spiegel [40]. Doyle [17] is also using a measure of association to produce word association maps, which diagrammatically portray the relationship of the terms used to index not just one document but an entire document collection. This technique will be discussed in more detail in Section 4.1.4.

Simmons [39] decided to index *all* content words in order to obtain maximum-depth indexing. The result is a language processing system that accepts questions worded in ordinary English and seeks to select appropriate answers from the information stored in natural language in computer memory. The total set of all of its content words constitutes the set of descriptors characterizing a given text (e.g., an article or a book). Every important word used by the author is listed, together with its location in the text.

As data for the Simmons program, a volume of the *Golden Book Encyclopedia* was keypunched. An exclusion list (words not to be indexed) was prepared, and with the use of a computer, an alphabetical list of all content words, together with the frequency of occurrence of each, was produced. A "VAPS" index number is recorded for each occurrence. VAPS stands for Volume, Article (or chapter), Paragraph, and Sentence—the number locates the position of the word in text. The program combines words with the same stem and cross-references some synonyms. Figure 4.1 is an example of the index.

A complete index is useful not only for document retrieval. As an ultimate extension of statistical indexing, the system has tremendous implications for fact retrieval and automated question answering systems.

Other researchers believe that techniques other than frequency counting must be used to select index terms. Edmundson [18] suggests that the selection of key words be based in part on positional clues, such as the occurrence of the word in the topic sentence of the paragraph, or

	V	A	P	S	V	A	P	S	V	A	P	S
FALL	1	9	8	3	1	10	3	1	1	10	3	2
	1	10	4	1	1	10	4	4	1	13	3	8
	1	13	5	3	1	16	2	2	1	19	1	1
	1	20	12	4	1	21	6	5	1	24	5	4
	1	27	6	2	1	28	3	4	1	28	4	1
	1	36	5	2	1	36	5	5	1	54	3	6
	1	54	8	2								
FALLS	SEE FALL											
FAMILIES	1	12	15	1	1	17	2	4	1	17	3	1
	1	17	3	2	1	23	2	3	1	23	8	5
	1	24	3	1	1	28	7	6	1	32	8	6
	1	44	2	2	1	44	2	3	1	44	3	2
	1	44	4	1	1	44	4	3	1	44	5	1
	1	44	5	5	1	44	6	1	1	44	7	1
FAMILY	SEE FAMILIES											
FAMOUS	1	3	3	5	1	5	6	1	1	5	7	1
	1	9	12	3	1	14	6	5	1	17	4	14
	1	17	4	20	1	18	3	7	1	20	9	2
	1	32	18	1	1	47	2	4	1	50	3	1
	1	56	3	7	1	57	2	2				
FANCY	1	33	3	4								
FANGS	1	15	2	2								
FAN	1	16	8	7	1	32	20	5				
FANS	SEE FAN											
FAR-OFF	1	57	4	2								
FARMER	1	1	5	4	1	2	5	4	1	2	6	6
	1	4	4	1	1	4	14	1	1	4	18	2
	1	4	18	3	1	8	8	3	1	12	6	5
	1	12	15	1	1	16	4	7	1	22	3	8
	1	22	4	1	1	32	19	1	1	32	19	3
	1	32	19	5	1	34	2	2	1	34	2	3
	1	34	3	1	1	34	3	2	1	34	8	5
	1	34	9	1	1	38	8	3	1	42	3	2
	1	43	4	6	1	43	8	1	1	43	8	3
	1	56	4	1	1	56	4	4	1	56	5	1
FARMERS	SEE FARMER											
FARMING	SEE FARMER											
FARMLANDS	SEE FARMER											
FARM	SEE FARMER											
FARMS	SEE FARMER											
FASTENED	1	33	2	5	1	33	5					

Figure 4.1 VAPS index

by semantic clues that would assign importance to the words following such phrases as "in summary," or "in conclusion." Climenson, Hardwick, and Jacobson assert that "the ability of a machine to adequately determine information relevancies depends strongly on its ability to recognize and manipulate the syntactic structure of the text" [12 p. 178]. They describe a syntax analysis program and discuss its use in machine indexing and abstracting.

Baxendale made use of syntactical analysis in her work on automatic indexing [3, 4]. She found, by empirical investigation, that the title used in technical periodic literature provided an acceptable source of index terms. Furthermore, she found that index terms are restricted, almost exclusively, to nouns or adjective-noun phrases. Her task, then, was to use the title as a source and to design a computer program that would select all noun or adjective-noun combinations from unedited titles. In the following title, the underscored words are the index terms selected by her program.

> Some electron-microscope investigations of the structure of photocathodes which have been subject to the effects of gaseous discharge. Pt. I.

4.1.2   Permutation Indexing.   Statistical indexing provides a means for determining the subject matter of a document, and is based on the assumption that a list of the document's content words adequately reflects the subject matter without regard to the arrangement of words in context. Nevertheless, meaning of a text depends in part on the arrangement, or syntactical relationships, of content words (e.g., "dog bites man" and "man bites dog"). Preserving the context increases the specificity with which content words may be interpreted.

There remains the problem of selecting a relatively small text rich in content words to be used as a source of index terms. Assuming that the author of a scientific paper tries to use an informative title, the document title contains more clues to document subject content than does any other sentence or clause. Therefore, the selection of content words can be limited to those contained in the title. Permutation consists of cycling the title so that each "significant" or "key" word is positioned successively (i.e., in order of occurrence in the title) in a fixed, or index word, position in one index line. A "significant" word is any not specifically excluded by being placed in a "forbidden word list" in computer memory. The list contains conjunctions, prepositions, articles, and other words of no index value.

The set of permuted titles is ordered alphabetically (see Figure 4.2) on the index word position. Thus, there will be an index entry for each key word in each title being indexed. A title containing five key words will have five index entries, each of which consists of (up to some maximum number of characters that may occupy one index line) the key word in the index word position and adjacent context words in corresponding arrangement on the line.

Ohlman published one of the first papers on permutation index design [9]. This was an index to the papers of the International Conference on Scientific Information held in Washington, D. C., in 1958. Luhn developed an almost identical procedure, which he entitled "Keyword-in-Context," or "KWIC" index [28]. Both Ohlman and Luhn, working independently and thousands of miles apart, developed the same punched card method of permuting titles, tested it on the same set of data, and distributed their reports at the same meeting.

In discussing the KWIC index, Luhn distinguished between the use of an index to retrieve previously published and stored information, and its use to inform interested readers of new and pertinent information published in their fields. The KWIC index is designed as a dissemination index that can be prepared quickly, automatically, and at reasonable cost. It can also be used for retrospective searches. *Chemical Titles,* a publication of the American Chemical Society, and B.A.S.I.C., published by BioSciences Information Service, are journals of permuted titles designed to inform scientists of new and relevant literature.

Note that the alphabetically arranged keyword in a permuted index is in the center column in the page. Note, too, that in this index the first and last word on the line may be incomplete; however, it is still possible to deduce or infer the sense of the title. The reference code at the right hand column is composed automatically during the machine manipulation of the data. It consists of the first four letters of the first author's last name plus the initials of his first and middle names, the last two digits of the year of the original publication, and the initial letters of the first three words of the title which are not one of the common function words. The complete reference may be found by looking up the reference code or the author index, both of which are separate indexes in the same volume.

Kennedy [22] proposed a permuted title index for internal documents. He reports that the Bell Telephone Laboratory bulletin of permuted titles serves a current awareness function, provides a multiaspect search facility, and provides each scientist and technician with his own desk copy index of company reports.

A slightly different form of permutation indexing was described by Veilleux, of the U. S. Central Intelligence Agency [47]. Her system was put into operation in 1952, but because of the nature of the agency, it was

LE AND BODY OF ASCARIS(	NEMATODA) AND LUMBRICUS(ANNELIDA)/	105313
ALYSIS OF ASCARIS-SUUM(	NEMATODA) ANTIGENS(RABBIT, PIG,-MAN	104100
TRONGYLUS-BRASILIENSIS(	NEMATODA) IN A THERMAL GRADIENT/ HOS	105176
H TRICHINELLA-SPIRALIS(	NEMATODA) IN DOGS(MOUSE)/ INCIDENCE	105189
CANINE DIRO FILARIASIS(	NEMATODA) IN NORTHERN-AUSTRALIA/ TRE	104428
AVES, COLEOPTERA, HOST,	NEMATODA) IN SIERRA-LEONE(AFRICA)/	105190
F CANINE SPIROCERCOSIS(	NEMATODA) IN THE FREETOWN AREA OF SI	105191
OF DIROFILARIA-IMMITIS(	NEMATODA) IN THE HEART OF DOGS EXAMI	105194
STUDY-(MAN)/ HOOK WORM(	NEMATODA) INFECTION AND ANEMIA. AN E	105181
PIDEMIOLOGY OF ASCARIS(	NEMATODA) INFECTION IN RELATION TO I	104300
STUDIES ON FILARIASIS(	NEMATODA). ISOLATION AND PURIFICATIO	104098
STRONGYLUS-CANTONENSIS(	NEMATODA)/ CARBOHYDRATE METABOLISM I	105349
ION) AND CEPHALOBELLUS(	NEMATODA)/ DISCUSSION OF THELASTOMA(	105223
WUCHERERIA-BANCROFTI)(	NEMATODA)/ ELECTRON MICROSCOPIC STUD	105353
PANAGRELLUS-REDIVIVUS(	NEMATODA)/ EXCRETORY-SYSTEM(STRUCTU	105357
TOMUM-QUADRISPINULATUM(	NEMATODA)/ IN-VITRO CULTIVATION OF 4	105355
VIRUS, BACTERIA, FUNGI,	NEMATODA)/ KANSAS PHYTO PATHOLOGICAL	105120
WORM TRICHURIS-VULPIS(	NEMATODA)/ PRODUCTION OF SUCCINATE B	105354
HS(CESTODA, TREMATODA,	NEMATODA)/ QUANTITATIVE DETERMINATIO	105312
OF ANCYLOSTOMA-CANINUM(	NEMATODA)/ ULTRASTRUCTURE AND HISTOC	105352
UTBREAK OF TRICHINOSIS(	NEMATODA, EPIDEMIC TRACED TO SAUSAGE	104302
F COTTON-D PLANT PESTS(	NEMATODA, HOMOPTERA, LEPIDOPTERA) IN	105159
OF DIROFILARIA-IMMITIS(	NEMATODA, ISOLATED FROM ANOPHELES-QU	105356
VIRUS, BACTERIA, FUNGI,	NEMATODA, NONPARASITIC) OF COTTON-D,	105125
CERCIASIS IN THE FIELD(	NEMATODA,-MAN)/ MASS THERAPY OF ONCH	104432
RIA-LUTRAE NEW SPECIES(	NEMATODA: FILARIOIDEA) FROM OTTERS(	105225
IOMAN ISLAND, MALAYSIA(	NEMATODA: GNATHOSTOMIDAE)/ GNATHOSTO	105224
TS IN SOIL FOR USE IN A	NEMATODE ADVISORY SERVICE(HIBISCUS-	105059
SCULENTUS-D)/ ROOT-KNOT	NEMATODE(MELOIDOGYNE-INCOGNITA) POP	105059
L BROMIDE FUMIGATION OF	NEMATODES IN SOIL UNDER GAS-PROOF SH	105109
N CONGO/	NEMATODES OF MYRIAPODS OF THE BELGIA	105222
)(CZECHOSLOVAKIA)/ THE	NEMATODES OF THE PEAT MOSSES(BRYOPH	105221
F TRANSPLANT INJURY AND	NEMATODES ON INCIDENCE OF VERTICILLI	105041
PLANARIA(TURBELLARIA)/	NEOBLASTS AND THE PHENOMENA OF INDUC	105347
E QUEENSLAND LUNG FISH,	NEOCERATODUS-FORSTERI(PISCES, AMPHI	102426
OF NEURONS IN IMMATURE	NEOCORTEX/ PROPERTIES OF SYNAPTIC AC	102779
CINNYRIS-CHLOROPYGIUS,	NEOCOSSYPHUS-POENSIS, AVES) OF BIRDS	105434
ND COLONIC IRRIGATIONS/	NEOMYCIN OTO TOXICITY. A CASE DUE TO	103207
HEPATIC ENCEPHALOPATHY(	NEOMYCIN, ANTI INFECTIVE FAILURES,-M	102009
AL ULCERS(IN RABBITS)(	NEOMYCIN, BACITRACIN, POLYMYXIN-B, A	104427
CHEMICAL COMPOSITION OF	NEOMYSIS-INTEGER(CRUSTACEA)/ BIOCHE	105370
SIS-K(VITAMIN-K)/ LATE	NEONATAL FORM OF ACUTE IDIOPATHIC AV	101839
TOLOGY, NOVEMBER, 1963/	NEONATAL HEMOPATHIES, SPECIAL SESSIO	100981
HEPATITIS VIRUS IN	NEONATAL LIVER DISEASE-(MAN)/	104216
LUCOSE TOLERANCE IN THE	NEONATAL PERIOD AND DURING THE 1ST 6	103544
ION OF VITAMIN-K IN THE	NEONATAL PERIOD-(MAN)/ ACT	101836
COPPER, AND ZINC IN THE	NEONATAL PERIOD/ INTAKES AND EXCRETI	103483
PLATELET ANTIBODIES IN	NEONATAL THROMBOCYTOPENIC PURPURA AF	104037
ELIAL FUNCTION(MOUSE)/	NEONATAL THYMECTOMY AND RETICULOENDO	102368
INFOLD THICKNESS IN THE	NEONATE TO SEX, LENGTH OF GESTATION,	101300
PATIENTS WITH MALIGNANT	NEOPLASIA/ INDIVIDUAL SPECIFIC LEUKO	103355
EUKEMIAS, AND MALIGNANT	NEOPLASIA: A HYPOTHESIS/ CONGENITAL	103376
FOR UNEXPLAINED FEVER(	NEOPLASM, INFECTION,-MAN)/ LAPAROTOM	101795
OF OBSTRUCTIVE NATURE(	NEOPLASM,-MAN)/ ANGIOGRAPHIC FEATURE	102808
E ETIOLOGY OF MALIGNANT	NEOPLASMS. REVIEW AND RESULTS/ STATI	103364
TIGENS IN AUTOCHTHONOUS	NEOPLASMS/ THEORETICAL BASIS FOR PRE	104060
AFTER INJECTION OF PRE	NEOPLASTIC AND NEOPLASTIC NUCLEIC-AC	103334
NXIETY IN PATIENTS WITH	NEOPLASTIC DISEASE/ A	102947
BITOR IN NORMAL AND PRE	NEOPLASTIC LIVER TISSUE OF THE RAT/	101954
N OF PRE NEOPLASTIC AND	NEOPLASTIC NUCLEIC-ACIDS/ TUMORS IN	103334
THE DIFFERENTIATION OF	NEOPLASTIC PROCESSES(MONOGRAPH)/ FU	103400
OF METHYLENE-BLUE(ANTI	NEOPLASTIC) AND BRILLIANT-CRESYL-BLU	103433

ASES IN THE CUTICLE AND	NERVE-CORDS OF 4 CYCLOPHYLLIDEAN CES	105345
S OF NORMAL RAT SCIATIC	NERVE/ UPTAKE OF CARBON-14 LYSINE IN	102742
RADIATION ON PERIPHERAL	NERVE, WITH OBSERVATIONS ON LOCAL HE	101362
DISTRIBUTION OF MEDIAN	NERVE,-MAN)/	103381
ITY OF PERIPHERAL MOTOR	NERVES IN MENTAL RETARDATION, DIABET	102803
DES OF SINGLE FIBERS OF	NERVES WITH INTACT SHEATH(NEURO PHY	102754
/ STUDIES ON ADRENERGIC	NERVES. USE OF RAT AND MOUSE IRIS(E	102772
TION OF THE SYMPATHETIC	NERVES/ BLOCKING ACTION OF DIMETHYLP	103190
RESSANT, DOG) ON HIGHER	NERVOUS ACTIVITY/ EFFECT OF STELAZIN	103248
PILEPSY, BEHAVIOR)/ 100	NERVOUS CHILDREN: 25-YEAR FOLLOW-UP(	103538
THE SPAYED RAT/ CENTRAL	NERVOUS MONO AMINES AND HORMONE INDU	102489
DISEASES OF THE CENTRAL	NERVOUS-SYSTEM BEFORE(1958-59) AND	104288
ES OF PERINATAL CENTRAL	NERVOUS-SYSTEM DAMAGE IN FULL-TERM B	102806
D METABOLISM IN CENTRAL	NERVOUS-SYSTEM DEGENERATIVES DISEASE	102807
OF SOME SECTIONS OF THE	NERVOUS-SYSTEM IN THE MECHANISM OF A	103184
SECTIONS OF THE CENTRAL	NERVOUS-SYSTEM OF RATS IRRADIATED IN	103592
CTRICAL REACTION OF THE	NERVOUS-SYSTEM OF THE MOLE CRICKET G	105376
STEROIDS ON THE CENTRAL	NERVOUS-SYSTEM OF THE MOUSE. PHARMAC	103186
STEROIDS ON THE CENTRAL	NERVOUS-SYSTEM OF THE MOUSE. SYNTHET	103198
IMULANTS OF THE CENTRAL	NERVOUS-SYSTEM ON THE STIMULATION(S	103181
AND RECALL(IN CENTRAL	NERVOUS-SYSTEM)/ ON MEMORY	102785
N CHARACTERISTIC OF THE	NERVOUS-SYSTEM(AVES, REPTILIA, AMPH	102776
-CORTEX AND THE CENTRAL	NERVOUS-SYSTEM(GUINEA-PIG)/ EFFECT	103132
E CENTRAL AND AUTONOMIC	NERVOUS-SYSTEMS IN THE MECHANISM OF	101943
OGLODYTES-AEDON, AVES)/	NEST CONSTRUCTION BY HOUSE WRENS(TR	105418
ULCER: THE ULCER VESSEL	NEST-(MAN)/ STUDIES ON THE BLOOD-VES	101971
AYTHYA-AMERICANA, AVES)	NEST(DESCRIPTION)/ AN UPLAND REDHEA	105420
CIDAE, TRYPOXYLONINAE)/	NESTING ACTIVITY OF THE MUD-DAUBING	105271
BUTION, AND FEATURES OF	NESTING FOR THE BLACK KITE(MILVUS-K	105432
MAMMALIA, DISTRIBUTION,	NESTING HABITS, BREEDING, GROWTH)/ A	105448
TTA, CYANOLISEUS, AVES,	NESTING HABITS, PAMPAS, ARGENTINA, P	105398
BOCAGEI(AVES, HABITAT,	NESTING), A NEW SPECIES FROM THE CON	105433
OBLAST(USSR)/ BIOLOGY(	NESTING, BEHAVIOR, MIGRATION) OF THE	105396
TIONS ON THE METHOD FOR	NET ENERGY DETERMINATION(CATTLE, CO	103692
CATTLE, COTTONSEED-D)/	NET ENERGY OF FAT AND MOLASSES FOR B	103692
HROUGH RESPIRATION, AND	NET PRODUCTION IN THE TROPICAL RAIN	101454
CETATE METABOLIC ON THE	NET PROTEIN UTILIZATION OF A 10-PER-	103116
RIETIES OF FIELD CROPS(	NETHERLANDS)/ 40TH LIST OF VA	104773
ASH FERMENTATION IN THE	NETHERLANDS/ DEVELOPMENT OF THE BREW	101858
THE CUTANEOUS LYMPHATIC	NETWORK BY COLLOIDAL GOLD-198/ INVES	102335
RAT, CAT, CHIMPANZEE)/	NEURAL AND BEHAVIORAL EFFECTS OF VIS	102706
DY/ REGENERATION OF THE	NEURAL RETINA FROM RETINA PIGMENT CE	103632
RESSANT)/ TIMING OF THE	NEURAL STIMULUS WHICH LEADS TO OVULA	103241
HE STRUCTURE OF THE MYO	NEURAL SYNAPSES/ EFFECT OF CARBO CHO	103239
OPTIC	NEURITIS DUE TO SINUSITIS-(MAN)/	102821
S IN AUTONOMIC GANGLIA(	NEURO ANATOMY)/ ADRENERGIC SYNAPTIC	102735
AT(DEGENERATION-STUDY,	NEURO ANATOMY)/ CORTICO FUBRAL PROJE	102737
AL EMINENCE IN THE RAT(	NEURO ANATOMY)/ ELECTRON MICROSCOPIC	102738
THE(BRAIN) CEREBELLUM(	NEURO ANATOMY, MAMMALIA)/ RELATIONSH	102734
OLOGICAL PICTURE OF THE	NEURO MUSCLE SPINDLES IN THE MUSCLES	103644
OTILE SENSORY CILIA AND	NEURO MUSCULAR JUNCTIONS IN A CTENOP	105336
TONOMIC DRUG) RESISTANT	NEURO MUSCULAR TRANSMISSION TO A PEL	103166
IN THE FUNCTION OF THE	NEURO MUSCULAR-SYSTEM(REVIEW)/ HORM	102484
ION-SICKNESS: 10 CASES(	NEURO PATHOLOGY,-MAN)/ CRIPPLING EFF	101806
MYELOGRAPHIC ANALYSIS(	NEURO PATHOLOGY,-MAN)/ SPINAL-CORD D	102809
UMENT) FOR TRANSFERRING	NEURO PHYSIOLOGICAL PULSE DATA AUTOM	102728
AMPAL(BRAIN) ABLATION(	NEURO PHYSIOLOGY) IN RATS: EFFECTS O	102768
E CLAMP DATA(AMPHIBIA,	NEURO PHYSIOLOGY)/ ACCOMODATION IN M	102761
OCHLEAR RESPONSES) CAT,	NEURO PHYSIOLOGY)/ ACTION OF ACETYLC	102698
MATIC STIMULATION(CAT,	NEURO PHYSIOLOGY)/ CENTRIFUGAL OPTIC	102783
E INFANT RHESUS MONKEY(	NEURO PHYSIOLOGY)/ DEVELOPMENT OF SL	102774
ENDING SPINAL PATHWAYS(	NEURO PHYSIOLOGY)/ DIFFERENTIAL SUPR	102749

Figure 4.2. Sample page from B.A.S.I.C. (Courtesy of BioSciences Information Service of Biological Abstracts.)

not well known. The permutation indexing systems of both Ohlman and Luhn use the author's title with no pre-editing; the CIA system provides for adding index terms to the title, a technique referred to as "title enrichment." The system uses a fixed field format that allows keypunching up to four "subject segments" for each 80-column punched card. More than one punched card may be used for a document, and, as stated previously, the title may be augmented at the discretion of the indexer. This procedure has the further advantage of allowing the printing of "see" and "see also" references. In addition, it can be handled entirely on card sorting equipment—it does not require the use of a computer. The CIA system has been found useful for retrieval, and economical to install and maintain.

Automatic permuted title indexing is being applied to an increasingly large number of reports, both within companies and agencies and within specialized disciplines, such as chemistry. It has been used primarily, though not exclusively, as a dissemination index for current awareness. As the volume of technical reports increases, many more information systems can be expected to use permutation indexing, or some variation, to cope with their documentation processing problems.

4.1.3 Citation Indexing.   The indexes examined up to this point are constructed from text contents—the author's words. Salton has studied "whether a similarity of bibliographic references or citations attached to two documents also implies a similarity of subject matter" [38, p. III-2]. The measure of similarity was based on the number of index terms shared by the two documents. A citation index is constructed* from the lists of references that accompany the text being indexed, on the assumption that if two texts cite the same references, they probably refer to the same subject. Kessler has termed this relationship "bibliographic coupling." He is testing the hypothesis that "scientific papers bear a meaningful relation to each other (they are coupled) when they have one or more references in common. Two papers that share one reference contain one unit of coupling" [23, p. 2]. Kessler has formulated two coupling criteria:

> *Criterion A*-A number of papers constitute a related group G_A if each member of the group has at least one reference (one coupling unit) in common with a given text paper P_O. The coupling strength between P_O and any member of G_A is measured by the number of coupling units between them. G_A^n is that portion of G_A that is linked to P_O through n

---

*A particularly clear, step-by-step description of the preparation of a citation index is provided in Lipetz [25]. The study used a group of 740 papers published in the *Proceedings* of two UN conferences on peaceful uses of atomic energy, and involved more than 11,000 citations.

coupling units. (According to this criterion there need not be any coupling between the members of G_A, only between them and P_O.)

Criterion B-A number of papers constitute a related group G_B if each member of the group has at least one coupling unit with every other member of the group. The coupling strength of G_B is measured by the number of coupling units between its members. Criterion B differs from Criterion A in that it forms a closed structure of interrelated papers, whereas Criterion A forms an open structure of papers related to a test paper.

Kessler, in studying the utility of bibliographic coupling, has demonstrated the existence of a logical relationship among papers in the G_A group, using reports published in *Physical Review*.

Garfield [19, 20] stresses the use of a citation index as a tool by which papers may be examined in historical perspective. He defines a citation index as "a directory of cited *references,* each accompanied by a list of citing *source* documents. The primary ordering of a citation index may be on the author of the reference, creating an author citation index; or on the publication in which the reference appeared, creating a journal citation index."*

As Tukey [46] has pointed out, most scientists conduct a literature search by following through the relationship of one article to another by means of the references provided by each author (directed browsing). The citation index enables one to do this more efficiently and more completely, since it lists articles that have referred to a particular paper, in addition to the articles cited by that paper. The researcher can thus search both forward and backward in time, with a given article as his reference point. The author citation index should reduce the labor of gathering the "historical" data needed to start a project and to prepare a scientific paper, and thus, should reduce the amount of unnecessary duplication of research. As the scientist traces through the references, he may find that his idea had already been pursued by another researcher and results published. Conversely, he may be stimulated by exposure to citations he might not otherwise have considered pertinent, but that, because they cite a reference he does consider pertinent, reveal unpredicted applications.

Figure 4.3 illustrates the format of the author citation index. An author can look up his own name in the index and quickly determine the names of other writers who have used his publications, thus learning of other researchers who are engaged in studying similar problems. He may find in this list some names that are unfamiliar to him, as well as references

---

*In addition to the cited references, Dr. Garfield has graciously provided the author with various pieces of unpublished material from the Institute of Scientific Information.

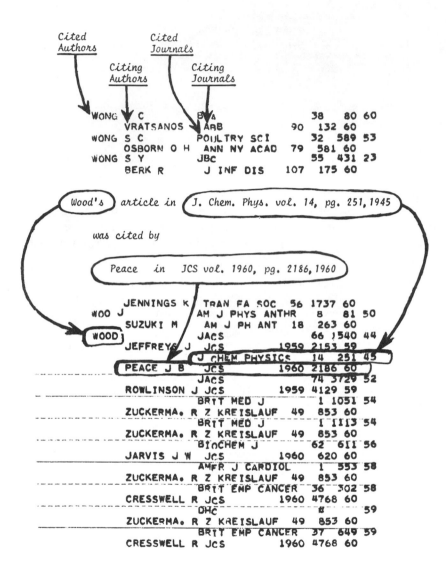

Figure 4.3 Author citation index printout. Courtesy *Institute for Scientific Information*

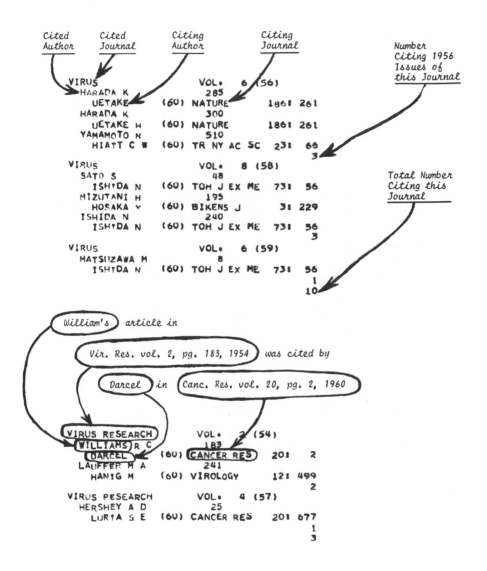

Figure 4.4   Journal citation index printout. Courtesy *Institute for Scientific Information*

to abstracts, reviews, and translations of his own work. Of special value in the academic environment, the citation index facilitates assessment of a scientific contribution, on the basis of the number of papers citing the contribution—that is, the degree to which it aided or stimulated other contributions.

The journal citation index (Figure 4.4) provides information concerning the use that scientists in a particular discipline (e.g., atomic physics) make of specific journals. By using this index we can determine, for example, the number of physicists who refer to chemical journals, or to *Science*, etc. This index helps guide or stimulates the direction of further scanning and may be analyzed to provide data about the journals themselves.

4.1.4 Association Indexing. A standard index, such as an index in the back of a book or a card catalog in a library, lists the index terms alphabetically. Users of the index are familiar with the alphabet and experience no difficulty in finding a given term. Thus, the alphabetical index is an efficient aid to document retrieval. Nevertheless, we may question whether other arrangements would work as well, or better.*

So far as we know, the human mind *associates ideas,* rather than storing terms alphabetically by topic. Can an index be organized in the same way? Doyle [15] suggested, early in 1961, the possibility of representing text-derived associations among index terms in a diagrammatic, or map-like, format. In more recent articles [16, 17] he examines, in detail, methods of measuring these associations and arranging the terms in an association map.

The map shown in Figure 4.5 was hand-drawn by Doyle. The strength of the correlations between the terms, based upon their co-occurrence in a body of 618 psychological abstracts, is represented graphically by the line of arrows for high correlation, the solid line for lower correlation, and dotted line for low correlation. Computer programs have been written which will draw the map automatically. Doyle suggests that the output of such a program would consist of a display of the map on a cathode ray tube, with printed maps being prepared off-line (i.e., from magnetic tape records).

Index terms are arranged in an association map in such a way that terms pertaining to similar concepts are clustered in the display space. Terms are grouped together, not because they start with the same letter of the alphabet but because they deal with similar subjects or related concepts. This association map can be viewed as a highly condensed and

---

*For example, one efficient way to obtain information is to ask an expert.

highly organized representation of a library. In conducting a search, the user would scan the map until he found the cluster of words pertaining to his topic. Having selected a topic, the user could then be shown an elaboration of the specified portion of the map containing the original cluster.

To illustrate the usefulness of the association map index, let us suppose that a researcher requested articles dealing with achievement programs

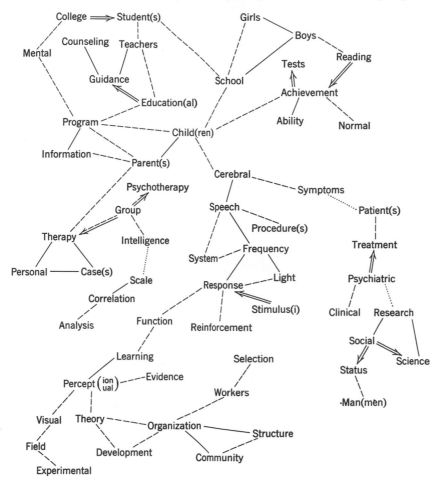

Figure 4.5   Association map based on Psychological Literature

in the public schools. In coordinate indexing, the terms "achievement" and "school" would elicit citations for some articles. However, compare this to the richness of the association map. As the searcher's eye scans the map area dealing with "school" and "achievement," he becomes aware that he can examine "achievement tests," "reading achievement," and "normal achievement," as well as "educational guidance programs for students who need counseling concerning their school progress." By providing the searcher with a map of the organized literature in the library, association indexing facilitates browsing and aids retrieval. The technique should prove very valuable, particularly if association maps can be generated automatically and disseminated quickly.

4.2 COMPUTER BASED CLASSIFICATION SYSTEMS

A classification system is a scheme for organizing a mass of material into groups, so that related objects are brought together in a systematic fashion. Objects that share more specified characteristics with one another than they share with other objects are classed together. By establishing nonoverlapping classes, the classificationist helps reduce to reasonable proportions the number of items one must scan to locate desired information.

Although the notion is conceptually simple, the practical problems involved in differentiating like objects are many. Consider, for example, a monograph dealing with coal mining in Germany. Should this be filed under "Germany" as one of its many industries, or should it be filed under "coal mining" with Germany being just one of a number of places in which coal mining is done? To solve this problem, we establish a convention; in this case the article would be filed under "Germany." This means that to do a study on coal mining throughout the world, one must look up "coal mining" as a subordinate subject under various country names. The point being made is that the efficiency of a particular method of classification is dependent upon the search strategy that will be used to retrieve the documents. Furthermore, no one method of classification will be equally efficient for all search techniques. This is an important point, and though obvious, is often overlooked.

Since it is impossible to anticipate the information need patterns and search requests of all users, why not eliminate classification categories altogether and file a reference to the document under all appropriate index terms? Some organizations have adopted this solution. However, the use of a descriptor list of 5,000 to 10,000 unique index terms, accumulated and arranged alphabetically, is slow and inefficient—especially for the inexperienced user attempting to formulate a search request. As the number of items in a file increases, whether the items are documents in a library or lists of index terms, some form of classification becomes necessary to facilitate a search of the file.

Apparently, then, rather than eliminating classification, we must select a classification system that will optimize the organization of the file. But, any static classification system, based upon a preconceived and logically organized set of categories, soon becomes outmoded and inadequate as the result of the dynamic growth of man's knowledge. What is needed is an empirically derived, dynamic system capable of describing a given set of documents at a particular point in time and capable of being reorganized with a minimum of duplicated effort. Such a dynamic system of classification is made possible by the use of modern computer technology.

4.2.1 Principles for Determining Class Membership. Classification is usually thought of in terms of "subject headings"; that is, documents are grouped according to their subject matter as determined by skilled librarians. Although this is one of the more common of the classification schemes, it is not the only one possible. Certainly, it is not a suitable principle on which to base an automated classification system. A computer cannot determine the subject content of a document the way a librarian does. A computer can process words, and the principle on which automated classification systems are based is statistical: *documents can be classified on the basis of the words they contain.* Documents on different topics use different sets of words. Therefore, documents can be ordered into classes on the basis of similarity or differences in vocabulary.

It is recognized that this principle will not guarantee 100-percent accurate classification. After all, one can express the same idea using different words, and it is also possible to use the same words to express different ideas. However, if we limit ourselves to scientific communication, these considerations should not cause serious difficulties, for the technical writer selects his words so as to inform and not to confuse. Classifying documents in accordance with the principle of similar word usage should result in a classification system analogous to, but not identical with, traditional subject categories and should be usable by both men and machines.

4.2.2 Procedures for Deriving Classification Systems. With the advent of large high-speed computers and complex statistical programming, it became possible to derive dynamic classification systems for collections of documents. The first attempts in this direction were made by Luhn, who showed that the content words of a document could be selected automatically, by computers. He also pointed out that documents containing similar content words tended to deal with the same content material, and, therefore, could be grouped together. Luhn (if I may thus interpret his work) considered that if documents were indexed by their key words, further classification would be unnecessary. "Rather than subtilize the artful classification schemes now in use," he wrote, "new systems would replace them in large part by mechanical routines based on rather elementary reasoning." [26, p. 309]

Tanimoto [43] took a different approach to the problem of classification. He argued that a scientific classification system is based upon determining a set of fundamental attributes of the objects to be classified. Furthermore, an effective scientific information system will enable one to predict the existence or nonexistence of an attribute. Tanimoto proceeded to describe a probabilistic theory upon which a system of classification and prediction could be based.

Parker-Rhodes [35] and Needham [32, 33] have derived a theory of clumps. A clump is a subset or class of elements (documents) selected from a universe (e.g., a library of documents). The essential problem of clumping is to choose, mathematically, those elements in a clump that have more in common with each other than the elements outside the clump. Different kinds of clumps, based on different techniques of grouping, are identified; for example, R-clump, GR-clump, AF-clump, etc. Parker-Rhodes does not state that the theory of clumps is a theory of classification. Nevertheless, the theory does provide a method for grouping together those elements in a universe of data that appear, by some definition, to belong together. This grouping, or clumping, is, in essence, classification—a point that has been recognized and that serves as a basis for some clumping experiments being performed by A. G. Dale and N. Dale [13, 14].

In discussing the application of mathematical methods to classification problems, Parker-Rhodes considered the use of factor analysis.

> "In so far as it is practically applicable this technique [factor analysis] has worked well enough; but I propose to suggest that it has two limitations (a) that some classification problems are in principle outside its scope, and (b) that it is not susceptible (at least as hitherto conceived) of adaptation computationally to the study of really large universes. [35, p. 2]

The limitation referred to in point (a) is that statistical techniques cannot be used to discover classes but are suited only to determine the probability that an item belongs to a given class. There is ample evidence in psychological literature that (if carefully applied) factor analysis can be used to map an area into its basic dimensions. Factor analysis has been used to determine primary mental abilities and the basic dimensions of personality. More can be done with this technique than simply calculating the probability that an item belongs to a particular class.

The second limitation, that the technique is not applicable to the computational study of large universes of data, was valid in the past, but is being corrected. Computer programs have been written that can handle a 90-by-90 matrix and, more recently, a 150-by-150 matrix. In process is a program for factoring a 1000-variable matrix. With the help of large high speed computers, we are learning to apply factor analysis to increasingly large universes of data. The method has no inherent capacity limitations, although economics may limit its application.

One of the first studies concerned with deriving a classification system by a factor analysis of document content was reported by Borko. The summary of this report follows:

> This study describes a method for developing an empirically based, computer derived classification system. Six hundred and eighteen psychological abstracts were coded in machine language for computer processing. The total text consisted of approximately 50,000 words of which nearly 6,800 were unique words. The computer program arranged these words in order of frequency of occurrence. From the list of words which occurred 20 or more times, excluding syntactical terms, such as "and," "but," "of," etc., the investigator selected 90 words for use as index terms. These were arranged in a data matrix with the terms on the horizontal and the document number on the vertical axis. The cells contained the number of times the term was used in the document. Based on these data, a correlation matrix, 90-by-90 in size, was computed which showed the relationship of each term to every other term. The matrix was factor analyzed and the first 10 eigenvectors were selected as factors. These were rotated for meaning and interpreted as major categories in a classification system. These factors were compared with, and shown to be compatible with but not identical to, the classification system used by the American Psychological Association. The results demonstrate the feasibility of an empirically derived classification system and establish the value of factor analysis as a technique in language data processing. [5, p. 279]

Borko [6] has continued his research in this area and has used factor analysis to derive a classification system that could describe the literature in the computer field. In addition, he has studied methods for automatically classifying documents into categories. The results obtained in these studies were comparable to those computed by Maron (See Section 4.2.3).

Other researchers are beginning to take an interest in the problems of classification and are studying the application of mathematical techniques to its solution. Baker [2] has proposed an information retrieval system based upon latent class analysis, a mathematical technique related to factor analysis. Latent class analysis was developed by Lazarsfeld [24], a sociologist, who used it to analyze questionnaires. Baker described the mathematical model for latent class analysis, and illustrated its application to information retrieval by means of a theoretical example. There is some question whether this particular technique allows derivation of a classification system or could best be used to test the adequacy of established categories. Since no empirical data were presented, the answer to this question awaits further research. Indeed, further research is required to demonstrate the effectiveness of any or all of the above mentioned mathematically derived classification systems, but the fact that classification systems can be mathematically derived from empirical data has been demonstrated.

4.2.3 Procedures for Classifying Documents. Maron [30] describes a procedure for "deciding in a mechanical way to which category (subject or field of knowledge) a given document belongs. It [the study] concerns the problem of deciding automatically what a given document is 'about'." This is an important study; it bridges the gap between the methods of deriving a classification system and those of automatically assigning index tags to documents without reference to classification.

In this "modest experimental study," as Maron refers to it, he used, as data, 405 abstracts of articles about computer technology published in the *IRE Transactions on Electronic Computers*. Maron considered the IRE classification system to be insufficiently discriminative; so he devised a set of 32 subject categories that he believed were more logically descriptive of the material. The 405 abstracts were divided into an experimental group of 260, called Set A, and a validation group of 145, called Set B. After classifying the documents of Set A, Maron selected 90 clue words that were good descriptors of the documents in their categories.

After completing the preliminary work, Maron proceeded to test his hypothesis that "a computing machine can correctly index documents on the basis of the occurrence of selected clue words in the document" [30, p. 411]. The results show "that if a document has at least two clue words (there were 210 such documents in group A), then the probability that the category with the greatest attribute number is a correct one is $191/210 = 91$ (percent)" [30, p. 411-12].

These results were validated by applying the same procedures to Set B, which was not used to select either the classification categories or the clue words. Of these 145 documents, only 85 contained two clue words; 44 of these, or 51.8 percent, were correctly and automatically placed in their proper category. These statistics clearly indicate the possibility of using a computer to assign automatically a document to its proper category in a classification system.

Borko and Bernick [6] applied factor analysis to the same 405 abstracts and derived 21 categories. Then, using human classification as the criterion, and using prediction equations based upon the factor scores, they attempted to classify automatically the documents into their proper categories. Of the validation group, 44 documents were classified identically by both the program and the humans. This is the same number reported by Maron. The results support the conclusion that automatic document classification is possible; although it may not be very practical as yet. These studies have even broader implications, for, as Maron says, "The problem of indexing brings us to the door of semantics and with it come all of the difficulties involved in an analysis of the concept of meaning" [30, p. 405].

In a later study by Borko and Bernick [7], aimed at improving the percentage of correct classification, they compared the factor scores with the Bayesian prediction equations. It was concluded that there was no statistically significant difference in the ability of these two procedures to classify documents automatically. However, the experiments did show that a slightly higher percentage of documents were correctly classified by mathematical means when using an empirically derived classification schedule as compared with a set of logically derived categories.

Trachenberg suggested that the efficiency of automatic document classification could be increased by improving the selection of clue words. He proposed to identify significant words by means of two information-theoretic measures and also used these measures as a basis for automatic classification of the document. He explained his criterion for the selection of clue words as follows:

> Thus the occurrence of the good clue word in documents must not only be strongly correlated with classification of these documents in one particular category, but the distribution of documents containing this word must markedly differ from the category distribution of all documents, i.e., it must supply more information than the *a priori* distribution of documents in categories did. [45, p. 349]

These concepts can be expressed mathematically by the proposed information-theoretic measures, which also enable one to select, as clues, not only single words but also word pairs, word triplets, and even higher order word combinations. Although no empirical data on the model are available, Trachenberg has proposed to test the validity of his model by conducting experiments on the same data base as that used by Maron and Borko.

Still another model for improving automatic document classification is the discriminant analysis method proposed by Williams [48]. This procedure classifies a document into the appropriate category by comparing the observed frequency of each significant word in the document with the corresponding theoretical frequencies computed for each of the possible categories. Using this system, a document can be classified into more than one category on the basis of the computed "relevance value." The initial report on the use of this discriminant model is encouraging.

Salton [37] suggested the use of two automatic methods as aids in improving automated content analysis of natural language texts. The first of these dealt with the use of syntactic analysis for the recognition of word associations and the second made use of bibliographic citations to determine document similarity. As discussed earlier, Garfield [19, 20] and Kessler [23] have shown that documents that cite the same references tend to deal with the same subject matter and that, therefore, citation indexes can be used as a method of grouping documents.

As the references indicate, there are a number of promising procedures enabling one to decide in a mechanical way to which category a given document belongs. By means of these statistical techniques, it is possible to overcome some of the semantic problems involved in determining the subject of a document.

4.3 SUMMARY AND CONCLUSIONS

Automated language processing techniques are being applied to the indexing and classification of documents so as to lead toward the establishment of an automated document storage and retrieval system. These mechanically produced indexes and classification categories are derived by means of statistical analysis of the words in the text. Much experimentation is taking place, and many varied and nonconventional methods of indexing and coding information are being developed.

How does one evaluate the usefulness of nonconventional indexes? As was pointed out in the introduction to this chapter, the fact that the mechanically produced index differs from the manually produced one makes evaluation difficult, but it does not mean that one is *ipso facto* better than the other. Ultimately, the usefulness of an index must be evaluated in terms of its effectiveness for retrieval of relevant documents in an information storage and retrieval system. A significant advance in evaluation methods has been made by Cleverdon [10, 11]. The ASLIB studies compared various manual indexing systems, and the resulting reports stirred up some healthy controversy [36]. Automated indexes were not included in the Cleverdon study and a comparative evaluation of their efficiency still needs to be done. Even though rigorous comparative studies of retrieval efficiency are not available, it is still possible to examine the mechanized indexing techniques in terms of what they are designed to accomplish.

First, while automated indexing does require computer processing, it does eliminate the need for a skilled librarian—a skill that is in short supply. Second, automatic indexing can be done faster than manual indexing, and making items in a collection accessible to users with least delay is often a critical consideration. Whether automatic indexing is less expensive than manual indexing is still an open question and is partially dependent upon the computer being used, and upon whether the writing of the program and the keypunching of the text is considered in the cost accounting. (Programs may be made available to all users, and keypunching may be eliminated by the use of character readers or by tape produced as a byproduct of automated type setting devices.) Third, automated indexing provides capabilities unobtainable by manual methods. VAPS and concordances allow for the indexing of a document by *all* important content words; KWIC shows all content words of a title in context; association maps arrange terms by strength of co-occurrence, rather than alphabetically; and citation indexing groups together all documents that cite similar references. Unquestionably, then, these nonconventional indexes do provide valuable aids for the researcher. Whether they should replace, or be used as an adjunct to, manual indexing awaits further research and experience.

Evaluating the utility of automated document classification procedures appears to be a more complex problem. It would be helpful to differentiate two aspects of the question and to examine each. The first aspect may be phrased

> Can documents be placed into classification categories with sufficient accuracy so as to facilitate the retrieval of relevant documents?

The only available experimental evidence by Borko and Bernick [6, 7, 8] and by Maron [30] indicates that human and automatic classification will agree in only slightly more than fifty percent of the cases. This is not a very high percentage, but before one dismisses automatic classification as being useless, it is necessary to point out that human classifiers agree with each other only about seventy-five percent of the time [8]. The real question is not how well the automatic procedure agrees with the human, but how much either method adds to the efficiency of the information storage and retrieval system. Unfortunately, no definitive answer can be given to this question, and so the value of using automated methods for putting documents into categories remains in doubt. All that can be said, at this time, is that machine methods of document classification are faster and more reliable than their human counterpart. The validity of the procedure is a subject for further investigation.

The second aspect of the evaluation problem may be phrased

> Are there any advantages to be obtained by deriving classification categories automatically (i.e., mathematically) as compared with a classification scheme derived by means of a logical analysis of a topic or field of study?

The available studies on mathematically derived classification systems are based on relatively small collections of documents. Even so, these required the use of considerable time on large computer systems. The resulting categories were quite broad. Therefore, although the computational techniques will undoubtedly be improved, a large general library should not attempt to classify its books according to mathematically derived categories. Furthermore, systems such as Dewey and Library of Congress are clearly superior where they exist. Large specialized libraries such as engineering, chemistry, or psychology libraries also have available specialized classification schedules and would find the derived categories too gross for practical use.

The major applications of mathematically derived classification categories are in situations where there are no existing classification schedules, such as:

a. Specialized collections of current technical reports on the leading edge of science and technology, e.g., in the field of artificial intelligence.
b. Specialized collections of current technical reports being produced by a particular corporation or organization, e.g., The RAND Corporation or the Harvard Computation Laboratory.
c. Specialized collections of information whose basic character is constantly changing so that new trends need to be identified and the organization of the data modified. Such a need exists in the processing of intelligence reports.
d. Accumulations of documents by individual researchers of small projects for their specialized, and often temporary, needs.

In each of these four cases, and in others that are similar, one must determine the basic dimensions into which the entire collection can be divided. A gross organizational pattern is needed as well as an efficient, objective method for finding this pattern by using a technique such as factor analysis. The fact that the classification system was derived mathematically makes for ease of modification as the collection changes. Thus, we see that automatic classification clearly supplements, but does not replace, manual systems of classification.

Studies in automated indexing and classification have been undertaken in response to a real need for improving the storage and retrieval of information. Some progress has already been made and, although much more needs to be done, it is obvious that these are important and fruitful areas of application for automated language processing.

REFERENCES

1. Artandi, S., A selective bibilography survey of automatic indexing methods, *Spec. Libraries,* v. 54, no. 10, 1963, pp. 630-34.

2. Baker, F. B., Information retrieval based upon latent class analyses, *J. of the ACM,* v. 9, no. 4, October 1962, pp. 512-21.

3. Baxendale, P., Machine-made index for technical literature—an experiment, *IBM J. of Research and Development,* v. 2, no. 4, 1958, pp. 354-61.

4. Baxendale, P., An empirical model for computer indexing, *Machine Indexing: Progress and Problems.* Washington: The American U., 1961.

5. Borko, H., The construction of an empirically based mathematically derived classification system, *Proc. 1962 Spring Joint Computer Conference,* v. 21, pp. 279-89.

6. Borko, H. and M. Bernick, Automatic document classification, *J. of the ACM,* v. 10, no. 2, April 1963, pp. 151-62.

7. Borko, H. and M. Bernick, Automatic document classification, Part II—additional experiments, *J. of the ACM,* v. 11, no. 2, April 1964, pp. 138-51.

8. Borko, H., Measuring the reliability of subject classification by men and machines, *Amer. Doc.,* v. 15, no. 4, October 1964, pp. 268-74.

9. Citron, J., L. Hart, and H. Ohlman, A permutation index to the preprints of the International Conference on Scientific Information, *SP-44,* Rev. ed. Santa Monica, Calif.: System Development Corp., December 1959. Orginally published November 1958.

10. Cleverdon, C. W., Final report on first stage of an investigation into the comparative efficiency of indexing systems. Cranfield, England: ASLIB, 1960.

11. Cleverdon, C. W., Report on the testing and analysis of an investigation into the comparative efficiency of indexing systems. Cranfield, England: ASLIB, October 1962.

12. Climenson, W. D., N. H. Hardwick, and S. N. Jacobson, Automatic syntax analysis in machine indexing and abstracting, *Amer. Doc.,* v. 12, no. 3, 1961, pp. 178-83.

13. Dale, A. G. and N. Dale, Some clumping experiments for information retrieval. Austin, Tex.: The U. of Texas Linguistic Research Center, February 1964.

14. Dale, A. G. and N. Dale, Clumping technique and associative retrieval. Austin, Tex.: The U. of Texas Linguistic Research Center, March 1964.

15. Doyle, L. B., Semantic road maps for literature searchers, *J. of the ACM,* v. 8, no. 4, 1961, pp. 553-78.

16. Doyle, L. B., Indexing and abstracting by association, *Amer. Doc.,* v. 13, no. 4, October 1962, pp. 378-90.

17. Doyle, L. B., *et al.,* Programmed generation of association maps from collection of keyword lists: final report, *TM-2083.* Santa Monica, Calif.: System Development Corp., 17 September 1964.

18. Edmundson, H. P. and R. E. Wyllys, Automatic abstracting and indexing-survey and recommendations, *Comm. of the ACM,* v. 4, no. 5, 1961, pp. 226-34.

19. Garfield, E., Citation indexes for science, *Science,* v. 122, no. 3159, 15 July 1955, pp. 108-11.

20. Garfield, E., Science citation index—a new dimension in indexing, *Science,* v. 144, no. 3619, May 8, 1961, pp. 649-54.

21. Jaster, J. J., B. R. Murray, and M. Taube, *The State of The Art of Coordinate Indexing.* Washington: Documentation, Inc., February 1962 (Preliminary Ed.).

22. Kennedy, R. A., Mechanized title word indexing of internal reports. *Machine Indexing: Progress and Problems.* Washington: The American U., 1961, pp. 112-32.

23. Kessler, M. M., An experimental study of bibliographic coupling between technical papers, *MITR-1,* November 1961, rev. June 1962.

24. Lazarsfeld, P. F., Latent structure analysis, Chapters 10 and 11 of The American Soldier, v. 4, *Measurement and Prediction,* S. A. Stouffer, ed. Princeton, N. J.: Princeton U. Press, 1950.

25. Lipetz, B., Compilation of an experimental citation index from scientific literature, Technical Report *IB 4000-19.* Itek Laboratories, June 1961.

26. Luhn, H. P., A statistical approach to mechanical encoding and searching of library information, *IBM J. of Research and Development,* v. 1, no. 4, October 1957, pp. 309-17.

27. Luhn, H. P., The automatic creation of literature abstracts, *IBM J. of Research and Development,* v. 2, no. 2, April 1958, pp. 159-317.

28. Luhn, H. P., Keywords in context index for technical literature (KWIC index), *Amer. Doc.,* v. 11, no. 4, October 1960, pp. 288-95.

29. *Machine Indexing: Progress and Problems.* Washington: The American U., 1961.

30. Maron, M. E., Automatic indexing: an experimental inquiry, *J. of the ACM,* v. 8, no. 3, July 1961, pp. 404-17.

31. Mooers, C. N., Zatocoding applied to mechanical organization of knowledge, *Amer. Doc.,* v. 2, no. 1, January 1951, pp. 20-32.

32. Needham, R. M., The theory of clumps II, *ML 139.* Cambridge, England: The Cambridge Language Research Unit, March 1961.

33. Needham, R. M., Research on information retrieval classification and grouping, *ML 149.* Cambridge, England: The Cambridge Language Research Unit, October 1961.

34. O'Connor, J., Some remarks on mechanized indexing and small-scale empirical results, *Machine Indexing: Progress and Problems.* Washington: The American U., 1961, pp. 266-79.

35. Parker-Rhodes, A. F., Contributions to the theory of clumps, *ML 138.* Cambridge, England: The Cambridge Language Research Unit, March 1961.

36. Rees, A. M., Review of a report on the ASLIB-Cranfield test of the index of metallurgical literature of Western Reserve University. Cleveland: Western Reserve U. Center for Documentation and Communication Research, October 1963.

37. Salton, G., Some experiments in the generation of word and document associations, *Proc. 1962 Fall Joint Computer Conference,* v. 22, pp. 234-50.

38. Salton, G., The use of citations as an aid to automatic content analysis, Scientific Report No. *ISR-2.* Cambridge, Mass.: Harvard U., September 1, 1962.

39. Simmons, R. F., and K. L. McConlogue, Maximum-depth indexing for computer retrieval of English language data, *SP-775.* Santa Monica, Calif: System Development Corp., April 1962.

40. Spiegel, J., *et al.,* Statistical association procedures for message content analysis, *SR-79.* Bedford, Mass.: Mitre Corp., Information System Language Studies, no. 1, 1962.

41. Stevens, M. E., *Automatic Indexing: A State of the Art Report,* NBS Monograph 91. Washington: National Bureau of Standards, March 1965.

42. Stiles, H. E., The association factor in information retrieval, *J. of the ACM,* v. 8, 1961, pp. 271-79.

43. Tanimoto, T. T., An elementary mathematical theory of classification and prediction. IBM, 17 November 1958.

44. Taube, M., C. D. Gull, and I. S. Wachtel, Unit terms in coordinate indexing, *Amer. Doc.,* v. 3, no. 4, October 1952, pp. 213-18.

45. Trachenberg, A., Automatic document classification using information theoretical methods, *Automation and Scientific Communication,* Part 2, H. P. Luhn, ed., American Documentation Institute, 1962, pp. 349-50.

46. Tukey, J. W., Keeping research in contact with the literature: citation indexing and beyond. Bell Telephone Laboratories and Princeton U. Mimeographed papers.

47. Veilleux, M. P., Permuted title word indexing procedures for a man-machine system, *Machine Indexing: Progress and Problems.* Washington: The American U., 1961, pp. 77-111.

48. Williams, J. H., Jr., A discrimination method for automatically classifying documents, *Proc. 1963 Fall Joint Computer Conference,* v. 24, pp. 161-67.

Extracting and Abstracting by Computer

Ronald E. Wyllys

5.1 CONDENSED REPRESENTATIONS OF DOCUMENTS

To provide a theoretical setting, any discussion of abstracting should begin with the more general concept of "condensed representations of documents."* This phrase is intended to include any bibliographic device which is associated with a given document and which, to a greater or lesser extent, reveals the content of the document. Thus the concept of condensed representation ranges from the subject classification portion of the call number of a book, at one extreme, to lengthy reviews of articles and books at the other. Excluded are only those devices that are generally quite unrelated to the content of a document, such as accession numbers. Familiar types of condensed representations include subject headings, titles, sets of index terms (or "descriptors"), lists of chapter or section headings, and abstracts.

Why should anyone be concerned with condensed representations of documents? Swanson answers this question by suggesting that one

> consider for a moment a 'thinkable' solution to the whole difficulty [of finding, in a library, information pertinent to a requester's interest]. Clearly, if the requester himself could read all existing literature [that is, every page of the entire library collection] and apply to each piece of information found therein expert intuitive criteria in order to ascertain its relevance to the requirement at hand, there would be, in principle, no problem of communicating recorded knowledge; the procedure suffers only from total impracticality. The historical answer to such impracticality is of course to organize, classify, index, and catalog the library and then search only a very small amount of catalog-type information. . . .
> In short, some kind of condensed 'representation' of the contents of the library is created. This representation, since it is condensed, is necessarily

*The term "condensed representation" was apparently first used by Swanson [46].

imperfect; the price paid for the convenience of having a practical and manageable search capability is the loss of at least some [and quite possibly most] of the accessible information in the library. . . . Intuitively, one knows that the larger and more detailed the index and catalog, the less the information loss but the greater the difficulty of searching. Indeed, in the extreme, if each sentence of each article of the collection were cataloged, the 'representation' of the library so created might approach high fidelity but would be almost as impractical as the library itself for conducting searches. [46, p. 1099]

One of the widely used traditional types of condensed representation is the abstract. In its usual form it is the product of a considerable amount of human time and effort, whether the abstract is that provided by the author of a scientific or technical article, by the editor of the journal in which the article appears, or by an independent reviewer-abstractor. And there is more than just time and effort involved; the traditional abstract is also susceptible to the biases, misplaced emphases, and misinterpretations—accidental or deliberate—of the writer of the abstract.

If methods can be developed of producing abstracts (or an essentially equivalent kind of condensed representation) by computer programs, such abstracts would have, at least, the advantages of reducing the amount of human time, effort, and misinterpretation embodied in the abstract. Whether other disadvantages of computer produced abstracts would be sufficiently offset by these advantages is still an open question. The most serious disadvantage of current computer produced abstracts is that they consist of individual sentences of the original text, extracted according to one or more criteria. Not only do the extraction criteria require further research, but the resulting sets of individual sentences present problems of disjointedness, incompleteness, redundancy, and the like.

The ultimate goal of research in automatic abstracting is to enable a computer program to "read" a document and "write" an abstract of it in conventional prose style, but the path to this goal is full of yet unconquered obstacles. To understand what these obstacles are and what some possible means of surmounting them may be, we need to review the work that has been done in automatic abstracting, the problems that have been solved, and those that remain. We begin by considering the basic functions to be served by abstracts and other condensed representations of documents.

5.1.1 Functions of Condensed Representations. A condensed representation of a document can serve either:

a. as a search tool, i.e., as a means of relating the represented document to the interest of a person seeking documents pertinent to that interest, or

b. as a means of revealing, more or less fully, the essential content of the represented document.

These two basic functions of condensed representations, which we shall call the search-tool and the content-revelatory functions, have been distinguished by other workers in the field of information retrieval, albeit the distinction has sometimes been only implicit. For example, Rath, Resnick, and Savage say

> Two functions of a lexical indicator of content [scil., a condensed representation] are: 1) to determine whether a document is relevant for a specific purpose, and 2) to find out some information from the document without having to read it in its original form. [35, p. 126]

Similarly, Edmundson and his colleagues distinguish the content–revelatory and search-tool functions—and point up a subfunction of the former—by stating:

> 1. The *summary* or digestive function is that of presenting to the reader substantive information on the most 'important' and 'significant' aspects of the abstracted paper. ...We include here also the current-awareness function, which is that of keeping the reader generally informed on new developments and publications in his field of interest.
> 2. Related to but clearly separate from the summary function is the *information retrieval* function. An abstract should contain informative clues to all potentially significant aspects of the article so that the reader can determine with reasonable certainty whether or not it is worth his time and effort to read the complete article. [34, p. 4]

To some extent the content–revelatory and the search–tool functions conflict with each other. As a search–tool, a document representation should ideally be as short as possible while still serving to relate the document to the searcher's interest. The shorter a tool can be while still serving this purpose, the more effective it will be. Yet brevity necessarily means that less of the content of the document can be revealed. Up to a point, the more fully a representation reveals the content of the document, the longer the representation must be.

It is clear that different types of condensed representations vary in their services to the search-tool and the content-revelatory functions. It is also clear that both these functions are needed, but needed to different degrees at different stages in a search. For example, at the beginning of a search for documents pertinent to one's interest of the moment, one is mainly concerned with using representations as search tools rather than as revelators of content. On the other hand, the final stage of a search consists of examining highly content-revelatory representations such as abstracts, reviews, and even the original documents.

An obvious implication of these considerations is that at each stage in the search process the type of condensed representation best suited to that stage should be used. With regard to semiautomated document retrieval systems, two less obvious implications are that the search tools used should be systematically ordered, and that we need not necessarily confine ourselves to traditional library tools or their analogs. The association map illustrates the second conclusion directly, since it is not only new but is (for practical use) wholly dependent on computers; it illustrates the first conclusion indirectly, in that the association map—like any other type of condensed representation, existing or potential—must be used at a suitable stage in the search process. (See Doyle [10] for the concept of the association map.)

5.1.2 Definition of Abstract.   Thus far we have been relying on the reader's intuitive notion of the meaning of the word "abstract." However, it is often difficult to determine whether a given condensed representation of a document is an abstract or something else. For instance, the difference between a "descriptive abstract" (see Section 5.2.3) and a "review" of a book is largely a matter of length. Similarly, annotations in a bibliography are often hard to distinguish from abstracts.

Because of these difficulties, a definition of "abstract" is needed. We offer the following working definition, intended primarily to distinguish abstracts from other types of condensed representations for the purposes of the discussions in this chapter: "An abstract is

a. a description of, or a restatement of, the essential content of a document

b. which is phrased in complete sentences (except for bibliographic data)

c. and which usually has a length in the range of from 50 to 500 words."

Three points should be noted. First, this definition, unlike Webster's, eliminates such condensed-representation types as association maps and descriptor sets from the category of abstracts, since it requires complete sentences. Second, the upper limit of 500 words, while admittedly arbitrary, eliminates such bibliographic devices as long reviews and *Reader's Digest*-type condensations. Third, the definition covers both human-produced and machine-produced abstracts, since the latter consist (at least currently) of sentences extracted from the original document. In Section 5.4.2 we shall discuss how this definition may have to be modified to deal with possible future types of abstracts and other condensed representations. For the moment, however, we turn our attention to the traditional human-produced abstracts.

5.2   ABSTRACTS PREPARED BY HUMANS

Traditionally, abstracts have been prepared either by specialists in the subject matter of the document being abstracted, or by persons such as librarians who are trained or experienced in abstracting as a technique in itself. There are advantages and disadvantages to both approaches. Aware of the difficulties, many abstracting journals have set up guidelines for their abstractors. Expecting that a consensus of these guidelines would reveal basic principles of traditional abstracting practices, Borko and Chatman recently surveyed a number of abstracting journals [8]. Their results are summarized below under the headings: function, content, and form.

5.2.1   Function.   The survey showed that abstracting journals reflect the distinction between search–tool and content–revelatory abstracts by recognizing two basic types of abstracts. One type is usually referred to as "informative" ("informational," "direct"); it provides the reader with the basic informational content of the article. The other is the "indicative" abstract ("descriptive," "alerting"), whose function is to "permit the reader to decide whether the article or book reviewed would be of value or interest to him."

Some of the abstracting services provided examples contrasting the two approaches. Following is a pair of such examples for a meteorological article, quoted from the survey:

Informative: Brinell and scratch hardness tests were made on single ice crystals with a modified Olsen Baby Brinell Hardness Tester and a Spencer Microcharacter, respectively. Hardness increased with decrease in temperature; Brinell hardness numbers ranged from about 4 at -5°C to 17 at -50°C. A similar temperature dependence for scratch hardness was noted. The single ice crystal was harder parallel to the c-axis than in the normal direction.

Indicative: The experimental procedures and results of Brinell and scratch hardness tests on single ice crystals are given. The effects of temperature and c-axis orientation on hardness are discussed, and the experimental data are tabulated and graphed. [4]

The survey revealed interesting differences in the writing styles associated with the two types of abstracts. Writers of indicative abstracts tend to use passive constructions (e.g., "are given," "are tabulated," "is indicated") and to emphasize the writing of the article being abstracted rather than the research reported in the article. Writers of informative abstracts tend to identify themselves grammatically with the author of the article being abstracted. They tend to state directly the actual experiments or investigations performed, and the behavior or state of being of the things studied (e.g., "scratch hardness tests were made," "hardness increased," "hardness numbers ranged," "a similar temperature dependence...was noted").

Some journals indicated a desire to perform *both* an indicative and an informative function. One reported policy was to write indicative abstracts for surveys, lectures, and other articles which "contain too much information (especially if it is a review); [or where] the information in the article is well known (a discussion); [or if] the article concerns mathematics which is difficult to verbalize" [1]. Informative abstracts, on the other hand, were called for in the case of research reports, so that the research could be disseminated widely.

The results of the survey, as they concerned the *function* of abstracts, were summarized as follows:

Abstract Type	Journals	
	Percentage	Number
Informative:	17.7%	23
Indicative:	36.9%	48
Both:	24.6%	32
Other or unclear:	3.1%	4
No information:	17.7%	23
	100.0%	130

These differences did not appear to correspond to any contrast in subject matter or field, as for example, the difference between pure science and technology.

5.2.2 Content. The survey found editors generally agreeing that abstracts should include the four main topics (purpose, methods, results, and conclusion) and, where applicable, specialized information, and should exclude all excessive verbiage, as in the case of detailed explanations and the repetition of known results.

The abstractor was frequently instructed to state the "purpose" of the article, or "the reasons for the work that was performed," the "objectives," the "nature of the problem," or the "goals." A few journals called purpose, "hypothesis." The term "methods" was generally used as a summary term for the "way," the "approach," the "treatment," that is to say, *how* the results were sought, rather than *what* was sought. Journals in the hard sciences and technology asked for a description of apparatus, equipment, and material or a categorization into "laboratory" or "field techniques." Although a few journals asked simply for "what was learned," the majority distinguished between *results* and *conclusions*, the dichotomy of classical experimental procedure, in which the experimenter obtains findings and then proceeds to interpret them. Obviously, it is sometimes necessary for the abstractor to make a selection among results. Conclusions were at least partially distinguished from results by being called the "interpretations" of the results or their "significance."

In addition to the four major categories of purpose, methods, results, and conclusions, instructions were often given regarding special or supplementary information to be included in the abstract. Some examples of these instructions are: give length of article; give status of research, as in progress reports; give new terms and their definitions. Instructions were sometimes highly specialized to meet the needs of certain subject fields, for example:

> *Pharmacology:* "how many individuals there were in the experimental series; whether human or animal, and the species; what percentage reacted, etc.; and in the case of a new drug, its composition." [32]
> *Chemical Market Analysis:* "company, location, plans, dates, capacity, trade name, nature of product, patents, unit consumption factor." [42]
> *Sociology:* "type of question (open-ended, multiple-choice, true-false, etc.), and the manner of administration. ... The N used in the study, the basic breaks made, the geographic or social characteristics of respondents or sources ... scales must be named: Guttman, Thurstone, Likert, etc." [44]

The attitudes of the editors toward the quotation of statistics, numbers, and formulas in the abstract were found to differ. One journal felt that "numerical results represent the heart of the abstract" [6]. Others asked that numerical results be included only "if necessary to support the author's conclusions; [if so, they] may be used in the final portion of the abstract" [29]. On the other hand, at least one journal suggested that numerical data not be included: "If at all possible, please avoid the use of mathematics" [3].

The abstracting journals typically wanted certain other categories of information excluded from their abstracts. For example: "Speculation by the author or general conclusions which do not follow immediately from the results...ought to be omitted" [43]; the abstractor should not include any "facts already well established" [15]. The most widespread exclusion pertained to information already implicitly included either in the title or the table of contents. A few journals warned against taking material from the author's own abstract verbatim.

5.2.3 Form (Length).   Many journals gave directions concerning the form in which the abstract was to be written. It is convenient to distinguish style, abstractor's comments, and length as aspects of form, and the survey covered each of these aspects. Style was taken to mean writing style (not format instructions such as paragraphing, typing, and abbreviations) and dealt with such matters as phrase and sentence structure, the voice (active or passive) of verbs, and verb tenses. Abstractor's comments dealt with whether or not the journals allowed critical comments rather than mere reporting, and with placing of the content (of the article being abstracted) in the context of other work in its field. Although the survey developed many interesting results as to style and abstractor's comments, the state-of-the-art is such that these aspects of form are currently not concerns of automatic abstracting. Hence we shall present here only those results of the survey that have to do with the length of abstracts.

As one might expect, practice varied widely concerning optimal abstract length. Indeed, even the measuring stick varied: number of words, percentage of the original article, number of lines, number of sentences, and amount of the page covered. Some examples of the various prescriptions are:

a. Number of words:

50-100	200
100+	250
100-500	300
125-150	400-800
150	2000

b. Percentage of the original article:
less than 3%
4%-6% of medium length articles but less for longer ones

c. Number of lines:
3-8
5-20
28

d. Number of sentences:
1 or 2

e. Amount of the page (8 x 11 double-spaced covered):
3/4 of a page
1-1/2 pages
not more than 3 pages

Few journals were so brave as to leave abstract length unspecified. The survey quoted one of the journals:

No specific limits on length of abstract have been set for survey reports. The author should keep in mind the value of a concise abstract to a busy reader and should write what is needed for the abstract but no more. Short, compact papers generally require actually shorter but proportionally longer abstracts than large, detailed papers. There are many different arbitrary limits set by scientific and technical journals on the length of abstracts, some in terms of a word limit and some in terms of a ratio or percentage limit. [48]

Most journals recognized that abstract length should be flexible to accommodate the different kinds of materials abstracted. Articles from foreign or difficult-to-obtain journals were frequently given longer treatment, while review articles were given quite brief abstracts.

5.2.4 The Contrasting Functions of Abstracts. The survey of the practices of abstracting journals points up the need to distinguish between the content-revelatory and the search-tool functions of abstracts. It also points up the fact that such a distinction has often been made—though not always clearly—in traditional abstracting practice. But when one attempts to apply some of the usual criteria for human-prepared informative or indicative abstracts to the problem of automatically producing abstracts, certain interesting difficulties arise, in the following way.

In their present stage of development, automatic abstracts consist of sentences selected from the original document. Hence they share the characteristic of informative abstracts (as opposed to indicative abstracts) of dealing directly with the research reported on, rather than with the process of writing the article. Current computer programs for preparing an automatic abstract of an article are forced, by default, to do what a human abstractor may choose to do in preparing an informative abstract: they identify themselves, in effect, with the author of the article, using his words to describe the experimental or investigative activities directly.

Automatic abstracts would appear, therefore, to fall naturally into the category of informative rather than indicative abstracts, i.e., to serve primarily the content-revelatory function rather than the search-tool function. Indeed, if sentences are to be selected for automatic abstracts on the basis of having scores above a certain threshold value, then it is appealing to try to guarantee adequate coverage of the content of an article by lowering the threshold value and including more sentences. Greater length, however, makes the abstract less effective (in the intuitive sense of Section 5.1.1) as a search tool, so that the conflict between these two functions of abstracts can become a problem. Perhaps a solution may lie in developing different techniques for producing search-tool automatic abstracts than for producing content-revelatory automatic abstracts, but how this might be done is not known at present. In any case, it is important to distinguish between the two functions in evaluating automatic abstracts.

Humans, in preparing abstracts, can make them serve a third function: to view an article from the perspective of the current state of knowledge in the field, and to highlight in the abstract what (if anything) is *new* in the article. This function ought to be at least a long-range goal of research in automatic abstracting. The survey of abstracting journal practice revealed that this function is explicitly desired by some, but by no means all, of the abstracting journals studied. Yet it is surely one of the most important services that an abstractor can perform in reporting on an article—and surely one of the most difficult for an automatic abstracting system to accomplish. For one thing, machine methods for recognizing what is new in an article are not known, except for special cases where the field of interest is quite narrow and the data are well structured. For another, an enormous memory capacity would be one of the necessary features in an automatic abstracting system designed to cover even a small portion of a scientific or technical field to the extent of being able to recognize what was new in an article in that field. The size of such a memory would, by itself, seem to put such a system well into the future. One can only hope that this prediction will prove to be as badly in error as comparable pessimism has proven in the past. Meanwhile, the function of evaluating the new contributions in an article and reporting on them in the abstract will have to be excluded from the functions that are desired of automatic abstracting systems, and evaluations of automatic abstracts must allow for this exclusion.

5.3   AUTOMATIC ABSTRACTS

5.3.1   Basic Concepts in Automatic Abstracting.   Credit is given to the late Hans Peter Luhn for first proposing that a computer program could produce a reasonable substitute for a human-prepared abstract. Luhn suggested that certain sentences in an article be identified as the few "most significant" sentences in the article, and that those sentences then be printed out, in the order of their appearance in the article, to form an automatic abstract of the article.*

*Though no one would wish to, or could, depreciate the originality and importance of Luhn's concept, some objections to his terminology have been voiced. For instance, Luhn used the term "auto-abstract" in his paper [25]. Since this really means "self-abstract," as the etymologically minded were quick to point out, we use the more nearly accurate "automatic abstract." The name "automatically produced abstract" would be better still, but some tribute has to be paid to brevity. Similarly, several people (including the present writer) have suggested that a more accurate name than "automatic abstract" would be "automatic extract," but this correction has gained only limited acceptance. Means for

A more general approach to choosing a subset of "most significant" or "best representative" sentences from the set of all sentences in an article might be the following. First, one would classify all the sentences in the article as either "definitely suited for extraction" (to form an automatic abstract), "possibly suited for extraction," or "definitely unsuited for extraction." Second, starting with the set of "definitely suited" sentences, one would add as many of the "possibly suited" sentences (presumably starting with the highest scored among the "possibly suited") as needed to form an abstract of the desired size.

Research in automatic abstracting has thus far concentrated on following Luhn's approach, attempting to improve one or more of the several steps. It is by no means certain that the more general approach would yield better results, but it should at least be experimented with. Automatic abstracting methods following Luhn's approach have, in general, consisted of three stages. In the first stage, measures of representativeness for the individual words in an article are developed. In the second stage, the representativeness scores for the words in each sentence are combined into a representativeness score for the sentence. In the third stage, various criteria are applied to the scores for the sentences in the article, in order to yield a set of desirable sentences for the automatic abstract.

At each of these stages numerous philosophical and practical difficulties are encountered that will be more understandable to the reader after a description of the techniques that have actually been used in automatic abstracting work. Hence, we shall postpone the discussion of the difficulties to Section 5.4.1, and turn next to a survey of the work to date in automatic abstracting. However, we must mention here one difficulty: the ambiguity that can arise from the fact that the word *word* has two distinct meanings. We shall follow the usual practice of distinguishing between these two meanings by using the technical terms *word-type* and *word-token,* or just *type* and *token,* where the word *word* would be ambiguous. Word-tokens are individual occurrences of the same word-type.

going beyond mere extracts—such as procedures for enabling computers actually to write English sentences dealing with the content of a paragraph (see Section 5.5.3)—are now becoming practicable, so that eventually the name "automatic abstract" will undoubtedly be justifiable. For the present, however, automatic abstracting systems rely entirely on the method of extracting sentences from the article to form an abstract of it. Finally, it has been pointed out that since the over-all goal in producing an automatic abstract of an article is to furnish a condensed representation of the essential content of the article, the sentences selected for the abstract would be better called the most "representative" sentences. Indeed, most of the sentences selected will not be "significant" in the ordinary intuitive sense of the word, but will be merely illustrative or exemplary (i.e., representative) of the content of the article.

5.3.2   Survey of Research in Automatic Abstracting.   The studies in automatic abstracting surveyed in this Section are presented in essentially chronological order. It may be helpful to observe here that most of them fall into one or the other of two categories: experiments with machine (or machine-like) methods of extracting sentences, and experiments in which human extraction of sentences is studied to ascertain basic principles for utilization in machine methods. One of the studies is in a third category since it deals with an examination of theoretical foundations for extracting.

5.3.2.1   *The Luhn Study.*   In his paper on automatic abstracting [25], the original paper in the field, Luhn held that the representativeness of a sentence was to be taken as a function of

a. the representativeness of each word-type in the sentence, and

b. the relative positions of the word-tokens within the sentence.

The representativeness of a word-type was to be a function of its (absolute) frequency in the document, in the following way:

a. function word-types, i.e., common words such as pronouns, prepositions, and articles, were not to be assigned any representativeness value;*

b. the *least frequent* content word-types were not to be considered representative;

c. content word-types with frequencies in the range above *least frequent* were to be considered representative.

In regard to the relative positions of the words, Luhn argued that

> whatever the topic, the [more closely] certain words are associated, the more specifically an aspect of the subject is being treated. Therefore, wherever the greatest number of frequently occurring words are found in greatest physical proximity to each other, the probability is very high that the information being conveyed is most representative of the article. ...The criterion is the relationship of the [representative] words to each other rather than their distribution over a whole sentence. It therefore appears proper to consider only those portions of sentences which are bracketed by [representative] words and to set a limit for the distance at which any two [representative] words shall be considered as being significantly related.

*The name "function word" has come to be the generally used term for words such as pronouns, prepositions, articles, auxiliary verbs, certain adjectives and adverbs (e.g., "more," "much," "very"), and conjunctions. In contrast to the function words are the "content words" that convey the principal ideas in the sentence. In what should be a clear extension of the meaning, we shall speak of "function word-types," "function word-tokens," "content word-types," and "content word-tokens," and also, shortly, of "representative" and "nonrepresentative word-tokens."

Luhn computed the representativeness value of a sentence in an article as follows:

a. The first step was to count the numbers of word-tokens of most of the word-types in the article, with the qualifications: (1) That function words (as given by a predetermined list) were not counted; and (2) that word-tokens beginning with the same letters were consolidated (i.e., treated as occurrences of the same word-type) if they had less than seven dissimilarities after their identical beginnings; otherwise such word-tokens were considered to belong to (in fact, to define) distinct word-types.

b. When the counting process had been completed, the frequency (i.e., number of tokens) of each content word-type was compared with a predetermined value V. A word-type whose frequency exceeded V was considered representative; a word-type whose frequency fell below V was considered nonrepresentative. Since Luhn also considered function word-types to be nonrepresentative, he used only a two-valued scale of representativeness; for he simply put each word-type into one or the other of two categories.

c. Next, the sentences in the article were individually considered. In each sentence, any representative word-token was called "isolated" if it was separated by more than four nonrepresentative word-tokens. Isolated tokens were disregarded.

d. Within each sentence, clusters of representative tokens (i.e., clusters having not more than four nonrepresentative tokens between any pair of representative tokens) were recognized, each cluster starting and ending with a representative token.

e. A representativeness value r_i for each cluster i was then calculated by squaring the number p_i of representative tokens in the cluster and dividing this square by the total number q_i of tokens in the cluster:

$$r_i = \frac{p_i{}^2}{q_i}$$

f. If a sentence had only one cluster of representative tokens, then the representativeness value of the sentence was taken to be that of the cluster. If a sentence had more than one such cluster, the representativeness value of the sentence was taken to be that of the highest valued cluster in the sentence.

g. Sentences with representativeness values above a predetermined value

R (or, for other purposes, a predetermined number of the sentences with highest representativeness values) were then printed out in the order of their appearance in the article, thus forming an automatic abstract for the article.

The program that Luhn used was written for the IBM 704. No details as to number of instructions or running time were given in his paper.

In view of the historical significance of Luhn's paper, we present in Figures 5.1 through 5.3 the contents (with a few minor terminological changes) of Exhibit 1 of Luhn's paper, the exhibit which contained the first published automatic abstract. This was an abstract of an article from the *Scientific American* entitled "Messengers of the Nervous System," by Amedeo S. Marrazzi.* The editor of the *Scientific American* supplied the following subheading (which was also quoted by Luhn) for this article:

> The internal communication of the body is mediated by chemicals as well as by nerve impulses. Study of their interaction has developed important leads to the understanding and therapy of mental illness.

Figure 5.1 exhibits the list of representative words in this article. Figure 5.2 gives Luhn's counts, on which the calculations of representative-

46 nerve	12 messengers	5 produce
40 chemical	10 signals	5 regulate
28 system	10 stimulation	5 serotonin
22 communication	8 action	4 accumulate
19 adrenalin	8 ganglion	4 balance
18 cell	7 animal	4 block
18 synapse	7 blood	4 disorders
16 impulses	7 drugs	4 end
16 inhibition	7 normal	4 excitation
15 brain	6 disturbance	4 health
15 transmission	6 related	4 human
13 acetylcholine	5 control	4 outgoing
13 experiment	5 diagram	4 reaching
13 substances	5 fibers	4 recording
12 body	5 gland	4 release
12 effects	5 mechanisms	4 supply
12 electrical	5 mediators	4 tranquilizing
12 mental	5 organism	

Figure 5.1   List of representative words and their frequencies—Luhn study

Scientific American, v. 196, no. 2, February 1957, pp. 86-94.

ness value were based. Figure 5.3 exhibits the automatic abstract, consisting of those sentences in the article that had representativeness values of 6.0 or more. The representativeness values are shown in the parentheses following each sentence.

Total number of word-tokens in the article	2326
Total number of word-types in the article	741
Total number of function word-types (deletion list)	170
Total number of content word-types	571
Ratio of total number of word-tokens to total number of content word-types	approx. 4:1
Total number of content word-types having a frequency of 5 or more	39
Number of word-tokens of such word-types	478

Figure 5.2   Word counts—Luhn study

It seems reasonable to credit the single-celled organisms also with a system of chemical communication by diffusion of stimulating substances through the cell, and these correspond to the chemical messengers (e.g., hormones) that carry stimuli from cell to cell in the more complex organisms. (7.0)

Finally, in the vertebrate animals there are special glands (e.g., the adrenals) for producing chemical messengers, and the nervous and chemical communication systems are intertwined: for instance, release of adrenalin by the adrenal gland is subject to control both by nerve impulses and by chemicals brought to the gland by the blood. (6.4)

The experiments clearly demonstrated that acetylcholine (and related substances) and adrenalin (and its relatives) exert opposing actions which maintain a balanced regulation of the transmission of nerve impulses. (6.3)

It is reasonable to suppose that the tranquilizing drugs counteract the inhibitory effect of excessive adrenalin or serotonin or some related inhibitor in the human nervous system. (7.3)

Figure 5.3   Automatic abstract—Luhn study

5.3.2.2   *The Baxendale Study.*   Although the goal of Baxendale's study [7] was the preparation of automatic indexes for documents, her research concerned methods of determining the representativeness of words and groups of words and, hence, deserves to be discussed here. She experimented with three methods of selecting words or groups of words from an article. In each case, the selected word-tokens were counted and the corresponding word-types were arranged in order of their frequencies. An index was then formed from the *n* words or phrases with the highest frequencies, n being chosen so as to yield an index with a suitable number of entries.

The first selection method was to delete function words by table look-up, thereby selecting all the other words in the article. According to Baxendale, the function "words—not exceeding 150—have in common a stability of use in the language which precludes their ever characterizing subject matter"* [7, p. 355]. Even this very rough selection method—which has the considerable virtue of being quickly and easily performed by a computer—eliminated over half the running text from further consideration.

The second method consisted in selecting the words in the first and last sentence in each paragraph. Baxendale argued that a paragraph, at least a well written one, has a "topic sentence" that is "the fulcrum on which the paragraph rests" [7, p. 355]. If one could assume that the topic sentence occurred fairly consistently in some fixed position in a paragraph, then it would be easy to program a computer to select the topic sentence. "An investigation of a sample of 200 paragraphs [revealed that] in 85 percent of the paragraphs the topic sentence was the initial sentence and in 7 percent the final" [7, p. 355]. Baxendale gave no details on the source of the 200 paragraphs, nor on her criteria for judging which sentence in a paragraph was the topic sentence. Should the latter objection strike the reader as mere quibbling, he is invited to consider the results of the Rath, Resnick, and Savage study (see Section 5.3.2.5) on the lack of consistency among the subjective judgments of different persons in choosing topic sentences.

The third method was to select the words in the prepositional phrases in the text. Baxendale considered it logical to speculate that the prepositional "phrase is likely to reflect the content of an article more closely than any other simple construction" [7, p. 357]. On the basis of a count of the average number of word-tokens in 350 prepositional phrases, she programmed her computer to recognize 50 English prepositions "by table lookup and then automatically select the next four words unless a second preposition or a punctuation mark is encountered" [7, p. 357].

Presumably the second and third selection methods also entailed deletion of function words before the frequency count was made.

---

*This comment is interesting in that it reflects a formerly widely held assumption about the behavior of function words which has only recently been scrutinized and found to be not entirely correct. This work was done by Wallace [49], who reported that frequency counts of two corpora, one drawn from the field of electronic computers and one from psychology, showed significant differences in the frequency rankings of function and other high-frequency words. The differences were sufficient to enable him to use the rank order of common words as the sole, and satisfactory, means of classifying further texts as belonging to either the field of psychology or the field of computer technology.

A rather surprising result (at least to the present writer) of Baxendale's experiment—and a very encouraging one for research in automatic analysis of document content—was the close similarity of the sets of representative words obtained by these three different selection processes. The same words, with very nearly the same relative frequencies, tended to be chosen by all the methods. This is shown in Figure 5.4, essentially a reproduction of the final table in Baxendale's paper, which lists the 12 most frequently occurring words in that paper as determined by the application of each of the three selection methods. Words that appear on only one list are italicized. The similarity of these sets of representative words suggests that for uniformity of result there is no special reason for choosing one selection method over the others. There is a practical reason, however, for preferring the second and third selection methods: the first method leaves about half of the original text to be frequency-counted, whereas the second and third methods both leave considerably less than half.

Baxendale went further and made a strong argument for preferring the third method over the second. She argued that the prepositional phrase offers a programmable means of coordinating single nouns into meaningful groups of nouns and, similarly, of coordinating nouns and their adjectival or participial modifiers. To illustrate her argument, she compared the single words "levels" and "forbidden," derived as representative words for an article on semiconductors, with the groups "discrete energy levels" and "forbidden energy region," yielded as parts of individual prepositional phrases.

There is unquestionably a worthwhile increase in representativeness to be gained through the use of word groups rather than single words in indexes. Unfortunately, computers find it far more difficult than humans do to distinguish meaningful groups of words. The programming alternative to the neat and simple method of using prepositions to determine word coordination would appear to involve at least some degree of syntactic analysis (e.g., as in the Synthex research, for which see Sections 7.1 and 8.5), which is a considerably more complicated programming problem. It may be observed in passing that the use of the preposition as a word-group determiner is of greater importance in English than in Russian, in which inflections often serve the purpose of prepositional phrases, or German, in which groups of basic words are often formed into single compound words rather than into phrases.

Baxendale's program was written for the IBM 650, the only machine available to her at the time of her study. She considered the 650 to be not especially appropriate for the needs of her study and, perhaps for this reason, she gave no details on running time or number of instructions.

Selection by Simple Deletion	Frequency		Selection by Topic Sentence	Frequency		Selection by Prepositional Phrase	Frequency	
Word	Abs.	Rel.	Word	Abs.	Rel.	Word	Abs.	Rel.*
1. index(ing)	30	.15	index(ing)	14	.17	index(ing)	21	.16
2. phrase(s)	21	.11	sentence(s)	8	.10	article	14	.11
3. sentence(s)	19	.10	vocabulary	7	.09	machine	11	.08
4. word(s)	19	.10	phrase(s)	7	.09	word(s)	11	.08
5. machine	17	.09	word(s)	7	.09	vocabulary	11	.08
6. unit(s)	17	.09	machine	6	.07	phrase(s)	10	.08
7. vocabulary	14	.07	noun(s)	6	.07	sentence(s)	10	.08
8. noun(s)	14	.07	unit(s)	6	.07	unit(s)	10	.08
9. article	14	.07	selection	6	.07	noun(s)	10	.08
10. frequency(ies)	11	.06	article	5	.06	language	10	.08
11. terms	11	.06	preposition(al)	5	.06	frequency(ies)	8	.06
12. selection	11	.06	content	5	.06	term(s)	7	.05
	198			82			133	

Figure 5.4   Lists of representative words—Baxendale study

*To 3 decimal places, 11/133 = .083 and 10/133 = .075.

She also made no mention of the rules she used for consolidating words, but they can be inferred from displayed entries such as "preposition(al)," "index(ing)," and "unit(s)" in her lists of index terms.

5.3.2.3 *The Oswald Study.* In his study, Oswald [13] set out to evaluate two basic ideas: (1) Automatically generated indexes should include not only single words but also groups of words as index terms; and (2) the choice of sentences, for an automatic abstract of an article, should be governed by the numbers of representative *groups* in the sentences. His approach resembled Luhn's, in that he first took the representative word-types to be the content word-types of highest frequency; second, he determined certain groups of representative word-types to be representative groups; and third, he chose as representative sentences those sentences that scored high in number of representative groups. Not having a computer available, he devised procedures that were intended to be programmable but could also be directly implemented by that ubiquitously useful tool, the graduate student.

Oswald's first step in dealing with a document was to count the tokens of "only words significant in the context of the document." [13, p. 5] Presumably Oswald and his assistants made subjective judgments of "significance in context." In the second step, the highest-frequency words were identified and every juxtaposition of one of them with "any other significant word with a frequency greater than 1 [was] recorded as a multiterm" [13, p. 5], i.e., as a significant word-pair. In the third step, each sentence having two or more multiterms was identified as potentially suited for extraction. From among these sentences, chosen first would be the sentence or sentences with the highest number of multiterms, then those with the next highest number of multiterms, and so on. If, at the final stage, not all the sentences with a given number (≥ 2) of multiterms could be included in the extract (e.g., because of a predetermined rule about the length of the extract), then such sentences were chosen in order of decreasing length.

Figure 5.5 presents the abstract that Oswald considered the best one resulting from his study.* The multiterms are italicized. Oswald commented most candidly that the automatic abstracts exhibited in his report appeared "to range in quality from fairly good to disappointing" [13, p. 17]. And he added: "The exhibits show that the abstracts of the longer articles studied tend to be more satisfactory than those of the

*The abstracted article was: Summerfield, M., Problems of launching an earth satellite, *Astronautics,* v. II, no. 4, November 1957, pp. 18-21, 86-88. Oswald estimated the number of running words in this article to be 4,000.

1. The fact that a 23-in. sphere weighing 184 lb. has been placed in an almost precise *circular orbit* indicated that a number of important technological problems such as high thrust *rocket engines,* lightweight missile structures, accurate guidance, stable autopilot control, and large scale launching methods have been solved, at least to the degree required for a *satellite project.*

2. In the years since 1945, the U.S. and the U.S.S.R. have invested large sums and great effort in advancing their respective science and knowhow of *rocket missiles,* and in recent years the race for the development and production of long-range *ballistic missiles* brought forth large *rocket engines,* large *rocket vehicles,* accurate guidance systems, effective instrumentation, reliable telemetering devices, and well-equipped *launching sites* and *firing ranges.*

3. If *C* is the *compass angle* of the *launching direction* measured from the East, and if *L* is the latitude of the *launching site,* then the *compass angle E* of the flight path crossing the equator is given by the formula:

$$\cos E = \cos L \cdot \cos C.$$

4. The *effective launching velocity* of a rocket is always a few percent larger than the actual *burnout velocity* because the former includes a *kinetic energy* increment equivalent to the *potential energy* at the burnout altitude.

5. Several considerations dictate the choice of *orbit altitude,* namely, lifetime of the satellite, communication with stations on the *surface of the earth,* possible errors in *launching velocity* and direction, and the required *launching energy.*

6. One way to discuss the problem is to assume that errors can occur in *elevation angle* and in *injection velocity,* and to inquire as to the necessary extra altitude at the *injection point* to overcome the effects of these errors.

7. If the total impulse of the propulsion system cannot be guaranteed under field conditions any closer than 3 percent, then the rocket should be designed to deliver 750 ft/sec greater *burnout velocity* than for the *circular orbit,* and the design orbit should be an ellipse with an apogee 500 miles higher than *injection point.*

8. If the guidance and autopilot system cannot be guaranteed any closer than 1 deg under field conditions, the *injection altitude* should be raised 70 miles and the corresponding *injection velocity* can in fact be reduced, but the *effective launching velocity* must be raised by 200 ft/sec.

Figure 5.5 Automatic abstract — Oswald study

shorter articles" [13, p. 19]. He ascribed this tendency to the difficulties inherent in using the absolute frequencies of the words in one article as the basic tool for determining the representativeness of the words.

Oswald also concerned himself with the question of forming an automatic index for a document. For the index he used both high-frequency

single words and high-frequency multiterms, and he determined the size
of the index by a manually convenient rule for including or excluding
potential index terms that yielded an index whose number of entries was
usually in the range of one to three percent of the number of word-tokens
in the document.

Figure 5.6 presents Oswald's automatic index for the article whose abstract was given in Figure 5.5. The numbers associated with the index

58	satellite	13	angle
	6 earth satellite		5 elevation angle
	5 low-altitude satellite		2 azimuth angle
49	orbit		2 compass angle
	8 circular orbit	12	circular
	5 equatorial orbit	12	missile
	4 elliptic orbit		3 ballistic missile
	2 circular satellite orbit		3 rocket missile
47	velocity	12	surface
	16 effective launching velocity		11 earth's surface
	5 burnout velocity	11	range
	4 injection velocity		3 firing range
	4 launching velocity	10	direction
	3 orbital velocity		2 launching direction
	2 exhaust velocity	10	error
	2 satellite velocity	10	vehicle
44	launching		3 rocket vehicle
	3 satellite launching		2 earth-escape vehicle
41	earth		2 research vehicle
33	altitude		2 satellite vehicle
	6 orbit altitude		
	2 injection altitude		*Additional Multiterms*
26	rocket		
	2 launching rocket	6	injection point
21	injection	4	energy required
18	path	4	launching site
	2 elliptic path	3	satellite project
	2 orbital path	3	earth's rotation
14	energy	2	rocket engine
	4 launching energy		
	3 potential energy		
	2 kinetic energy		

Figure 5.6   Automatic index — Oswald study

terms are their absolute frequencies in the article. The "Additional Multiterms" are those that were excluded by the inclusion-exclusion rule mentioned above; they are included here for comparison. In contrast to his comment on his automatic abstracts, Oswald felt that his automatic "indexes ... appear quite attractive ... [being] more elaborate than those composed of" only single words [13, p. 19].

An interesting feature of Oswald's experiment was that he had a technical librarian (D. V. Black) prepare an abstract and a set of subject headings for each of the articles that were automatically abstracted and indexed in the experiment. The abstract and subject headings thus prepared for the Summerfield article are presented in Figure 5.7.

Conventional Subject Headings
Satellites, Artificial
Rockets (Aeronautics)
Celestial mechanics

Conventional Abstract
Historical aspects of earth satellites are traced back to 1903.
Orbit selection is discussed with the aid of graphs. Launching energy requirements for various orbits and orbit altitudes are presented. Comparisons are made among the following:

    Launching velocity of a satellite,
    V-2 launching velocity,
    ICBM launching velocity.

Necessary observation requirements are also presented, followed by guidance problems. The effects of various errors on the orbit are shown, and conclude the article.

Figure 5.7 Conventional subject headings and abstract—Oswald study

5.3.2.4 *The ACSI-Matic Study.*   The first information-handling system to use automatic abstracting as one of its regular operational procedures was the ACSI-Matic system of the Department of the Army (*A*ssistant *C*hief of *S*taff, *I*ntelligence). The automatic abstracting portion of this system was developed by the Advanced Systems Development Division of IBM. So far as is publicly known, this is (to date) the only operating system that actually used automatic abstracting.

The automatic abstracting procedures used in ACSI-Matic were basically those suggested by Luhn, with some interesting variations. One set of variations concerned the treatment of documents with an unusually high proportion of low-frequency words, and of documents with longer-than-average sentences. The other variations, an important advance over the original Luhn process, concerned procedures aimed at reducing or eliminating redundancy in the content of the sentences finally selected for the abstract.

The majority of ACSI documents were found to contain between 48 and 56 percent function words, and to have average lengths in the range from 18 to 26 words. Documents with these characteristics were handled by the following "normal procedure." Words with frequency equal to or greater than the average word frequency in the document were designated as representative words. Sentences were scored by adding the total number of representative words in the sentence to the sum of a set of fractions calculated from the pattern of the nonrepresentative words in the sentence. Each sequence of n nonrepresentative words was assigned the fraction $\frac{1}{2}^n$. For example, if x denotes a representative word and $-$ denotes a nonrepresentative word, the sentence "$x--x---x$" would have the score: $1+\frac{1}{4}+1+\frac{1}{8}+1=3\frac{3}{8}$. This procedure is an elaboration of Luhn's treatment of the density of representative words, which consisted simply of counting only those clusters of representative words that were separated by not more than four nonrepresentative words.

When a document had an average sentence length greater than 26 words, it was found that "the discriminating power of the [normal procedure] diminishes" [19, p. 7]. In such cases a further step was added, consisting in the division of "each of the sentence values by the square root of the number of words in the sentence, [resulting in the selection of] somewhat longer and considerably more adequate sentences" [4, p. 33]. However, when more than 10 percent of the sentences in the document are more than 40 words in length, the normal procedure is used once again. In short, if the sentences in a document are too long, the normal procedure is unsatisfactory; but if the sentences are very much too long, then the normal procedure once again becomes satisfactory. Undoubtedly this is a result of empirical considerations and, as such, is an interesting reflection of the facts of life in natural language.

The foregoing sentence-scoring procedures were based on designating as "representative" all words whose frequency equals or exceeds the average word frequency in the document. This procedure for determining representativeness was followed when 48 to 56 percent of the document consisted of function words. Two interesting special cases outside this range were distinguished:

> ...very general or 'blah' documents and very specific or 'detailed' documents. [Blah documents] are characterized by considerable verbiage and little content. They have two main characteristics: (1) the percentage of [function] words is high, and (2) the highest-frequency [content] words are so general as to be useless. In cases where the percentage of [function] words is greater than 56 percent, the list [of words whose frequencies equal or exceed] the average is further reduced by deleting words which occur with a frequency greater than 1 percent of the total document size. [19, pp. 7-8]

"Detailed" documents were those containing

> such specific information that the high-frequency words do not accu-
> rately reflect the depth of detail in the individual sentences. These doc-
> uments are usually characterized by [their having] less than 48 percent
> [function words] and a high proportion of [unit]-frequency words.
> When the percentage of [unit]-frequency words is greater than 35 per-
> cent of the different words in the text, and the percentage of [function]
> words is low, the detailed document procedure selects as [representative]
> those words whose frequency is *less than* or equal to the average word
> frequency. [19, p. 8]

When all the sentences in a document had been assigned a score, two
final steps remained: to choose a set of sentences potentially forming the
automatic abstract, and to attempt to eliminate overlapping sentences
from this set.

The number of sentences to be extracted was found by the following
procedure, for which no rationale was offered:

> The number of sentences in the document is divided by ten. If the quo-
> tient is more than 20, 20 is subtracted from the result and the remainder
> is divided by 32. The number of sentences in the abstract is this quo-
> tient plus 20. If the document has less than 200 sentences, the abstract
> has 10 percent of the total number of sentences. [18, p. 150]

Apparently, whatever the number n determined by the foregoing procedure, the n sentences with highest scores were tentatively chosen for
extraction and were called "abstract sentences." The $n/4$ sentences with
next highest scores were called "reserve sentences."

Word-tokens were consolidated by a process analogous to Luhn's
(see the fourth paragraph of Section 5.3.2.1), and each distinct content
word-type was assigned a "dictionary number." Pairs of "abstract sentences" were examined for possible redundancy in the following way:

> The dictionary numbers for every sentence are compared with the
> dictionary numbers of every other sentence, [and] the number of match-
> ing dictionary numbers [is noted]. If the total number of dictionary num-
> bers in [a pair of] sentences exceeds four times the number of matching
> dictionary numbers, the sentences do not match. [The next step] is to
> find the abstract sentence with the greatest number of matches, and, if
> two sentences have an equal number of matches, the lower [score].
> [18, p. 152]

The program, taking into account some special cases and exercising certain controls too intricate to be detailed here, deleted the most heavily
matched (the most overlapped or redundant) sentences and replaced
them with reserve sentences until either (1) there were no matching sentences in the set of abstract sentences or (2) the set of reserve sentences

was exhausted. The sentences that were in the set of abstract sentences at the end of this process formed the automatic abstract for the document.

The above programs were written for the IBM 704 computer. The processing speed was reported as 1000 words of running text abstracted per 42 seconds of 704 time.

5.3.2.5 *The Rath, Resnick, and Savage Studies.*   Undertaken as a part of the ACSI-Matic project, but later published separately, were studies by Rath, Resnick, and Savage on what sentences would be chosen as representative by humans using only their subjective judgments, and on comparisons of human-chosen representative sentences with machine-chosen sentences. They began by having 6 subjects read 10 articles from the *Scientific American,* choose the 20 most representative sentences from each article, and then rank the 20 sentences in decreasing order of representativeness. Similarly, 20 sentences were picked from each article by computer programs essentially equivalent to Luhn's. They found that

> both the human-selected sentences and the [computer]-selected sentences differed significantly from randomness. There is a wide range of individual differences [among] the human subjects. ... There was very little agreement between the subjects and the machine methods on the sentences selected as being representative. [36, p. 140]

Several followup studies were reported separately by one or more of the Rath, Resnick, and Savage trio. In the first [37] of these, Resnick asked five of the original six subjects to read some of the original articles again eight weeks later and to carry out the same operations (selecting and ranking sentences) as before. He found that

> each subject on the average selected the same sentences only 55 percent of the time. ...[The subjects] were able to correctly identify their previous selection 64 percent of the time. The lack of inter- and intra-subject reliability seems to imply that a single set of representative sentences does not exist for an article. It may be that there are many equally representative sets of sentences which exist for any article. [37, p. 143]

A second followup study [35], by all three authors, compared the relative usefulnesses of full texts and three types of condensed representations: titles; automatic abstracts produced by the Luhn technique, called "auto-abstracts" in the study; and automatic abstracts produced by extracting the first five percent and the last five percent of the sentences in an article, called "pseudo-auto-abstracts" in the study. As their evaluation criterion, the experimenters employed the tried—but not necessarily true—method of deriving, from the articles, questions to be answered from the condensed representations. They divided their subjects into a control group, a "full-text" group, and a group for each of the three types of condensed representations. The subjects were to evaluate the relevance of the documents in answering the questions, and to answer the questions.

The results were hardly surprising. With respect to the search-tool function, the experimenters found that titles alone led to the selection of a high percentage of irrelevant documents, whereas "there were no major differences" among the full-text group and the groups using the two kinds of abstracts "in their ability to pick appropriate documents." [35, p. 130] With respect to the content-revelatory function, the full-text group "obtained a significantly higher score" [35, p. 130] in answering the questions. However, it was of interest to find that the members of the group using pseudo-auto-abstracts had the highest confidence in their judgments as to relevance. The experimenters speculated that this "significantly high confidence . . . may stem from the high literary quality of the pseudo-auto-abstracts over the auto-abstracts as the former contain sentence to sentence continuity." [35, p. 129] Another interesting sidelight, whose importance is hard to judge in view of the small size of the sample, was that "the auto-abstracts contained about 25 percent of the answers, while the pseudo-auto-abstracts contained 18 percent and the titles only 1 percent" [35, p. 130].

A third study [39], by Resnick and Savage, explored the possibility that the previous study [35] might have been "strongly influenced by the type of subject population utilized and the artificiality of the task for such a subject population, and [that] different results might have been obtained using a more homogeneous subject population and a criterion test with greater face validity" [39, p. 141]. To counter these criticisms, Resnick and Savage utilized reports selected from military intelligence documents, used questions prepared by intelligence analysts, and employed intelligence analysts as subjects. As was expected, the full-text group again did better than the other groups in answering the questions. Rather unexpectedly, however, the experimenters found that although "in the previous study, the text and abstract groups [had] outperformed the title group in determining the relevance of documents . . . in the present study all groups did equally well" [39, p. 146].

This latter result, since it contradicts the previous study [35], would seem to be rather inconclusive. It is at least partially supported, however, by the results of a fourth followup study [38], conducted by Resnick. This study pursued—in a different and not wholly comparable context— the question of the value of abstracts in judging relevance, by comparing "the effectiveness of titles with that of abstracts when they were used for the purpose of notifying research workers of the availability of documents which might be relevant to their work interests" [38, p. 1004]. Having been notified of incoming documents by titles alone or by titles and abstracts, the research workers selected documents they thought potentially relevant to their work interests, and then reported whether they, in fact, considered the documents relevant. Resnick found neither a "significant difference in ordering rates for documents when titles [alone] are used... and when a combination of titles and abstracts is used" nor a significant difference in the percentages of documents judged relevant after being ordered by the two methods [38, p. 1005].

On the basis of the foregoing experiments Savage has contended that abstracts do not usefully serve the search tool function. Quite aside from criticisms that might be made of the experiments, one important counter-argument is simply to point out the widespread existence of titles that obviously do not in themselves give any usable clue as to the content of their article. Mathematicians are among the worst offenders in attaching clue-poor titles to their articles, for such titles as "Note on a Theorem of Smith" are frequently encountered in the mathematical literature. The percentages of clue-poor titles for articles in various scientific fields would be an interesting subject for further study, but it is clear that in absolute number such titles constitute a serious problem for information retrieval, and that some condensed representation—whether an abstract or something else—is often needed to supplement the title.

5.3.2.6 *The Ramo-Wooldridge Study.*

In variety of approaches the Ramo-Wooldridge study [34], directed by Edmundson, was the largest yet undertaken in the field of automatic abstracting; and it was probably the most thorough in exploring some of the subtler questions. The group followed four main lines: (1) An investigation of the extent to which people are consistent in extracting sentences from an article; (2) a mathematical study, conducted primarily by J. L. Kuhns, of the logical foundations of the process of extracting sentences, essentially a study of how to formulate the inductive probability of a given sentence's being selected for extraction by computer programs;* (3) a study, conducted primarily by P. L. Garvin, of types of relationships expressed by sentences, with a view toward using relationship categories as criteria for extracting sentences; and (4) writing and experimenting with computer programs to

---

*The "inductive probability" under discussion is that developed by Rudolf Carnap. The primary reference is: Carnap, R., *Logical Foundations of Probability,* 2nd ed., U. of Chicago Press, Chicago, Illinois, 1962. For a brief and very lucid treatment, see Carnap, R., *What is probability? Scientific American,* v. 189, no. 3, September 1953, pp. 128-138.

utilize the attributes of human-extracted sentences, as developed in (2) and (3).

The investigation of human consistency in extracting began with the devising of a correlation coefficient that would measure the similarity of two sets of sentences extracted from a given article, taking into account the sizes of the abstracts relative to the original article and relative to each other. The correlation coefficient was applied to "the results of a study of about seventy extracts originated from a dozen articles each processed by six or so people" [34, p. 8]. It was found—in contrast to the results of the Rath, Resnick, and Savage study (see Section 5.3.2.5)—that "the extent to which people are consistent in extracting is sufficiently large to justify the study of the attributes of the material which they extract. It is not large enough to rely on any single individual to furnish the extracted material for any one article, however" [34, p. 12].

The mathematical study of sentence selection furnished the first philosophical basis for the process of forming extracts of articles by assigning representativeness scores to the sentences in the article. For this reason, and because the notion of inductive probability—as opposed to statistical probability—may be unfamiliar to many, we shall treat the mathematical portion of the Ramo-Wooldridge study in greater detail than the other portions.

The study assumed that simulation of human extraction of sentences would be an acceptable short-range goal for automatic abstracting research. Such simulation entails the concept of the probability that a given sentence will be selected by a human, where—in contradistinction to the usual statistical sense of probability—this is not a probability statement based on past observations of the relative frequency of selection.

As the report stated in part, one may consider the situation of

> two gamblers X and Y who are told that a certain document has been extracted and [to whom] certain characteristics of a particular sentence of that document are described. [These characteristics, together with] the total information available on past sentence selection by extractors [are] summarized in a proposition which we shall call 'E' [for 'evidence']. Let S be the hypothesis that the particular sentence has been extracted. The ratio of [i] the stake offered for a bet on S to [ii] the total stake, is called the betting quotient q for the bet on S. Suppose that the amount bet on S is q, and the amount bet against S is 1-q. [We can assume] there exists some value q such that x would be [equally] willing to bet on the hypothesis S with quotient q or against S at quotient 1-q. This value is, as far as X is concerned, the psychologically fair betting quotient for S relative to E. [That is, q] indicates the support that X believes E confers on S. Assuming that Y 'processes' the evidence in the same way as X, he too would accept either betting role.

In this case, the value q is said to be the *fair betting quotient* for the hypothesis S relative to the evidence E for these bettors. To test whether q is indeed fair, suppose that this same document was extracted by many extractors. If X and Y made a series of bets, X for S with quotient q, Y against S with quotient $1-q$, then we could compute the total balance of wins and losses. It is clear that X's net gain (and hence Y's) is zero if and only if the ratio of occurrence of S is exactly q. In this case q is deemed statistically fair relative to the system of bets. [34, p. 25]

It follows that a representativeness score for the sentence of hypothesis S should incorporate: "(1) the degree of evidential support that E confers upon S; (2) the fair betting quotient for S relative to E; (3) an (E-based) estimate of the relative frequency of the occurrence of S. These are well-known properties of [Carnap's] quantitative logical conception of probability" [34, pp. 25-26]. These three characteristics were further investigated, utilizing empirical data from a sample library (100 documents for each of which an extract was prepared by 3 different persons), to develop a programmable betting function.

The investigation yielded three requirements for an adequate betting function. First, such a function should be "fair" on the sample library; i.e., if the probability of a particular sentence's being selected is given by the betting function, the expected value of the number of sentences selected should equal the mean number of sentences extracted by each of the human extractors. Second, the function should be "proper" on the sample library; i.e., the expected value of the total number of word-tokens in the selected sentences should equal the mean number of word-tokens extracted by each of the extractors. Third, the length of a sentence and the probability of its being selected should be linearly uncorrelated. This requirement was based on the empirical finding that in the sample library the mean length of all sentences did not differ significantly from the mean length of the sentences chosen for the extracts.

In conclusion, it was shown that a betting function that satisfied these three requirements, and was in that sense a satisfactory measure of the probability of a particular sentence's being extracted, could be constructed as follows. Let p_i be the ratio of (i) the number of tokens of word-type W_i occurring in sentences extracted from the sample library to (ii) three times (since there were three extracts made of each article) the number of tokens of W_i in the sample library. Then, for a particular sentence j, sum the various p_i's for all the word-tokens in j, and divide by the length of j (i.e., the total number of tokens in j). The resulting quotient q_j is the desired betting function or probability of extraction. In other words, the process of extracting sentences on the basis of normalized sums of weights for word-tokens in the sentences can be justified mathematically.

The third portion of the Ramo-Wooldridge study explored the possibility of assessing the representativeness of portions of a document by examining the

> semantic structure of the individual sentences . . . A method would have to be developed which would allow for a systematic description of the content of sentences in terms of a relatively small number of semantic categories. [Such a method] was developed under the name of predication-typing. It was found possible to reword a large majority of the sentences in natural-language documents in a standardized form [which] can be expressed by the general statement: 'A stands in relation X to B'. [34, pp. 58-59]

Sentences that lent themselves to such rewording were called "predications"; those that did not, "non-predications." The number of predication types necessary appears to be surprisingly small. Only 33 types sufficed for the processing of some 2700 sentences in 25 documents. Figure 5.8 exhibits several predication types and the symbols denoting them in the notation developed for the predication-typing study.

A	statement of accompanying circumstances	A is accompanied by B
Cp	statement of comparability	A is comparable to B
Ef	indication of effect	A affects B
Ma	description of movement away	A moves away from B
Rm	description of result of motion	A arrives at B
U	description of use	A is used for B

Figure 5.8   Predication types and their notation

Preliminary work on a calculus for predication typing, together with some interesting explorations of difficult cases and recommendations for the course of further research, constituted the remainder of the work done in this portion of the Ramo-Wooldridge study. It was felt that the results justified the assertion "that we are in the process of developing a workable empirical technique for semantic analysis." [34, p. 73]

The fourth part of the Ramo-Wooldridge study was the development of computer programs for sentence extraction. As the report stated in part, these programs were based on the hypothesis that "material consistently selected by humans as being of high value for an abstract is rich in what we shall call here *cue* words and phrases which, *independently of the subject content,* tend to indicate or suggest that the sentence in which they appear is of high significance or importance. In addition a significant role will almost certainly be played by subject-rich *key* words" [34, p. 7, emphasis added].

The programs were written for, and run on, an IBM 7090. With the qualification that

> in our research, the optimization of computer programs was considered of secondary importance [and] that our programs could be somewhat faster (perhaps 25 percent), we achieved the following average rates. The edit program requires about 22 milliseconds per word while the abstracting program takes 37 milliseconds per word. Thus the total time to take natural language text in free form from cards to a printed abstract is about 59 milliseconds per word; or, in other terms, we can abstract 63,000 words each hour. This makes the cost per word about one cent (1.03 cents) on the basis of a cost of $650 an hour for computer time. [34, p. 23]

In a retrieval experiment with interesting results, a library of 11 short articles from the *Physical Review* served as the information store to which four experimenters made 50 requests each. The "documents were retrieved 118 times, of which 94 instances [80 percent] were relevant retrieval; 24 [20 percent], irrelevant retrieval" [34, p. 52], presumably as judged subjectively. Next the 11 articles were replaced by (1) extracts prepared by a physicist, (2) extracts prepared by the computer, and (3) titles alone. These representations of the article were searched (no details were given on who searched or how) with the following results [34, p. 52]:

(a) *Search Using Physicist's Extracts*
    Relevant information surviving search = 60 percent
    Irrelevant documents eliminated = 68 percent
    Average size of extract = 24 percent
(b) *Search Using [Computer–Prepared] Extracts*
    Relevant information surviving search = 54 percent
    Irrelevant documents eliminated = 72 percent
    Average size of extract = 27 percent
(c) *Search Using Titles*
    Relevant information surviving search = 7 percent
    Irrelevant documents eliminated = 100 percent.

Although it is not clear just what is meant by "relevant information surviving search," it is of interest to compare the foregoing percentages of retrieval with those obtained by Rath, Resnick, and Savage (see Section 5.3.2.5). However, the sample size in all three experiments is probably too small for any final conclusion to be drawn.

In a second research effort [47], the Ramo-Wooldridge group continued their research by developing computer programs to accomplish four different methods of weighting words in the sentences of a document, and by experimenting with the effects of combining these weighting methods. The four methods were called the Cue, Key, Title, and Location methods.

In the Cue method a list of general words occurring frequently in scientific and technical prose was developed and called the Cue Dictionary. Various weights (positive, zero, and negative) were subjectively assigned to the words. The computer program assigned to a sentence the algebraic sum of the weights of the word-tokens in the sentence contained in the Cue Dictionary.

In the Key method all words in a particular document, except those occurring in the Cue Dictionary, were frequency-counted. The word-types with frequencies above a predetermined threshold were defined to be Key words, and each Key word-type was assigned a weight equal to its frequency. The computer program assigned to each sentence the sum of the weights of the Key word-tokens occurring in the sentence.

In the Title method, a Title Glossary for a particular document was developed that consisted of the content words found in the title, subtitles, and headings of the document, with the exception of those content words possessing weights of zero in the Cue Dictionary. One of two weights was assigned to each word-type in the Title Glossary: a larger weight to word-types occurring in the title, a smaller weight to word-types occurring only in subtitles or headings. The computer program assigned to each sentence the sum of the weights of the word-tokens in the sentence contained in the Title Glossary.

In the Location method sentences were assigned weights in two steps. A Heading Dictionary was developed that consisted of about 100 general words occurring frequently in the headings of sections of scientific and technical articles, e.g., "aims," "findings," "investigation," "method," "requirements," "summary," and "work." These words were subjectively assigned weights. A word's Heading Dictionary weight was not necessarily equal to its weight in the Cue Dictionary if it also occurred there; but words with zero weights in the Cue Dictionary were excluded from the Heading Dictionary. As the first step in assigning a weight to each sentence, the computer program assigned to the sentence the sum of the weights of the word-tokens in the sentence contained in the Heading Dictionary. As the second step in the Location method, certain sentences were assigned weights based on their position within the text of the document being processed. Each sentence in the first and last paragraphs of the document was assigned one weight; in each intermediate paragraph, the first and last sentences were assigned another, smaller weight. The final weight for each sentence in the document was the sum of the weights assigned it in these two steps.

In each of the four methods—Cue, Key, Title, and Location—the computer program finally ranked all sentences in order of decreasing weight. The sentences selected for the extract were the 25 percent of the sentences with highest weights. All headings were also selected, and in the final extract, the selected sentences were merged with their proper headings and printed out in the order of their occurrence in the original document.

Besides experimenting with each of the four methods individually, the Ramo-Wooldridge group also compared the automatic abstracts resulting from various combinations of the methods. As their report stated in part, they expected that of the 15 possible (non-void) combinations

> the Cue-Key-Title-Location combined method would produce the best abstract, since all of the four categories of machine recognizable clues come into play. However, the experimental data show that the combined Cue-Title-Location method, excluding the Key method, gives as good or better abstracts as the combination of all four methods. [Also] considerable computer storage will be saved by omitting the Key routine. The data support a conjecture made during the previous study that Key words, while important for indexing, are not as important for abstracting. [47, p. 19]

It may be observed here that this is a quite surprising result. Certainly, one would expect the additional information provided through the use of Cue-, Title-, and Location-clues to improve the process of selecting sentences. But it is hard to understand why, in general, the use of the information provided by the Key method—which, after all, was essentially the method originally used by Luhn—should actually degrade the selection process. One is led to suspect that some circumstances peculiar to the texts being used may have caused the degrading. It is to be hoped that further research can be undertaken to try to shed more light on this paradoxical result.

5.3.2.7 *Other Studies.*   In Sections 5.3.2.1 through 5.3.2.6 we have reviewed the principal published experiments in automatic abstracting, with the exception of the few Soviet papers in the field, which have reported on Luhn-type automatic abstracting and have discussed other possible techniques. In addition to the reports on experiments, some papers have been published dealing with theoretical, speculative, and conceptual problems of automatic abstracting. To conclude our survey of research in automatic abstracting, we summarize two of these papers, which suggest alternative and fundamentally different approaches to the central problems of automatic abstracting.

Edmundson and Wyllys, in a study that was originally reported as a part of the Oswald study [13] but was later published separately [14], took issue with Luhn's use of the number of occurrences (i.e., the absolute frequency) of a word in a document as the sole basis for measuring the word's representativeness of the content of the document. Instead, the report pointed out that

> very general considerations from information theory suggest that a
> word's *information* should vary inversely with its frequency rather than
> directly, its lower probability evidencing greater selectivity, or delibera-
> tion, in its use. It is the rare, special, or technical word that will indicate
> more strongly the subject of an author's discussion. Here, however, it is
> clear that by 'rare' we must mean *rare in general usage*, not rare within
> the document itself. In fact, it would seem natural to regard the contrast
> between the word's relative frequency f within the document and its
> relative frequency r in general use (scil., $0 < f < 1$ and $0 < r < 1$) as a more
> revealing indication of the word's value in indicating the subject matter
> of a document. [14, p. 227]

We suggested ways in which this "relative-frequency approach" might
be tested.

We observed also that

> a further refinement ... would be the development of [a reference set of
> relative] frequencies for special fields of interest. This would have two
> benefits: it would become possible to classify documents as to [subject]
> field, and it would become possible to note the significance of words
> which are frequent in the document and frequent in a very large refer-
> ence class c_0 of literature (i.e., these words would not be [representative]
> with respect to c_0) but which are rare in the special field. [14, p. 228]

For example, the word "love" is common in general literary English but
rare enough in electrical engineering so that its use in a document in
that field (perhaps in an article on robots) would suggest not only that it
was highly representative of the content of the document but also that
the field of electrical engineering had come to encompass "love." If an
automatic document-content analysis system found similar uses of "love"
in other electrical engineering documents shortly thereafter, the system
could call the attention of its human operators and users to the possible
emergence of a new area of interest within the field of electrical engineering. This potential application of the relative-frequency approach may
be termed "trend detection"; its usefulness in fields such as military intelligence should be obvious. Meadow [28] has experimented with a
classification and indexing program utilizing the relative-frequency approach, which she developed independently. Williams has also reported
[50] on experiments indicating that this approach, with suitable modifications, appears to be useful in classifying documents.

Another potential basis for automatic abstracting, again fundamentally different from the Luhn technique, was suggested by Climenson,
Hardwick, and Jacobson [9]. They proposed a syntax–analytic approach to the problem of extracting the essential content of a document.
The first part of their work consisted of writing a program for automatic
syntax analysis by a computer. The second part, according to their re-

port, consisted in the application of Harris's theories of transformation analysis and discourse analysis to the sentence analyses derived by the computer. However, it was not clear from their report that they had made any greater use of Harris's theories than merely to base their work one one of the premises of transformation analysis: namely, that the sentences of a document can be broken down into "a set of minimal sentences, developed from the sentences of the document, each of which [minimal sentences] makes an assertion of importance to the readers of the document sentences" [9, p. 181].

The main results of the experiment by Climenson, Hardwick, and Jacobson were stated by them, in part, as follows:

> The automatic syntax analysis program disposes a sentence in such a way that it is possible to recognize its syntactically indispensable portions. . . . It is assumed in document condensation that [these portions] are also the major information-carrying units. As an example, an English speaker would probably feel that the sentence:
>
> > The recently expelled Cuban consul was recalled by his infuriated government.
>
> when reduced to *the consul was recalled* had not lost its main information content. The omissions only reduced the information somewhat. . . . The sentence as given above could be an expansion of any of the following sentences:
>
> > The consul was recalled.
> > The Cuban consul was recalled by his government.
> > The expelled Cuban consul was recalled by his infuriated government.
>
> The first of these sentences might be the underlying sentence for all the expansions, while the other sentences add information which supplements but does not alter the basic information. . . . The string-connecting and nesting characteristics of English illustrated above suggest the notion of central/peripheral structures which might have a relation to central/peripheral information. Machine implementation of a limited set of word- and phrase-deletion rules based on these ideas produced a reduction to about 35 percent of the original length of the text. Although there is no satisfactory measure of information significance of the machine condensation, it appears that the condensation does retain the gist of the original. [9, p. 182]

5.4 PROBLEM AREAS IN AUTOMATIC ABSTRACTING

One of the purposes of surveying past work in automatic abstracting is to shed light on some of the difficulties, both practical and philosophical, that have confronted researchers. We now turn our attention specifically to these difficulties, the principal fields of future research in automatic abstracting. It is convenient to group the problems into three categories, by no means exclusive: problems in the quantification of meaning, problems of language, and problems of application.

5.4.1 Problems in the Quantification of Meaning. The central problem in automatic abstracting is that of measuring the representativeness of units of text: words, word groups, phrases and clauses, sentences, paragraphs, and so on. At present there is, quite frankly, no satisfactory means of measuring the representativeness of text units. The various techniques that we have mentioned in our survey of automatic abstracting experiments are at best merely plausible guesses about things that intuition tells us ought to indicate representativeness.

The problem is twofold. First, much further work remains to be done in experimenting with already suggested representativeness criteria and in trying to develop new and better criteria. Representativeness criteria fall conveniently into three categories, under which they are discussed below: statistical, syntactico-semantic, and textual. Second, research is needed to develop objective measures of the representativeness of text units, that is, measures of the information content of text units relative to the information content of the document of which they are a part.

5.4.1.1 *Statistical Criteria of Representativeness.* The fundamental criterion that Luhn (see Section 5.3.2.1) used was the word's absolute frequency in the document; i.e., his fundamental criterion was a statistical one. The absolute-frequency procedure operates on the quite reasonable assumption that an author uses terms pertinent to the topic of his document with greater frequency than terms not pertinent to his topic. But the use of absolute frequency as the only criterion encounters the difficulty that certain general terms—such as "importance," "connection," and "theory"—tend to have high frequencies without having a comparably high pertinence to the specific topic of an individual document.

One answer to this difficulty is to include such general words in the list of words to be excluded from the frequency-counting process, as was done in the second Ramo-Wooldridge experiment (see Section 5.3.2.6). To prepare a comprehensive list of such words is tedious at best; and at worst its use could be very troublesome since these general words, unlike most function words, might be topically pertinent in certain cases.* Even

---

*An often used example of a function word that can be a topically pertinent content word is "will," which is an auxiliary verb and a term in law and in psychology.

if this difficulty could be satisfactorily met, there would remain still another difficulty: namely, that a highly specialized term, rare in general or even professional usage, might be importantly representative of the content of a document in which it did not occur often enough to rank high in the frequency count.

It was as a possible solution to these difficulties of the absolute-frequency approach that Edmundson and I proposed our relative-frequency approach (see Section 5.3.2.7). Although this relative-frequency approach has not been tested on an adequately large scale, some small-scale manual experiments suggest that a combination of both the absolute-frequency and the relative-frequency approaches may yield the best results as a statistical estimator of word representativeness.

A third type of statistical estimator of representativeness might be based on co-occurrence measures such as those used by Doyle [10]. In measuring co-occurrence, one is interested only in whether a word (or more generally, a text unit) occurs in a given body of text, not in how frequently it occurs there. The usual application of co-occurrence measures involves a collection of documents, with interest being focused on the number of documents that contain a given text unit. It has been suggested that it might be fruitful to investigate the application of co-occurrence measures to the problem of measuring representativeness, for example, by changing the scale of application and trying to develop a representativeness estimator based on the number of subdivisions (e.g., paragraphs) of a document that contain a given word.

5.4.1.2 *Syntactico-Semantic Criteria of Representativeness.* Besides statistical criteria, other plausible clues are words that authors frequently use in sentences of more than average representativeness: e.g., "conclusion," "demonstrate," "disclose," "prove," "show," and "summary." It would seem reasonable that the occurrence of such a word should increase the sentence's chance of being selected to form part of the automatic abstract for the article. To follow such a procedure would be to base the representativeness of a sentence in part on the meaning of certain of the words in the sentence. For this reason we shall refer to such a procedure as the use of "semantic" criteria.

Clearly, certain phrases would be usable as semantic criteria. Indeed, the occurrence in a sentence of such a phrase as "it was found that ...," "the experiment proves ...," or "the central problem is ..." would indicate, probably more sharply than any single word, that the sentence was likely to be representative of the topic of the article. The point of mentioning words and phrases separately is that it will be more difficult to use phrases as representativeness indicators than to use single words;

for single words can be utilized through simple table-lookup methods whereas phrases will require syntax analysis methods for the handling of their more varied possible appearances.

We have rather arbitrarily labelled the use of certain words and phrases as the use of "semantic criteria." Equally arbitrarily, we now group under the heading of "syntactic criteria" those clues to the representativeness of words or of sentences that consist in structural patterns within sentences. A simple example would be the assumption that long, compound sentences tend to be of more than average representativeness in an article—if only because longer sentences can contain more ideas than shorter sentences. This assumption was, in fact, used by the research group at Ramo-Wooldridge in one of their studies [34, p. 21] and yielded useful results.

It appears reasonable to expect that other, and more subtle, syntactic criteria could be found. This expectation is supported by a study by Ford and Holmes [16] on the behavior of humans in summarizing documents. Although it was not required that the subjects use the exact terminology of the article, they tended to do so rather than to use synonyms or circumlocutions. Ford and Holmes discovered that the subjects tended to extract, with high frequency, phrases having certain structural patterns. For example, there was strikingly frequent use by the subjects of the patterns "noun (or adjective): noun (or phrase) and noun (or phrase)" and "noun (or adjective): noun (or phrase), noun (or phrase), and noun (or phrase)"; as in "Two factors are important: the value of imports and the actual outflow of gold."

5.4.1.3 *Textual Criteria of Representativeness.*   The third main class of representativeness criteria is that of "textual" criteria—those criteria defined basically by the appearance of the printed (or typewritten) page. The class of textual criteria can in turn be divided into "positional" and "editorial" criteria. The chief positional criteria are the position of a sentence with respect to the document as a whole, and with respect to a paragraph in the document, as first pointed out by Baxendale (see Section 5.3.2.2) and later utilized in the second Ramo-Wooldridge experiment (see Section 5.3.2.6).

Editorial criteria include such features as italicization, capitalization, and punctuation. Less dependable as indicators of representativeness than positional criteria, they also vary more from journal to journal, so that their use will have to be tied to the editorial practices of individual journals.

Italicization appears in a variety of equivalent forms, and is used not only to indicate the author's or editor's desire to emphasize the word or words thus marked, but also to distinguish words in foreign languages, citations of reference material, and for other purposes having nothing to do with the representativeness of the italicized material. Similarly, capitalization has a variety of functions other than its obvious uses in beginning sentences and proper nouns. Special sizes and styles of type are also used for a variety of functions, sometimes including that of emphasis. Investigation of such editorial features will have to include investigation of means of determining when the various features are being used for purposes, such as emphasis, that can be related to assessing the representativeness of words and sentences.

Special editorial practices of other kinds can also be used in estimating representativeness. A good example of such a practice is to be found in the *Scientific American*. Articles in this magazine are liberally supplied with pictures, tables, and diagrams that illustrate the major points being made in the articles, and these illustrations are closely tied to the text of the articles. When a statement in the text is thus illustrated, the sentence is ended by an italicized instruction, such as *"see illustration on page*_____,"* enclosed in square brackets. Almost always a sentence so ended is highly representative of the content of the article. Because of the strong editorial control on articles in the *Scientific American* (more control than professional journals usually find practicable), its articles have a homogeneity of style that can be expected to make even manual investigation of editorial criteria for representativeness fruitful.

5.4.1.4 *Semantic Information Content.* The problem of measuring representativeness is, of course, closely linked to—and, in fact, can be viewed as a part of—the problem of measuring the importance of information. That this latter problem is an extremely difficult one has long been recognized by philosophers and logicians, as well as by documentalists and other information system scientists. One line of attack has been to try to set up a "semantic space," in which each of the dimensions would be some fairly general attribute. A word would be viewed as a point in the semantic space, whose projections on the various axes would yield a measure of the word's meaning. This is the approach taken by, for example, Osgood [31] and Quillian [33].

A different approach is that of MacKay [26] , who would relate semantic information content to the degree of change producible in the receiver of the information. MacKay suggests viewing an intelligent organism as embodying

> a vast constantly changing matrix of *conditional probabilities*. . . . determining the relative probabilities of various patterns . . . of behaviour in all possible circumstances. . . . Unless the organism happens to be organ-

ized exactly to match the current state of affairs (in its environment), *work* must be done to bring it up to date: work, not only in a physical, but in a *logical* sense. This 'logical work' consists in the adjusting and moulding of the conditional-probability structure of the organizing system: the formation, strengthening, or dissolution of functional linkages between various basic acts or basic sequences of acts. The total configuration of these linkages embodies what we may call the total 'state of readiness' of the organism. ...[That portion of] the total configuration that keeps the organism matched to its field of purposive activity ...[we shall call] the *orienting* system, and the corresponding total state of readiness the *orientation* of the organism.

Information can now be defined as that which does logical work on the organism's orientation (whether correctly or not, and whether by adding to, replacing, or confirming the functional linkages of the orienting system). Thus we leave open the question whether the information is true or false, fresh, corrective or confirmatory, and so on.

The *amount of information* received by an organism can then be measured (in various ways) by measuring if we can (in various ways) the logical (organizing) work that it does for the organism. ...The *meaning* of an indicative item of information to the organism may now be defined as its selective function on the range of the organism's possible states of orientation, or for short, its *organizing function* for the organism. ... (It must be clearly distinguished from the *organizing work done* on the organism, which is *the result of the exercise* of this organizing function. Much confusion is caused by attempts to identify meaning with the change produced in the receiver.) [26, pp. 470-71, MacKay's italics]

MacKay's suggestion would doubtless be very difficult to experiment with in terms of human intelligence, but this should not deter researchers from trying to apply his concept to simpler animal intelligences and to machines. For instance, it might prove fruitful to review, in the light of MacKay's "states of readiness," some of the experiments with computer programs that "learn."

At a given point in the running of a learning program, the learning that has taken place could be interpreted as constituting the program's state of readiness and, typically, would be expressed in terms of the set of strategies (states of orientation) available to the program for its next step. The information received by the program in the next step could be identified, as could the changes in the program's state of readiness, namely, the modifications in the set of available strategies resulting from the program's acting upon the information received. The information's selective function on the range of the program's possible states of orientation—its MacKay *meaning*—could thus be assessed, and the MacKay *amount of information* could be related to the amount of organizing work done on the program. It seems possible that research employing such interpretations of the concept of amount of information could eventually contribute greatly to the solution of the problem of measuring the amount of semantic information conveyed by a linguistic unit.

Another potentially fruitful approach to the measurement of semantic information content is to be found in a paper by Katter [23]. His approach begins by defining the "Communication Effect of a language expression . . . as the probability that the *preferred definition* [of the expression]; offered by a randomly selected member from a language-using population, will be recognized as specifying that expression when given to another randomly selected member" [23, p. 1]. Direct measurement of the communication effect of a language expression is costly, but the communication effect was shown to correlate very strongly with a function of "the Diversity/Fluency ratio of the frequency distribution of linguistic definitions given for the expression. Diversity is the number of different kinds of definitions given by (a large number of) respondents. Fluency is the average number of definitions given by a single respondent." [23, p. 1]

The production of condensed representations of documents can be interpreted, from the viewpoint of Katter's communication effect, in the following way. The extent to which a condensed representation of a document satisfies the search-tool function is directly related to the probability that a searcher, upon examining the condensed representation, will be able to predict accurately the degree of his interest in the document itself. In the context of a document-search process, it seems reasonable to take this probability as equal to the probability that the search can accurately predict the essential content of the document. In this sense, the text units extracted (or generated) for the condensed representation should be those units having the highest predictive power — the highest communication effect for the searcher — with respect to the document. This suggests that instead of talking about the representativeness of a text unit *in vacuo*, we ought to think in terms of the unit's representativeness for a given searcher, or at least for a given class of searchers. Then, in relation to a particular document, we could say that the representativeness of a text unit for a searcher is equivalent to the communication effect of the text unit with respect to the document, rather than with respect to the whole body of linguistic knowledge of the searcher as in Katter's definition of communication effect.

At this point it is interesting to recall the Rath, Resnick, and Savage studies (Section 5.3.2.5) and a part of the Ramo-Wooldridge study (Section 5.3.2.6) concerning human consistency in selecting sentences from a document to form a pseudo-automatic abstract. In both studies it was found that people are consistent neither with each other nor with themselves in choosing sentences to be extracted. Yet the various pseudo-automatic abstracts of a given document in these experiments must be assumed to have been of roughly the same order of satisfactoriness, even though the abstracts consisted of different sentences; for otherwise the experimenters would have found, not inconsistency among the sentence sets, but simply that some of the sentence sets formed better, and other sentence sets poorer, abstracts. In fact, Resnick states explicity that his group's findings suggest there may be "many equally representative sets of sentences" [37, p. 143] for a given document.

Given these experimental results, one is naturally led to ask just what it is that makes these different sentence sets equally representative. We suggest that an answer to this question may be found in the communication-effect approach. If one assumes that pairs of alternative sentences, chosen by different persons to cover a particular aspect of a document, are equivalent in communication effect with respect to that aspect, then the supposed inconsistency no longer exists. In other words, it should not be considered reasonable to require consistency, *in the sense of identity*, in the selection of sentences to form an automatic abstract of a document, just as it would not be reasonable to require that traditional abstracts of the document, prepared by different individuals, be written in identical sentences. In both cases, the desideratum is only that the abstracts, traditional or automatic, be equivalent in their communication effect with respect to the document.

5.4.2   Problems of Language.   In the previous section we have dealt at some length with the problems of quantifying meaning, because these problems are the most serious, the most difficult of solution, and probably destined to be the longest-lived of the problems confronting automatic document-content analysis. There remain the problem areas of language and of application, which we shall treat briefly in this section and the one following.

5.4.2.1 *Ambiguity.*   One of the chief problems of natural language is ambiguity. As Kaplan [22, p. 39] metaphorizes: "Ambiguity is the common cold of the pathology of language. The logician recognizes equivocation as a frequent source of fallacious reasoning. The student of propaganda and public opinion sees in ambiguity an enormous obstacle to successful communication. Even the sciences are not altogether free of verbalistic disputes that turn on confused multiple meanings of key terms." Ambiguity causes trouble enough when humans are using language. When attempts are made to use natural language in computers, ambiguity causes even more trouble.

The first type of ambiguity we shall discuss is that of multiple meanings, the "monster of polysemy" as Rhodes, a leading researcher in machine translation, picturesquely put it [12, p. 384] in commenting on the difficulties that the multiple-meaning problem creates in the computer processing of natural-language data. Polysemic ambiguity may reside in single words, or in word groups that express a conceptual unit, such as compound nouns; or it may reside in the whole of a larger unit of language, such as a phrase, clause, sentence, or paragraph. The reason for making this distinction is that these two types of polysemic ambiguity have different implications for machine handling of natural language. In the case of a single word, or a unit-concept group, the ambiguity consists in there being more than one meaning for the word or group. In the case of phrases, clauses, sentences, and paragraphs, the ambiguity may or may not be the result of multiple meanings for some of the individual words or unit-concept groups in the larger linguistic unit.

If the ambiguity of a larger unit is the result of multiple meanings for an individual word or group, then the problem can be reduced to that of handling the ambiguity of the word or group. But—and here is the real point of the distinction we are making—if the ambiguity of a larger linguistic unit arises in the interpretation of the entire linguistic unit, and not merely from multiple meanings of individual words or groups within the unit, then the ambiguity must reside in the *relations among the words* rather than in the words themselves. We shall refer to such ambiguity as "string ambiguity"; the terms "word ambiguity" and "group ambiguity" will be used for the ambiguity of single words and of unit-concept groups, respectively. Other expressions have also been used: for instance, "syntactic ambiguity" for "string ambiguity" and "semantic ambiguity" for "word (or group) ambiguity." However, these expressions seem unsatisfactory to us, since thus to contrast "syntactic" with "semantic" implies that the problem of multiple meaning in strings is not a problem of semantics, i.e., is not a problem of meaning.

Examples of word and group ambiguity have been frequently provided and discussed by philosophers, by linguists, and undoubtedly most profitably, by humorists. Dostert [12, p. 425] points out that "flying planes can be dangerous," a striking example in English, cannot be ambiguous in French, where it must be rendered in forms equivalent to either *les avions en vol peuvent être dangereux* or *il est dangereux de piloter des aéroplanes*. Robert Hayes invented the delightful sentence, "The hungry dog turned on the spit," for which he claims upwards of 16 possible interpretations. In these examples, the ambiguities clearly arise from multiple meanings for the individual words.

Examples of string ambiguity are also all too plentiful; in fact, string ambiguity is probably the most common disease of current technical writing. Does "scientific information handling" mean "the handling of scientific information" or "the scientific handling of information"? Does "computer program design procedures" mean "procedures for designing computer programs" or "procedures, in the form of computer programs, whose function is to design"? Do advertising gems like "Brand X is 99.9% pure" and "Soap Y cleans better than any soap" mean anything at all? In these examples the ambiguity stems from the multiplicity of possible modifying relations among the words—or, as with the advertising slogans, from the total absence of meaningful modifying relations—and not from multiple meanings for the individual words. To illustrate this assertion, we observe that we can remove the ambiguity in the first example simply by inserting a hyphen to indicate which relation is intended: compare "scientific-information handling" with "scientific information-handling." Unfortunately, the second example is not so easily cured of its ambiguity; although "computer-program design procedures" and "computer-program design-procedures" probably would convey the intended ideas, rewriting would be a better solution. The advertising slogans are another matter entirely—the ambiguity is not unintentional.

Both word ambiguity and string ambiguity create problems in the automatic processing of natural language. Solutions to the problems raised by string ambiguity can be expected to result from research in automatic syntactic analysis, which has largely been the province of machine-translation researchers and is discussed in detail in Chapter 7. To the solution of the problems raised by word and group ambiguity, there have thus far been two basic approaches. One approach is to try to limit the number of alternative meanings that a given word or unit-concept group might have in a given context. The other approach is to provide the user of the output of the automatic processing with several or all of the alternative meanings of a given word or group, either with or without some sort of ranking in order of likelihood of pertinence, so that the user can choose the alternative he thinks is best or, at least, most likely.

Other types of ambiguity can also cause trouble in automatic processing of natural-language data. Homographs create difficulties that require both syntactic and semantic techniques for solution. For example, in the text of legal documents and of articles in psychology the word "will" occurs both as an auxiliary verb and as a noun with specialized technical meanings, meanings that are different in law and in psychology. It seems clear that only some type of syntactic analysis will be able to distinguish between the verb and noun uses of "will"; certainly, semantic analysis will be required to distinguish the two noun uses of "will," at least for documents in which both uses occur, such as an article on the psychological barriers to writing one's will.

Advertising gems of nonmeaning constitute still another source of difficulty in automatic document-content analysis. One can easily imagine a syntax-analysis routine trying to locate the carefully omitted comparison in a slogan like "Brand Z smokes cleaner, purer, longer" and winding up in a loop as a result of its vain search. Another troublesome type of ambiguity is exemplified by the sarcastic use of "What a lovely day!" in a drenching downpour. One is inclined to be quite pessimistic about the possibilities of successfully handling such ambiguity in automatic natural-language processing. Fortunately for automatic processing—though perhaps unfortunately for the readers thus deprived of candor and levity— sarcasm is rarely inserted into technical reports and even more rarely allowed by editors to reach print.

5.4.2.2   *Unit–Concept Groups.*   One of the principal difficulties that English offers to automatic document-content analysis results from the expression of a single concept by two or more words. In speaking here of a "single concept," we mean what might be called a minimal level of single concept, the level typically expressed by a single noun or verb. The difficulty arises when a single concept on this minimal level is expressed by two or more words, as in compound nouns such as "computer program" and "information retrieval"; in adjective and noun pairs such as "near synonym" and the notorious example, "red herring"; and in verb-preposition pairs such as "refer to" and "look up."

It will be recalled (from Section 5.3.2.3) that Oswald set out to evaluate in his study [13] the thesis that automatically generated indexes should include not only single words but also groups of words. Surprising as it seems, Oswald's study appears to have been the first automatic indexing study that attempted to employ unit-concept groups as index terms. Previous studies had either ignored word groups entirely, or merely mentioned them in passing as desirable but unattainable, or assumed that word groups could be broken into single words at the indexing stage and then successfully recombined at the searching stage. However, Oswald did not develop a means for the automatic recognition and use of word groups. Instead, his study employed humans who were to simulate the automatic processing of natural-language data, and these humans were instructed to use unit-concept groups for index terms as though automatic recognition of such groups had already been achieved. A "brute force" attack on the problem—dictionary storage of commonly used unit-concept groups—has been tried in connection with machine-translation research and has shown itself to be useful. Dictionary storage, however, can obviously never be a complete solution, for unit-concept groups are constantly being created for new concepts. Undoubtedly, a combination of semantic and syntactic analysis will be necessary.

5.4.2.3 *Intersentence Reference.* In discussing problems of word and string ambiguity, we need not confine ourselves to difficulties occurring within the boundaries of single sentences; at a next higher level occur problems involving more than one sentence, one of which is the problem we call "intersentence reference." By this, we mean the kind of problem exemplified in the sentence you are now reading; for the first two words of this sentence, "by this," refer to an idea expressed in the sentence immediately preceding. In an abstract formed by the automatic extraction of individual sentences from a larger body of text, the strong possibility exists that any individual sentence selected may be incomplete; though the sentence may have fulfilled various criteria of representativeness, phrases or concepts necessary to its full understanding may not be contained in the sentence itself. The problem of intersentence reference has been the subject of intensive study by Olney and the reader is referred to his recent report [30] for further discussion.

5.4.3 Problems of Application.   Inevitably, the application of automatic abstracting techniques in an actual information-storage and -retrieval system will be closely linked with the use of automatic data–processing equipment. Equipment is not within the scope of this chapter, however; and so, except for this passing tribute to hardware's high importance in the realization of information-handling systems, we confine our attention to problems on the "software" side.

Software problems fall rather easily into two categories: input and output. Under the heading of input we can place those problems that deal with the wealth of information contained in the appearance of a page of printed matter, and with the interpretation and utilization of that information. Under the heading of output we can place those problems concerned with preparing and presenting the abstract in a suitable form and, perhaps most important, in a form that humans will be readily willing to use. This does not include, by way of specific example, the typical, densely packed, 120-character line, wholly upper-case printout from today's high-speed printers. Automatic abstracts must be presented in an attractive format and made easily readable if they are to be used on a large-scale or for more than purely experimental purposes. To achieve this attractiveness and readability, format–controlling computer programs will have to be linked with more flexible printing equipment than is generally available today. The recent development of printing equipment utilizing electronically controlled photographic composing processes would seem to be amenable to the kind of programmed format control needed.

We have been implicitly assuming that the printed page will continue to be as important in the future as it has in the past as a carrier of information. It is indeed possible that other forms of publication may supplement, and even to some extent supplant, the printed page in the future. For instance, one can envision a central information system, say for a large corporation, whose natural-language entries would consist largely of inputs from teletypes and Flexowriter tapes prepared directly from manuscripts. Eventually it should even be possible for automatic processing to turn the spoken word into electrical or magnetic representations of numbers, letters, words, and appropriate punctuation. But it seems hardly possible that such forms of information transmission will completely replace the printed page in the foreseeable future, and hence it remains important to think in terms of the printed page. Especially is this so with respect to the problems of input; for at least some of the present store of knowledge, essentially all of which is in printed form, will serve as input to most of the information systems to be developed in the next few decades.

Let us assume, then, that the printed page will be a major source of input material for an automatic abstracting system. Let us assume also that automatic character readers will soon exist that are capable of correctly interpreting all the characters appearing on the printed pages used as inputs to the system. One of the problems confronting us is to decide which part of the information contained on the page to use, and which part to ignore. We have already discussed (in Section 5.4.1.3) some of the kinds of information, appearing on a printed page as the result of the author's and editor's work, which are possibly useful as indicators of sentence representativeness. Experimentation is needed to determine which of these possibilities is actually useful.

Another input problem is that of handling nonverbal material, such as mathematical and chemical formulas, charts, and tables. At present, such material is usually pre-edited by humans before the document reaches the first stage of automatic processing. It will be desirable to develop means of automatically accomplishing some of this work. A character reader might be programmed to recognize a mathematical formula and arrange for photographic reproduction of the formula in the output of the automatic abstracting system. An allied output problem is illustrated by the difficulties involved in incorporating in the output a diagram referenced in a highly representative sentence selected for an automatic abstract.

Finally, in this sketch of input problems, we may mention that of preparing an automatic abstracting system, or more generally any automated document-processing system, to deal with the diversity of editorial and printing practices encountered in the handling of many different journals and other sources of input. Among the various inputs there will be many differences in page sizes, kinds of paper, means of binding, type styles and sizes, page formats, page numbering, and rules governing the use of footnotes, references, citations, captions, punctuation, and paragraphing; these are just a few of the characteristics that the system will have to handle. Attention to such details can be expected to consume a good deal of time in setting up any information-processing system that does not make heavy use of human intervention in the preparation of the inputs, whether the humans act in the role of pre-editors or merely as keypunch operators.

5.5 SOME POSSIBLE DEVELOPMENTS IN AUTOMATIC ABSTRACTING

5.5.1 Tailored Abstracts. Throughout this chapter we have implicitly considered automatic abstracts as analogs of traditional human-produced abstracts. One of the limitations inherent in the analogy is that we are led to think of producing a single abstract for a given document, to be used by all persons potentially interested in the document without regard to differences in their individual interests.

We must not overlook the fact that in automated systems we shall *not* necessarily be limited to analogs of the traditional library search-tools. Two principles for designing automated document-retrieval systems should be kept in mind:

(1) We are free to develop new tools that will take advantage of the speed of computers in performing routine tasks;

(2) We can utilize the communication between the user and the automated document-retrieval system to make both the old and the new tools more effective.

In keeping with these principles, Doyle and I have conjectured [51] that in searching a document-retrieval system for documents pertinent to the interest of a user, it might be feasible to select, by various methods, a small set of possibly pertinent documents and then, as the final stage in the search process, to prepare "tailored" automatic abstracts reflecting (1) the pertinence of each document to the user's request, and (2) the distinctions among the documents in the set. Thus, if some of the same documents turned up as part of the set of responses to a different request, it would be not only possible but expected that somewhat different automatic abstracts would be prepared for them.

An initial means of implementing such tailored abstracts, undoubtedly capable of being improved by further research, could be to give increased weight in the automatic abstracting process to content words that occurred in the search request, and diminished weight to content words that were shared by many or all of the documents in the possibly pertinent set. Naturally, the concept of preparing tailored abstracts could be extended to other types of condensed representations as well. The extension to Doyle's association maps [10] would probably be especially easy.

5.5.2 Abstracting in Foreign Languages.   Despite the enormous volume of scientific research currently underway in the United States and the British Commonwealth, and despite the tendency of scientists to publish in English in preference to their native languages, about half the world's scientific and technical literature is published in languages other than English, according to a recent estimate*. This foreign-language material must be translated into English to be usable by most American scientists, but translation, whether human or automatic, is a costly process. The fertile mind of Luhn recognized, early enough for inclusion in his original paper on automatic abstracting, the contribution that this new technique could make toward solving the problem of translation costs. He wrote that automatic abstracting "could also be used to alleviate the translation burden. To avoid total translation initially, [automatic] abstracts of appropriate length could be produced in the original language and only the abstracts translated for subsequent analysis" [25, p. 165]. Users would then read the English translations of the abstracts and, presumably, choose only some fraction of the original set of foreign-language articles for complete translation, thus saving part of the cost of translating the whole of the original set.

Actually, of course, the whole original set is not currently translated, because of the cost involved. The articles are screened for their potential interest for English-speaking scientists, and only a fraction are judged worthy of translation in full, with resultant savings in time and money. There is, however, a hidden loss in the fact that the screening of a foreign-language article must be done by persons who know the language. Such persons, dedicated and competent though they may be, cannot judge as

*Scientific and Technical Translating, UNESCO, Paris, 1957, pp. 13-19. Accurate estimates of percentages for languages of publication appear to be extremely difficult to formulate. An excellent discussion is to be found in: Bourne, C. P., The world's technical literature: an estimate of volume, origin, language, field, indexing, and abstracting, *Amer. Doc.*, v. 13, no. 2, April 1962, pp. 159-168.

well as a scientist himself whether the article is of interest. Consequently, some uninteresting articles get translated while some potentially interesting articles are left untranslated.

Edmundson and I [14, pp. 233-234] illustrated Luhn's idea with computations of the potential savings from foreign-language abstracting before translating. Even if our estimates of the savings are too high, as seems likely to me in retrospect, there can be little doubt that savings could be achieved by abstracting before translating.

5.5.3 Computer Writing of Natural-Language Text. The ultimate goal in automatic abstracting is to develop a set of methods by which a computer program could read a document and write a natural-language summary of it. As the reader will be well aware, the state-of-the-art is still a good distance from the achievement of this goal. Nevertheless, some recent research in linguistics indicates that the goal may be reached.

The work done in transformation analysis by Chomsky and in transformation and discourse analysis by Harris (see also the discussion of the work of Climenson, Hardwick, and Jacobson in Section 5.3.2.7) seems especially pertinent to the problem of enabling a computer to read natural-language text with some degree of "understanding." Recent work by Klein [24] contains a promising first start toward computer writing of a summary of an input text. The problems in research in computer writing of natural-language text are too complex to discuss in detail here. We wish merely to point out that automatic abstracting will offer an important area of application of the research.

5.6 EPILOG

In this chapter we have surveyed the first five years of research in automatic abstracting. If it seems that relatively little has been accomplished in the field, it should also be realized that very few people have concerned themselves with automatic abstracting. Currently, for instance, there are probably not more than a dozen people engaged in automatic abstracting research, compared to well over a hundred working on machine translation. Continuing the comparison, we note that MT research is over 10 years old now and has been well supported, in terms of both money and personnel, throughout that decade. In contrast, as a leading researcher in both MT and automatic abstracting, Edmundson, recently observed, "various United States government agencies have invested several millions of dollars in automatic translation since 1953, while only several hundred thousand dollars have been made available for research on automatic abstracting since 1958" [11, p. 259].

Despite these handicaps, research in automatic abstracting has made progress, especially in the area that is perhaps the most important for any kind of research: the discovery and recognition of the fundamental problems involved. It has become clear that the fundamental problems of automatic abstracting research are essentially, first, the linguistico-philosophical problem of meaning and its measurement, and second, the philosophico-linguistic problem of developing the logical analysis of natural language. We cannot imagine a pair of problems more intimately concerned with that uniquely characterizing ability of mankind—the power of verbal communication.

REFERENCES

1. American Petroleum Institute, API technical abstracts manual for *API Abstracts of Refining Literature,* New York.
2. American Society of Mechanical Engineers, Instructions for reviewers of ASME papers, New York.
3. American Society of Mechanical Engineers, Review preparation guide for *Applied Mechanics Reviews,* New York.
4. American Society for Metals, Abstractors' manual of the *ASM Review of Metal Literature,* Metals Park, Novelty, Ohio.
5. Armed Services Technical Information Agency, ASTIA guidelines for ... cataloging and abstracting, *Technical Abstract Bulletin.* Arlington, Va. (ASTIA now has the name: Defense Documentation Center (DDC).)
6. Battelle Memorial Institute, Reviewers' instructions for *Semiconductor Abstracts,* Columbus, Ohio.
7. Baxendale, P. B., Machine-made index for technical literature—an experiment, *IBM J. of Research and Development,* v. 2, no. 4, 1958, pp. 354-61.
8. Borko, H. and S. Chatman, Criteria for acceptable abstracts: a survey of abstractors' instructions, *Amer. Doc.,* v. 14, no. 2, 1963, pp. 149-60.
9. Climenson, W. D., N. H. Hardwick, and S. N. Jacobson, Automatic syntax analysis in machine indexing and abstracting, *Amer. Doc.,* v. 12, no. 3, 1961, pp. 178-83.
10. Doyle, L. B. Semantic road maps for literature searchers, *J. of the ACM,* v. 8, no. 4, 1961, pp. 553-78.
11. Edmundson, H. P., Problems in automatic abstracting, *Comm. of the ACM,* v. 7, no. 4, 1964, pp. 259-63.
12. Edmundson, H. P. (Ed.), *Proc. of the National Symposium on Machine Translation.* Englewood Cliffs, N. J.: Prentice-Hall, 1961.
13. Edmundson, H. P., V. A. Oswald, Jr., and R. E. Wyllys, Automatic indexing and abstracting of the contents of documents, Los Angeles, Calif.: Planning Research Corp., 31 October 1959. (The Oswald study is reported on pp. 5-34 and pp. 59-133.) (Also catalogued as RADC-TR-59-208 and DDC AD 231606.)
14. Edmundson, H. P., and R. E. Wyllys, Automatic abstracting and indexing—survey and recommendations. *Comm. of the ACM,* v. 4, no. 5, 1961, pp. 226-34.
15. Excerpta Medica Foundation, Abstractors' instructions, New York.

16. Ford, J. D., Jr. and E. H. Holmes, A comparison of human performance under natural language and term diagram procedures for the production of report summaries, *TM-662.* Santa Monica, Calif.: System Development Corp., 6 February 1962.

17. Institution of Electrical Engineers, Notes for abstractors, *Science Abstracts, Section B: Electrical Engineering Abstracts,* London, England.

18. International Business Machines Corporation, Advanced Systems Development Division, ACSI-matic auto-abstracting project, final report, v. l, Yorktown Heights, New York, 22 February 1960.

19. International Business Machines Corporation, Advanced Systems Development Division, ACSI-matic auto-abstracting project, final report, v. 3, Yorktown Heights, New York, 31 March 1961.

20. International Statistical Institute, Instructions for new abstractors for *The International Journal of Abstracts: Statistical Theory and Method,* Edinburgh, Scotland: Oliver and Boyd, Ltd.

21. *Journal of the American Leather Chemists Association,* Abstractors' instructions, U. of Cincinnati, Cincinnati, Ohio.

22. Kaplan, A., An experimental study of ambiguity and context, *Mechanical Translation,* v. 2, no. 2, 1955, pp. 39-46.

23. Katter, R. V., A predictor of semantic communication effect, *TM-663.* Santa Monica, Calif.: System Development Corp., 1 August 1962.

24. Klein, S., Automatic paraphrasing in essay format, *SP-1602/001/00.* Santa Monica, Calif: System Development Corp., 1964.

25. Luhn, H. P., The automatic creation of literature abstracts, *IBM J. of Research and Development,* v. 2, no. 2, 1958, pp. 159-65.

26. MacKay, D. M., The informational analysis of questions and commands, *Information Theory, Fourth London Symposium,* C. Cherry (Ed.). London, Butterworths, 1961, pp. 469-76.

27. MacKay, D. M., Operational aspects of some fundamental concepts of human communication, *Synthèse,* v. 9, no. 3-5, Issue 3, 1953, pp. 182-98.

28. Meadow, H. R., Statistical analysis and classification of documents. Rockville, Md.: International Business Machines Corp., 1962.

29. Modern Medicine Publications, Style guide for science writers, Minneapolis, Minn.

30. Olney, J. C., Using discourse analysis procedures to reduce context dependence, *SP-1606/001/00.* Santa Monica, Calif.: System Development Corp., July 1965.

31. Osgood, C. E., *The Measurement of Meaning.* Urbana, Ill.: U. of Illinois Press, 1957.

32. Parke, Davis and Company, Suggestions to abstractors, *Therapeutic Notes,* Detroit, Michigan.

33. Quillian, M. R., A notation for representing conceptual information; an application to semantics and mechanical English paraphrasing, *SP-1395.* Santa Monica, Calif.: System Development Corp., 1963.

34. Ramo-Wooldridge, A Division of Thompson Ramo Wooldridge, Inc., Final report on the study for automatic abstracting, Canoga Park, Calif., 1 September 1961. (Also catalogued as RADC-TR-61-230.)

35. Rath, G. J., A. Resnick, and T. R. Savage, Comparisons of four types of lexical indicators of content, *Amer. Doc.,* v. 12, no. 2, 1961, pp. 126-30.

36. Rath, G. J., A. Resnick, and T. R. Savage, The formation of abstracts by the selection of sentences—part I. Sentence selection by men and machines, *Amer. Doc.,* v. 12, no. 2, 1961, pp. 139-41.

37. Resnick, A., The formation of abstracts by the selection of sentences—part II. The reliability of people in selecting sentences, *Amer. Doc.,* v. 12, no. 2, 1961, pp. 141-43.

38. Resnick, A., Relative effectiveness of document titles and abstracts for determining relevance of documents, *Science,* v. 134, no. 3484, pp. 1004-06.

39. Resnick, A. and T. R. Savage, A re-evaluation of machine-generated abstracts, *Human Factors,* v. 2, no. 3, 1960, pp. 141-46.

40. Savage, T. R., H. C. Fallon, and M. E. Saxon, ACSI-matic auto-abstracting project, interim report. Yorktown Heights, N. Y.: International Business Machines Corp., 28 August 1959.

41. Sherrod, J., Preparing the technical abstract, *Amer. Meteorological Society Bulletin,* v. 38, no. 8, 1957, pp. 496-97.

42. Snell, Foster D., Inc., Abstractors' instructions for *Chemical Market Abstracts,* New York.

43. Society for Research in Child Development, Guide for the preparation of abstracts, *Child Development Abstracts and Bibliography,* Lafayette, Ind., Purdue University.

44. *Sociological Abstracts,* Abstracting instructions, New York.

45. Stein Engineering Services, Inc., Abstracting instructions for *Strain Gage Readings,* Phoenix, Ariz.

46. Swanson, D. R., Searching natural language text by computer, *Science,* v. 132, no. 3434, 1960, pp. 1099-1104.

47. TRW Computer Division, Thompson Ramo Wooldridge Inc., Automatic abstracting, Canoga Park, Calif., 2 February 1963. (Also catalogued as RADC-TDR-63-93.)

48. United States Geological Survey, Dept. of the Interior, Abstractors' instructions, *Geophysical Abstracts.* Washington: U. S. Government Printing Office.

49. Wallace, E. M., Rank order patterns of common words as discriminators of subject content in scientific and technical prose, *SP-1505.* Santa Monica, Calif.: System Development Corp., April 1964.

50. Williams, J. H., Jr., A discriminant method for automatically classifying documents, *Proc. of the Fall Joint Computer Conference, 1963.* Baltimore, Md.: Spartan Books, Inc., 1963.

51. Wyllys, R. E., Document searches and condensed representations, *FN-6170.* Santa Monica, Calif.: System Development Corp., 10 January 1962.

6

Stylistic Analysis

Sally Yeates Sedelow and
Walter A. Sedelow, Jr.

The use of the computer for stylistic analysis of natural language,* a field we have defined as "computational stylistics" [46, 48] has just begun to emerge as a major mode of computer-based research. If style is the patterning formed in the linguistic encoding of information and stylistic analysis is the detection of such pattern, much of the work encompassed under indexing, concordancing, author-attribution studies, content analysis, and syntactic analysis† is also a part of stylistic analysis. Style, in a verbal context, is associated with traditional literary analysis; thus, one might say that studies of form, of texture, of tone, of rhythm, and even of influence are also aspects of stylistic analysis.

As these examples suggest, the study of style in its largest sense is not necessarily statistical. But in the strictest sense, stylistic analysis is frequently dependent upon some, often very simple, implicitly statistical procedures. In the case of stylistic analysis which does not use the computer, the "statistics" or "protostatistics" may exist as no more than an informal inexplicit feeling about, for instance, the relative importance of a particular theme, or no more than an undimensionalized sense of a particular tone. Computational stylistics, on the other hand, is explicit and often will include precise counts, such as the frequencies of each word appearing in the text, or a numerical indication of the precise location of a given word in a particular text.

Some studies, such as the Mosteller-Wallace work on the *Federalist Papers* [37], are sophisticated statistical studies—in fact, refinement of

---

*The term "natural language" is common among computer users to distinguish between programming languages (languages used by human beings to communicate with the computer) and languages used by human beings to communicate with each other.

†This chapter will not include a discussion of syntactic analysis, because a survey of the state of the art in that area occupies another section of this book.

a statistical procedure was one goal of the Mosteller-Wallace study. The location of this chapter on stylistic analysis within the part of this book entitled *Statistical Analysis* does not imply sophisticated statistical procedures—although we welcome those that can be used for computational stylistics—but it does recognize the quantification potential in stylistic study.

6.1 WORD INDEX AND CONCORDANCE CONSTRUCTION

The state of the art is, at present, most mature in construction of word indexes and concordances. Chapter 4 in this book discussed the role of indexing as applied to information retrieval. For stylistic analysis, indexing serves a different purpose. The emphasis is upon word usage, and indexing is valuable because it "places" a word in its context. Given this information, a scholar can look for patterns of word occurrence and co-occurrence.

A concordance may show not only where a word occurs in the text, but also the context in which the word occurs. With only an index of word occurrences, the scholar must look up every entry in order to select those of interest to him. By providing the immediate context as well, the concordance may greatly improve the researcher's efficiency.

6.1.1 Word Indexing Procedures. As a computer procedure, word indexing is quite simple. If, for instance, a novel is being indexed, a small number of computer registers is set aside as counters, to record the number of occurrences of each substantive word according to its chapter, paragraph, sentence, and position within the sentence. Before the first word is "read in" to the computer, the chapter, paragraph, sentence, and word counters are set to zero, assuming that we are proceeding from the start of a book. When the first word is sensed by the computer, the word counter advances to 1. The word count increases by 1 as each subsequent word is sensed by the computer until the end of a sentence is reached. At this point, the sentence count increases by one and the word count begins again at zero. The paragraph and chapter counts are manipulated analogously.

There are a number of satisfactory indexing systems that can be used in stylistic analysis. The general procedure described above is an adaptation of the Simmons-McConlogue "depth-indexing" technique [50]. Clayton has a program that lists the lines in which a given word occurs [10] and Smith describes a program [51] that supplies the number of the sentence in which a word occurs. Since word indexing also can be an intermediate step in the construction of concordances, concordance-building programs have an indexing procedure, as do many other programs useful to stylistic analysis.

6.1.2 Concordance Building Projects and Methods. Major concordance-building projects are underway at the Centro Atomazione Analisi Linguista in Gallarate, Italy, at Cornell University, at New York University, at Boston College, and at Tufts University. In addition to these projects, focused upon a specific author or work, other research directed toward perfecting generalized techniques for constructing concordances has been undertaken. A programming procedure developed by Kay and described in Section 6.1.2.2, exemplifies such research.

6.1.2.1 *Concordances Focused Upon Particular Authors or Works.*
The project at Gallarate, under the direction of Roberto Busa, S. J., is focused upon the works of St. Thomas Aquinas; in addition, concordances of the Dead Sea Scrolls, and of works by Aristotle, Kant, and Goethe have been undertaken as part of the same project [8, 9]. By the end of 1964, approximately 15 million words had been processed. Sheer volume of words has forced Father Busa and his colleagues to alter the concordance for St. Thomas to the extent that function words (prepositions, conjunctions, etc.), which occur hundreds and even thousands of times, appear only in indexes and not in the concordance proper. To exemplify the kinds of conclusions concordances enable scholars to make, Father Busa notes that analysis of the Aquinas concordance indicates that St. Thomas predominantly used the word "virtus" to mean "strength" or "driving power," rather than "self-control."

The concordance-building project at Gallarate has also explored the possibility of filling in missing words or groups of words in a given manuscript. In an article describing the work on the Dead Sea Scrolls, Tasman says that

> Replacing obliterated words...is not always a serious problem since the analysis of the text reveals the frequency, sequence, use and context of all visible words. This information forms a rudimentary system for analyzing the writing style of an author and provides a tool to interpolate missing words or to detect foreign additions uncommon to the author. While it will not be absolutely certain that exact substitution will be made, machine substitution is much more accurate than manual methods. Up to five consecutive words have been "rewritten" by the data processing machine in texts where the words were intentionally left out of the text and blank spots indicated. [54, pp. 11-12]

Tasman's description of literary data processing [53] and the work on the Dead Sea Scrolls are good introductions to general problems and procedures for textual inventories. As is well known, the seven scrolls were discovered in a cave near the Dead Sea by an Arab shepherd, searching for his stray goats. At the time of their discovery, the scrolls were more than 2,000 years old and contained about 400 manuscripts, represented by 40,000 fragments, written in three languages: Hebrew, Aramaic, and Nabatean. The task of scholars was to identify these thousands of fragments by language, scroll, and scribe, and to combine them into their original form. Modern computer technology was enlisted to help accomplish this tremendous task.

Even the relatively straightforward work of keypunching took on new complexity. Ancient Semitic characters were used in the keypunching operation. The Hebrew alphabet of the scrolls does not include vowels; there are twenty-two consonants, five of which have a final form, or twenty-seven different Hebrew letters. To accommodate the text material, normally written from right to left, a modified card punch was devised to permit cards to be punched this way rather than in the conventional left-to-right direction. This modification reduced opportunities for error by saving the keypunch operators the necessity of transposing from right to left as they read and punched the text.

Six separate index lists of the scrolls were prepared:

(1) *Each Word List*—an alphabetically-arranged list in which each word in the text, together with its identifying data, is printed out as many times as it occurs.

(2) *Different Word List*—a summary list of graphically different words and the frequency of occurrence of each.

(3) *Identity Word List*—prepared by the scholar who separates the homographs and groups each word into its graphic-semantic family.

(4) *Lexicon*—combines the features of the *Different Word List* and the *Identity Word List*.

(5) *Reverse Index*—combines the features of the *Each Word List* and the *Identity Word List*.

(6) *Concordance*—for each appearance of the word, this list contains a section of the line or lines of text in which the word is embedded.

Tasman speculates that the time involved in the preparation of this material using automatic data processing techniques was only 1/299th as long as would have been required to do the work manually. Card punching and verifying of the approximately 30,000 words took less then 4 weeks; programming, 3 months; card-to-tape conversion, 3 hours; processing of the text into the 6 different indexing lists, 1 ½ hours on the IBM 705; and the printing of the lists, 9 hours.

In 1962, Fogel of Cornell University noted that "The only convention-ally-produced large concordance to an English or American poet which has appeared since the end of 1941 seems to be Professor Eby's concord-ance to Whitman's *Leaves of Grass* and selected prose." [15, p. 16] Cornell University has taken the lead in production of concordances using the computer [39]; initially those for the poetry of Matthew Arn-old [40], and William Butler Yeats [41], more recently for the work of William Blake and Emily Dickinson. Painter [38] describes the Cornell concordance construction procedure as follows:

> Input to the program consisted of either Hollerith punched cards or a magnetic tape prepared from such cards by off-line card-to-tape equip-ment. The Concordance program operated in three phases. The first phase scanned the line of poetry from the input cards. It broke the line into its component words and appended an identification of source line. After all the lines of text had been scanned, the words were sorted into alphabet-ical order. This was phase two. Phase three retrieved the source line, edited it, and prepared the printed output.

The Arnold volume [40], edited by Parrish, is approximately the length of Eby's Whitman concordance but is sold for less than half the cost of Eby's manually produced concordance.

A section of the Arnold concordance is reproduced in Figure 6.1 and reveals the value of a concordance to the scholar. Every instance of the use of the word is recorded. Word sequences and lingustic preferences

Word Sweep	Source Page#	Title (abb)	Line#
Sweep in the sounding stillness of the night	10	Mycerinus	46
Off they *sweep* the marshy forests	13	Church Brou 1	19
And his closed eye doth *sweep*	133	Tristram 1	90
Let her *sweep* her dazzling hand	134	Tristram 1	121
And sent me with my dogs to *sweep*	148	Tristram 2	176
And sent him with his dogs to *sweep*	148	Tristram 2 V	176
Sweep through my soul	185	Strayed Revel	6
Sweep through my soul	194	Strayed Revel	297
Free to the *sweep* of light and wind	223	Epilog Laocoon	72
Houses with long white *sweep*	242	Summer Night	18
Behind me on their grassy *sweep*	274	Stanzas Carnac	9
The sickle-*sweep* of Quiberon Bay	274	Stanzas Carnac	27
Widend her *sweep* and surveyd	280	Haworth Church	16
An arm aloft for help then *sweep* beneath	358	Merope	833
One arm aloft for help then *sweep* beneath	358	Merope V	833
The wind *sweep* man away	421	Empedocles 1 2	260

Figure 6.1.   Portion of Parrish's concordance to Arnold's poetry. [40, p. 94]

peculiar to the author can be identified. The scholar no longer need devote his energies to the tedious task of amassing examples; he is able to use his time and skill to interpret the evidence provided for him by the computer. He is freed from a clerical task to pursue a creative one.

A concordance of the extant remains of Old English poetry, comprising some 168,000 words, is being prepared at New York University under the direction of Bessinger [5]. Smith [51] says that the concordance-generating program being used for the Old English project "isolates each occurrence of each word in a text, and presents it in the full sentence in which it occurs."

Figure 6. 2 illustrates yet another type of concordance, which is being used for the works of Tertullian in a project directed by Siberz and Devine [49]. This type of concordance is widely known as the KWIC (Key-Word-In-Context) index, and was developed by the late H. P. Luhn [26]. As is evident, the word being "indexed" occurs in the middle of the line and is accompanied by a sufficient quantity of preceding and succeeding words to make up a printout line. The information at the right shows where in the works of Tertullian the word in question occurs.

An *Althochdeutsches Glossenwortenbuch* (concordance to the Old High German glosses) is being prepared under the direction of John Wells and Taylor Starck [57]. The starting material, *Die althochdeutschen glossen,* published in five volumes, 1879-1922, by Elias Steinmeyer and Eduard Sievers, consists of approximately 2,700 double-column pages of Latin and German words, plus supplementary material published by other scholars since that time in about forty separate articles. The number of German words totals about 140,000. The listing and indexing of both German and Latin words is to be performed by the computer.

Other major concordance-building projects, directed toward the preparation of concordances as material for historical dictionaries, are in progress in Jerusalem for Hebrew, in Prague for Czech, in Leiden for Flemish, in Nancy for French (120 million words are to be processed), in Budapest for Hungarian, and in Bonn for Kant's *Sammtliche Werke.* Except for the Bonn project, these efforts might be described as the characterization of some components in stylistic analysis of the language habits of a culture or ethnic group.

6.1.2.2 *A General Procedure for Building Concordances.* In order to provide some idea of programming procedures involved in constructing a concordance, this section provides a rather detailed description of a program devised by Martin Kay [23]. This program is designed for general use, rather than for analysis of the works of a particular author.

Five principal options (concordances, indexes, lists, punch, and mon-

, SI CONTRA EUM FECERINT,	AUT AB ADUERSARIIS EIUS, SI PRO EO	MR	6, 2
T COLERE+, NEC ALII OBEST	AUT PRODEST ALTERIUS RELIGIO. +SED	SC	2, 2
TOR UNIUERSITATIS, ODORIS	AUT SANGUINIS ALICUIUS. +HAEC ENIM	SC	2, 8
EA NOS PATI QUAE OPTAMUS,	AUT ULTIONEM A NOBIS ALIQUAM MACHI	SC	2,10
, NE GAUDEANT +CHRISTIANI	AUT SPERENT +CHRISTIANAE. POSTEA C	SC	3, 4
GARIBUS ENIM NON DICIMUS)	AUT A DAEMONIIS AUT UALETUDINIBUS	SC	4, 5
DICIMUS) AUT A DAEMONIIS	AUT UALETUDINIBUS REMEDIATI SUNT +	SC	4, 5
O RENUNTIAUIT, IN CARCERE	AUTEM ETIAM CARCERI. +NIHIL INTERE	MR	2, 5
QUO UELIT TRANSFERT. +UBI	AUTEM ERIT COR TUUM, ILLIC ERIT ET	MR	2,10
GERE OMNIUM EST, INIMICOS	AUTEM SOLORUM +CHRISTIA NORUM. 4.	SC	1, 3
TIOSI SUNT+, CONTESIOSUS	AUTEM +DEUS NON EST. 3. +DENIQUE Q	SC	2, 2
IN SACRILEGIO. 4. +OMNES	AUTEM QUI TEMPLA DESPOLIANT, ET PE	SC	2, 4
PABULA SUNT. 9. +DAEMONAS	AUTEM NON TANTUM RESPUIMUS, UERUM	SC	2, 9
NFESSOS DAMNARE, NEGANTES	AUTEM AD TORMENTA REUOCARE+, +UIDE	SC	4, 2
NFESSIONE NON UULTIS. +SI	AUTEM CONTENDITIS AD ELIDENDOS NOS	SC	4, 2
AM EXPUGNATIS. 3. +QUANTI	AUTEM PRAESIDES, ET CONSTANTIORES	SC	4, 3
ARMATOS= QUIA PAX UESTRA	BELLUM EST ILLI. 6. +QUAM PACEM QU	MR	1, 5
SPONDIMUS. +NEMO MILES AD	BELLUM CUM DELICIIS UENIT, NEC DE	MR	3, 1
PACE LABORE ET INCOMMODIS	BELLUM PATI IAM EDISCUNT, IN ARMIS	MR	3, 2
FFUMIGATUS. +NEC ILLI TAM	BENE SIT IN SUO REGNO, UT UOS COMM	MR	1, 5
UT AD STADIUM TRIBUNALIS	BENE EXERCITATI INCOMMODIS OMNIBUS	MR	3, 5
A FEMINIS, UT UOS QUOQUE,	BENEDICTAE, SEXUI UESTRO RESPONDEA	MR	4, 3
. +INTER CARNIS ALIMENTA,	BENEDICTI MARTYRES DESIGNATI, QUAE	MR	1, 1
ERINT. 3. +INPRIMIS ERGO,	BENEDICTI, NOLITE CONTRISTARE +SPI	MR	1, 3
EI SUSTINET. 4. +QUO UOS,	BENEDICTI, DE CARCERE IN CUSTODIAR	MR	2, 4
AURUM. 3, 1. +SIT NUNC,	BENEDICTI, CARCER ETIAM +CHRISTIAN	MR	3, 1
UMULTUM. 3. +PROINDE UOS,	BENEDICTI, QUODCUMQUE HOC DURUM ES	MR	3, 3
INAMBULAUERUNT. 2. +HAEC,	BENEDICTI, NON SINE CAUSA +DOMINUS	MR	5, 2
CONTREMISCITIS, AD CUIUS	BENEFICIA GAUDETIS. +CETEROS ET IP	SC	2, 1
EM ADUOCATIS, QUI ET IPSI	BENEFICIA HABENT +CHRISTIANORUM, L	SC	4, 4
RUCEM EXCELSAM, ET RABIEM	BFSTIARUM, FT SUMMAM IGNIUM PEONAM	MR	4, 2
IXUS, TOT CRUCES SENSIT.	BESTIAS FEMINA LIBENS APPETIIT, ET	MR	4, 6
T GLADIUM, IGNEM, CRUCEM,	BESTIAS, TORMENTA CONTEMNAT SUB PR	MR	4, 9
AUILUM IDEM +CAECILIUS AD	BESTIAS DAMNASSET, STATIUM HAEC UEX	SC	3, 5
PROMPTUS. +NON ERGO NOBIS	BLANDIAMUR, QUIA +DOMINUS CONSENSI	MR	4, 1
C SIT PERFECTA ET PROPRIA	BONITAS NOSTRA, NON COMMUNIS. +AMI	SC	1, 3
MI ET CORPORIS DEPUTATE.	+BONUM AGONEM SUBITURI ESTIS IN QUO	MR	3, 3
TUS, CORONA AETERNITATIS,	BRABIUM ANGFLICAE SUBSTANTIAE, POL	MR	3, 3
OPHI= +HERACLITUS, QUI SE	BUBULO STERCORE OBLI TUM EXCUSSIT+	MR	4, 5
S +CAPELLA IN ILLO EXITU	+BYZANTINO= CHRISTIANI GAUDETE. E	SC	3, 4
E +CHRISTIANUS DECESSIT.	+CAECILIUS +CAPELLA IN ILLO EXITU +	SC	3, 4
DRUMETICUM +MAUILUM IDEM	+CAECILIUS AD BESTIAS DAMNASSET, ST	SC	3, 5
IMPUBICITIA CELEBRANTIUM	CAEDERIS+, NON IN LOCA LIBIDINUM P	MR	2, 7
GIS AEDIFICARI SCIAS, CUM	CAEDI UIDETUR. +QUISQUE ENIM TANTA	SC	5, 4
AD CONSECUTIONEM GLORIAE	CAELESTIS ET DIUINAE MERCEDIS. +SI	MR	4, 9
E SUBSTANTIAE, POLITIA IN	CAELIS, GLORIA IN SAECULA SAECULOR	MR	3, 3
T IN NERUO, CUM ANIMUS IN	CAELO EST. +TOTUM HOMINEM ANIMUS C	MR	2,10
NT, IN ARMIS DEAMBULANDO,	CAMPUM DECURRENDO, FOSSAM MOLIENDO	MR	3, 2
POSSENT+, UT+UESPRONIUS	+CANDIDUS, QUI +CHRISTIANUM QUASI T	SC	4, 3
NUS DECESSIT. +CAECILIUS	+CAPELLA IN ILLO EXITU +BYZANTINO=	SC	3, 4

Figure 6.2. Sample of the Tertullian concordance

itor) are available to the user of Kay's program. The *concordance* option provides an alphabetically arranged list of words, each embedded within a specified amount of text. The *index* is the alphabetical list of words accompanied by references to text location of each. The *list* is an index without the location references. The *punch* option provides the list on punched cards, one word per card. The final option, *monitor*, prints out words in the list format, but in order of first occurrence rather than in alphabetical order.

When punching up a text for which a concordance is to be made, the references (specified by the user) to the text location of the citation must be punched into the cards along with the textual words. Kay provides two conventions for indicating references. The first is to include an identification word at the beginning of each card. Because each citation includes 131 characters and there can be only 80 characters on any single punched card, the citation always includes either the identification word from the card on which the word itself was punched or the immediately following one. When using this system, the identification word need not be treated differently from other words by the machine.

The second convention is to use a special identification word (again, specified by the user), recognizable by the program, which is appended to every citation. It is not necessary to have such a word on every card because the program will print out the last one to occur before the occurrence of the given word, however far back the identification word may be.

Kay urges the scholar, when punching up the text, to include more information than he thinks he will use. For example, his initial goal may be simply to make a concordance of words exactly as they appear in the text. At some later point, the scholar may wish to consider stems and endings separately. To facilitate such study, he might, when punching the text, separate stems from endings by a character such as +. For his initial concordance, the program will operate on the text, treating + like any other non-blank character. For his later study, the computer may be instructed to operate upon the same text, replacing + by a space. This procedure would cause stems and endings to be treated independently.

The concordance building program operates in three major stages: first, the text is given a broad alphabetical sort so that major sections are sequenced correctly; second, individual words are arranged alphabetically; and third, citations for the concordance are formed. To make these procedures possible, a "token" record of the occurrences of each word is kept in addition to the record of each word, or "type."

To exemplify the initial stages of the program, let the sentence "Here's a tentative survey of a tentative concordance program" be considered.

The sentence is examined from left to right; therefore "Here's" is the first word entered in the TOKEN table and the first word entered in the TYPE table. In order to conceptualize the procedure, it is also useful to think of "Here's" as the top node of a tree structure. All the words subsequent to the top node appear on the left side of the tree if they alphabetically precede "Here's" and on the right side of the tree if they alphabetically follow "Here's." The tree structure for the sentence might appear as it does in the center of Figure 6.3.

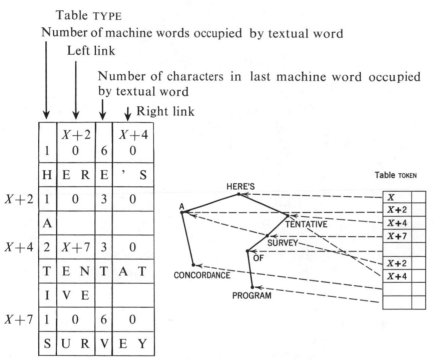

Figure 6.3.   Tree structure for sample sentence

Table TYPE, as is apparent in Figure 6.3, consists of at least two machine words for each textual word. The first machine word contains four kinds of information: the number of machine words the textual word occupies; a link to a textual word, if any, which alphabetically precedes the textual word being examined; the number of characters in the last machine word of the entry occupied by that textual word; and a link to a textual word, if any, which alphabetically follows the textual word being examined. "Here's" occupies one machine word; the left and right links are initially set to zero because "Here's" is the first word and, therefore, there are no words to which to link it; there are six characters in the last (and only) machine word occupied by "Here's." "A" has no link, initially, because there is nothing on its left or down to its right. As soon as "A" is entered in Table TYPE, the left link of "Here's" is changed from 0 to $X + 2$ because "A" alphabetically precedes "Here's." Double rowed entries in the link sections in Table TYPE represent successive alphabetizing as words are added to the table. Notice that the words are considered sequentially; although both "survey" and "tentative" are to the right of "Here's," the linking is from "Here's" to "tentative" on the right, and then from "tentative" to "survey" on its left.

Table TOKEN, at the right of Figure 6.3, contains the addresses of the types for each of the occurrences, or tokens, of the type. For example, the "Here's" entry begins in the machine word indexed by X, in Table TYPE, "A" in the word indexed by $X + 2$, etc. The two tokens of "A" both contain $X + 2$, the address of the type "A" in Table TYPE. The entries for "concordance," "of," and "programs" are not filled in because Table TYPE, in Figure 6.3, is not carried out through those words.

The information in Tables TYPE and TOKEN is manipulated during the second and third parts of the program. For convenience of explanation, a more abstract example will be used to illustrate those sections. See Figure 6.4. The left link of F, the head of the tree, is checked to see if it is nonzero. If it is, the link to the left is broken (is set to 0 in Table TYPE), and links to the right from D are examined until a zero link is reached (in this case, E has a zero in its right link). At this point, F and all its branches are linked to E's right. This procedure down the main left branch and appropriate right subbranches of the tree continues until the tree looks like Figure 6.4b.

Next, the program, beginning on the left, examines node (type) A and succeeding nodes until a node with a left link is reached. In our example, J will be the first such node. The links between F and J and, subsequently, J and H will be broken, so that the final section of the tree will appear as in Figure 6.4c. When the procedure is repeated the final section of the tree will, of course, be as in Figure 6.4d. When all left links are gone, this section of the program is completed.

The final stage of the program, which forms the concordance citations, uses the now empty left links of Table TYPE and the entries in Table TOKEN. The explanation will be based upon the diagram in Figure 6.4e.

Table TOKEN is processed from the bottom up. The type for token F is indexed, or pointed to, by the entry in $XX + 10$. Therefore, the *left* link of type F is set to $XX + 10$ (in Figure 6.4e, the contents of the left link are recorded below the appropriate node). Token E is indexed by the contents of $XX + 9$, token B by $XX + 8$, and token C by $XX + 7$. Token E

Table TOKEN

Entries in Table TYPE

Links to next occurrence
of same token

Links to Table TYPE

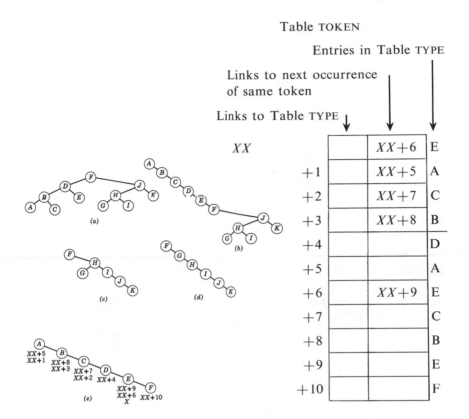

XX		XX+6	E
+1		XX+5	A
+2		XX+7	C
+3		XX+8	B
+4			D
+5			A
+6		XX+9	E
+7			C
+8			B
+9			E
+10			F

Figure 6.4. Tree structure analysis example

occurs again at position $XX + 6$. Therefore, the left link in the entry for type E is placed in the right half of $XX + 6$ in table TOKEN and the location of the more recent occurrence of token E is placed in the left link of the "E" entry in Table TYPE. This procedure continues until all of Table TOKEN has been processed. Thus, when compiling the citations for any given type, the program starts at the top of Table TOKEN and, when the first token is found, direct links are available to each subsequent occurrence of the token. The direct links make the construction of the concordance a very fast process.

6.2   AUTHOR ATTRIBUTION STUDIES

Certain author attribution studies are more appropriately reserved for discussion later in this chapter, but there are at least three that, because of the nature of their focus, should be described separately. One of the studies applies Bayes' Theorem to the problem of author discrimination; the second examines certain kinds of word frequencies; and the third uses a variety of tabulations to examine the provenance of the Pauline epistles.

Whatever the aim of the author attribution studies, the means by which the aim is achieved is the analysis of the style of authors studied. Many authors write about the same subject, but the way each puts words together and, in part, the words each chooses serve as stylistic signatures discriminating one author from another. The work described in this section is, therefore, in the mainstream of stylistic analysis that uses the computer.

6.2.1   Application of Bayes' Theorem to *The Federalist Papers.* Mosteller and Wallace's study of *The Federalist Papers* [37] was primarily an effort to test a particular statistical measure, commonly referred to as Bayes' Theorem, on a textual discrimination problem. The Federalist papers were written during 1787 and 1788 by Alexander Hamilton, James Madison, and John Jay, and were published to help convince the citizens of New York to ratify the United States *Constitution.* In all, seventy-seven papers were published anonymously. Jay is credited with writing five of the essays, Hamilton with forty-three, and Madison with fourteen. Three papers (numbered 18, 19, and 20) are known to have been written jointly by Hamilton and Madison. This leaves twelve papers (numbered 49—58, 62, and 63) whose authorship is in dispute, although it is known that either Hamilton or Madison was the author.

Scholars have been interested in resolving the problem of disputed authorship, and recent research — particularly the work of Adair [1, 2] — attributes all twelve of the disputed papers to Madison. The task that Mosteller and Wallace set for themselves was to determine the authorship of these twelve papers by first making an analysis of some of the statistically isolatable properties of the known writings, and then to predict the authorship of the unknown papers.

They tried a number of discriminators. Sentence length proved to be of no help because both Hamilton and Madison wrote long, complex sentences. Mosteller and Wallace recorded the mean sentence length of the known Hamilton and Madison papers respectively as 34.55 and 34.59 words with an average standard deviation of 19.2 and 20.3. Content words (nouns, adjectives, verbs) were considered to be too subject-dependent to be good discriminators. High-frequency function words (prepositions, conjunctions, etc.) did provide good clues as to authorship. Function words, as opposed to content words, presumably are not so heavily subject-dependent; rather, the use of function words seems to provide a sort of unconscious continuity in a given author's style. At least, this is the case in the known works of Hamilton and Madison. Figure 6.5 indicates the discriminative power of the function words "by," "from," and "to." From these data, Mosteller and Wallace concluded "High rates for 'by' usually favor Madison, low rates favor Hamilton; for 'to' the reverse holds true. Low rates for 'from' tell little, but high rates favor Madison." [37]

Rate	Word by		Rate	Word from		Rate	Word to	
	H.	M.		H.	M.		H.	M.
1-3	2		1-3	3	3	20-25		3
3-5	7		3-5	15	19	25-30	2	5
5-7	12	5	5-7	21	17	30-35	6	19
7-9	18	7	7-9	9	6	35-40	14	12
9-11	4	8	9-11		1	40-45	15	9
11-13	5	16	11-13		3	45-50	8	2
13-15		6	13-15		1	50-55	2	
15-17		5				55-60	1	
17-19		3						
Totals	48	50		48	50		48	30

Figure 6.5   Frequency distribution of rate per thousand words for "by," "from," and "to," in 48 Hamilton and 50 Madison papers

On the basis of the statistical properties of the words used in the papers, the odds are very much in favor of Madison having written all twelve of the disputed papers and the major part of Papers 18 and 19, which were jointly authored by Hamilton and Madison. The authorship of Paper 20 is undetermined because of a possibility that other people contributed to the writing. These findings are far more rigorously derived than earlier author attribution studies.

6.2.2   Word Use Frequencies as Applied to the Junius Problem. In 1962, the English Department of the University of Goteborg published Ellegard's *A Statistical Method for Determining Authorship: The Junius*

Letters, 1769-1772 [14]. The paternity of the Junius Letters, a series of political pamphlets written in England, has been much disputed, with Ellegard himself summarizing the history of the disputation in *Who Was Junius?* [13]. In the Goteborg study, he argues for a statistical characterization of distinctive word usage. Having applied such a characterization to the Junius letters, he concludes that they were written by Sir Philip Francis, rather than by any one of forty other possible authors, including Lord Chatham, Lord Chesterfield, Edmund Burke, and Edward Gibbon. Ellegard also urges the general applicability of his statistical analysis.

The procedure amounts to determining, for some group of mutually contemporaneous authors, the respective frequencies of their uses of certain words. Those used more often by a given author than by his contemporaries were designated "plus" words and those used less often were called "minus" words. Ellegard's goal was to translate statements as to use-frequency differentials into statements of authorship. He concluded that for his approach to reach its target, a sample on the order of one million words from contemporary authors working in a similar genre and one hundred thousand words from the works of a particular author would be required. The method

> ...is sensitive enough to select correctly practically all the author's works of the same general kind if they amount to 10,000 words or more, and to reject correctly practically all texts of the same size by other authors. We have also found that the power of separation that the test possesses is good down to the text sizes of about 4,000 words, and considerable even down to text samples of about 2,000 words. [13, p. 77]

Ellegard argues for an application of his procedure comprehensively with reference to both the totality of a literature's genres and its eras. To do so would be further to perfect these statistical-linguistic analyses, and to apply them to phrases and, possibly, constructions as well as to words; the result, he foresees, would be of great utility in studying persistence, change, and individuality in language communities.

As is true of Mosteller and Wallace, there is an acknowledgment of indebtedness to Yule [61] and Ellegard notes parallels in his approach with that of Guiraud [20]. Although he makes use of Yule's *Biometrika* article on sentence length [60], he does not mention George Zipf's work.

6.2.3 Authorship of the Pauline Epistles.   The other author attribution study which might appropriately be discussed here is the work of Morton* on the Pauline epistles [36]. Fourteen New Testament epistles have

---

*During a recent conference at Yale, the Rev J. W. Ellison disputed Morton's findings. Ellison said that, using Morton's technique, he was unable to find continuity of style in Morton's article about the Pauline epistles.

commonly been attributed to Saint Paul. Morton decided to use computer-based stylistic analysis as a means of testing the validity of this common assumption. Like Mosteller and Wallace, Morton tabulated occurrences of certain commonly occurring words. The best discriminator seems to have been the word "kai," which is roughly equivalent to the English word "and." Distances between occurrences of the words tabulated were also taken into account. On the basis of his study, he concluded that Saint Paul probably wrote only five of the epistles in question—*Romans, First* and *Second Corinthians, Galatians,* and *Philemon.* The others, Morton says, were written by an, as yet, unknown hand.

6.3   STUDIES BASED UPON TRADITIONAL STYLISTIC CHARACTERISTICS

Traditional literary analysis of style has employed such concepts as *form, tone, texture, influence* and many others having in common a vagueness of definition so great as to allow each scholar a different point of departure when talking about the style of a given text. Linguistic researchers have also been concerned with the problem of style; and they have tended to talk of *rhythmic structures, syntactic structures,* and, more recently, of *graphemic, phonemic,* and *morphemic structures.* A volume edited by Sebeok on style [45] provides a good general survey of linguistic research in this area as well as including some commentaries by literary critics. So far as computer-based stylistic analysis in concerned, linguists have thus far focused upon syntactic analysis in an effort to solve the continuing problems associated with achieving adequate machine translations. Their work on style is, therefore, described elsewhere in this book (Chapters 7 and 9).

The stylistic analysis produced manually that most closely approximates research using computers is that undertaken by Miles, who has analyzed sound, syntax, and context in the vocabularies of poetry in the 1740's, 1840's and 1940's, as well as the work of other periods and poetic movements [28-34]. Other studies that might be mentioned are Whaler's [58] attempt to work out the statistics of the rhythm in *Paradise Lost* and Yule's work [61] on the *De Imitatione Christi* and the religious works of Gerson. Yule was an avocational student of literature—his major work was in the field of statistics and his literary explorations attracted the attention of Mosteller in his days as a graduate student.

6.3.1   Studies Focused upon Individual Authors.   Recent attempts to use the computer to deal with aspects of style while solving questions of authorship, have been reported by McDonough [27], by Dearing [12], by Wachal [55], and by Milic [35].

McDonough set out to examine the structural metrics of the *Iliad*, which has 112,000 words arranged in 15,694 dactylic hexameter lines. An example of the dactylic hexameter line in English poetry is the well known:

"This is the forest primeval, the murmuring pines and the hemlocks." The dactyl is composed of a long syllable followed by two short syllables. The final foot —a spondee—consists of two long syllables. The first five feet in a dactylic hexameter line are dactyls, although a spondee may be substituted for a dactyl in any of the five positions. McDonough suggests that a word that is itself a single dactyl (such as "murmuring") could be used to fill any of the first five feet. In the *Iliad* there are 5,542 such words; thus, if the only factors were the supply of such words and of positions in which they could theoretically fit, one might expect to find about 1,100 of them in each of the first five feet. Actually, McDonough reports, not one of these 5,542 words is used to fill the third foot; only 346 in the second foot; but 2,064 in the fifth foot. Obviously, more is involved in the positioning of the word than the basic framework of the dactylic hexameter. McDonough says that this

> ...study of the "right" and "wrong" places for words of a given rhythm and related questions such as the proper places within the line for pauses in the meaning and grammar, we call somewhat arbitrarily "structural metrics." Others use the term "inner" metrics. [27]

McDonough notes that a manual study of the *Iliad's* metrics would entail first the preparation of an index that would list every word in the *Iliad* not by its spelling but by its rhythmic function. This task would require indicating the rhythmic function of each of the 112,000 words on, say, 112,000 index cards; then, sorting these cards into 157 different categories; next, counting and comparing the contents of each category; and, finally, copying the information down so that it could be set in type, proofread, and printed.

In order to do a complete study of metrics in the *Iliad*, McDonough coded the rhythm of each line and had it punched on IBM cards, which were fed into the IBM 650 for isolation, sorting, and counting of the individual words, and printing of a complete list. McDonough describes the code as follows:

> It was based on the logic that (in the <u>Iliad</u>) any given syllable in any given line was either long or short, and that (in any language) any syllable is either the first syllable of its word, the last syllable, an interior syllable, or the entire word. Thus <u>1</u> represented a long syllable

beginning a word; 2 a long syllable within a word; 3 a long syllable ending a word; 4 a long monosyllabic word; 5, 6, 7 and 8 represented the
corresponding short syllables. [27]

"This is the forest primeval, the murmuring pines and hemlocks"
would be coded: 4 8 8 1 7 5 2 7 8 1 6 7 4 8 8 1 3. Whenever a two-syllable
spondee replaced a three-syllable dactyl, a 9 was inserted to show that
the third syllable which might have occurred did not occur. Thus, every
line was represented by exactly 17 digits.

McDonough's study showed that word types appearing with relatively
high frequency were evenly distributed throughout the *Iliad*. A count of
a given item in one section of the *Iliad* could be used to predict the count
of that item in another section. For some students, these results might
seem to authorize the inference that the *Iliad* was written by one hand.
Perhaps more important, so far as stylistic analysis in general is concerned,
is the fact that McDonough's study enables one to make precise statements about a stylistic characteristic in the *Iliad*. It is no longer necessary,
in this case, to fall back on such phrases as "rather more frequently" or
"somewhat less often." As similar studies are conducted, other general
statements, always based upon rigorously complete factual information,
can be made about the structural metrics of a particular culture or a particular genre, such as the classical epic. For the first time, literary critics
will have at least one precise measure in their critical repertoire.

Dearing's work on Dryden [12] was concerned not with metrical
structure but with orthographic structure. Are there certain patterns of
spelling, used by Dryden, which discriminate his work from that of other
authors? Dearing's study suggests that there are and that they can be used
to resolve the problem of attribution in some cases.

Another effort to analyze the style of a particular author was undertaken by Milic [35] with reference to the works of Johnathan Swift.
Milic took a 3,500-word sample from Swift and each of four control
authors (Addison, Johnson, Gibbon, and Macaulay), analyzed the samples into word-class equivalents, and then examined the resulting frequency distributions. Milic designated 24 word classes, based on Fries'
[18] classification into parts of speech and function words. The class
designators were entered on punch cards and tabulated by an IBM 1620
computer. The results are data about the arrangement and frequency of
overlapping three-word patterns in each sample and author.

Milic reports that

> ...the statistical study shows that Swift's style is quantitatively con-
> sistent and different from the control authors, in certain specific features,
> especially verbals, introductory connectives and three-word patterns.

> These three criteria permit the identification of a pamphlet previously
> considered uncertain—*A Letter of Advice to a Young Poet*—as the definite
> work of Swift, subject only to the reservation that another hand may have
> tampered with the first few pages. [34]

Milic's work —as was the case with that of McDonough and Dearing—
used the computer for statistical manipulations and summaries; judgments as to metrical structure or word classes were made and indicated
manually.

Wachal is engaged in trying to devise a generalized solution to the problem of "text paternity," by working out a vector of indices for textual
discrimination. He also hopes to have discriminating results as to the indices themselves. [55]

6.3.2   An Analysis of Stylistic Influence. The detection of the influence of one author upon another sometimes amounts to little more than
noticing that the "influenced" author specifically names the "influencing"
author. More commonly, however, perception of influence depends upon
some stylistic similarity between two or more authors. Raben [43] has
used the computer to detect an influence of Milton upon Shelley by comparing the vocabulary used in *Paradise Lost* with that of *Prometheus
Unbound*. Raben was led to this investigation by the discovery that
Shelley's translation of Dante's *Inferno* included borrowings from Milton's phraseology. According to Raben, "Shelley believed that every
age had its master poet, and so he used the phrases of one master poet
to translate another. It seemed natural to him." This discovery suggested
to Raben that perhaps Shelley had used Milton's diction in his own poetry.
Focusing his search upon *Paradise Lost* and *Prometheus Unbound*, Raben found sections of the two poems that had a high incidence of either
identical words or words using the same root. For instance, when Shelley
and Milton both described the bower in Eden, seventeen words appeared
in common. Words used as evidence of influence did not, of course, include function words such as "of," "and," and "the."

The research algorithm and its implementation that made Raben's
conclusions possible were developed by Goodman and Villani [19]. In
order to demonstrate the difficulty in manually finding a common vocabulary, Goodman cites the two sentences from *Prometheus Unbound* and
Paradise Lost, which appear in Figure 6.6. A reading of these two sentences suggests a similarity of tone. It is, in fact, the case that the sentences
have a number of words in common—but locating the common vocabulary
even in these relatively short sentences is a tortuous business.* A manual

---

*Words in common (based on root forms) are "bear," "live," "behold," "reproach,"
"earth," "build," "secure," "wonder," "wrath," "forth," and "fear."

Prometheus Unbound   (Act III, Scene I)

All else had been subdued to me; alone
The soul of man, like unextinguished fire,   5
Yet burns towards heaven with fierce reproach and doubt,
And lamentation, and reluctant prayer,
Hurling up insurrection, which might make
Our antique empire insecure, though built
On eldest faith, and hell's coeval, fear;   10
And though my curses through the pendulous air,
Like snow on herbless peaks, fall flake by flake,
And cling to it; though under my wrath's night
It climbs the crags of life, step after step,
Which wound it, as ice wounds unsandalled feet,   15
It yet remains supreme o'er misery,
Aspiring, unrepressed, yet soon to fall:
Even now have I begotten a strange wonder,
That fatal child, the terror of the earth,
Who waits but till the destined hour arrive,   20
Bearing from Demogorgon's vacant throne
The dreadful might of ever-living limbs
Which clothed that awful spirit unbeheld,
To redescend, and trample out the spark.

Paradise Lost   (Book XI)

The conquered also, and enslaved by war,
Shall, with their freedom lost, all virtue lose
And fear of God: from whom their piety feigned
In sharp contest of battle found no aid   800
Against invaders; therefore, cooled in zeal,
Thenceforth shall practice how to live secure,
Worldly or dissolute, on what their lords
Shall leave them to enjoy; for earth shall bear
More than enough, that temperance may be tried: 805
So all shall turn degenerate, all depraved;
Justice and temperance, truth and faith forgot;
One man except, the only son of light
In a dark age, against example good,
Against allurement, custom, and a world   810
Offended: fearless of reproach and scorn,
Or violence, he of their wicked ways
Shall them admonish; and before them set
The paths of righteousness, how much more safe
And full of peace; denouncing wrath to come   815
On their impenitence; and shall return
Of them derided, but of God observed
The one just man alive; by his command
Shall build a wonderous ark, as thou beheldst,
To save himself, and household, from amidst   820
A world devote to universal wrack.

Figure 6.6 Excerpts from *Prometheus Unbound* and *Paradise Lost*

search of all of *Prometheus Unbound* and *Paradise Lost*, both very long poems, would be practically impossible.

Goodman's computer search procedure consisted of a number of steps. First, concordances using the sentence as the basic structural unit were prepared for both poems using Smith's program [51]. Next, the computer examined these indices or concordances for words occurring in both texts. These words were recorded with, in numerical order, the sentence numbers in which they appeared in *Prometheus Unbound* followed by the sentence numbers for *Paradise Lost*. This information was then expanded so that there was one listing for each Shelley sentence number containing a particular word along with all sentences by Milton that contained the same word. A second expansion designated all pairs of sentences containing the same word. For example, 584 1702 WRINKLE indicates that "wrinkle" occurs in sentence 584 in *Prometheus Unbound* and sentence 1702 in *Paradise Lost*. Next, the two sentence numbers that constituted a pair were treated as a single combined number (e.g., 5841702) and sorted into numerical order. This numerical sorting brought together all words co-occurring in any pair of sentences from *Prometheus Unbound* and *Paradise Lost*. Following this sorting, sentences sharing only one word were eliminated so that the printout listed only sentences containing multiple occurrences. (The printout lists both the sentence numbers and the words occurring in the sentences.) Combinations having the largest number of words in common were listed first. "In this manner," Goodman concludes, "a few hours of machine time disclosed a sentence in *Prometheus Unbound* that contained 17 words in common with a single sentence in *Paradise Lost*. This accomplishment would probably have taken a human investigator using conventional methods the better part of a lifetime if it could have been done at all." [19]*

6.3.3 Computer-Based Exploration of Stylistic Characteristics. The computer-based research on stylistic analysis described thus far in this chapter has been concerned with the style of a particular author or authors. In "A Preface to Computational Stylistics" [46], Sally and Walter Sedelow suggest the importance of using the computer for an attack upon the nature of stylistic characteristics, without reference to a specific author. With style defined as "patterns formed in the linguistic encoding of information," they argue that further work is needed on the nature of, for instance, rhythm, before the rhythm in the works of a particular author can be operationally described.

*In 1959, a highly prescient commentary on some currently emergent general issues associated with influence studies was included in a discussion by Walker of Joseph Priestley's phlogiston writings [56].

6.3.3.1 *Definition and Discovery of Aspects of Style.* In an effort
to find ways of examining language, which might make characteristics
of style more obvious, Sally Sedelow and Daniel Bobrow devised a program (MAPTEXT) that would "map" certain textual elements, such as function words and content words, onto a nonverbal representation [47].
For example, function words might be represented by an asterisk and
content words by a zero. Thus removed from semantic context, distributional patterns of occurrence should be more obvious. In addition, MAP-
TEXT can be used to explore patterns of punctuation, the use of specific
words, or groups of specific words, or any linguistic feature or complex
patterns of features—whether deterministically or probabilistically char-
acterizable. After a promising pattern has been revealed, the computer
can be used to perform statistical analyses; the analyses can be performed
either upon the abstracted form of the pattern or upon the input text
itself. The Sedelows point out that

> "MAPTEXT will have provided a sequentially multi-dimensional view
> of the text; the specified representations may suggest others not specified
> but nonetheless apparent in the graphic form. Statistical summations
> alone, while evidently useful, are not so likely to add new dimensions to
> the researcher's knowledge nor, therefore, to suggest new directions for
> research as are a combination of the statistical summations *and* the
> MAPTEXT representations." [48]

6.3.3.2 *The Perception of Theme.* When we see that theme, narra-
tive surface, and other such features of a text are themselves among an
author's stylistic choices, then it is apparent that computer-based programs of content analysis are coping with some of the properties of style.
Two such programs are Sedelow and Ruggles' VIA program [48] and
Stone's General Inquirer program [52].

The VIA (verbally-indexed associations) program is based on the assumption that the perception of theme is dependent, in part, upon the
perception of semantic similarity among words in a given text and, in part,
upon the perception of words that are contiguous with the semantically
related words. According to this perhaps minimal definition, theme is a
function of semantic content and textual context. Because conventional
thesauri are organized on the basis of putative semantic relationships, the
thesaurus form is used as the basis for the VIA program.

The relationship for theme analysis and style can be illustrated in the
operation of the current VIA program. First, the frequency of all the content words in the input text is determined. The text is "canonized"—that
is, words are grouped on the basis of a common root—and the frequency
count is based on the root. For instance, if there were three occurrences

of "madly," two of "madness," and one of "mad," the count would be six. A list of all canonized words occurring more than any specified number of times, together with an index indicating where in the text each word appears, is then printed out. After this list has been made available, conventional thesauri, Brown's *Composition of Scientific Words* [7], dictionaries of synonyms, and the immediate textual context of the high-frequency words are explored for conceptually associated words. This presently manual exploration is scheduled for computer implementation.

The computer searches the text for each of the suggested associated words and enters any that it finds on a list headed by the high-frequency word with which it is conceptually associated. Thus, when working with a scene from *Hamlet,* the words "ill" and "disease" appeared on a list headed by "mad." The lists of high-frequency words and their associates, together with all suggested associates, constitute the beginnings of the computer's own special thesaurus, and these lists are saved in a form to which the computer has access. Following examination of the next section of text for high-frequency words, the computer searches its own special thesaurus for associated words. At present, the computer procedure determines whether the high-frequency word appears anywhere in its thesaurus—in which case a search is made for all other words appearing in the same thesaurus entry. If one or more of the words in the entry heads yet another entry, a textual search is made for words appearing under that entry. For example, it the word "disease" is a high-frequency word, the input text is searched for occurrences of the word "mad." If the word "insane" appeared in the "mad" entry and also headed another entry, the text would be searched for occurrences of "insane" as well as for occurrences of all words in the "insane" entry. As the computer thesaurus grows, the need for manual searching for possible associated words is reduced. This "learning" characteristic of the program is one of its great strengths and differentiates it from other programmed techniques for thematic analysis.

The basic VIA program, as described above, is currently being altered to enable the computer to save all suggested associated words, although only those appearing in the text would be a part of the computer thesaurus. Optimum depths for carrying out searches within the thesaurus still need to be determined for particular applications.

The VIA program results in a thematic or conceptual outline—in the form of a crossreferenced thesaurus—of a particular literary work, or group of works by the same author, or works by a series of authors. Features of this program that are particularly important and distinctive are (1) the self-adapting characteristic, and (2) the construction of the thesaurus on the basis of words that appear in the work under examination. There is no pre-prepared word list, as is the case with thesauri conventionally used for retrieving documents or information.

Stone has developed a program for content analysis known as the General Inquirer [52]. The General Inquirer procedure consists of four parts: dictionary procedures, retrieval operations, data preparation, and special procedures for syntax identification.

A dictionary with words grouped into themes or concepts is prepared manually. The psychosociological dictionary currently contains 3,450 entries—including the 3,000 most frequently used words in the Thorndike-Lorge list plus other words of special interest to the behavioral scientist. Because suffixes are eliminated in the dictionary entry, more than 10,000 words can be identified by reference to this dictionary. The dictionary represents a theory, or point of view, to be used as a basis for analyzing text material. The dictionary for a research project on psychoanalytic theory can be expected to differ considerably from a dictionary used by a political scientist interested in studying political trends. The themes or concepts (for example, kinship relationships or emotions) are further subdivided into first order and second order tags.

After the words in an input text have been associated with a particular tag or group of tags, the number of times each tag concept has been used in a given section of text is tallied. The investigator can also request the program to retrieve all sentences containing specified words, or all sentences that deal with a tag concept. Sometimes, a retrieved sentence lacks clarity because it depends for its subject upon a pronoun that has no immediate referent. When preparing data for input to the General Inquirer, such pronouns can be identified by enclosing the referent in parentheses, so that a sentence might read, "It (cake) was good," or "He (John) went home." Similar editing can be used to provide the computer explicitly with information assumed to be known implicitly by the reader (e.g., "Europe in 1942 was an unpleasant and unhappy place" implies war, destruction, food shortages, fear, etc.).

The raw text can be edited to reduce content ambiguity and to identify syntactic relationships among the words. The sentences "Man bites dog" and "Dog bites man" require syntactic codes to enable the computer to distinguish between their meanings. The General Inquirer system makes nine syntactic codes available to the user.

The General Inquirer has been a popular research program and has been used to distinguish between real and simulated suicide notes, to analyze psychotherapy interviews [16], and to compare themes in folktales [11].

6.4 RESEARCH ANCILLARY TO STYLISTIC ANALYSIS

There are several research projects which do not deal directly with automated stylistic analysis but do contribute to such exploration. Research on the automation of bibliographies and on the compilation of word lists for use in computer-based research are examples of such projects.

Bibliographies contribute to work on stylistic analysis by making available to the investigator exhaustive inventories of the work of an author or genre that is to be analyzed. Word lists, especially those stored on punch cards, magnetic tape, or discs, provide a standard of word usage against which the vocabulary of a given author or genre can be compared.

6.4.1 Bibliography Construction. Research on ways to use the computer to compile bibliographies is underway at both the University of Colorado and New York University. The Colorado project, under the direction of Sawin and Nilon [44], is focused upon bibliographies in English studies, and the New York University project, recently described by Pollin [42] and Heller [21], has been concentrated initially upon compiling a bibliography based upon the *Revista de Filologia Espanola*.

The goal of Sawin's work is to provide an integrated bibliography, which he defines as a "single bibliographical compilation containing every item which has ever been listed in any bibliography prepared in the subject-field, with provision for continuous addition of new items." This bibliography is to be "indexed in depth and stored in such a way that retrieval of any discrete segment of the total record can be accomplished quickly and accurately on demand of the individual teacher or researcher." [44]

The New York University bibliographical aid is described as an "index or guide to the forty-three volumes of the *Revista*." Pollin says that "the first section of the index is an alphabetical listing of the 313 authors of the 920 scholarly articles which appear in the *Revista*. The articles by each author appear chronologically, in the order of their appearance in the *Revista*. The exact form of each author's signature is also reproduced." [42] The second section of the bibliography is devoted to book reviews and is organized in the same manner as the first section. The third part of the bibliography is an alphabetical listing of all authors whose works have been the subject of *Revista* book reviews, as well as of all anonymous works which have been reviewed. The last two sections of the bibliography are subject indices in which the articles and book reviews, respectively, have been categorized under headings (history, literature, musicology, and linguistics) likely to be consulted by students and scholars working in Hispanic letters, history and philology. Each subject index consists of some 250 categories arranged in patterns considered logical and, whenever possible, chronological.

6.4.2 A Standard Corpus of American English.   Francis [17] has directed a computer-aided research program to compile a standard corpus of present-day American English. The 1,014,294-word corpus stored on magnetic tape is based upon samples of text from the categories "Informative Prose" and "Imaginative Prose" as shown in Figure 6.7. The figures within parentheses indicate the number of 2,000-word samples examined under each category.

6.5 COMPUTER-DERIVED APPLICATIONS OF STYLISTIC ANALYSIS

The research described thus far in this chapter involves using a computer to assist with, or take over, tasks previously done manually. Stylistic analysis is also of great importance for tasks that have been created by the development of computers. In fact, work on these computer-derived tasks has helped lead to a realization both (1) of the necessity of being able to specify characteristics of style and (2) of the difficulty with which such specification is achieved, using the tools that literary and linguistic critical traditions have provided. Research in the fields of automatic abstracting and machine translation are cases in point.

6.5.1 Stylistic Distinctions Among Types of Abstracts.   With reference to automatic abstracting, Borko and Chatman [6] have advanced the view that it seems possible to make some stylistic distinctions between informative and indicative abstracts. They discussed such distinctions in terms of form, noting differences in voice, tense, and focus of the abstract (the informative abstract "discusses the research" and the indicative abstract "discusses the article which describes the research"). Borko and Sedelow have suggested that an effort be made to specify stylistic discriminators so that stylistic algorithms for the automatic production of different types of abstracts (e.g. psychological abstracts, abstracts of English studies, etc.) may be developed. Wolf is using a computer to search for variations in the use of function words among types of abstracts [59].

In early studies focused upon indexing procedures, Baxendale experimented with analytical techniques that are also applicable to automatic abstracting [3, 4]. In an effort to determine whether differences in the pattern of writing distinguished articles in the field of engineering from

```
  I. Informative Prose                                    (374)
       A. Press: Reportage                                 (44)
            Political
            Sports
            Spot News
            Society
            Cultural
            Financial
       B. Press: Editorial                                 (27)
            Institutional Editorials
            Individual Columns
            Letters to the Editor
       C. Press: Reviews                                   (17)
       D. Religion                                         (17)
       E. Skills and Hobbies                               (36)
       F. Popular Lore                                     (48)
       G. Belles Lettres, Biography, Memoirs, etc.         (75)
       H. Miscellaneous                                    (30)
            Government Documents
            Law Cases
            Industry Reports
            Foundation Reports
            House Organs
       J. Learned                                          (80)
            Physical Sciences
            Mathematics
            Life Sciences
            Medicine
            Political Sciences and Law
            Behavioral Sciences
            Philosophy
            Literary Criticism and Scholarship
            Art and Music Criticism and Scholarship
            Technology and Engineering
 II. Imaginative Prose                                    (126)
       K. General Fiction                                  (29)
       L. Mystery and Detective Fiction                    (24)
       M. Science Fiction                                   (6)
       N. Adventure and Western Fiction                    (29)
       P. Romantic and Love Story Fiction                  (29)
       R. Humor                                             (9)
```

Figure 6.7   Standard corpus of present-day American English

those in the social sciences, Miss Baxendale examined relative positions
of grammatical elements and, on the basis of this examination, derived
modal sentences. To distinguish major themes, which might serve as keys

to the articles' contents, she compared the relative retrieval performance of, respectively, the selection of words ocurring in topic sentences, the selection of single words on the basis of frequency, and the selection of words occurring in prepositional phrases. Her research showed remarkable similarity of results among these three procedures.

6.5.2 Stylistic Variables in Machine Translation. Research on style by scholars working on the problem of machine translation has been focused upon syntax and their work is discussed in Chapter 9. Sedelow and Sedelow [48] have stressed the necessity of dealing with other stylistic variables in order to achieve adequately readable translations. The MAPTEXT research described earlier in this chapter is, in part, directed toward this goal.

6.6 COMPUTATIONAL STYLISTICS: SOME PROSPECTIVE IMPACTS

The late Wilbur Marshall Urban of Yale once said that language was the last and deepest problem of the philosophic mind. At present, it is certainly a focus of attention for many scientists and scholars. What may we expect from replicable stylistic investigations during the next several decades?

6.6.1 Literary Scholarship. Automated stylistic investigations of literature will resolve many problems of authorship and make possible precise statements about a particular work or the works of a particular author. Careful investigation of works representing a genre should enable scholars to eliminate the vagaries too often associated with the definition of tragedy, or epic, or romance. So, too, attempts to use the computer to analyze such stylistic attributes as rhythm will force a clarity of definition —or, at least, a recognition of lack of clarity. At the very least, the computer will free scholars from drudgery and allow more time for creative thought. The scholar no longer needs to count manually the occurrences of the dactyl, nor need he ask himself, "Did I count accurately?" Imaginatively used, the computer will free scholars from the morass of ill-defined critical jargon that has inhibited communication and fostered petty controversies. A scholar will not need to ask so often of another author's work, what, textually and exactly, he is talking about. Instead, he can devote himself to truly humanistic issues.

6.6.2 Social Sciences. World-wide, during the past several decades, political participation has accelerated. In a project led by Lasswell, [24, 25], Lerner, de sola Pool and others, much research has been done on the recruitment of political elites and the linguistic behavior of different styles of political leadership. They are, in effect, studying certain phases of *persuasion*, one of the central events of high-participation societies and a generator of words and patterns of words to which stylistic analysis may be applied. The transformation of effective civic utterances into a set of explicit and reliable verbal procedures would be a significant social event.

To develop rhetorical algorithms, a rigorous set of procedures for characterizing style appears essential. The analytical net must be small-meshed enough to catch an abundance of verbal detail and to characterize it with sufficient precision to allow its computer-programmed reproduction. Without such a 'net,' we cannot discover, even on a probabilistic basis, what patterns of address do work and under what circumstances. Even these circumstances are significantly verbal: the effects of a style seem to be, in part, a matter of the prior verbal experiences of the auditors. To cope with the masses of presumably relevant detail, computer-based analysis, storage, and retrieval are necessary.

Despite disagreement about the extent and distribution of psychic strains and maladies, the combination of (1) accelerated cultural change and improved diagnostic technique, (2) higher expectations for therapy, (3) more intra-familial independence, and (4) more intra-social dependence may create an over-demand for the supply of available traditional clinical services. Programs for screening patient-respondent statements in accord with criteria of syndrome revelation may become a matter of course. Insofar as decision rules can be formulated and put to work on protocols so that the psychologist and psychiatrist do not themselves have to process a great deal of verbiage to detect likely diagnostic leads, this area of health practice will profit from computer assistance.

Computer programs could be designed to aid sociolinguistic research such as that foreshadowed in the paper read by Raven McDavid, of the University of Chicago, at the Sociolinguistic Conference held in the spring of 1964 at the University of California at Los Angeles. McDavid urges the same close attention to the conditions for intra-lingual usage change that, for many years, workers at the University of Michigan have been bringing to bear on second-language learning. The social implications and motivations for the eradication of disvalued dialectal differentiae and for the acquisition of prized usage characteristics may serve to guarantee wide interest in this work. If it is to be practically useful to migrants from one class or dialect group to another, then the economies provided by computer-assisted analysis of individual verbal habits and prescription for changes doubtless will be necessary. It may be that a heightened demand for learning additional languages by 'jet-set' businessmen, government men, and academic men, will also create demand for the custom-tailoring of language training to prior individual language experience that computer-based stylistic analysis may be able to provide.

One of the most promising implications of stylistic analysis by computer is its utility for psychological anthropology, a specialty closely identified, in the United States, with the work of Hsu [22]. Just as patient protocols can be subjected to computer analysis, so, too, can the open-ended questions of surveys and in-depth interviews. One expects to see the use of these techniques by psychological anthropologists increase as they seek to determine, partly through verbal style, modal personality attributes in national populations.

Work on folklore thematic analysis has already been summarized, and a multidimensional exploration of folklore style should add to the richness and value of such studies.

6.6.3 Scientific Innovation. An exposition of the stylistic dimensionalities of creative acts in science also constitutes a social lien upon stylistic analysis. The discrepancies between human aspirations or demands and their current fulfillment may soon appear to be the great driving engine of science. If science is more and more often harnessed to pulling out of ignorance the prerequisites for a technology of world abundance, then an imperative demand for a science of science presumably will become acute. It is the creative functioning of scientists which will most demand investigation. Are there, for instance, certain recurrent features in the verbal conduct of scientists when they pursue significant new ideas? Are there alterations in their more abstract characterizations of the phenomena they may be studying—as has been found to be the case in a simple way by small-group researchers studying the preludes to consensus? If there are, content analysis by itself will be inadequate, however necessary. We may suppose that 'scientific style' may come to be as highly regarded and intensively studied as literary style and that the scientists themselves will contribute to the imposition of norms of accomplishment for the requisite stylistic analysis. Such norms will include discourse generation by computer according to stylistic specifications (synthesis), as evidence that the analysis is as accurate and complete as it may claim to be.

6.6.4 Information Retrieval. Time sharing, remote accessibility, and other various new data processing capabilities are as much responsible as the general increase in knowledge for the developing expectation that, at least as to location and retrieval, knowledge will come to be centralized and integrated. Well before this century is over, we may ask one or more giant computer systems for answers to specific questions, rather than asking libraries for books or articles that seem appropriate to a general theme. When we have our words and equations about the world neatly, easily, and unifiedly stored and accessible, it seems likely that one part of the capability required will be access to statements and sets of statements by their stylistic features. If so, we may say that a necessary precondition for a comprehensive data base will include computational stylistic procedures of the sort adumbrated in this chapter.

6.6.5 Automated Language Production.   Cartoons and other popular comments on the 'computer revolution' seem, generally, to represent the machines as laconic: enormous machines fed mountains of data to produce mousey, or at least midget, outputs. This perception may be deflecting attention from some of the newer phases of computer usage. We may need the image of a large reservoir breaking, in order to imagine the out-flow of words that will come forth when computers are initiating and producing "natural" language, either as responses to specific questions or as (a) periodic reporting functions of system programs.

To require computer-generated language to conform in detail to all, or most, of a human's linguistic conventions is analogous to requiring early printers to make their output resemble manuscript writing. Initially, just such 'magic realism' may be demanded, to demonstrate the machine's true virtuosity and intelligence as well as fully to achieve communication. Later, we may learn to accept as satisfactory very different output language from the computer. But, at least for an interval, a computer talking to a noncomputer specialist must do so very much in accordance with the latter's everyday language expectations. And here we have another area in which stylistic analysis will be required to do much. In order to meet a Turing-like test of stylistic adequacy, it seems that—barring the discovery of an unexplicated but workable and relevant mode of partial self-organization in verbal analysis—we will need to find one or more complete methods of characterizing the stylistic features of language.

Literature … persuasion … individual and cultural linguistic analysis and change … scientific creativity … unified storage of knowledge … language-by-computer—to cope with the verbal behavior components in each of these areas of current interest, we may expect that much will be asked of computational stylistics research.

REFERENCES

1. Adair, D., The authorship of the disputed *Federalist Papers*, Part I, *The William and Mary Quarterly*, v. 1, no. 2, April 1944, pp. 97-122.

2. Adair, D., The authorship of the disputed *Federalist Papers*, Part II, *The William and Mary Quarterly*, v. 1, no. 3, July 1944, pp. 235-64.

3. Baxendale, P., A statistical analysis of the pattern structure of the English sentence, IBM Report *RR-Mr-27*, September 1958.

4. Baxendale, P., Machine-made index for technical literature—an experiment, *IBM J. of Research and Development*, v. 2, no. 4, October 1958, pp. 354-61.

5. Bessinger, J. B., Computer techniques for an Old English concordance, *Amer. Doc.*, v. 12, no. 3, July 1961, pp. 227-29.

6. Borko, H. and S. Chatman, Criteria for acceptable abstracts: a survey of abstractors' instructions, *Amer. Doc.*, v. 14, no. 2, 1963, pp. 149-60.

7. Brown, R. W., *Composition of Scientific Words*. Baltimore: 1956.

8. Busa, R., S. J., Human errors in preparing the input for computers, Paper presented at NATO Symposium on Communication Processes, Washington: 17 August 1963.

9. Busa, R., S. J., An inventory of fifteen million words, *Proc.*, IBM Literary Data Processing Conference, 9-11 September 1964, pp. 64-84.

10. Clayton, T., The preparation of literary text for multiple automated studies: comprehensive identification and the provision of discriminants, *Proc.*, IBM Literary Data Processing Conference, 9-11 September 1964, pp. 171-199.

11. Colby, B. N., G. A. Collier, and S. K. Postal, Comparison of themes in folktales by the General Inquirer system, *J. of Amer. Folklore*, October-December 1963, v. 76, no. 302, pp. 318-23.

12. Dearing, V. A., The use of a computer in analyzing Dryden's spelling, *Proc.*, IBM Literary Data Processing Conference, 9-11 September 1964, pp. 200-210.

13. Ellegard, A., *Who was Junius?* Stockholm: Almquist and Wiksell, 1962.

14. Ellegard, A., *A Statistical Method for Determining Authorship: the Junius Letters, 1769-1772*. Goteborg Acta Universitatis Gothoburgensis, 1962.

15. Fogel, E. G., Electronic computers and Elizabethan texts, *Studies in Bibliography*, F. Bowers (ed.) Bibliographical Society of the U. of Virginia, 1962, pp. 15-31.

16. Ford, J. D., Jr., Automatic detection of psychological dimensions in psychotherapy transcripts by means of content words, *SP-1220*. Santa Monica, Calif.: System Development Corp., 12 July 1963.

17. Francis, W. N., A standard corpus of edited present-day American English for computer use, *Proc.*, IBM Literary Data Processing Conference, 9-11 September 1964, pp. 79-89.

18. Fries, C. C., *The Structure of English: an Introduction to the Construction of English Sentences*. New York: 1952.

19. Goodman, S., and R. Villani, An algorithm for locating multiple word co-occurrences in two sets of texts, *Proc.*, IBM Literary Data Processing Conference, 9-11 September 1964, pp. 275-292.

20. Guiraud, P., *Les Caracteres statistiques du Vocabulaire*. Paris: Presses Universitaires de France, 1954.

21. Heller, J., A proposed system for the collection, correction and rearrangement of large masses of data, *Proc.*, IBM Literary Data Processing Conference, 9-11 September 1964, pp. 98-112.

22. Hsu, F. L. K., *Psychological Anthropology: Approaches to Culture and Personality.* Homewood, Ill.: Dorsey Press, 1961.

23. Kay, M., *Manual For A Concordance Routine.* RAND Corporation Summer Seminar on Computational Linguistics, July 1963 (in preparation).

24. Lasswell, H. D., N. Leites, *et al., The Language of Politics: Studies in Quantitative Semantics.* New York: G. W. Stewart, 1949.

25. Lasswell, H. D., R. D. Casey, and B. L. Smith, *Propaganda and Promotional Activities, An Annotated Bibliography.* Minneapolis, Minn.: U. of Minnesota Press, 1935.

26. Luhn, H. P., Keyword-in-Context index for technical literature (KWIC index), IBM ASDD Report, *RC-127,* 31 August 1959.

27. McDonough, J. T., Jr., Homer, humanities, and IBM, *Proc.,* IBM Literary Data Processing Conference, 9-11 September 1964, pp. 25-36.

28. Miles, J., *The Primary Language of Poetry in the 1640's.* Berkeley and Los Angeles: U. of California Press, 1948.

29. Miles, J., *The Primary Language of Poetry in the 1940's.* Berkeley and Los Angeles: U. of California Press, 1951.

30. Miles, J., *The Primary Language of Poetry in the 1740's and 1840's.* Berkeley and Los Angeles: U. of California Press, 1950.

31. Miles, J., *Wordsworth and the Vocabulary of Emotion.* Berkeley and Los Angeles: U. of California Press, 1942.

32. Miles, J., *Pathetic Fallacy in the Nineteenth Century.* Berkeley and Los Angeles: U. of California Press, 1943.

33. Miles, J., *Major Adjectives in English Poetry from Wyatt to Auden.* Berkeley and Los Angeles: U. of California Press, 1946.

34. Miles, J., *Renaissance, Eighteenth-Century, and Modern Language in English Poetry: A Tabular View.* Berkeley and Los Angeles: U. of California Press, 1960.

35. Milic, L. T., *A Quantitative Approach to the Style of Jonathan Swift.* Ann Arbor, Mich.: University Microfilm, 1964.

36. Morton, A. Q., A computer challenges the church, *The Observer,* 3 November 1963, p. 21.

37. Mosteller, F. and D. L. Wallace, Inference in an authorship problem, *J. of the Amer. Statistical Assoc.,* LVIII (1963), pp. 275-309.

38. Painter, V. A., Computer preparation of a poetry concordance, *Comm. of the ACM,* v. 3, no. 2, February 1960, pp. 91-95.

39. Parrish, S. M., Problems in the making of computer concordances, *Studies in Bibliography,* F. Bowers (ed.) Bibliographical Society of the U. of Virginia, 1962, pp. 1-14.

40. Parrish, S. M., ed., *Concordance to the Poems of Matthew Arnold.* Ithaca, N.Y.: Cornell U., 1959.

41. Parrish, S. M., and V. A. Painter (eds.), *Concordance to the Poems of W. B. Yeats.* Ithaca, N.Y.: Cornell U., 1963.

42. Pollin, A. M., The construction of a bibliographic aid using electronic techniques and devices, *Proc.,* IBM Literary Data Processing Conference, 9-11 September 1964, pp. 90-97.

43. Raben, J., A computer-aided investigation of literary influence: Milton to Shelley, *Proc.,* IBM Literary Data Processing Conference, 9-11 September 1964, pp. 230-274.

44. Sawin, L., and C. Nilon, The integrated bibliography plan and its history. Memorandum, November 1963.

45. Sebeok, T. (ed), *Style in Language.* New York: M.I.T. Technology Press and John Wiley and Sons, 1960.

46. Sedelow, S. Y. and W. A. Sedelow, Jr., A preface to computational stylistics, *SP-1534.* Santa Monica, Calif.: System Development Corp., 17 February 1964.

47. Sedelow, S. Y. and D. G. Bobrow, A LISP program for use in stylistic analysis, *TM-1753.* Santa Monica, Calif.: System Development Corp., 17 February 1964.

48. Sedelow, S. Y., W. A. Sedelow, Jr., and T. L. Ruggles, Some parameters for computational stylistics: computer aids to the use of traditional categories in stylistic analysis, *Proc.,* IBM Literary Data Processing Conference, 9-11 September 1964, pp. 211-229.

49. Siberz, J. K., S. J., and J. G. Devine, S. J., Computer-made concordances to the works of the early Christian writers, *Proc.,* IBM Literary Data Processing Conference, 9-11 September 1964, pp. 128-141.

50. Simmons, R. F. and K. L. McConlogue, Maximum-depth indexing for computer retrieval of English language data, *Amer. Doc.,* v. 14, no. 1, January 1963, pp. 68-73.

51. Smith, P. H., Jr., A computer program to generate a text concordance, *Proc.,* IBM Literary Data Processing Conference, 9-11 September 1964, pp. 113-127.

52. Stone, P. J., R. F. Bales, J. Z. Namenwirth, and D. M. Ogilvie, The General Inquirer: a computer system for content analysis and retrieval based on the sentence as a unit of information, *Behavioral Science,* v. 7, 1962, pp. 484-98.

53. Tasman, P., Literary data processing, *IBM J. of Research and Development,* July 1957, pp. 249-56.

54. Tasman, P., *Indexing the Dead Sea Scrolls by Electronic Literary Data Processing Methods.* IBM Brochure, November 1958.

55. Wachal, R. S., Linguistic tests of authorship, Research proposal, U. of Wisconsin, 2 December 1963.

56. Walker, R. A., Jr., *Joseph Priestley and the Phlogiston Controversy.* Honors thesis. Amherst, Mass.: Amherst College Library, 1959.

57. Wells, J. C., A concordance and dictionary to the Old High German glosses, *Proc.,* IBM Literary Data Processing Conference, 9-11 September 1964, pp. 148-159.

58. Whaler, J., *Counterpoint and Symbol and Inquiry into the Rhythm of Milton's Epic Style.* Copenhagen: Rosenkilde, 1956.

59. Wolf, M. H., The IBM 1620 as a tool for investigating principles of auto-abstracting, *Proc.,* IBM Literary Data Processing Conference, 9-11 September 1964, pp. 293-305.

60. Yule, G. U., On sentence-length as a statistical characteristic of style in prose, *Biometrika,* v. 30, 1939, pp. 363-90.

61. Yule, G. U., *The Statistical Study of Literary Vocabulary.* Cambridge, England: University Press, 1944.

Part III

SYNTACTIC ANALYSIS

7

Syntactic Theories in Computer Implementations

D. G. Bobrow

A statement in a spoken language may be regarded as a one-dimensional string of symbols, its dimensionality being limited by the need for presenting the symbols in a single time sequence. Evidence indicates, however, that most information is not stored in the mind in one-dimensional arrays. A speaker apparently transforms stored information into a linear output string, and a listener decodes this linear string. For communication to take place, then, two conditions must prevail: the information maps of both the listener and the speaker must be similar for a given universe of discourse, and—more important—the listener's decoding process must be an approximate inverse of the speaker's encoding process. Language education is, in large part, an attempt to standardize the coding process.

A certain preferred class of utterances is defined by an educated native speaker to be "sentences" of the language, and members of this class are the principal vehicles of written communication in the language. (Communication via sentences occurs less frequently in speech.)

Two kinds of information processing are apparently involved in constructing and deciphering sentences. *Semantic* processing deals with the meanings of individual symbols (words); *syntactic* processing deals with words as members of word classes and with the structural relationships between classes. It is difficult to draw a sharp line between the two, especially when definition of membership in a class of words is dependent upon the meaning of a word. Katz and Fodor [33] discuss the distinction and outline the structure of a semantic theory.

In this chapter we are concerned mainly with syntactic processing. In Section 7.1 we discuss the problems of syntactic classification of words. Section 7.2 surveys theories of grammar that have served as a basis for syntactic processing by computer. Many different methods have been proposed for syntactic processing of English sentences, and a number of these methods have been implemented on digital computers. All such processes associate additional structures with the sentences of a language. Some programs demonstrate the generation of grammatical sentences from a set of syntactic rules for English. Other syntactic processors are used as preliminary processors for translation of English sentences to other representations of the same information (e.g., other natural languages, structures within the computer used for information retrieval, etc.). A third set of programs is used for studying English grammar and finding allowable parsings for a sentence on the basis of given rules. The form of the rules for each grammar and a description of the syntactic structure associated with a sentence by each processor are given. We review the goals and present † success of computer programs that have been written. Syntactic analysis programs written only for application to languages other than English are not described, nor are theories of grammar unique to such programs.

7.1   DETERMINATION OF WORD CLASSES

Conventional school grammars usually divide English words into eight classes, or "parts of speech"—noun, pronoun, adjective, verb, adverb, preposition, conjunction, interjection—which are supposed to be the "natural" divisions of words into classes. Sentences are parsed, i.e., associated with a syntactic structure, in terms of these classes. Difficulty arises, however, when one tries to determine which words are in what class. For example, * a noun is usually defined as "the name of a person, place, or thing." "Blue" and "red" are the names of colors, but in expressions such as "the blue tie" or "the red dress" we do not call "blue" and "red" nouns, but adjectives, because an adjective is a "word that modifies a noun or pronoun." Much of the difficulty here is that these two definitions are not parallel— the first tries to classify a word in terms of its lexical meaning, the second in terms of its function in the sentence.

Modern linguistic practice avoids this difficulty by placing two words in the same word class if they appear in the same environments. Thus word classes are co-occurrence equivalence classes. An example of this type of definition of word classes is given in Fries [17]. He assumes that

> all words that could occupy the same 'set of positions' in the patterns
> of English single free utterances must belong to the same part of speech
> ... (we) make certain whether, with each substitution (into the sample

*These examples are taken from Fries [17].

†See postscript, p. 251.

frame), the structural meaning is the same as that of our first example or different from it.

The frames Fries uses are the sentences:

    A. The concert was good (always).
    B. The clerk remembered the tax (suddenly).
    C. The team went there.

Words that can fit into the position occupied by "concert" in frame A, "clerk" and "tax" in frame B, and "team" in frame C are called Class 1 items. Class 2 items can replace "was" in frame A, "remembered" in frame B and "went" in frame C. The words in Class 3 can replace "good" in frame A (with appropriate lexical changes for consistency). However, this does not define Class 3 uniquely, and so frame A was modified, and Class 3 words are defined as only those that can fit into both blanks in:

    The _____concert was_____.
          Class 3   Class 3
Class 4 words must fit into the indicated position in:
        Class 3 Class 1 Class 2 Class 3 Class 4
    (The)_____is/was _____ there
                                    here
                                    sometimes

or in: Class 1   Class 2   Class 1 Class 4
    (The)_____remembered (the)_____ clearly
                                    so
                                    repeatedly

or: Class 1 Class 2 Class 4
    (The)_____ went   clearly
                                  away
                                  safely

Although there is a large measure of overlap between Classes 1, 2, 3, and 4, and the traditionally defined noun, verb, adjective, and adverb, respectively, Fries keeps the names distinct because, for example, Class 1 both excludes certain words traditionally classified as nouns, and includes words not traditionally classified as nouns.

In addition to the four major word classes, Fries defines 15 groups of function words—words that serve as structural markers within a sentence. Although in normal text these function words make up only about seven percent of the number of distinct lexical items, the total number of function words can be approximately one-third of the total number of words. Unlike most words in the four major classes, the lexical meaning of a function word is not clearly separable from its structural meaning in the sentence. For example, it is not difficult to define or associate appropriate nonverbal experiences with such words as "horse," "computer," "run," "fall," "smooth," or "rapidly." For such words as "the," "shall," and "there" (in "there is nothing wrong"), experiential definition is an almost impossible task. These function words must be known as individual items to allow us to determine the structure (and then the meaning) of a sentence.

Having placed large numbers of words in the four major word classes, one notes that words in each class have certain common formal characteristics (with the exception of the function word groups). For example, many of the Class 4 words, such as "rapidly," "slowly," "fairly," "badly," etc., end in the suffix "-ly." We can immediately classify "argled" as derived from the verb "argle" by its suffix. There are many other such formal clues to word classification. Such clues and patterns in English allow parsing a sentence such as, "The oolywop stiply argled a golbish flappent," without definitions of the meanings of any of the content words.

Most English syntactic analysis programs, rather than using the formal characteristics and immediate context of a word to determine its part of speech, use a dictionary look up operation to find the word's possible classifications (e.g., "yellow" can be a noun, verb, or adjective), and to resolve ambiguities during the parsing operation. One program, however, written by Klein and Simmons [38, 39, 41], actually computes syntactic classifications for English words. Using a dictionary of suffixes and prefixes, common exceptions, and function words, the program tries to classify each word in a sentence. Most ambiguities are resolved by consulting the immediate context. For example, if an unknown word might be an adjective or noun, and is the blank in a context "the (adjective)____ (verb)," the program unambiguously classifies this word as a noun. The program successfully labeled more than 90 percent of the words in a large text. Computation of word class is fast compared to dictionary lookup for a large vocabulary, but dictionary lookup must be done for the remaining 10 percent, whose class cannot be computed. Klein and Simmons use these computed classifications as input for a parsing program.

Resnikoff and Dolby [61] have reported briefly on another program that computes a part of speech for "any English word, though not always correctly." They report the accuracy on a trial of 150 sentences as "evidently high." Their criterion of correctness is agreement with *either* the *Oxford Universal* or *Merriam-Webster International* dictionaries. The dictionary size and affix lists used were significantly smaller than those used in the Klein-Simmons program. The authors use neither context to resolve ambiguity, nor the computed parts of speech in further linguistic processing, although their program may eventually be used as a preprocessor for a parsing program written at Lockheed.

Only after classification of word types (by computation or lookup) can further syntactic analysis be done. Using only those word classes defined thus far, we discover the following anomaly. The two sentences:

"The boy which stood there was tall"

and

"The bookcase which stood there was tall"

must both be considered grammatical, since the only change from one to the other is a substitution of one member of an equivalence class for another. However, an educated speaker of English would call only the second grammatically correct. If we wish our grammar to act as a characteristic function for a language (and accurately specify which strings are sentences and which are not), then we must divide "nouns" into at least two subclasses, those associated with "which" and those with "who."

Actually, as pointed out by Francis [16], we can recognize 11 pronoun substitute-groups in present-day English:

Pronouns (singular-plural;
"/" indicates alternatives)   Examples
 1. *he-they*   (man, father, brother, monk, king)
 2. *she-they*   (woman, mother, sister, nun, queen)
 3. *it-they*   (house, tree, poem, rock, complication)
 4. *he/she-they*   (parent, child, friend, cook, tutor)
 5. *he/it-they*   (bull, ram, rooster, buck, steer)
 6. *she/it-they*   (cow, ewe, hen, doe, heifer)
 7. *he/she/it-they*   (baby, dog, cat, one, other)
 8. *it/they-they*   (group, committee, team, jury, crew)
 9. *he/she/they-they*   (somebody, someone, anybody, person)
    (or no plural)
10. *it* (no plural)   (dirt, mathematics, poetry, music, nothing)
11. *they* (no singular)   (pants, scissors, pliers, clothes, people)

These subclasses can be determined in terms of co-occurrence in sentences containing the given pronouns and nouns, but the classification system is now more complex.

Further problems arise when we consider the following:

John admires sincerity.
Sincerity admires John.

The first string is certainly a grammatical sentence, but how should we classify the second string? We can call it a "grammatical but meaningless sentence"—it is well formed according to our rules of grammar, but we can attach no meaning to it. Although such sentences would not be expected to occur in discourse, a system of analysis is complete only if it provides a means for distinguishing between such meaningless strings and grammatical sentences whose meaning can be understood. Whether this analysis should be done syntactically, or in further semantic processing, is moot.

One method proposed for including this discrimination in a syntactic processor involves further subdividing the word classes thus far defined. For example, a noun would be classified as *abstract* or *concrete* ("sincerity" is abstract, "John" is concrete), a countable or a mass noun ("apple" is a countable noun; "water" is not), etc. A verb could be classified by the type of subject it can have (e.g., an abstract noun cannot be a subject for the verb "admire"). Then "sincerity" is an abstract noun, and "admire" requires a concrete subject. Notice, however, that we have started to define noun subclasses by meaning; we thus enter the shadowy land between syntax and semantics. If our purpose is to process the parsed sentences further, this uncertain division is unimportant. But a theory of syntax based on a nonsemantic association of signs with signs must define this line more precisely. Perhaps a distributional basis for defining all necessary subclasses can be found.

7.2   SYNTACTIC STRUCTURES AND COMPUTER IMPLEMENTATIONS

The processes by which a human being generates and decodes verbal communications are not well understood. Somehow a speaker chooses a sequence of symbols from a repertoire to represent an "idea." He uses these symbols, together with structural markers, in a linear string to communicate to another person. A symbol may be a morpheme, a word, or a sequence of words.

In order for a speaker to be understood, he must use his content words in a preferred sequence and separate them by appropriate structural markers. A listener then uses this sequence and the structural markers to perform an inverse of the transformation made by the speaker, and decodes the sentence. Only certain preferred sequences of words can be decoded; one large class of these preferred sequences contains the "sentences" of a language. One of the primary goals of linguistic theory is to provide a grammar—a set of rules—for a language that will distinguish between the sentences and nonsentences of that language, and simultaneously associate a useful structure with these linear strings. This associated structure should show the similarities of sentences that are largely independent of particular lexical items, and should reflect similarities in the processing needed to understand these sentences.

Many different types of grammars have been proposed for English. We distinguish types of grammars by the form of the grammar rules, and by the type of structure the grammar associates with a word string. Following Chomsky [13], we shall call two grammars *weakly equivalent* if they generate the same set of sentences from the same initial vocabulary or, analytically, if they classify the same strings as sentences or nonsentences. Two grammars are *strongly equivalent* if there is isomorphism between the structural diagrams each associates with a given sentence.

A minimum criterion for any acceptable grammar of English is that it be weakly equivalent to the implicit grammar of a native speaker of English; that is, it should accept as sentences just those the speaker does. However, this implies a different grammar for each speaker, and there is a wide divergence in dialect between a university educated person and a street urchin. Although an uneducated speaker probably will accept more strings as sentences, the standard usually taken for a grammar is weak equivalence to the dialect of the educated person. However, grammars can be developed for both.

The following further criteria are also used as a basis for the acceptability of a grammar:

(1) Two sentences such as "John hits the ball" and "Mary lifts the baby," which are considered structurally the same, must be associated with the same structural diagram by the grammar.

(2) A sentence such as "They are flying planes," which is ambiguous, should be associated with a different structural diagram for each interpretation of the sentence.

(3) Chomsky [12] discusses the "explanatory power" of a grammar as a criterion for acceptability. By this he means that an adequate grammar should provide an explanation, for example, of why "John hit the ball" and "The ball was hit by John" are semantically identical although the strings and associated structural diagrams are not similar.

(4) All other things being equal, the simpler of two grammars is the better. However, no standard of simplicity (except conciseness) has ever been agreed upon.

(5) A nonlinguistic criterion is the usefulness of the syntactic structure for further processing. Some examples of processing beyond syntactic analysis will be given later in this chapter.

7.2.1 Dependency Grammars. Conceptually, one of the simplest grammars is the dependency grammar developed by Hays [26, 28]. According to this grammar, a sentence is built up from a hierarchy of dependency structures, where each word in the sentence, except an origin word (usually the main verb), is related to the sentence by dependence on another word in the sentence.

> The concept of dependency is a broad generalization of syntactic relatedness. Adjectives depend on the nouns they modify; nouns depend on verbs as subjects and objects, and on prepositions as objects; adverbs and auxiliaries depend on main verbs; prepositions depend on words modified by prepositional phrases. In semantic terms, one occurrence depends on another if the first modifies or complements the meaning of the second—this includes rules of agreement, government, apposition, etc. [26, p. 4]

For example, the string "the house" is made up of two elements, with "the" dependent on "house." The article "the" delimits "house," and is, thus, dependent upon "house" for its meaning in the sentence. (This is a very pragmatic use of the word "meaning.") In the phrase "in bed," "bed" is dependent upon the preposition "in" to connect it to the rest of the sentence, and thus depends upon this preposition.

A word can have more than one dependent. In the phrase "boy and girl," both "boy" and "girl" are dependent upon the *governor* of the phrase, the conjunction "and." Similarly, in the phrase "man bites dog," both "man" and "dog" are dependent upon the verb "bite." In the dependency analysis used by Klein and Simmons [38, 41] this is not so.

A graphic representation of the syntactic structures associated with some strings by a dependency grammar is shown in Figure 7.1. These structures are downward branching trees. Each node of the tree is labeled with a word of the string. There is no limit to the number of branches from a node. A word is directly dependent upon any word immediately above it in the tree.

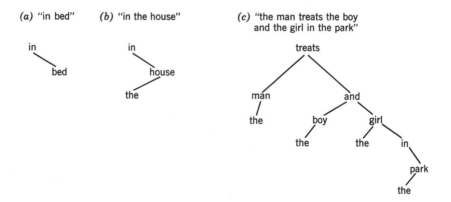

Figure 7.1. Dependency trees

Such trees are constructed by investigating all possible connections between words in the initial string. The defining postulate of a dependency grammar is that "two occurrences can be connected only if every intervening occurrence depends directly or indirectly on one or the other of them" [29]. Thus, local connections may be made first, and then more distant connections may be tested for validity. This localization assumption is convenient for computer processing.

Another important property of a dependency grammar is the isolation of word order rules and agreement rules. The structure tables for the grammar define allowable sequences of dependencies in terms of word classes. For example, a noun followed by a verb may be in subject-verb relationship. If this word order criterion is met, agreement in number may then be checked.

If, for each successful connection made, the rule that generated the dependency connection is recorded, the *use* of a particular word occurrence in the sentence (e.g., as subject, object, object of preposition, etc.) can be attached to the tree.

Several computer applications have been made of the ideas of dependency grammars. The initial efforts were made by Hays [29], and much effort by his group has gone into making a dependency grammar for Russian. A number of interesting heuristics are used in this analysis program to find a single preferred parsing of a sentence. First, closest linkages are given preference. Hays proposed making a statistical study of the frequency of occurrence of connections, and, in parsing, those connections with maximum weight would be tested first. Another scheme focuses on a specified occurrence that can be independent. Any connection that can be made to this occurrence is checked first. Thus the Hays system tends to make ambiguous nouns into subjects or objects of verbs rather than modifiers of other nouns. Hays states that Garvin calls this the "fulcrum" approach to syntactic analysis. In a later program, Hays [25] utilizes a code matching scheme which gives very fast dependency analyses of Russian sentences.

Hugh Kelly, while at The RAND Corporation, also used a dependency grammar in a parsing program for English. Although the grammar developed was not extensive, it was sufficient for several applications. One use of this parser was as a preliminary processor of English input for a heuristic compiler of Simon [67].

Gross [22] wrote a general parsing program for dependency grammars, which, in one left-to-right scan, generates all structures compatible with a given dependency grammar table. No extensive grammar was developed for this program.

The concept of word dependency is also used by Klein and Simmons

[38, 41] in a computer program designed to generate coherent discourse. In general, when a grammar is used to generate sentences, most of the sentences are semantic nonsense. Such meaningless but grammatical sentences as "The colorless green ideas sleep furiously" or "John frightens sincerity" are more the rule than the exception. However, Klein and Simmons use a base text of English sentences and observe the dependency relations among words of this text. For example, the adjective "original" may be dependent upon the noun "ideas"; however, in ordinary discourse, "green" will never be dependent upon "ideas." Thus, by following the ordinary grammar restrictions, plus these additional relevance dependency restrictions, the authors are able to generate surprisingly coherent sentences.

In later work, Klein [37] uses dependence as a transitive relation. Then, using the transitive dependencies in an entire base text, his program is able to generate a coherent paraphrase of this base text following a given outline. In addition, by adjusting the frequencies of use of different rules in the generative grammar, controlled variation of style is achieved [36].

Very little foreign work in syntactic analysis programs for English has been published in English. The available translations indicate that most of the Russian work is being done with dependency grammars. Moloshnava [55], for example, writes of using "the known tendency (of words) to combine with other classes of words." Andreyev [3] describes a dependency analysis for translating English into an intermediate language, which is then to be translated into Russian. However, none of this has yet been fully implemented on a computer.

7.2.2 Immediate Constituent Grammars. Another type of grammar used to describe English syntax is an immediate constituent grammar. The basic premise of this type of grammar is that contiguous substrings of a sentence are syntactically related. Brackets or labeled brackets are used to demark syntactically significant substrings. These brackets may be nested, but they may not overlap. The sentence is enclosed in the outermost bracket pair. A formal theory of grouping as a basis for analysis is given by Hiz [30]. Chomsky [13] calls this type of grammar a context-free phrase structure grammar.

Consider the sentence:

"The man ate the apple."

Bracketing the syntactically significant phrases, we get:

((the man) (ate (the apple)))

These unlabeled brackets demark the three principal substructures of the sentence. Usually, when bracketing is done with a phrase structure grammar, the brackets are labeled in some way. For example, we can use "{ }" to enclose a sentence, "[ ]" to enclose a verb phrase, and "( )" to enclose a noun phrase. Then the bracketed sentence would be:

$$\{ \text{ (the man) [ate (the apple)] } \}$$

The more common way to represent the constituent structure of a sentence is with a tree diagram:

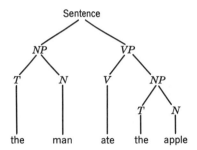

Read from bottom to top, the diagram shows that "the" is a member of word class *T* (definite articles), "man" and "apple" of *N*(nouns), and "ate" of *V* (verbs). A *T* and *N* combination forms the syntactic unit *NP* (noun phrase); *V* and *NP* form a *VP* (verb phrase). An *NP* followed by a *VP* is a *Sentence*.

Note that these trees are unlike those generated by a dependency grammar (Section 7.2.1). The nodes of a dependency grammar tree are labeled with words of the sentence, and the structure shows relations between words. A constituent structure tree has the names of syntactic units as labels for all nodes except the bottom nodes of the tree. Only at the lowest nodes do the words of the sentences appear. The tree structure shows the combination of syntactic units into higher level constituents.

The rules of these context-free phrase structure grammars are of the following simple form:

$$A_1 + A_2 + \cdots + A_n \rightarrow B_i$$

$A_1, A_2, \ldots, A_n$ and B_i are labels for syntactic units, and this rule is to be interpreted as stating that if a string of syntactic categories $A_1 + A_2 + \ldots A_n$ appears in a sentence, the elements of the string may be combined into a single unit labeled B_i. The "+" indicates concatenation. B_i may even be one of the A_i occurring in the left side of this rule. This is not uncommon in English—for example, if A is an adjective and N is a noun, then $A + N \rightarrow N$ is a rule of English; that is, an adjective followed by a noun may be treated as if it were a noun.

The rule form given was for the decoding or parsing of English. However, this type of rule can be easily modified to provide a generation scheme for sentences. The rule given earlier may be rewritten as:

$$B_i \rightarrow A_1 + A_2 + \ldots + A_n$$

We now interpret this rule as the instruction, "rewrite B_i as the string $A_1 + A_2 + \ldots + A_n$." The initial symbol with which we start is *Sentence* and by successive rewriting we can generate a string of words which is a grammatical sentence (according to our grammar).

The following simple grammar illustrates this process:

(i)	*Sentence* $\rightarrow NP + VP$
(ii)	$NP \rightarrow T + N$
(iii)	$N \rightarrow A + N$
(iv)	$VP \rightarrow V + NP$
(v)	$T \rightarrow$ the
(vi)	$A \rightarrow$ green, red
(vii)	$N \rightarrow$ man, apples
(viii)	$V \rightarrow$ ate, hit

The following lines are a "derivation" of the sentence "the man ate the green apples." The numbers to the right refer to the rules used in generating this sentence from the rewrite rules.

Sentence	
$NP + VP$	(i)
$T + N + VP$	(ii)
the $+ N + VP$	(v)
the $+$ man $+ VP$	(vii)
the $+$ man $+ V + NP$	(iv)
the $+$ man $+$ ate $+ NP$	(viii)
the $+$ man $+$ ate $+ T + N$	(ii)
the $+$ man $+$ ate $+$ the $+ N$	(v)
the $+$ man $+$ ate $+$ the $+ A + N$	(iii)
the $+$ man $+$ ate $+$ the $+$ green $+ N$	(vi)
the $+$ man $+$ ate $+$ the $+$ green $+$ apples	(vii)

The second line of this derivation is formed in accordance with rule (i) by rewriting *Sentence* as $NP + VP$, and so on.

This derivation can be represented by the following tree structure:

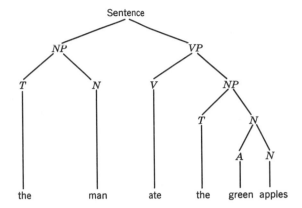

This diagram does not indicate the order in which the rules of the grammar were used, and many derivations would yield this same tree structure. However, only the information in the diagram is necessary to determine the constituent analysis of the sentence.

A substring is defined to be a "constituent" of a sentence if, from all the words of the substring (and only those words), we can trace back to some single node of the tree. If this node is labeled Q, then we say that this substring is a "constituent of type Q." Note that "the green apples" is a constituent of type NP, but "the green" is not a constituent of the sentence, because both these words cannot be traced back to a single node from which *only they* originate.

It is sometimes possible to construct two correct distinct diagrams for the same sentence. Chomsky calls this phenomenon "constructional homonymity" [12]. When this occurs, the sentence in question is ambiguous. Ambiguities arise in two ways. The first type of ambiguity is exemplified by the phrase, "the boy and girl in the park." In this string the prepositional phrase "in the park" may be thought of as modifying either the noun "girl" or the entire noun phrase "boy and girl." There are two distinct trees corresponding to the two choices for bracketing this string, representing a genuine ambiguity in meaning.

The second type of ambiguity is caused by the frequent occurrence of homographs in English. Two words are homographs if they look identical, but are different parts of speech. For example, the "run" in "we run" and the "run" in "the run in her stocking" are homographs. To parse a sentence, all classifications given in the dictionary must be tried for each word. Local context is sometimes sufficient to decide which homograph of a word is present, but homographs often cause ambiguous interpretations of a sentence. An interesting example is a short sentence, "They are flying planes," analyzed by Oettinger [57], for which he finds three distinct parsings because of homographs.

In the first parsing, "are" is classified as a copulative, and "flying" is an adjective modifying "planes." We can bracket this as "(they (are (flying planes)))." For the second parsing, "are" is an auxiliary for the verb "flying," and "planes" is the object of this verb—this parsing corresponds to the parenthesizing "(they (are flying) planes)." The third parsing, which is left as an exercise for the reader, would probably be accepted by few English speakers.

The rules given above for this simple phrase structure grammar allowed each constituent to be rewritten as, at most, two subconstituents. Although such binary rewrite rules are sufficient to link all connected constituents, linguists debate whether the resulting structure adequately represents the structure of the language. In most cases, binary structures are obviously adequate, but where one has a string of coordinate adjectives, such as in "the old, black, heavy stone," one might like to think that each of the adjectives in this phrase modifies the meaning of just "stone," rather than that "black" modifies the noun phrase "heavy stone," etc. The two diagrams of Figure 7.2 show the difference between the binary structure and the multiple-branching coordinate structure.

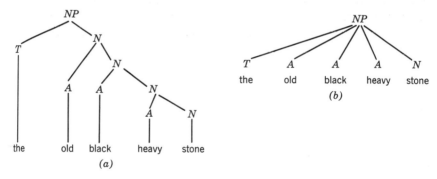

Figure 7.2 (a) Binary structure, (b) coordinate structure

For computational simplicity, most computer parsing programs that perform immediate constituent analysis use binary rewrite rules. An extensive immediate constituent grammar for English is being developed by Robinson [64]. The grammar uses binary combination rules and a complex four-digit coding scheme for the classification of the constituents of English. Early testing of this grammar was done with a parsing program written in the list processing computer language IPL-V. Currently, the grammar is being used by, and tested on, a parsing program written for John Cocke of IBM. Cocke's program is much faster than the IPL program, since it is written in machine code for the IBM 7090. An efficient algorithm invented by Cocke, and described in an article by Hays [29], is used for generating all possible parsings for a sentence. By using two-word constituents and individual words, the program generates all three-word constituents. Similarly, all constituents of length n are generated sequentially from constituent strings of smaller length, until all constituent strings of length s, the length of the sentence, are generated. Constituents are generated by a fast hash-code table lookup for pairs of subconstituents.

The time for parsing a short sentence (fewer than 10 words) is less than one second. All possible parsings for a sentence of 30 to 40 words can be found in less than one minute. The number of possible parsings grows rapidly with the length of a sentence. Usually, long sentences contain many prepositional phrases, and each such phrase may modify any of several nouns. Each ambiguity increases the number of parsings multiplicatively. However, these multiple parsings are carried forward with no redundancies.

The output of Robinson's parsing program is a printout of the resulting tree, with grammar codes associated with each node. Later versions of the program also attach flags to the word, at each node of the tree, indicating in more readable terms the function of the word within the sentence. The grammar has been extended and refined so that identical labels are attached to comparable elements of structurally different paraphrases, such as the two that make up an active-passive pair [63].

An extensive set of linguistic processing programs has been written at the Linguistics Research Center of the University of Texas. The theory of language propounded by Lehman and Pendegraft [46] is an explication of Morris's [56] theory of signs, with language processing stratified into at least three levels. These strata are syntactics, the relationship of signs to signs; semantics, the relationship of signs to the things they denote; and pragmatics, the relationships of signs to their interpretations.

Operational programs perform lexical analysis, and then syntactic analysis for any immediate constituent grammar (not restricted to binary constituents). The lexical analysis program acts as a preprocessor for the syntactic analysis program. It accepts as input a string of allographs (indivisible lexical constants, such as letters or strokes) and gives as output a list structure of all segmentations of the input string, which includes all items in the input in some acceptable lexical segment. These lexical segments are denoted by "syntactic constants" used as parts of the structures constructed by the syntactic processor. Syntactic processing is stochastic in that a probability of occurrence is associated with each syntactic structure. All ambiguities are carried forward in a list structure with no redundancies. At each step in a construction, either all possible structures, or only a specified number of highest-probability alternatives may be used.

There is no restriction on the length of an input string. The system is designed for high-volume processing. Corpus maintenance programs in the current system maintain about 850,000 words of English text, 750,000 in German, 3,000 in Chinese, and 30,000 in Russian. Immediate constituent grammars are being developed for each of these languages. At present, the English grammar consists of approximately 5,400 rules. With the addition of semantic rules, pragmatic rules, and interlanguage-transfer rules, it is hoped that this system will provide good computer-produced translations.

A parsing program utilizing a simple phrase structure grammar has been written by Klein [40]. A notable feature of this program is that, as mentioned earlier, words are classified primarily by computation, rather than by dictionary lookup. From the phrase structure parsing, certain dependency relationships are extracted, which are useful in question answering by the Synthex program [38, 39, 41]. For example, to answer the question "Do worms eat grass?," the following facts are noted about the question.* It is an active construction, with "worms" as subject and "grass" as part of a verb-modifying phrase. These relationships imply certain dependency relationships among "worms," "eat," and "grass." From these, it follows that the second of the following two "information rich" statements

"Birds eat worms on the grass."

"Most worms usually eat grass."

is the better of two potential answers—though both contain the same content words: "worms," "eat," and "grass."

Klein [37] has written a parsing program that simultaneously computes a phrase structure analysis and dependency analysis for an English sentence. The dependency relationships found are those needed for his scheme for generation of coherent discourse, discussed earlier.

Parker-Rhodes [59] has proposed a lattice model for language from which all possible parts of speech, syntactic units, and grammar rules may be derived. Not all syntactic structures appear in all languages. A form of dependency analysis is superimposed upon this immediate constituent grammar, and items are grouped (from right to left) only if a governor (head of a dependency structure) is found surrounded by an arbitrary number of dependents. The output of the parser is a bracketed

*See also chapter 8.

structure. A program embodying the Parker-Rhodes procedures for English has been written for the Cambridge University Computer EDSAC II.

Green [19] has written a "multiple path heuristic parsing program." Written in the list processing language IPL, it is designed to be used as a tool to test any immediate constituent grammar. It recursively generates all legal substructures, cutting off generation when there are more empty nodes in these substructures than items to fill the nodes. Further heuristics to reduce search are planned but have not yet been coded.

Brown [10] has built an utterance generating and resolving device utilizing an immediate constituent grammar. He has developed a small grammar for this for English and a complete one for Loglan [11]. All his programming was done in COMIT. (Programs to generate grammatical strings from arbitrary immediate constituent grammars are trivial if programmed in a list processing language. This author programmed one in LISP in half an hour, and debugged it in two runs.)

There is a straightforward isomorphism between syntax in Backus notation [4] and in an immediate constituent grammar. Although any syntax directed compiler could act as a parser for English, none has been developed for this application. Floyd [15] gives an excellent review of this field, and an extensive bibliography of related work.

7.2.3 Categorial Grammars. Syntactic analysis performed on the basis of rules of an immediate constituent grammar involves two independent dictionary lookup operations. Parsing operations handle words as members of classes. Therefore, on a first pass, each word occurrence in a sentence is associated with its possible syntactic categories. Subsequent references to the list of grammar rules determine which adjacent constituents in a string can be combined into higher level constituents. This lookup operation is iterated each time a new word category replaces two lower level syntactic markers.

With large vocabulary lists and many grammar rules, these lookups take a disproportionate amount of time, and this time increases rapidly with list size. The limited storage capability of the immediate (fast) memory of a computing system requires that much necessary material be placed in slow auxiliary storage, thus further slowing the parsing operation. (As mentioned, Simmons, *et al.* are using computation instead of dictionary lookup to resolve the problem of word classification for most words.)

Studies are also in progress with the goal of avoiding a lookup operation for grammar rules. The original work was done by Ajdukiewicz

[1] and has been continued by Bar-Hillel [6] and Lambek [44]. This work is based on the following approach (as expressed by Lambek):

> In classical physics it was possible to decide whether an equation was grammatically correct by comparing the dimensions of the two sides of an equation. These dimensions form an Abelian group generated by L, M, and T with these quantities admitting fractional exponents. One may ask whether it is similarly possible to assign 'grammatical types' to the words of English in such a way that the grammatical correctness of a sentence can be determined by a computation of this type.

Obviously, such a language coding could not be commutative. (For example, the sequence "the boy" is allowable as a syntactic unit in a sentence, and "boy the" is not.) However, some codings for parts of speech have been developed that have certain of the properties of dimensions in physics. Bar-Hillel's "categorial grammar" and Lambek's "calculus of syntactic types" both use grammatical types denoted by complex symbols that have dimensional properties. Let us illustrate this class coding with an example. Recall that a pronominal adjective has the property that the resulting adjective-noun string can again be treated in the same way as the original noun. Bar-Hillel assigns a noun the grammatical code n, and an adjective the code $\frac{n}{[n]}$ (written as (n/n) in Lambek's notation). The string has type $\frac{n}{[n]} \cdot n$ (where "." indicated concatenation). Performing a "quasiarithmetic" cancellation from the right, we compute the code for the string type as $\frac{n}{[n]} \cdot n = n$. As another example, an intransitive verb, such as "eats" in "John eats," is given type $\frac{s}{(n)}$. The string "John eats" therefore has type $n \cdot \frac{s}{(n)} = s$. The indicated resulting type is s, or sentence, after cancellation.

If the basic grammatical categories are denoted by s, n_1, n_2, ..., m_1, m_2, ..., then the operator categories of a grammar are denoted by:

$$\frac{s}{(n_1)\,(n_2)\,\ldots\,(n_i)\,[m_1]\,\ldots\,[m_j]\,\ldots} ; i+j \geq 1$$

As indicated, a term enclosed by parentheses, e.g., (n_k), can be canceled from the left; a term enclosed in brackets, e.g., $[m_k]$, can be canceled from the right. (Lambek used the notation $(n\backslash s)$ and (s/n) for left and right cancelable terms.)

In his initial paper, Bar-Hillel makes use of only two basic categories, s and n. As an example of the complexity of structure types that occur, consider "very" in the derivation of the syntactic type of the phrase "very large house," which follows:

phrase: very large house

types:

$$\frac{\dfrac{n}{[n]} \cdot \dfrac{n}{[n]} \cdot n \;\to\; \dfrac{n}{[n]} \cdot n \;\to\; n}{[\dfrac{n}{[n]}]}$$

Note that this algebra is not associative. The derivation starts by combining the two left-hand terms to get a derived type of $\frac{n}{[n]}$ for the substring "very large." Then the right-hand cancellation is made, yielding the grammatical type n for the entire string. If, in attempting to compute the type of this substring, we combined the right-hand pair first, we would be left to find the type of a string with two constituent codes:

$$\frac{\dfrac{n}{[n]}}{[\dfrac{n}{[n]}]} \cdot n$$

This pair is not further reducible. Thus, the pairing must go the other way if this substring is to have a single derived category.

A derivation leading to a single operator category or a single basic category is called a *proper derivation*. A derivation is a sequence of lines in which each succeeding line differs from the one immediately preceding it, in that exactly one pair of adjacent elements has been combined to form a new derived category. A *parsing* for a sentence is any proper derivation whose terminal symbol is s.

The figure below shows the only proper derivation of the simple sentence "Poor John sleeps."

Poor   John   sleeps

$$\frac{n}{[n]} \quad \cdot \quad n \qquad \frac{s}{(n)}$$

$$n \quad \cdot \quad \frac{s}{(n)}$$

$$s$$

In a categorial grammar, one defines a substring t to be a constituent of a sentence s if in a proper derivation of s there is included a proper derivation of t. This definition is equivalent to our earlier definition of *constituent* in terms of nodes of a tree.

The derivation given can be represented by a tree:

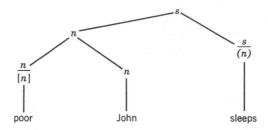

Each substring of a constituent can be traced back to a single node. Note that the boundaries of a constituent are dependent on the context of the substring. For example, "John sleeps" has an immediate derivation to a single category maker, s; however, in the context "poor John sleeps" there is no proper derivation in which "John sleeps" is reduced to a single constituent.

The mathematical problems implicit in dealing with strings of markers of the type shown have been further investigated by Bar-Hillel [5] and his associates, by Lambek, and by Mitchell [54]. Lambek has exhibited a decision procedure for this algebra as a deductive system. However, very little has been done to develop an extensive grammar of this form for English.

The combination rules for a categorial grammar, or Lambek algebra, are implicit in its markers for the word classes. This method of avoiding an iterated grammar rule lookup has been utilized in two different parsing programs. One was written by Glenn Manacher of the Bell Telephone Laboratories in Murray Hill, New Jersey (personal communication), in the COMIT programming language. At present, it can parse sentences that do not contain conjunctions, commas, appositive clauses, or elliptical constructions. However, Manacher believes that these restrictions are not inherent in this type of grammar.

The program is a multipass scanner that makes local linkages first and recursively builds up the parsed structure. Ten basic categories are used, and the operator categories for the grammar are defined in terms of these basic categories. The grammar and program successfully handle such complex constructions as "he wants a man to see the car work." The output of the program is a parenthesization of the sentence, showing the constituent structure, and a list indicating the use of each word within the sentence (e.g., "he" is the subject of the verb "want").

Kay [34] has also written a very fast, general parsing program for categorial grammars. The program is available for experimentation on an IBM 709/7090 as a FAP-FORTRAN II symbolic package, or as a binary deck. In the operation of this program grammatical tags are put into a parenthesis free format. For example $\frac{s}{(n)}$ and $\frac{s}{[n]}$ become *Pns* and *Fns*. These tags are then compiled into lists of computer instructions, which are executed by the parsing routine to give high speed comparison of grammatical types. The techniques used are explained in detail in the cited reference.

7.2.4 Predictive Syntactic Analysis.   Predictive syntactic analysis is based upon a restricted form of immediate constituent grammar. The restrictions are associated with the order in which words in the input string are scanned during analysis. In most immediate constituent parsers, many passes are made over the input string. Substructures internal to the string are often determined before constituents containing the initial words are considered. A predictive parser analyzes a sentence in one left-to-right scan through the words. Before describing the structure of the syntactic rules in terms of an immediate constituent grammar, let us first consider the mechanisms used in predictive analysis.

When a person reads the word "the" in a construction, he expects a noun, delimited by this occurrence of "the," to follow. Similarly, he predicts, from the appearance of an initial noun phrase, the later occurrence of a verb phrase (if he expects to read a sentence). Predictive analysis works in a similar manner. An initial prediction is made that the string to be scanned is a sentence. From this prediction and the initial word in the sentence, further, more detailed predictions are made of the expected sentence structure. For example, if the first word in the sentence is "they," the grammar table states that with an initial pronoun the prediction of a sentence s may be replaced by predictions of a predicate and then a period, or by a prediction of, successively, an adjective phrase, a predicate, and then a period—or by seven other sets of predictions.

One set of these predictions at a time is placed on a pushdown list. The prediction that must be satisfied first appears at the top of this list. A pushdown list has the property that the last item placed in the list will be the first item retrievable from the list. (It is analogous to a dish stack in a cafeteria, in which the last dish placed on top of the stack must be the first taken from the stack.)

As each successive word of a sentence is scanned, its syntactic type s_j and the topmost prediction in the stack p_i are compared. It may happen that this prediction p_i can be completely satisfied by a member of the class s_j. For example, if the prediction is "noun phrase," the proper noun "Tom" completely satisfies this prediction, and "noun phrase" would be removed from the top of the list. If not, new predictions compatible with s_j and p_i are generated, and these new predictions are placed on top of the pushdown list. If no new predictions can be made, we infer that earlier predictions were incorrect and an alternative path must be tried. If the terminal punctuation mark of the sentence is reached and all the predictions made have been satisfied, then this set of predictions represents a parsing for the sentence. If some predictions remain unsatisfied, or if there are no more predictions in the stack, but words remain, then this parsing has failed. If all sets of predictions fail, the sentence is ungrammatical.

Each set of predictions for a word class marker s_j and a top prediction p_i is a form of an immediate constituent binary rewrite rule for the predicted structure p_i. The two constituents of p_i are always of the following restricted form. The left element is always a terminal marker (in fact, s_j). This element can only be rewritten to give a single symbol, i.e., a word of the sentence. The right subconstituent of p_i is a complex symbol—a list of further predictions. Gross [22] has shown that predictive grammars are weakly equivalent to the class of unrestricted immediate constituent grammars. His paper also contains a proof of the weak equivalence of immediate constituent grammars and both dependency and categorial grammars. The original proof of equivalence for dependency grammars was done by Gaifman [18]. (Weak equivalence of two grammars means that both grammars recognize exactly the same set of strings as the set of grammatical sentences or, equivalently, generate the same strings.)

Computer implementations are based on work first done by Rhodes [62] for a Russian parsing program. The most extensive grammar for English for predictive analysis by computer has been developed by Kuno and Oettinger [43, 57]. By making use of a set of "prediction pools" (i.e., a number of pushdown lists) they have been able to obtain all the parsings of syntactically ambiguous sentences:

> Branchings caused by homography and by multiple functions of a given word class are followed in a systematic loop-free sequence in which each partial path is traversed only once. Different paths that reach the last word in a sentence correspond to acceptable syntactic structures of the sentence.

The program is written in machine code for an IBM 7090 and has, for example, found the four possible parsings for a 23-word sentence in 1.2 minutes.

Several heuristics are used to increase the efficiency of the program. For example, if at any time the sum of the minimum number of words needed to fulfill all the predictions in the pushdown list exceeds the number of words left in the sentence, this set of predictions is immediately discarded. This technique is extraneous to the theory of predictive analysis, but does not change the class of sentences to be parsed. The depth of nesting of a predicted structure is another cutoff measure. Evidence given by Miller [53] indicates that a person cannot understand sentences with a nesting depth greater than about seven. Thus, structures whose pool of predictions implies a greater depth are discarded on the assumption that such depths are rarely if ever reached by well formed sentences. Theoretically, but not practically, this changes the set of parsable sentences for the program.

Kuno and Oettinger use a coding trick in the grammar to obtain greater efficiency. Some predictions may be dropped so that two separate parallel paths need not be followed. For example, the prediction of an adverb immediately after a verb may be dropped, because the structure of the remainder of the sentence is, essentially, independent of such an occurrence. Using such a coding, the initial segment of the sentence need not be analyzed twice, once for the prediction set with the adverb and once without it. Another favorable feature of this program is the complete separation of the rules of the grammar from the active program, so that the active program need not be changed when a change is made to a grammar rule. As mentioned previously, this program finds all possible parsings of a given sentence compatible with its grammar. Lindsay [47-49] has written a parsing program based upon predictive analysis techniques. His program finds just one parsing for a sentence, even for ambiguous sentences, and not always the "correct" parsing, i.e., the one that would be understood by a person. However, the parsing found usually contains sufficiently correct substructures for the additional semantic processing done by Lindsay's program.

Lindsay was interested in the problem of extracting certain information from text, and being able to answer certain questions on the basis of this information. The universe of discourse for the questions was the relationship of one member of a family to another (e.g., uncle, brother-in-law, etc.). The input text could contain extraneous information, as in

"Tom bought his daughter Jane a candy bar."

After a complete syntactic analysis, including linking the "his" in this sentence to "Tom," the noun phrases dealing with family relationships are examined and the information is stored on a representation of a family tree. Questions about relationships are answered by finding the points on the tree representing the individuals and, using this tree structure, by computing the relationship corresponding to the path through the tree between these points.

This predictive syntactic analysis program served adequately for further processing of the sentences. It had, however, two restrictions. First, the language was limited to Basic English, a system extracted from normal English by C. K. Ogden [58] containing approximately 1,500 vocabulary items. The words are chosen sufficiently carefully (they are not the 1,500 most common words of English, but the most useful) that most thoughts that can be expressed in unrestricted English can be expressed in this dialect. None of the simplifications involved contradict standard English grammar or semantics.

The second limitation of Lindsay's parsing program centers around its inability to handle quotations, appositive phrases that have no function indicating the right end, interjections, or certain special constructions frequently used with questions. However, Lindsay is continuing work on the problem of syntactic analysis by computer, and may extend the scope of his program.

Another parsing technique closely related to predictive analysis is that implemented on an IBM 7090 for Sydney Lamb* at the University of California, Berkeley. The program works with any binary nondiscontinuous immediate constituent grammar with the following additional information. In each pair of "tactic codes" (syntactic names), one of the pair is marked as presupposing the other. For example, in the construction $A + N \rightarrow N$, the adjective A presupposes the noun. Since the adjective occurs first, we say that A predicts N. If the presupposer is the second member of a pair, we say it "retrodicts" the other tactic code. Retrodictions are related to the "hindsight" technique of Rhodes [62], and the predictions to predictive analysis. However, these presuppositions are strictly local in nature. Using these presuppositions, the program determines all possible analyses in one left-to-right scan.

Program efficiency is gained by grouping all construction formulas for one presupposer. The addresses in the grammar table correspond to syntactic codes, and the entries are computer instructions to be executed. English and Russian grammars are being developed for this program as one portion of a much larger computer language processing system.

7.2.5 Phrase Structure Grammars with Discontinuous Constituents. The phrase structure grammars we have considered thus far have allowed only contiguous elements of a string to be syntactically related. In generating a sentence, a single syntactic constituent may be replaced by two contiguous subconstituents (for *binary* immediate constituent grammars). Rewrite rules of the form $A \rightarrow B + C$ are sufficient to generate most syn-

*Now at Yale University.

tactic structures found in English. However, consider the following sentence:

"He called her up."

The word "up" is part of the verb structure, and intuitively we think of "call up" as one constituent. However, to account for the syntactic connection between "call" and "up," and to restrict the rewrite rules to contiguous subconstituents, a large number of rules would have to be added to the grammar—one for each type of element that might appear between "call" and "up."

To provide a concise notation to describe this type of discontinuous syntactic form, which appears in many languages, Yngve [72] added another rule format to simple phrase structure grammars. Rules in this format are called binary discontinuous rewrite rules.

These rules take the form:

$$A \rightarrow B : C$$

The interpretation for such a rewrite rule is as follows. If, in generating a sentence, we have a string XAY, where Y is a single syntactic marker, we may rewrite the string, using the rewrite rule above, as $XBYC$. In general, when using the rule shown, A is replaced by B, and C is inserted in the string to the right of B, but separated from B by exactly one constituent marker. This rewrite rule is undefined if A is the right hand element of the string. The set of rules shown below is used to generate the sentence, "He called her up."

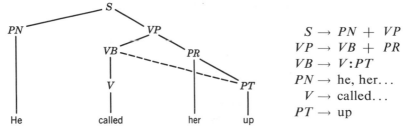

$$S \rightarrow PN + VP$$
$$VP \rightarrow VB + PR$$
$$VB \rightarrow V:PT$$
$$PN \rightarrow \text{he, her...}$$
$$V \rightarrow \text{called...}$$
$$PT \rightarrow \text{up}$$

Note that the structural diagram is no longer a simple tree structure; therefore, relationships within the sentence cannot be indicated just by bracketing. Thus, this type of grammar is not strongly equivalent to the immediate constituent grammars discussed previously. Matthews [51] has shown that the two types of grammar are weakly equivalent.

One of the earliest computer programs utilizing a discontinuous constituent grammar was written by Yngve [71] for the generation of English sentences. A grammar was written that was sufficient to generate the first ten sentences of a children's story book. Then, using the rules of this grammar and the vocabulary in this text, 100 sentences were generated randomly. The sentences generated were "for the most part quite grammatical, though of course non-sensical."

Another program for generating English sentences from a discontinuous constituent grammar was written in the COMIT programming language by B. K. Rankin at the National Bureau of Standards. The grammar used was one in a series of languages that are subsets of English, and that are to be used for information retrieval. Rankin intends to be able eventually to generate sentences describing pictorial information, and to answer questions in English about previously stored pictorial and textual information.

Donald Cohen, also of the National Bureau of Standards, has invented an algorithm and written a program that will recognize and analyze any sentence according to the rules of an arbitrary discontinuous constituent grammar. The result of the analysis is essentially a nested listing of the order in which rewrite rules could have been applied to generate the sentence, and the results of applying these rewrite rules. The program gains efficiency by making a preliminary examination of the sentence to determine which rules can possibly "cover" which elements. Only those pairs in which both elements can be covered by one rule need to be considered as candidates for combination into a single constituent. Kirsch [35] reported on the use of Rankin's grammar and Cohen's parsing procedure in an application to computer interpretation of English text and pictures. Further work by Kirsch and Hsu at NBS is in progress.

A parsing program for a discontinuous constituent grammar, with a "self-organizing heuristic program," has been written by Knowlton [42]. Knowlton used a grammar containing some extreme overgeneralizations. He then provided a training sequence for his parsing program. He showed it correct hand-parsings for sentences. The program abstracted probable partial structures from within these sentences. Using this information, the first parsing found by the program for a sentence was most often the "correct parsing," although the overgeneralizations implied by the rules of the grammar would have allowed many incorrect parsings. The program attempted to parse 300 sentences written in Basic English. It used at each attempt its experience on previous sentences and the hand-parsed correct answer given for these sentences. An effort (processing time) limit was imposed for the parsing of each sentence, and the attempt to parse a sentence was abandoned if the effort expended exceeded this level. Of the approximately 150 sentences for which a parsing was found within the time limit, about 90 percent were parsed correctly. The results indicate that learning can be successfully applied to the problem of finding a good parsing for a sentence.

Another discontinuous constituent grammar for English, written by

Harman [23], will be discussed after an exposition of transformational grammars.

A number of different parsing algorithms for context free grammars have been described in this section. The relative efficiency of each algorithm is hard to assess on the basis of the information given in the literature, because of the differences in programming languages and computers used. The only reasonable comparison was made by Griffiths and Petrick [21], who programmed each process for a simulated pushdown store automata, and compared parsing time and storage requirements for each.

7.2.6   Transformational Grammars.   All the syntactic theories thus far described are weakly equivalent to what Chomsky calls a context-free phrase structure grammar. He raises several objections to such restricted grammars, and proposes additional types of rules to be added to phrase structure grammars [13].

First, he proposes that the form of the rewrite rules be generalized to $ZXW \rightarrow ZYW$. Z and W are the context of the single symbol X, and Y may be a string of one or more symbols. Although Z and W may be null, the set of elements Y that may be substituted for X is usually dependent upon Z and W. A grammar with such rules is called a context-sensitive phrase structure grammar.

To illustrate the necessity for such rules in the generation of English sentences, consider the generation of the two parallel sentences "he runs" and "they run." The generation for both proceeds from the initial symbol S to the string $PR + VI$ (PR = pronoun, VI = intransitive verb). Then if PR is rewritten as "he," VI must be rewritten as "runs" to be grammatical. Similarly, if PR is rewritten as "they," "run" for VI is necessary. Of course, two separate rules could be used, specifying either both pronoun and verb as singular, or both as plural. However, one context-sensitive rewrite rule would express this more concisely.

Another more serious objection to phrase structure grammar is the mathematical limitation on the type of strings producible by such grammars. Chomsky [14] has shown that strings of indefinite length and of the form $abca'b'c'$, in which a' is dependent on a, b' on b, and c' on c, cannot be produced by a phase structure grammar. An example in English, pointed out by Bar-Hillel, is the construction involving "respectively," e.g., "Tom, Jane, and Dan are a man, woman, and programmer, respectively."

Another linguistic objection raised by Chomsky is that the strong intuitive relationship between two such sentences as "The man drives the car" and "The car is driven by the man" is not explained in any way by a phrase structure grammar. Similarly, "the dog is barking" and "the barking dog" should be related.

As a solution to these problems, Chomsky has proposed an additional set of rules beyond the usual phrase structure rewrite rules. Chomsky* proposes that after the generation of sentences by a phrase structure grammar, there be transformation rules that can transform one sentence into another sentence of the language. For example, one such transformation would transform a sentence in the active voice ("The man drives the car") into a sentence in the passive voice ("The car is driven by the man"). Other transformations applied to pairs of sentences, may combine the pair into one sentence. One such transformation would transform the two sentences "The boy stole my wallet" and "The boy ran away" into the complex sentence "The boy who ran away stole my wallet." As Chomsky points out [12], such transformations have sets of "*P*-markers" as domain and range, that is, tree structures associated with strings by a phrase structure grammar. They are not defined on terminal strings. In addition to specifying how a terminal string is to be changed, a transformation must specify the "derived" *P*-marker of the new sentence.

The introduction of transformation rules simplifies the basic phrase structure grammar. Only a simple set of "kernel sentences" need be generated. All other complex sentences can be generated by applying transformation rules to these kernel sentences. In addition, if certain semantic restrictions are to be included in the grammar (e.g., "frightens" may have "John" as an object, but "sincerity" may not), these restrictions need be listed only once. For example, restrictions on the generation of objects for active verbs need not be repeated for the passive construction. (Since the passive is taken from a fully developed sentence in the active voice, these restrictions will be carried over implicitly.) On the other hand, for a simple phrase structure grammar, such restrictions would have to be listed explicitly for both voices.

Walker and Bartlett [70] are developing a parsing program based on a transformational grammar for use with an information retrieval system. Sentence analysis is performed by generating possible strings of constituents, as suggested by Matthews [50, 52]. Each terminal string is then matched against the input sentence. When a match is achieved, a parsing has been found and the parsing routine has determined the kernel sentence of the input string. The program also records the transformations used to embed the kernel sentences in the input string. To limit the large search space of possible kernels and transformations that might be generated,

*For recent changes in transformational theory see Chomsky, N., *Aspects of the Theory of Syntax,* MIT Press, Cambridge, Mass. 1965, p. 251. (Mass. Inst. of Tech. Research Laboratory for Electronics. Special Technical report no. 11) (AD-616 323)

certain heuristics are used to find plausible transformations. For example, if a sentence ends in a question mark, it is certain that at some point the question transformation was used.

Walker and Bartlett give an example of the types of kernels to be found in analysis of a question for the sentence "What are the airfields in Ohio having runways longer than two miles." The kernel sentences found are:

1. X's are the airfields.
2. The airfields are in Ohio.
3. The airfields have runways.
4. The runways are long.
5. Two miles are long.

Using the information about how the kernel sentences are transformationally related, these kernels will be translated into information retrieval language. Since this portion of the program has not yet been implemented, the value of this type of syntactic analysis as a preliminary processor has not been determined for this task.

Andress [2] is constructing a general purpose program to facilitate study of generative grammars of the type proposed by Chomsky. Given a set of context-sensitive phrase structures rules and a set of transformation rules, the program generates exactly one structure of each syntactic type possible within the grammar. The rules can be inserted in a compact notation. At present, only the phrase structure rule-generating portion has been programmed, but Andress expects to be able, eventually, to handle all of Lees's [45] transformational grammar.

A sophisticated transformational grammar and parsing program for English has been developed by Petrick [60] at AFCRL. The program utilizes an ordered list of inverse transformations—each associated with an inverse structural index, which is a sequence of terminal symbols and syntactic types. The parser begins at the top level by determining whether or not the last-ordered transformation could have been applied, on the basis of its inverse structural index. If not, the next-ordered transformation is considered; if so, this inverse transformation is applied, and the resulting structure is used by the parsing program. At present, the grammar consists of about 200 phrase structure rules and about 40 transformations. The program takes from about 15 seconds to 10 minutes to parse a sentence on an IBM 7090. A more extensive grammar for English for this program is being written at IBM by Syrell Rogovin.

7.2.7 A Phrase Structure Grammar with Complex Constituents. As mentioned earlier, Harman [23] has written a generative grammar, without transformation rules, that overcomes most of the difficulties associated with a discontinuous-constituent phrase structure grammar. Additional generative power is introduced into the grammar by the use of complex symbols for syntactic markers. The rewrite rules of the grammar are written in terms of these new notational abbreviations. An example of such a complex syntactic marker is: "SENT/SUBJ ABSTR, OBJ ANIM," a phrase marker for a sentence having an abstract subject and an animate object. Since this notation is based upon COMIT programming language capabilities, it is easily manipulable on a computer. The rewrite rules allow either the top or the subscripts (after the "/") to be rewritten independently, and certain properties (i.e., subscripts) may be carried to a subconstituent or discarded.

One useful property of this type of grammar is that semantic restrictions can be accounted for at a high level, instead of when specifying the terminal string. In addition, since both passive and active constructions are generated from one sentence specification, the close relationship between these forms is indicated. This compares favorably with this same property of transformational grammars.

Harman based his grammar on the most comprehensive transformational grammar of English he could find,* and claims that his program will generate roughly the same set of sentences as the transformational grammar will. The two grammars are approximately the same length. The phrase structure grammar, because it has an unordered set of rules, may be somewhat easier to write. The use of this complex subscript notation, then, appears to overcome the principal difficulties that led to the introduction of transformational grammars. Then two grammars are not equivalent. It remains to be seen which type of analysis and which structures are most fruitful for further use on the computer. The additional generative power of transformational grammars should be acknowledged, although it may not be needed in practice.

7.2.8 String Transformation Grammars. Harris and his associates have developed a method of syntactic analysis that is intermediate between constituent analysis and transformational analysis. Harris's lucid account of his work [24] is summarized below.

The basic assumption underlying the string analysis of a sentence is that the sentence has one "center," an elementary sentence that represents the basic structure of the sentence. Additional words within the sentence are adjuncts of these basic words, or of structures within the sentence. Analysis consists of identifying that center and adjoining the remaining words, in segments, to the proper elements of the sentence. Harris gives the following example:

*An improved version of Lees's [45] transformational grammar.

Today, automatic trucks from the factory which we just visited carry
coal up the sharp incline.
trucks carry coal is the center, elementary sentence
today is an adjunct to the left of the elementary sentence
automatic is an adjunct to the left of trucks
just is an adjunct to the left of visited
etc.

In the analysis, each word is replaced by a marker for its syntactic
category. Several constituents are strung together in such a way that the
resulting pluri-constituent can be replaced by a marker of a constituent
within it. This endocentric construction (i.e., one expanded from an elementary category by adjoining) can then be split into this head and its
adjuncts. Iterating over all segments of the input string, one obtains the
center of the string.

In later work by Joshi [32], the results of a string analysis resemble
the results of a Chomsky transformational analysis. A sentence is resolved
into a number of kernel sentences such that each main verb in the sentence is part of its own kernel. Some phrases containing implicit verbs are
also resolved; for example, "the violinist arrived late" is resolved into
"N_1 arrived late" and "N_1 plays the violin." These kernels are identified
only from the string, not from the structure of the associated syntactic
tree (as in a Chomsky transformational analysis). Programming effort in
connection with this procedure was made in cooperation with A. W. Holt,
and partly reported in his thesis [31].

Each method of syntactic analysis developed by Harris has been designed for computer implementation. The method reported in Harris's
book [24] was implemented on the UNIVAC I computer, and was run successfully in 1959. The transformational decomposition program described
by Joshi was never completed.

The general arrangement of the work done by the UNIVAC program
was as follows:

(1) Dictionary lookup of each word, and replacement of the word by its
    category mark or marks.
(2) Resolution, where possible, of multiple category marks for single
    words by the use of local context.
(3) Multiple scans through the string — some passes from the left, some
    from the right. Each scan tries to segment the sentence into "first-
    order strings."

For example, to find noun phrases, the text is scanned from right to left.
Whenever a noun is found, a noun-phrase bracket is opened on the right.
The scan continues to the left, accepting all words that can be a part of

this phrase. When a left delimiter is found, such as an article, the phrase is closed and the scan is continued until no more groupings into the first order strings can be made. The form of this string of symbols (zero and first order) is then checked against a set of standard patterns. Alternative segmentations are checked and all resultant successful parsings are given. This UNIVAC program will analyze a large class of English sentences. (Space limitations within the UNIVAC were, in general, the reason for the omission of other sentence types.) The same general methods would work for almost all sentences.

Sager [65], another associate of Harris, has directed the programming of a predictive procedure for string analysis. At each position, all possible extensions of the center string are predicted, plus right-side adjuncts of the current category, left-side adjuncts of the next category, etc. The procedure is analogous to phrase structure predictive analysis. The program is written in IPL, and recursively finds all possible string analysis of a sentence.

Another syntactic analyzer based upon Harris's methods was that used in the Baseball [19] program. This program accepted and answered a restricted class of English questions about a limited universe of discourse — baseball statistics. The syntactic analysis portion of this program performed, essentially, the first three steps of the procedure given above for Harris's program. The segmented string was then converted into a standard set of questions—a specification list—which was then used to obtain the answer to the question asked. In this case, a phrase structure grouping was the only syntactic analysis necessary for further processing.

Householder and Thorne [69] use some of Harris's techniques for bracketing syntactic units, but the result of their analysis is a string in a different order than the input string—a linearized dependency order. Much of the processing done by their program is described by a sequence of *ad hoc* rules for unambiguously determining the word class of English homographs, and defining clause boundaries. The output of the syntactic analysis is a list of the kernel sentences of the input sentence.

7.2.9 Other Parsing Systems. A number of programs exist that parse and process English language text, whose operations are not describable in terms of the theories discussed thus far. In general, their processing is based on transformation into canonical forms that serve as a semantic base. For example, Bobrow's STUDENT program [7, 8] analyzes discourses that express algebra story problems. STUDENT takes a problem such as "If Mary is twice as old as Ann was when Mary was as old as Ann is now, and Mary is 24, how old is Ann?"; transforms it into the set of simultaneous equations which express the relations given in this discourse; then, solves the problem and generates the English sentence, "Ann's age is 18," which expresses the solution. The analysis used in STUDENT depends on matching linguistic forms that express arithmetic relations specific to its semantic base, and on a match calling a subroutine that performs the corresponding transformation on the input.

Another system with a strong canonical data base representation is the DEACON system designed by Thompson [68]. In this system, each word has a part of speech that reflects how it is stored in memory. For example, data corresponding to a noun referent word are stored as a list in the computer. Thus, a word like "ship" is stored as list of ships and has part of speech L, for list. For each syntactic rule, a semantic rule indicates how to process a stored structure to obtain a structure corresponding to a combination of words. For example, the syntactic rule which combines "red" and "ship" to produce the phrase "red ships" keys a semantic rule, which produces from the list of ships the sublist of just those ships that are red. Utilizing these transformations, DEACON is able to obtain answers to queries of its data base.

Instead of utilizing a specific semantic base, Bohnert [9] uses the predicate calculus as a canonical form into which input English is transformed. Bohnert's Project LOGOS is attempting to construct a sequence of English-like languages (closer and closer approximations), each supplied with an algorithm that will translate it back into ordinary logical symbolism for use in machine deduction or other forms of content retrieval.

7.3.   CONCLUSION

This chapter has reviewed a variety of theories of grammar and modes of output resulting from many types of syntactic analysis programs. Without a further goal than syntactic analysis for its own sake, we are limited to judging these programs by arbitrary, nonoperational criteria of elegance, explanatory power, and simplicity. The adequacy of these theories must be judged according to their usefulness for further processing. Until a method of syntactic analysis provides, for example, a means of mechanizing translation of natural language, processing a natural language input to answer questions, or generating some truly coherent discourse, the relative merit of each grammar will remain moot.

7.4 POSTCRIPT

During the interval of time that elapsed from the original writing of this chapter until its final review before publication, work in the area of syntactic theories of language has, of course, continued. The recent computer implementations are predominantly improvements of systems described in the text, with no surprising advances. The three survey articles listed below are recommended for a review of more recent work in the field.

BOBROW, D. G., FRASER, J. B. and QUILLIAN, M. R.
  Automated Language Processing. In: Cuadra, Carlos (ed.) *Annual Review of Information Science and Technology, 1966* (American Documentation Institute. Annual Review series, vol. 2). Interscience Publishers, New York, 1967.
KUNO, SUSUMU. *Computer Analysis of Natural Languages.*
  Presented at Symposium on Mathematical Aspects of Computer Science; American Mathematical Society, New York, April 5-7, 1966.
SIMMONS, ROBERT F. Automated Language Processing.
  In: Cuadra, Carlos (ed.) *Annual Review of Information Science and Technology, 1965* (American Documentation Institute. Annual Review series, vol. 1). Interscience Publishers, New York, 1966.

REFERENCES

1. Adjukiewicz, Die syntaktische konnexitat, *Studia Philosophica*, v. 1, 1935, pp. 1-27.
2. Andress, J., A program for the study of generative grammars, IBM Research Paper *RC-820*, 9 November 1962.
3. Andreyev, N. D., Linguistic aspects of translation, *Proc. of 9th International Congress of Linguistics,* Cambridge, Mass., 1962.
4. Backus, J. W., The syntax and semantics of the proposed international algebraic language of the Zurich ACM-GAMM conference, *ICIP*, Paris, June 1959.
5. Bar-Hillel, Y., C. Gaifman, and E. Shamir, On categorial and phrase structure grammars, Research Council of Israel, v. 9F, no. 1, June 1960.
6. Bar-Hillel, Y., A quasi-arithmetical notation for syntactic description, *Language*, v. 29, no. 1, January-March 1953.
7. Bobrow, D. G., *Natural Language Input for a Computer Problem Solving System.* Ph.D. thesis, Dept. of Mathematics, M.I.T., 1964. (Available as *MAC-TR-1*, Project MAC, M.I.T.)
8. Bobrow, D. G., A question answering system for high school algebra word problems, *Proc.* FJCC. Washington: Spartan Press, November 1964.
9. Bohnert, H. G., Logical linguistic studies for machine text perusal, Semiannual report *AF49(638)-1198*, January 1964.
10. Brown, J. C., Simulation model-making and the problem of system-controlled human behavior, *Faculty Conference on Computer Applications.* Tallahassee, Fla.: Florida State U., April 1962.
11. Brown, J. C., Loglan, *Scientific American,* June 1960.
12. Chomsky, N., On the notion "rule of grammar," *Proc. of the Symposium in Applied Mathematics*, v. 12, p. 6, 1961.
13. Chomsky, N., *Syntactic Structures.* 'S-Gravehage: Moulton and Co., 1957.

14. Chomsky, N., Three models for the description of language, *IRE Trans. on Information Theory*, v. IT-2, September 1956.

15. Floyd, R. W., The syntax of programming languages, *Trans. on Electronic Computers*, v. EC-13, no. 4, August 1964.

16. Francis, W., *The Structure of American English*. New York: Ronald Press, 1958.

17. Fries, C. C., *Structure of English*. New York: Harcourt Brace and World, 1952.

18. Gaifman, H., Dependency systems and phrase structure systems, *Information and Control* (in press).

19. Green, B. F., A. K. Wolf, C. Chomsky, and K. Laughery, Baseball: an automatic question-answerer, *Proc. of the Western Joint Computer Conference*, Los Angeles, Calif., May 1961.

20. Green, L. D., A multiple path heuristic parsing program. Pasadena, Calif.: Electro-optical Systems, Inc., 1963.

21. Griffiths, T. V., and S. R. Petrick, On the relative efficiency of context-free grammar recognizers, *AFCRL-TM-64-2*. Bedford, Mass., 1964.

22. Gross, M., On the equivalence of models of language used in the fields of mechanical translation and information retrieval, *Information Storage and Retrieval*, v. 2, April 1964.

23. Harman, G. H., and V. H. Yngve, Generative grammars without transformation rules, *RLEQPR #68*. Cambridge, Mass.: Massachusetts Institute of Technology, 1962.

24. Harris, Z. S., *String Analysis of Sentence Structure*. The Hague: Moulton and Co., 1962.

25. Hays, D. G., Connectability calculations, syntactic functions, and Russian syntax, *Mechanical Translation*, v. 8. no. 1, August 1964.

26. Hays, D. G., Dependency theory: a formalism and some observations, *RM-4087-PR*. Santa Monica, Calif.: The RAND Corp., July 1964.

27. Hays, D. G., Automatic language-data processing, in H. Borko, ed., *Computer Applications in the Behaviorial Sciences*. Englewood Cliffs, N. J.: Prentice-Hall, 1962.

28. Hays, D. G., Basic principles and technical variation in sentence-structure determination, in C. Cherry, ed., *Information Theory*. Washington: Buttersworth, 1961.

29. Hays, D. G., Grouping and dependency theories, *Proc. of the National Symposium on Machine Translation*. Englewood Cliffs, N. J.: Prentice-Hall, 1961.

30. Hiz, H., Steps toward grammatical recognition, *International Conference for Standards on a Common Language for Machine Searching and Translation*, Cleveland, Ohio, 1959.

31. Holt, A., *A Mathematical and Applied Investigation of Tree Structures for Computer Analysis*. Ph.D. thesis, U. of Pennsylvania, 1963.

32. Joshi, A., A procedure for a transformational decomposition of English sentences, *TDAP 42*. Philadelphia: U. of Pennsylvania, 1962. (Presented at the ACM national conference, August 1963.)

33. Katz, J. J., and J. A. Fodor, The structure of a semantic theory, *Language*, v. 39, no. 2, April-June 1963.

34. Kay, M., A parsing program for categorial grammars, *RM-4283-PR*. Santa Monica, Calif.: The RAND Corp., September 1964.

35. Kirsch, R., Computer interpretation of English text and picture patterns, *Trans. on Electronic Computers*, August 1964.

36. Klein, S., Control of style with a generative grammar, *SP-1633/001/00*. Santa Monica, Calif.: System Development Corp., July 1964.

37. Klein, S., Automatic paraphrasing in essay format, *SP-1602/001/00*. Santa Monica, Calif.: System Development Corp., July 1964.

38. Klein, S., and R. F. Simmons, Syntactic dependence and the computer generation of coherent discourse, *Mechanical Translation,* August 1963.

39. Klein, S., and R. F. Simmons, A computational approach to grammatical coding of English words, *J. of Assoc. for Computing Machinery*, July 1963.

40. Klein, S., *Automatic decoding of written English*. Ph.D. thesis, U. of California, Berkeley, 1963.

41. Klein, S., and R. F. Simmons, Automated analysis and coding of English grammar for information processing systems, *SP-490*. Santa Monica, Calif.: System Development Corp., August 1961.

42. Knowlton, K., *Sentence Parsing with a Self-organizing Heuristic Program*. Ph.D. thesis, M.I.T., August 1962.

43. Kuno, S., and A. G. Oettinger, Syntactic structure and ambiguity of English, *Proc. of the International Federation of Information Processing Congress*, 1963.

44. Lambek, J., On the calculus of syntactic types, *Proc. of Symposia in Applied Mathematics,* v. 12, 1961.

45. Lees, R. B., The grammar of English nominalization, Part II, *International J. Amer. Linguistics,* v. 61.26, no 3.

46. Lehmann, W. P., and E. D. Pendegraft, Machine language translation study report #16. Austin, Texas: Linguistics Research Center, U. of Texas, June 1963.

47. Lindsay, R. K., Inferential memory as the basis of machines which understand natural language, in *Computers and Thought*. New York: McGraw-Hill, 1963.

48. Lindsay, R. K., Toward the development of machines which comprehend. Austin, Texas: U. of Texas, 1961.

49. Lindsay, R. K., *The reading machine problem*. Unpublished Ph.D. thesis, Carnegie Institute of Technology, 1960.

50. Matthews, G. H., Analysis by synthesis in the light of recent developments in the theory of grammar, *Proc. of Colloquium on Algebraic Languages*, Prague, 1964.

51. Matthews, G. H., Discontinuity and asymmetry in phrase structure grammars, *Information and Control*, v. 6, no. 2, June 1963.

52. Matthews, G. H., Analysis by synthesis of sentences in a natural language, *Proc. of the 1961 International Conference on Machine Translation and Applied Language Analysis.* London: H.M.S.O., 1962.

53. Miller, G. A., The magical number seven-plus-or-minus-two, *Psychological Review*, v. 63, 1956.

54. Mitchell, R. P., A note on categorial grammars, *Proc. of the 1961 International Congress on Machine Translation of Languages and Applied Language Analysis.* London. H.M.S.O., 1962.

55. Moloshnava, T. N., An algorithm for translating from the English to the Russian. *Translation in Foreign Developments in Machine Translation and Information Processing*, no. 11, USSR.

56. Morris, C. W., Foundation of the theory of signs, *International Encyclopedia of Unified Science*, v. 1, no. 2. Chicago, Ill.: U. of Chicago Press, 1955.

57. Oettinger, A., and S. Kuno, Multiple-path syntactic analyzer, *Proc. of the International Federation of Information Processing Congress*, Munich, 1962.

58. Ogden, C. K., *A System of Basic English*. New York: Harcourt Brace and World, 1934.

59. Parker-Rhodes, A. F., A new model of syntactic description, *Proc. of the 1961 International Conference on Machine Translation and Applied Language Analysis*. London: H.M.S.O., 1962.

60. Petrick, S. R., A recognition procedure for transformational grammars, AFCRL, Bedford, Mass., 1964.

61. Resnikoff, H., and J. L. Dolby, Automatic determination of parts of speech of English words, *Proc. of the IEEE*, July 1963.

62. Rhodes, I., A new approach to the mechanical syntactic analysis of Russian, *Mechanical Translation,* v. 6, November 1961.

63. Robinson, J., Automatic parsing and fact retrieval: a comment on grammar, paraphrase, and meaning, *RM-4005-PR*. Santa Monica, Calif.: The RAND Corp., February 1964.

64. Robinson, J., Preliminary codes and rules for automatic parsing of English, *RM-3339*. Santa Monica, Calif.: The RAND Corp., December 1962.

65. Sager, N., A procedure for syntactic analysis, *Proc.of the International Federation of Information Processing Congress*, Munich, 1962.

66. Simmons, R. Γ., S. Klein, and K. McConlogue, Co-occurrence and dependency logic for answering English questions, *SP-1155*. Santa Monica, Calif.: System Development Corp., April 1963.

67. Simon, H., Experiments with a heuristic compiler, *J. of Assoc. for Computing Machinery*, v. 10, no. 4, October 1963.

68. Thompson, F. B., et al., Deacon breadboard summary, *RM-64TMP-9*. Santa Barbara, Calif.: General Electric Co., 1964.

69. Thorne, J. P., Automatic language analysis, *RADC-TDR-63-11*. Bloomington, Ind.: Indiana U., ASTIA No. 297381.

70. Walker, D. E., and J. M. Bartlett, The structure of languages for man and computer: problems in formalization, *First Congress on the Information Sciences*, 1962.

71. Yngve, V. H., Random generation of English sentences, *Memo 1961-4*. Cambridge, Mass.: Massachusetts Institute of Technology, Machine Translation Group, RLE, 1961.

72. Yngve, V. H., A model and an hypothesis for language structure, *Proc. of the Amer. Philosophical Society,* v. 104, no. 5, 1960.

8

Answering English Questions by Computer

R. F. Simmons

Of the many varied approaches toward computer processing of natural languages during the last decade, the majority has focused on mechanical translation. Computer based document retrieval systems, supporting stylistic and content analysis of documents, have been developed. More than a dozen systems for answering English questions have been reported.*

The term "question answering machine" as used here covers a range from conversation machines to machines that generate sentences in response to pictures, and systems that translate from English into logical calculi. All of these may be interpreted as attempting to use natural English in a manner very closely related to the question and answer pattern.

Research toward natural language question answering systems began in 1959. Currently, fifteen or sixteen programs—experimental rather than operational—for answering some type of English question are being studied. Each shows that some aspects of the panorama of verbal meaning can be reproduced successfully by machine, but none as yet offers general solutions to the problem of high quality language processing or attacks the engineering problems, which a practical device would encounter. Although each question answering system so far built deals comparatively trivially with a trivial set of English questions, in the early stages of a research discipline, the effectiveness and generality of the systems developed are of considerably less interest than are the principles that

*This survey was conducted under ARPA Contract SD-97 and has also been reported in *Comm. of the ACM,* v. 8, no. 1, January 1965, which is available as SDC document *SP-1556/000/01.*

emerge from the experimentation. This paper explains some principles and techniques of question answering that have emerged during the past five years and summarizes the state of the art of language processing.

8.1 A LOGIC OF QUESTIONS AND ANSWERS

In English, the question mark, intonation, and the rearrangement of subject and verb constitute a small set of rules for transforming any statement into a question. In addition, a vocabulary of special question words— "who," "why," "where," etc.—provides clues to the nature of the desired answer. Linguistic differences between declarative statements and questions are well cataloged and understood; not so with logical differences. Harrah [24] and Belnap [1] suggest that a question is a special subclass of assertions whose propositional truth or falsity can be determined; Hamblin [22, 23] and MacKay [38] take a contrary view.

In the Belnap classification, a question has two parts: (1) a set of alternatives and (2) a request. The request part of the question indicates the acceptable form of a *direct* answer by showing which and how many of the alternatives must be present. A direct answer is that particular set of alternatives that is a complete answer to the question. For example, in the question, "What are two primes between 1 and 10?" the set of numbers between 1 and 10 is presented as alternatives from which an answer is to be selected. The request states that any two of these will be a direct answer. There exist also *partial* answers, *eliminative* answers, *corrective* answers and *relevant* answers, each of which offers something less than the questioner hoped for.

Questions may also be classified as *complete* (disjunctive), e.g., "Is Reagan the governor of California?" and as *incomplete:* "Who is the governor of California?" It is also desirable on occasion to classify questions as *safe, risky, foolish,* etc. A safe question is one that divides the universe in two as in "Did she wear the red hat or not?" and for which there is a direct answer. A foolish question is one which cannot have a direct answer, e.g., "What is the largest number?" Risky questions include those with built-in assumptions such as "Have you stopped beating your wife?"

Closely related to questions are imperative statements. "Go to the store," "Set course 180, speed 500," and "Set Dodgers equal win over Boston at Detroit" are all imperatives. Imperative statements ordinarily call for a physical action not involving language, while a question usually dictates a language response. In terms of question answering programs, however, the difference becomes mainly one of output mode; the analysis phase for each type of statement is similar. Like the question, the imperative contains a request and outlines an environment of alternatives. In such commands as "Name the signers of the Constitution," where the desired behavior is linguistic, the difference disappears entirely. Logic developed for question answering systems applies almost directly to machines for doing useful nonlinguistic work in response to English commands.

The main features of the Belnap classification system are considered in the analysis of question answering systems that follows. The distinction between commands and questions tends to be of minor importance for these machines.

8.2   PRECURSORS

Question answering systems are a recent development, but the desire to translate language statements into symbols to use in a calculus has existed as long as formal logic. Attempts to build machines to test logical consistency date back at least to Ramon Lull in the thirteenth century. Several logic machines for testing the validity of propositions were constructed in the nineteenth century [18]. However, only in recent years have attempts been made to translate mechanically from English into logical formalisms.

8.2.1   The Conversation Machine. This program by Green, Berkeley, and Gotlieb [21] allows a computer to carry on a seemingly intelligent conversation about the weather. The problem was originally posed in the context of Turing's definition that a computer could be said to be thinking if it could participate in a conversation in such a manner that the human participant could not establish that he was not speaking to a real person. By choosing a conversational topic as stereotyped as weather, the experimenters hoped to gain some experience with the meaning of Turing's idea.

The conversation machine dealt with three factors: meaning, environment, and experience. Meaning is expressed in terms of dictionary entries for words, combinations of these entries for remarks, and preference ratings (like or dislike) for certain types of weather. The environment of the system is an input of the day's weather, and its experience is a general knowledge of the type of weather experienced at various times of the year.

Words are categorized as *ordinary*, e.g., "snow," "rain," etc.; *time*, e.g., "today," "December," etc.; and *operator*, e.g., "not," "change," and "stop." The meaning of each word is stored as an attribute-value pair. For time-words, the attribute is a type of time—calendar or relative

—and the value is a code for the amount. For operator words, the attribute is a code for a function to be accomplished, and the value is the degree to which it is to be executed. Thus, "change" and "stop" call a subroutine for negation but the degree code for "stop" is greater than that for "change." Such ordinary words as "dew," "drizzle," and "rain" are coded for successively higher values of the attribute "wetness."

The meaning of a remark is calculated by looking up each word and coding it by its attribute-value pair from the dictionary. "Meaningless" words—not in the dictionary—are assigned the code zero-zero. The set of codes for words in a remark represents the word's "meaning." The program compares the meaning of a remark with its own store of coded "remarks," selects a reply frame, and fills in the blanks with words originating from the remark, from its experiences, or from its preference codes.

The authors use the example, "I do not enjoy rain during July." The "not" operator word acts on "enjoy" to give "dislike," which is a meaningful word to the program. The resultant meaning for the remark is the set, "dislike," "rain," and "July." Looking up the time-word "July," the program discovers that "July" is associated with "heat" and "blue skies." Since these two terms do not relate to "rain," the program records an *essential disagreement*. On this basis it selects a reply frame and fills in the blanks as follows:

"Well, we don't usually have *rainy* weather in
July so you will probably not be disappointed."

The conversation machine avoids the whole problem of syntactic analysis and is obviously limited to a few simple constructions. However, it does analyze a statement into a set of meaningful parameters, which are then used to select an answer. Its principle of coding the meaning of words as an attribute-value pair is still basic to far more recent and advanced question systems.

8.2.2 The Oracle.   As a Master's thesis under John McCarthy, then at M.I.T., Phillips programmed an experimental system to answer questions from simple English sentences, by syntactically analyzing both the questions and a corpus text that may contain an answer [42]. This analysis transforms both the question and the sentence into a canonical form showing the subject, the verb, the object, and nouns of place and time. The system was written in LISP, which simplified the programming task.

Its principle of operation can be appreciated by following the example in Figure 8.1. The example sentence is analyzed into subject, verb, and (essentially) object. The analysis is limited to simple sentences and breaks down if the sentence has two or more subjects or objects. The first stage of analysis is to look up each word in a small dictionary to discover its word class assignment. At this point such words as "school," "park," "morning," etc., are also coded as time or place nouns. During the analysis, the question is transformed into declarative order and auxiliary verbs are combined with their head verbs so that both question and potential answering statement are in the canonical form, subject-verb-object, as shown in Figure 8.1.* A comparison is then made to determine if the elements of the sentence match those of the question. In the example, all three elements match and the program would print out "to school" followed by the entire sentence. Had the input been a complete question, i.e., "Did the teacher go to school?" the Oracle would have modified its behavior to respond, "Yes."

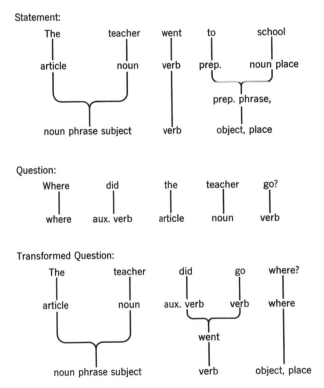

Figure 8.1 Oracle-type analysis of question and answer

The Oracle exemplifies the principle of answering questions by structural matching of syntactic-semantic codes. Within the range of very sim-

---

*Details of the types of syntactic analysis commonly used are not covered in this chapter. See Bobrow [4] or Chapter 7.

ple English structures, the method is uncomplicated and easily achievable. The principle of double coding—for syntactic and semantic word class— will be seen to generalize to much more complicated structures than the Oracle used.

The conversation machine and the Oracle are two prototypes of question answerers, which even in 1959 demonstrated that *if* statements can be coded semantically and syntactically they can be matched to discover how closely they resemble each other. For the conversation machine, the match was against a coded data base and the selection of a reply to a remark was a function of the type of correspondence between the remark after coding and the program's coded store of statements and rules. For the Oracle, the comparison was between an English question and an English sentence, both of which were inputs.

8.3 LIST-STRUCTURED DATA BASE SYSTEMS

A list-structured data base question answering system is one that deals with data that are strongly organized into list form. SAD SAM reads Basic English* sentences and extracts from them data which can be appended to a list-structured data base. The Baseball system answers questions from lists that summarize a Major League's season's experience. The recent DEACON system is designed both to build a data structure from English sentences and to answer English questions from it. All of these programs illustrate and explore the principle of well organized but limited information structures as a basis for experimenting with methods of answering English questions.

8.3.1 SAD SAM. This acronym stands for Sentence Appraiser and Diagrammer and Semantic Analyzing Machine. It was programmed in IPL-V by Lindsay [37] as part of a dissertation at Carnegie Institute of Technology. SAD SAM is divided into two parts: a parsing section and a section for handling meanings. The system is designed to accept simple sentences limited to a Basic English vocabulary concerning family relationships. The data base is in the form of a family tree represented in the program by a hierarchical set of lists. A sentence is parsed as it is read, the information that a person bears a relationship of "brother," "mother," "father," etc., to someone else is extracted, and the name so represented is appended to the appropriate lists or branches of the family tree.

*Basic English is a subset of English limited to a vocabulary of 300—1600 words and the simplest grammatical constructions. See Ogden [41].

The parsing system is an independent program using a form of the predictive analysis techniques described in detail by Oettinger and Kuno [35]. Although it was designed for relatively simple structures, Lindsay reports that it can handle relative clauses and at least some appositional strings. As a result of the parsing, the input to the semantic analysis program is (1) a sentence whose parts are labeled noun, verb, noun phrase, etc.; and (2) a tree structure showing the relationships among these grammatical features.

The semantic analyzer searches for subject-complement combinations that are connected by the verb "to be" and cross-references these to indicate equivalence. Words that modify equivalent words are then grouped together. Next, the sentence is searched for any of the eight words in Basic English that characterize kinship relations. Thus, for the sentence,

"John's father, Bill, is Mary's father,"

the term, "John's father" would be set equivalent to the complement, "Mary's father." The two kinship terms would be recognized and the proper names which modify them would be discovered. The word "Bill" modifies the subject and, since subject and object are equivalent, it also modifies the object. Triplets are constructed to show the relationship between each pair of names as follows:

Bill (father) John

Bill (father) Mary

These relationships are added to the family tree, which has then the following structure:

Family unit (name)	
(Attribute)	(Value)
Husband	Bill
Wife	Unknown
Offspring	John, Mary
Husband's parents	Unknown
Wife's parents	Unknown

Since this data structure is in the form of IPL lists, instead of actual names of family members, pointers may be used to indicate the location of a family list containing the names. The result is an interlocking data structure that allows a fairly significant level of inference. In the example above, since John and Mary are offspring of a common parent, it is known that they are siblings. If a following sentence states that Jane is Bill's wife, it will be immediately known that Jane is the mother of John and Mary (since no multiple marriages are permitted).

Lindsay's primary interest was in machine comprehension of English and he attempted to show that an important component of understanding lay in building large coordinated data structures from the text that was read. He found it necessary to use a syntactic analysis to discover relationships between the words his program "understood," and then to transform the "understood" portions of the sentence into a form that could map onto his data structure.

8.3.2 Baseball. The baseball program, originally conceived by Frick, Selfridge, and Dineen and constructed by Green, Wolf, Chomsky, and Laughery [20], answers English questions about the scores, teams, locations, and dates of baseball games. The input questions are restricted to single clauses without logical connectives such as "and," "or," or "but" and excluding such relation words as "most" or "highest." Within the limitations of its data and its syntactic capability, Baseball is the most sophisticated and successful of the first generation of experiments with question answering machines. It is of particular interest for the depth and detail of its analysis of questions.

Baseball is programmed in IPL and uses list structures to organize data. The data are set up with a major heading of months. For each month there is a list of places in which games were played. For each place there is a list of days, for each day a list of games, and for each game a list of teams and score values, exemplified by the following data format:

$$\begin{aligned}
&\text{Month} = \text{July} \\
&\quad \text{Place} = \text{Boston} \\
&\qquad \text{Day} = 7 \\
&\qquad\quad \text{Game Serial} \# = 96 \\
&\qquad\qquad \text{Team} = \text{Red Sox, Score} = 5 \\
&\qquad\qquad \text{Team} = \text{Yankees, Score} = 3
\end{aligned}$$

The program also contains a dictionary that includes the part of speech of a word, its meaning, an indication of whether it belongs to an idiom, and a code to show if it is a question word. The first part of the program's task is to use the dictionary, parsing routines, and content routines to translate from the English language question into a specification (or spec) list which is similar in format to the data structure.

The first step is to substitute dictionary codes for the English words. A parsing using a modification of Harris's approach [25] results first in bracketing the phrases of the question, then in determining subject, object, and verb. For example, the question "How many games did the Yankees play in July?" gives the following bracketing:

"(How many games) did (the Yankees) play (in (July))?"

The brackets distinguish noun phrases and prepositional phrases and locate the data needed for the spec list. The parsing phase resolves some ambiguities of the noun-verb type; while others, such as "Boston = place" or "Boston = team" are resolved later.

A semantic analysis phase actually builds the spec list from the parsed question. In this phase, the dictionary meanings of the words are used. The meaning may be an attribute, which is part of the data structure, as "team" means "team = (blank)," or "who" means "team" = ?"; or the meaning may be a call to a subroutine. For example, "winning" means "routine A1," which attaches the additional condition "winning" to "team" on the spec list. The output of these routines is a spec list used to search the list structures of the data store for an acceptable answer.

After the spec list is completed, the processing phase takes over. In some cases, this consists of matching of a blank item on the spec list—such as the place in which a given team played on a given day. In other cases, as with the words "every," "either," and "how many," processing is a very complicated searching and counting procedure. The output of the program is in the form of a "found" list, which shows all of the acceptable answers to the question.

In the Baseball system, three aspects of the question answering problem stand out clearly. A first phase of syntactic analysis merges into the second phase, semantic analysis. However, for the first time a third logical processing phase becomes explicit. In this phase, even though the relations between words and the meaning of words are already known, a wide range of operations are performed as a function of these meanings.

Having considered the manner in which Lindsay's SAD SAM reads text to append data to a list structure similar to that used by the Baseball system, it is apparent that Baseball could become a completely self-contained (though limited) automatic language processor. To achieve this goal, factual statements would be read and analyzed into their spec lists and a new processor would be required to add the data to the storage lists.

8.3.3 The DEACON Breadboard. Thompson [58, 59] and Craig [13] have reported on DEACON*—a data based question answerer which is part of a man-machine communication system that may eventually allow operators to communciate with each other and with the computer in a subset of natural English. The question answerer is programmed in a special list processing language, KLS-II, developed for this system.

In general, DEACON depends on a list-structured data base. Thompson makes explicit the importance of a well understood data structure and in-

*DEACON stands for Direct English Access and CONtrol.

troduces a principle of equivalence between the word classes of syntactic analysis and the semantic categories of the data base. As a result, his programs do not break neatly into a parsing system, a semantic analyzer, and a data processor, although these phases remain distinguishable. His language analysis parses a sentence into the names of lists and the calls to operations to be performed (immediately) on the lists. The resulting sublists are tested for their truth value in the last phase of data processing.

   An example presented by Thompson [59, pp. 17-23] will clarify the operation of these programs. The question to be answered is: The cost of what Air Force shipments to Omaha exceeds 100,000 dollars? The data base from which this question is to be answered is outlined in Figure 8.2. This table can be read as a list structure of shipments, with sublists of Air Force, Army, and Navy shipments. Each of these sublists has attributes of cost, origin, and destination, and values as shown in the cells of the table.

SHIPMENTS	COST	ORIGIN	DESTINATION
Air Force			
Shipment *a*	39,000	Detroit	Washington
Shipment *b*	103,000	Boston	Omaha
Army			
Shipment *a*	-	-	-
Shipment *b*	-	-	-
Navy			
Shipment *a*	-	-	-
Shipment *b*	-	-	-

Figure 8.2. DEACON-type data base

   The first step in analyzing the question is that of assigning word classes as follows:

the	F	to	F
cost	A	Omaha	V
of	F	exceeds	$R(V,V)$
what	F	100,000	N
Air Force	M	dollars	A
shipments	L	?	

The word "shipment" is classified L as a major list. The term "Air Force" is classified M as a list modifier (or major sublist). "Cost" and "dollars" are assigned A for attribute. "Omaha" is designated V for value and "100,000" is designated N for number. Each of the words coded F represents some function for the system to perform. The parsing is accomplished with a phrase structure grammar in which each rule is accompanied by a transform to operations on the data list structure. For example, the following rule,

$$L_1 = M + L : T_1 (M,L)$$

means that when the combination of word classes $M + L$ is found, substitute for L_1 the list which is generated by T_1 operating to extract the sublist M from the major list L. The word "what" is a function word interpreted as a quantifier, which generates all cases of the structure it modifies. At the conclusion of the analysis there is the rule,

$$T = V + R(V,V) + V : T_7(V,R,V),$$

which translates roughly into "Is it true that the value of the data generated in the first clause exceeds the value of the data generated in the second clause?"* By the time this rule is applied, the first and second clauses are each represented by a list. $R(V,V)$ is a function that tests a member of the first list as greater in value than a member of the second. In this case, the second list has one entry: value 100,000 dollars. For each member of the first list, the indicator for true or false is assigned as a result of the comparison.

The DEACON system accepts the occurrence of ambiguous analyses, but usually these are resolved in terms of the data context of the sentence. Each remaining analysis is dealt with as a separate statement or question. It generalizes to a broad range of data and to a reasonably complex subset of English. The system is self-contained in that it both reads its own data and answers questions. It makes explicit the principles of structure and question analysis which, although previously implicit, were not fully conceptualized in such systems as Baseball, SAD SAM and the PLM (see below). DEACON is important theoretically in showing the continuity between syntactic, semantic, and symbolic-logical analyses of English in a data base system.

8.3.4   Other Data Base Approaches.   Work by Walker and Bartlett [63], Sable [48], and several classified systems under Air Force sponsorship are further examples of systems which attempt to query a data base in some subset of English. The outline of a special problem-oriented language for translating from a subset of English into operations on a data base was reported by Cheatham and Warshall [7].

*For example, is clause 1 (cost of AF shipments, etc. = 103,000) greater than clause 2 (100,000 dollars = 100,000); thus, is 103,000 > 100,000?

8.4   GRAPHIC DATA BASE SYSTEMS

Two systems that depend on graphic data bases are described in this section. One clearly shows the power of translating from English or from graphic data into a subset of the predicate calculus. The other takes a probabilistic learning approach toward the generation of valid English statements from the diagrams it reads. Together, they add further support to the idea, suggested earlier by Lindsay [37] and others, that a well structured data base offers great potential for making inferences as well as for providing explicitly stored data.

8.4.1   The Picture Language Machine (PLM). At the National Bureau of Standards, Kirsch [29-32], Cohen [8,9], Rankin [44] and Sillars [50] have devised a program system that accepts pictures and sentences as input. It translates both the pictures and the English statement into a common intermediate logical language and determines whether the statement about the picture is true. This set of programs is of particular interest in this review since it seems to be one of the first to explore the principle of translating from a subset of English into a formal language and to point out a reasonable method for doing so.

The PLM is composed of three subsystems — a parser, a formalizer, and a predicate evaluator. Its language is limited to a small subset of English suitable for making statements and asking questions about three geometric figures. The parsing system is based on an immediate constituent grammar that includes the discontinuous-constituent operator. Parsing is accomplished by a recognition routine, which successively substitutes symbols from the dictionary for words in the sentence, or for an intermediate symbol string, until the top of the parsing tree is reached.

After the sentence has been parsed to produce one or more tree structures representing it, the formalizer translates the parsed sentence into the formal language. The formal language is a first-order functional calculus with a small number of constant predicates. The primitives of the language include brackets, parentheses, the terms "and," "if...then," "for all," "there exists," "not," "identity," certain other quantifiers, variables, and three types of predicates. The singular predicates are typified by the following examples:

$$\mathrm{Cir}(a) \qquad a \text{ is a circle}$$
$$\mathrm{Bot}(a) \qquad a \text{ is at the bottom}$$
$$\mathrm{Bk}(a) \qquad a \text{ is black}$$

Some typical binary and ternary predicates follow:

Bgr(a,b)	a is bigger than b
Lf(a,b)	a is to the left of b
Smc(a,b)	a is the same color as b
Bet(a,b,c)	a is between b and c
Mort (a,b,c)	a is more to the right of b than c
Mmid(a,b,c)	a is more in the middle of b than c

The formalizer is designed to work with each parsing that the grammar produces. A formalization rule exists for each rule in the grammar. Translation consists of substituting formalization symbols for grammar symbols, beginning at the top of the parsed tree and working down. More than simple substitution is required to insert quantifiers and implication symbols, but essentially the process of translating to the formal language bears a great similarity to that of generating a language string from a phrase structure grammar. For each parsing of a sentence, the translation into the formal language results in a unique, unambiguous, well formed formula. An example sentence "All circles are black circles" has only one parsing, which finally translates in the following formal statement:

$$(\forall X_1)[CIR(X_1) \supset (\exists X_2)[CIR(X_2) \& Bk(X_2) \& (X_2 = X_1)]]$$

The structure of this formula is explicit and unambiguous; the relationships between the geometric variables are clearly specified and the truth value may be tested by the predicate evaluator. If true, the answer to the implied question "Are all circles black?" is "Yes."

The predicate evaluator translates from pictures to the formal language. It is designed to accept inputs that have been processed by SADIE, a scanning device. The inputs are limited to three sizes each of triangle, square, or circle, each of which may be in outline or filled in. A technique called "blobbing" is used to distinguish objects resulting from the scan and each such object is then circumscribed with a rectangle. Maximum and minimum x-y coordinates are computed and the ratios of these serve to distinguish triangles from circles or squares. Circles are distinguished from squares on the basis of covering less area. A "black" figure is one whose area is filled in, while a "white" figure is an outline. These relatively simple computations suffice to generate the valid predicates from the picture matrix.

Some of the interesting features of the PLM can be appreciated only by close study of its documentation. For example, the grammar used is a modified phrase structure system with a remarkably compact notation [30]. The problem of ambiguity of syntactic analysis is accepted, and each possible interpretation of the sentence is tested for validity as a well formed formalization. There is a practical scheme for translating at least a small subset of English into the predicate calculus and an equally feasible system for testing the formalization against that resulting from the picture matrix.

8.4.2 Namer. Simmons and Londe [51] programmed a system to generate natural language sentences from line drawings displayed on a matrix. The primary intent of this research was to demonstrate that pattern recognition programs could be used to identify displayed figures and to identify the relationships among them. After this had been established, a language generator was used to generate simple sentences such as "The square is above, to the right of, and larger than the circle." The sentences that are generated are answers to possible explicit relational questions.

The pattern recognition aspects of Namer were derived from work by Uhr and Vossler [62]. When a picture is presented on the input matrix, a set of 96 characteristics is computed. The algorithms or operators compute these as functions of the size, shape, and location of the pattern in the matrix. Typical characteristics that are derived include one-bit indications of the presence or absence of parts of the figure in sections of the matrix, of protuberances, of holes in the pattern (as in a circle), and of indentations as in a "u." A first-level learning stage of Namer selects a small subset of the 96 characteristics that correlate most highly with correct recognition of the name by which the experimenter designates the pattern.

The second level of Namer operates in a comparable fashion to obtain characteristics of the sets of coordinates representing two patterns. At this level, the operators generate characteristics of comparative size, separation, density, height, etc. Subsets of these 96 characteristics are learned in the same fashion as at the earlier level, to correlate with such relation terms as "above," "below," "thicker than," "to the right of," etc.

The language generator uses a very brief phrase structure grammar to generate simple sentences that are true of the picture. For example:

"The dog is beside and to the right of the boy."

"The circle is above the boy."

"The boy is to the left of and taller than the dog."

A great variety of drawings can be learned. Once a relationship is learned between any two figures, the system usually generalizes successfully to most other pairs of figures.

Both the PLM and Namer show the capacity of making geometric inferences based on a set of computational operations on line drawings. Unique sets of characteristics resulting from the computations can be mapped onto English names and words expressing spatial relationships. In this respect these systems anticipate some recently developed inference systems (see later paragraphs on the SQA). The PLM has the additional feature of being able to answer questions about those English language statements permissible in its grammar. Since it can translate from English into a formal statement, the formalization for the question can be compared to that for the proposed answer. By the addition of predicates that go beyond simple spatial relations, the PLM may generalize into a much broader inference system than any yet available.

Namer, on the other hand, is not strictly a question answerer. In order to answer English questions selectively, it would be necessary to match the valid statements that can be generated against an analysis of the specific question. However, Namer offers a probabilistic learning approach for learning names and relationships in a data base. This approach may generalize far beyond spatial relationships and their expression in language and may suggest a method for dealing with inference in nongraphic data bases as well.

8.5   TEXT BASED SYSTEMS

In the previous two sections, question answerers that query a well-structured but limited data base have been described. The text based systems, in contrast, attempt to find answers from ordinary English text. As a consequence, neither the language to be used nor the data to be queried lend themselves to fractionation into convenient small packages of vocabulary or simple syntax. Although current experimental text based systems deal with relatively small amounts of text (from 100,000-500,000 words), they are designed for larger amounts. They resemble information retrieval systems in their use of indexing and term matching techniques, but they deal at the level of English questions and sentences instead of term sets and documents. In addition, the text based question answerer adds linguistic and semantic processing phases to evaluate the material discovered in the retrieval phase. Three such systems will be described here — Protosynthex, the Automatic Language Analyzer, and the General Inquirer.

8.5.1   Protosynthex.   Simmons and McConlogue with linguistic support from Klein [52, 53] have built a system that attempts to answer questions from an encyclopedia. The goal in this system was to accept natural English questions and search a large text to discover the most acceptable sentence, paragraph, or article as an answer. Beginning at the level of ordinary text, Protosynthex makes an index, then uses a synonym dictionary, a complex intersection logic, and a simple information scoring function to select those sentences and paragraphs that most resemble the question. At this point, both the question and the retrieved text are parsed and compared. Retrieved statements whose structure or whose content words do not match those of the question are rejected. A final phase of analysis checks the semantic correspondence of words in the answer with words in the question.

Keypunched natural langue text that has been stored in the computer system is first indexed. An index entry is constructed for each content word in the text. A root-form logic is used to combine entries for words with similar forms. For example, only one index entry exists for "govern," "governor," "government," "governing," etc. Posted against each term entry are a set of VAPS numbers that indicate the *V*olume, *A*rticle, *P*aragraph and *S*entence address of each occurrence of the indexed word.

The first step in answering the question is to look up each of its content words in the index and retrieve all appropriate VAPS numbers. A dictionary of words of related meaning is used to expand the scope of any word in the question to any desired level. Thus the question, "What animals live longer than man?" might result in the following lists of content words as a query to the index.

Query Word	*Words of Related Meaning*
animals	mammals, reptiles, fish
live	age
longer	older, ancient
men	person, people, women

The intersection test finds the smallest unit of text, preferably a sentence, in which the greatest number of query words occur. A simple information score, based on the inverse of the frequency of occurrence of the word in the large sample of text, is used to weight some words more heavily than others in selecting potential answers. All of this computation is done with the VAPS numbers obtained from the index. The highest scoring five or ten potential answers are then retrieved from the tape on which the original text was stored. These constitute an information-rich set of text corresponding to the set of alternatives proposed by the question (within limits of the available text).

The question and the text are then parsed, using a modification of the dependency logic developed by Hays [26]. For example, Figure 8.3 shows the dependency structures of a question and some potential answers that were retrieved. The parsing system learns its own word classes as a result of being given correctly analyzed text. The human operator interacts frequently with this parser to help it avoid errors and ambiguities. In the simple examples in Figure 8.3, the principle of dependency structure matching can be seen. All of the potential answers included "worms" and "eat," the content words from the question. But only those statements in which the dependency of "eat" on "worms" is maintained need be considered further as possible answers.

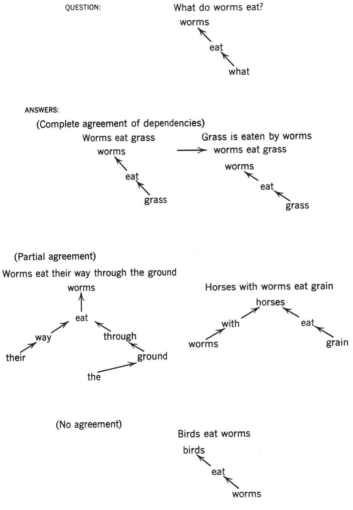

Figure 8.3 Dependency structures of a question and
some potential answers (Protosynthex)

The actual matching is accomplished by a fairly complex set of programs, which build a matrix containing all the words from the question and from its possible answers. The matrix is examined to discover the structure matches and the part of the statement that corresponds to the question word. For the example question, this evaluation program would output as follows:

$$
\begin{array}{lll}
\text{worms} & = & \text{worms} \\
\text{eat} & = & \text{eat} \\
\text{what} & = & \text{grass} \\
\text{what} & = & \text{their way} \\
\text{what} & = & \text{through the ground}
\end{array}
$$

A semantic evaluation system is now required to score each of the words in phrases corresponding to "what." This system is essentially a dictionary lookup whose entries can grow as a function of use. If certain words are found to be answers to "where" questions they will be so coded in the dictionary. If the question had been "Worms eat what food?" the words "ground," "way" and "grass" would have been looked up and compared in semantic coding with "food." Those that corresponded most closely would have been scored as best answers. The semantic evaluation system is still in early stages of experimentation but is expected to resemble the parsing system in that its dictionary will be developed and modified as a function of experience with text under the control of an on-line operator.

The approach of Protosynthex is to filter out successively more and more irrelevant information, leaving only statements that have a high probability of being answers to the question. This system is an attempt to deal with a large and syntactically complex sample of natural text. It is a symbiotic system in which man works with the computer to help resolve both syntactic and semantic ambiguities. Only in this fashion is the program able to overcome the problems associated with multiple, apparently valid interpretations of the same sentence or question.

8.5.2 The Automatic Language Analyzer (ALA). From Indiana University, a series of reports [27, 60] by Householder *et al.*, and Thorne describe the progress toward completion of a rather complicated automatic language analysis system.* This system is designed to handle the breadth and complexity of language found in a book on astronomy. As a question answering system, it introduces a variation of the principle of translating from English into an intermediate language that bears a strong

---

*For the sake of convenience, this has been abbreviated to the ALA system and the present summary is based on the final report by Thorne.

relationship to dependency structure. When translated to the intermediate language, FLEX, the question or text is also augmented by semantic
codes obtained from *Roget's Thesaurus*—or from a specially constructed
thesaurus. The degree of matching between question and text is then computed to select a best answer.

The primary information store for the ALA is a preanalyzed set of
sentences stored on tape. The preanalysis includes assignment of FLEX codes
and of thesaurus references. The thesaurus is a list of clusters, each of
which indexes the portions of the text in which members of the cluster
appear. A dictionary of word-stems and phrases provides cross references
to clusters in which the word appears. The question is analyzed and assigned FLEX and thesaurus codes; sentences are selected and matched;
and the paragraphs that contain sentences supposedly answering the
question are printed out with their scores.

English is transformed into the FLEX language by looking up each
word in a dictionary to assign ordinary syntactic word classes. Special
routines, using additional cues available in the sentence, resolve word-
class ambiguity. The words are ordered into clauses and phrases and the
accuracy of this ordering is checked. The breaking into clauses is accomplished by the use of marker words such as verbs and absolute markers
such as "because," "how," "if," "when," etc. When the sentence has
been analyzed into subject, verb, and their qualifiers, the translation into
FLEX is accomplished as shown below:

> The old man ate stale food reluctantly.
>
> | $S1$ | $S2$ | $P1$ | $P2$ | $P3$ |
> |------|------|------|------|------|
> | man | old | ate | food | stale |
> | | | | reluctantly | |

The notation is to be read, "$S1$ means subject, $S2$ is the first qualifier, $P1$
means the verb, and $P2, \ldots, Pn$ refer to verb modifiers." The importance
to the sentence of each FLEX symbol is rated separately for subject and
predicate in order of the numbers assigned. Thus an $S1$ or a $P1$ are most
heavily weighted in the later comparison process.

Each word also carries a semantic coding. This code is simply a list of
the thesaurus clusters in which it is found. For semantic matching of
words a and b, the following formula is used:

$$\text{Semantic Correlation} = \frac{n_{ab}}{[(n_a)(n_b)]^{1/2}}$$

where n_a and n_b are respectively the number of clusters in which a and b
are found, and n_{ab} is the number they share in common. When a question

and a sentence are matched, "mutual relevance" is scored* by considering the following three comparisons in a weighting scheme:

1. Relative importance of the category (i.e., $S1$ or $P1$ more important than $S2\ P2$).
2. Match of FLEX category ($S1\ =\ S2$ better than $S1\ =\ S3$, etc.).
3. Cluster matching score (according to the formula above).

The paragraphs containing the best scoring sentences and their scores are then recovered and printed out.

Although programming of this system is apparently not yet completed, and it may be claimed that the FLEX transformation leaves much to be desired as an intermediate language, the ALA is unquestionably one of the more ambitious and sophisticated systems so far described. How well the semantic correlation will correspond to meaning matches between statements needs to be established. In any case, ALA is a clearly formulated realization of what has hitherto been a rather vague idea that a thesaurus may be helpful in question answering.

8.5.3   The General Inquirer.   A paper by Stone [56] describes a COMIT program system useful for analyzing the content of text. As a question answerer, the General Inquirer recovers all sentences containing a given set of concepts. As in the Householder-Thorne ALA, a thesaurus is used for coding words as to concept membership and, if desired, an intermediate language may be used which makes explicit the syntax of the text and question. However, the General Inquirer differs from most of the systems so far described in that syntactic manipulations are done as a manual pre-editing phase for the text and the questions.

Probably the most interesting feature about these programs is the dictionary and thesaurus operation. The thesaurus is built especially for the content to be studied. For example, a thesaurus for psychological studies includes headings such as "Person," "Behavioral Process," "Qualities," etc. As subheadings under "Behavioral Process," such cluster tags as the following are found: "react," "see," "hear," "smell," "defend," "dream," "escape," etc. For an anthropological study, the thesaurus would contain many different headings.

The dictionary includes about 3,000 common English words and words of special interest to any particular investigation. The dictionary lookup is accomplished by first filtering out function words such as "and," "or," "to," "of," etc., then looking up the remaining portion of text (about 50 per cent) in the complete dictionary. Each of the words in the main dic-

*For other associative scoring techniques see Doyle [16].

tionary is defined by the thesaurus tags or clusters to which it belongs. Thus, the dictionary entry for "abandon" has the following format:

ABANDON = GO + REJECT + END + DANGER + ALONE

In the processing phase, each word in the text to be examined may be tagged by its cluster memberships and matched against the terms of the request.

Content analyses may be as simple as frequency counts of tag concepts in a discourse or they may be requests for all sentences in the discourse with the tags "reject" and "person." A great deal of useful analysis can be accomplished using just the semantic portion of the General Inquirer. However, to avoid apparent matches that are structurally dissimilar (as in the overworked example, "man bites dog" versus "dog bites man"), a syntactic analysis is often desirable.

The following semantic-syntactic categories are used in the manual pre-editing phase:

1. Subject and incorporated modifiers
2. Nonincorporated subject modifiers
3. Predicate verbs
4. Verb modifiers including time referents
5. Object and incorporated modifiers
6. Nonincorporated object modifiers
7. Indirect object and modifiers
8. Attributive nouns
9. Attributive verbs

The use of these codes is indicated in the following example (from a suicide note).

IN THE LAST/4 WEEK/4 A NUMBER/1 OF OCCURRENCES/1 HAVE FORCED/3 ME/5 INTO A POSITION/4 + WHERE I/8 FEEL/9 MY LIFE/1 IS NOT WORTH/3 CONTINUING/3.

The " + " separates two clauses that were coded as separate "thought sequences." For the case of pronouns or ellipses, the referent words are added in parentheses. The grammar distinguishes between metaphrases such as "I feel that" and declarative statements about apparent facts.* Like the Householder-Thorne ALA, the General Inquirer finds that a limited syntactic analysis is sufficient for its purpose.

Additional applications of the General Inquirer or simulations of it can

---

*With codes 8 and 9, "attributive" meaning "metaphrase."

be found in North [40] and Ford [17]. It has already proved itself useful in supporting several types of content analysis.

8.5.4 Remarks on Text Based Systems. The three text based systems described introduce some principles not usually dealt with in data base systems. The first of these is a semantic principle of indexing large bodies of text at a depth such that words in a question or their semantic tags can serve as queries to the index. The text processors each faced the problem of bringing explicit organization into the relatively loose flow of ordinary English, and each attempts to solve it by use of some combination of indexing, and syntactic and semantic analysis. The dependency structure matching principle of Protosynthex, and translation into the FLEX language of ALA, or the "thought sequences" of the General Inquirer are examples of analyses that go beyond the purely syntactic. In all three systems, additional semantic coding is explicitly undertaken. The data organization in each of these systems is distributed among indexes, thesauruses, and synonym dictionaries, and among the rules for text analysis. Although information categories are overlapping (rather than unique as in the data base questioners), a strong data organization is present in text based systems.

8.5.5 Other Text Questioners. Swanson [57] has attempted to measure the effectiveness of natural language queries for retrieving documents. Salton has considered aspects of the structure-matching principle and means for measuring its degree in a given pair of sentences [49]. Giuliano [19] and Spiegel [55] have given a great deal of consideration to the use of word associations as a basis for question answering and retrieval systems. Associative indexing may also prove a valuable adjunct to other techniques of comparing questions and their answers. The association nets described by Doyle [16] offer an interesting approach toward question answering. Finally, the whole area of classification systems, auto-abstracting, and document retrieval can be expected to contribute increasingly toward the development of general purpose question answerers.*

8.6 LOGICAL INFERENCE SYSTEMS

Transformation from subsets of English to formulation is represented by six (five of which are recent developments) question answering pro-

*See also a recent discussion by Robinson [47].

grams. The earliest work in this area, reported by Williams [65], concerned translating from natural English to the predicate calculus. More recent work by Williams [64] and a series of papers by Bohnert [5, 6] develop algorithms for translating from important small subsets of English into predicate calculus forms. Bohnert's Project LOGOS has developed computer programs that translate samples of English ranging from a simple language to be used in a marriage bureau to a "war novel" command language.

The five most recently developed question answering systems use explicit rules of logical or mathematical inference. Four of these are associated with artificial intelligence or linguistic laboratories at M.I.T. All are programmed in forms of COMIT or LISP, and all suggest a line of descent from McCarthy's Advice Taker model [39] and bear a relationship to the family of problem-solving and theorem-proving systems.

8.6.1 The Darlington Logic Programs.   A series of COMIT programs by Darlington [14, 15] at the M.I.T. Mechanical Translation Laboratory translate a subset of English into various forms of the propositional and predicate calculi, then test the validity of arguments using a modification of the Davis-Putnam algorithm. The propositional system is able to discover clause separations and so recognize propositions using only an elementary type of syntactic analysis. A more complete phrase structure analysis is accomplished in programs concerned with translating relational statements into the predicate calculus.

The first phase of the translation is a dictionary lookup, which assigns one of two word classes to each word in the text. A word is either a P for punctuation or a W for all other types. The P type words are such words as "if," "then," "and," "or," "but," "therefore," "either," "neither," "nor," "that," and several others that have significance as logical separators. Additional word class subscripts are assigned subsequently. The P words are further subcategorized as to the type of connection or separation that they perform and as to the particular subroutine to be called for special processing. For example, "or," "nor," and "and" call a special subroutine that looks for "either ... or," "neither ... nor," and "and ... both," respectively. The W words are assigned syntactic word classes such as "noun plural," "auxiliary verb," "adjective," "gerund," etc.

Verbs and gerunds are simplified into abbreviated infinitive forms (to be = be), and some sentences are expanded. For example, "The box and the chair are wooden" is processed into the transform, "The box be wooden and the chair be wooden." Every string of W words separated by a P word is then examined to determine if it is a sentence. These strings qualify as sentences only if each contains at least one noun and one verb. Propositional symbols such as A/V, B/V, etc., are then substituted for each string of W words followed by a P word. These strings are then compared and, where identical, are assigned the same propositional symbol.

Each proposition is then parenthesized according to a fairly complex set of priority rules in accordance with the P words that separate them. The output is then ready to feed into the program, which uses the modified Davis-Putnam algorithm to test the validity of the propositions. The modifications to this algorithm simplify and speed up the process of testing consistency by eliminating redundant clauses.

In the functional logic translation program, sentences are parsed into a phrase structure tree whose nodes are labeled in a manner that makes transformation to quasilogical formulae a simple process. For example, the sentence "All circles are figures" transforms into the quasilogical formula, "All $+$ Variable A $+$ Noun Phrase $1A$ $+$ is $+$ some $+$ Variable A $+$ Noun Phrase $2A$." This formula is then transformed to the logical format by looking up its elements in a table of equivalents. The logical analysis proceeds through three levels. At the most detailed level, all elements of the sentence will have been transformed into relational terms and existence assertions. Darlington is presently working toward the development of an algorithm which the system can use to choose automatically the level of analysis required to prove or disprove the argument.

The Darlington system can be appreciated as a specialized question answerer, which tests a verbal argument for internal consistency. The example "All circles are figures. Therefore all who draw circles draw figures" was translated into logical form and proved valid in a total of about 0.3 minutes. (Note that "Do all who draw circles draw figures?" is the question that is being answered.)

Weaknesses of the Darlington System are the usual ones of limited ability to handle such complexities of English as pronomial reference, ellipsis, metaphor, etc., and its use of a tiny subset of the language. Its approach to syntactic analysis tends to be rather rough-and-ready, using assumptions that oversimplify the problem and cast some doubts on the generality of the solutions. However, the system does exemplify a well rounded attack on the problem of translating a small segment of English into logical notation and then evaluating the arguments. It indicates quite clearly that logical translators are an interesting and profitable line of research toward the aim of high quality language processing by computers.

8.6.2 **The Cooper System.** An elegant example of translation from simple English statements into Aristotelian logic has been programmed in COMIT by Cooper [11]. This system accepts a small subset of statements such as "Magnesium is a metal," "Gasoline burns rapidly," and "Magnesium oxide is a white metallic oxide." Such statements, or questions in the same form, are translated into one of the four basic Aristotelian sentence types, "All x is y, no x is y, some x is y, and not all x is y." The resulting logical form is tested for deducibility from the information already in the system.

Cooper very carefully defines the subset of English and of English grammar with which he is working. This subset includes adjectives, modifying nouns, substantives, "is" predicates, and intransitive verb predicates. He also defines a logical language L^*. Within this logical language, a certain amount of syllogistic inference is possible. The translation algorithm includes phases of syntactic analysis and transformation into forms belonging to L^*. The process of parsing and transformation is comparable to those already described in the Darlington system and the Kirsch PLM [29]. The system correctly answers "false" to the assertion "sodium chloride is salt," "salt is compound," and "elements are not compounds." It also discovers that the assertion "magnesium is a metal that burns rapidly" is true, after finding in its information store that "magnesium is a metal" and "magnesium burns rapidly."

Cooper's system translates from a subset of English into Aristotelian syllogistic logic; its obvious limitations in the generality of the approach, the usefulness of the subset of English, and the efficiency of the proof algorithm do not detract from the propaedeutic value of a system simply devised and clearly executed.

In this area of translation from natural language to logical formalisms, books by Reichenbach [46] and Copi [12] are basic texts. Recent papers by Kochen [33], Krulee [34] and Travis [61] discuss important aspects of the problem of building question answering systems based on formal languages.

8.6.3 The Specific Question Answerer (SQA). Black [2] has programmed the SQA to find brief answers to short English questions. It is called a Specific Question Answerer because it can extract only brief specific answers that are either directly stated in or deducible from its corpus of text. The program consists of a basic system written in LISP and a corpus containing formal and informal rules of inference as well as declarative statements. In most of his examples, Black avoids the problems of syntactic analysis by requiring exact matching of structure between questions and possible answers. (In the latest version, the input is in a formal language.)

The corpus is organized as a set of conditional statements of the form,

"If ..., then ... ." A declarative statement such as "Mercury is a planet" is considered to be a conditional with an empty antecedent. A typical corpus is made up of such declarative statements and such complete conditionals as the following:

Mercury is next smaller than Pluto
Pluto is next smaller than Mars
Mars is next smaller than Venus
If X is next smaller than Y, then X is smaller than Y.
If X is next smaller than Y and Y is smaller than Z then X is smaller than Z.

Primitives of the system include variables such as X, Y, etc.; words (which include variables as well as English words such as "Mars," "Venus," "is," "next," etc.); and phrases, which are strings of words.

The system compares a question with each of the consequents in the corpus. For example, the question "What is next smaller than Pluto?" matches immediately with the first consequent of the corpus, "Mercury is next smaller than Pluto." If the question is "Pluto is smaller than what?," the answering process is more difficult. In this case, there are two matches with the consequents, "X is smaller than Y" and "X is smaller than Z." The word "Pluto" may immediately be substituted for X in each consequent. The first antecedents for each of these two consequents are then used as questions, i.e., "If Pluto is next smaller than Y and Y is smaller than Z" for the first question and "If Pluto is next smaller than Y (then Pluto is smaller than Y)" for the second. (Parentheses indicate that the enclosure is not an antecedent.) It will be left as a tree-searching exercise for the reader to follow the resulting net to obtain the answers, "Mars" and "Venus."

Recent work with minor modifications to this program has shown that it can solve at least some of the Advice Taker problems [39]. Black has also suggested that the parsing of English syntax may be dealt with by conditional substitutions. For example, one question transformation is "If X is a Y, then is X a Y." This rule transforms from one form of question to one form of declarative statement. To what extent such a transformational approach will actually account for English syntax remains to be supported by experimental evidence. Although the inference approach is undeniably powerful, two drawbacks remain. The first is that the SQA requires an exhaustive search of the network of matching consequents, and with even a few hundred consequents the time requirement must be very large. The second is the apparent requirement that the corpus of consequents be internally consistent. However, Black has suggested approaches toward easing these difficulties.

8.6.4 The Semantic Information Retriever (SIR). From the point of view of exploring a model of meaning as communicated in natural language, Raphael [45] has built a program that accepts a class of simple English statements and, in interaction with the questioner, answers some questions about them. The model considers English words as objects and certain relationships as holding between them. The formalization of the model is a limited relational calculus. The model also takes advantage of the property list characteristics of LISP. Although only a few meanings are specifically dealt with, Raphael suggests that by modeling words in their interrelationships, the meaning is preserved for a human reader.

This program avoids the complexities of syntactic analysis by limiting itself to a small number of fixed formats for sentences. The present system recognizes about 20 simple sentence formats, which include both interrogative and declarative types. By comparison with these basic patterns, an input sentence such as "Every boy is a person" is translated into the logical form:

SETR   (Boy Person).

This means that "person" is in a superset relation to "boy." If a sentence or question does not correspond to a known format, it is rejected by the program with an appropriate comment to the operator.

Figure 8.4 shows a set of example inputs to this program and the resulting data structure for them. In answering the question, "How many fingers are on John?" the system is able to match the question form "(finger, John)" successively with "(finger, hand)," "(hand, person, 2),", "(John, boy)" and "(boy, person)." The "How many" requirement was not fully satisfied, so it asks for further information. With the additional data "(finger, hand, 5)" in the numerical part-whole relation, it is able to calculate the answer: 10.

The Raphael program is another example of a system that uses a limited set of logical predicates such as subset, part-whole, left-right, etc., to allow study of deducing or inferring answers to questions. Like the Black program, this one essentially ignores syntactic problems, and depends on internally consistent data. However, Raphael's model tests a sentence for consistency before accepting it as data and it also makes explicit the interaction with the questioner.

Both the SQA and SIR are examples of deductive systems that understand some aspects of the meaning of words. They put particular emphasis on various relational terms and use rules of logical inference to follow trees of axioms and theorems. In both cases, if the statement form of the input question can be deduced from information in memory, the answer

INPUT STATEMENTS:	FORMALIZATION:
Every boy is a person	SETR (Boy, Person)
John is a boy	SETR (John, Boy)
Any person has two hands	PARTRN (Hand, Person, 2)
A finger is part of a hand	PARTR (Finger, Hand)
QUESTION:	
How many fingers are on John?	PARTRNQ (Finger, John)
COMPUTER RESPONSE:	
How many fingers per hand?	
INPUT STATEMENT:	
Every hand has five fingers	PARTRN (Finger, Hand, 5)
ANSWER:	
The Answer is 10	

Figure 8.4. An example from the Raphael program

is "Yes;" if its negation is deduced, the answer is "No." If the statement cannot be deduced, the answer is "Don't know." SIR recognizes when information is missing and requests it, but is limited to those relational terms for which it has corresponding functional routines. The SQA seems to be a more general approach, in that it can accept a very broad range of relational terms without the necessity of reprogramming. That is, the SQA, following the Advice Taker paradigm, allows the question asker to program the machine by giving it additional information. Both systems provide relatively simple and comparatively efficient algorithms for deducing answers to questions.

8.6.5 Student. Bobrow [3], for an M.I.T. doctoral thesis, has programmed an algebra problem solver that accepts problems phrased in a limited subset of English and transforms these into equations, which can be solved arithmetically. The limited subset of English is mainly sufficient to account for the phrasing found in a high school algebra text. The system is programmed in LISP and is currently operable on the time-shared 7094 computer system at M.I.T.'s Project MAC.

Student is based on a theoretical relational model whose objects are variables such as words, numbers, or phrases that name numbers. The relations are the ordinary arithmetic operations of adding, subtracting, multiplying, dividing, exponentiation, equality, etc. The means for expressing the relations among objects are sets of simultaneous equations. The problem that Student attacks is that of transforming a set of English statements in which a set of equations is implicit into an explicit formulation of those equations.

Background data, which help Student to "understand" the meaning of certain words and phrases, are provided by a part of the system that accepts simple English statements such as "twice always means two times" or "three feet equals one yard." This subprogram builds what is essentially a dictionary of transformations from one form of English into an equivalent formalism that the program can use, or into a form identical with one used previously in a problem.

Bobrow's first step in transforming an English statement into a set of equations is to make mandatory substitutions such as "two times" for "twice," "square" for "the square of," and several others. His next step is to identify terms such as "plus," "percent," "times," etc., and to tag them as operators. In addition to tagging operators in this phase, the program identifies certain verbs, question words, and the terminal question mark. The process is accomplished by dictionary lookup. After these operations, an example problem appears as follows:

IF THE NUMBER (OF/OP) CUSTOMERS TOM (GETS/ VERB) IS 2 (TIMES/OP 1) THE (SQUARE/OP 1) 20 (PER- CENT/OP 2) (OF/OP) THE NUMBER (OF/OP) ADVER- TISEMENTS (HE/PRO) RUNS, AND THE NUMBER (OF/ OP) ADVERTISEMENTS (HE/PRO) RUNS IS 45, (WHAT/ QWORD) IS THE NUMBER (OF/OP) CUSTOMERS TOM (GETS/VERB) (QMARK/DLM)

A most critical phase of the processing is the next step, in which two simple heuristics are used for breaking the problem statement into simple sentences. The first is to look for an "if" followed by anything, followed by a comma, followed by a question word, and transform it to two sentences. For example, "If ... customers Tom gets ... is 45, what is ... Q MARK" transforms to "... customers Tom gets ... is 45. What is ... Q MARK." The second heuristic, applied after the first, is to divide strings followed by "and" into two simple sentences. Following these operations the following simple sentences result from the example above:

THE NUMBER *OF* CUSTOMERS TOM *GETS* IS 2 *TIMES* THE *SQUARE* 20 *PERCENT OF* THE NUMBER *OF* AD- VERTISEMENTS *HE* RUNS.

THE NUMBER *OF* ADVERTISEMENTS *HE* RUNS IS 45.

WHAT IS THE NUMBER *OF* CUSTOMERS TOM *GETS*
QMARK

The operators and function terms are underlined in the above sentences.

All of the simple sentences are now of the form, "*P*1 is *P*2." In the first sentence, *P*1 represents "The number of customers Tom gets" and *P*2 is the remainder following "is." (In cases of sentences in the form "*X* does/has *Y*" the program transforms them to "The thing *X* does/has is *Y*.")

Each of the operators now calls for a special function to be performed. For example (OF/OP) checks to see if "of" is immediately preceded by a number; in that case it is treated as the multiplication operator. Otherwise, its operator tag is stripped off and ignored. A (PERCENT/OP 2) looks at the preceding number and divides it by 100. Other such operators not only are more complicated but require consideration of precedence levels. The result of applying these operations is to put the equations into the explicit form that LISP can use in solving them.

Many hazards may still exist to block the explicitness of the equations. Because of pronouns, ellipses, shifts in measuring units (as from feet to inches, or from dollars to cents), or because of synonymic references such as "people" for "customers," the variables and units in the equations may not match. If these difficulties arise, Student takes recourse to its memory of background data, which can be manipulated by the user to provide unit transformations, sentence transforms, and synonyms. Heuristics for guessing the referent of pronouns are also provided.

There are numerous interesting features about Student, not the least of which are its use of a fund of background information and its substitution of a heuristic approach to sentence analysis for the more usual analytic one. The meaning of a problem is first resolved into simple sentence units, then into variables and operators. The meaning of the operators is the function they cause to be performed. For variables, the only pertinent question is "does the string *Pi* identically correspond to the string *Pj*." If not, possible transformations are considered to bring about such a result.

Although the system is obviously limited to a well controlled, specialized subset of English, it has proved sufficiently versatile to solve a large number of high school algebra word problems. It contributes significantly to language processing technology in its heuristic approach to syntactic analysis, its use of background information, and its direct approach toward translating a small class of English operator words into their mathematical equivalents.

8.7 ANALYSIS AND CONCLUSIONS

Although the question answerers described express a wide variety of approaches, there are striking similarities in processing requirements. A strong organization of data storage is a common requirement. Even in the case of English text questioners, an additional phase of index processing is usual to obtain this degree of organization. The language must be analyzed syntactically and, in the more sophisticated systems, semantic analysis is also required. Question and data are transformed into some canonical form and a matching and sometimes a scoring is undertaken to determine whether or not an answer is present. In the list-structured data base systems, the output is usually a list of the matching terms from the lists that were the referent of the question. In addition, for each of the systems, there may be a level of inference-drawing, although only a few make this level explicit.

8.7.1 Data Organization.   The data base programs understand text and/or questions by transforming them into the categories and subcategories of a well structured data storage system. Usually, this data system is in terms of lists in which each headlist has sublists organized by attributes and values. The chief advantage of this structure is that a given item may be a member of many lists that address it (and so interrelate it), while the item need be recorded only once. The papers by Lindsay [37] and by Thompson [58] make explicit the value and importance of coding information by the structure in which it is embedded. The resulting structural relations permit some degree of inference.

In the text processing programs, the natural English language text has an additional organization imposed upon it through a preprocessing indexing, usually supported by lists of synonyms and a dictionary of concept codes. The data structure in these systems is less explicit and less centralized but quite as essential as in the list structured data base programs.

8.7.2 Syntactic Analysis.   Although this paper has not emphasized the description of the special techniques of syntactic analysis, it is an important phase in all question answering systems—even in those where simplifying assumptions are used to avoid it. Generally an immediate constituent model is used and generally the problem of ambiguous interpretations is encountered. In the data base systems, where a small subset of English constitutes the vocabulary, the problems of ambiguity sometimes can be resolved in terms of the referent data structures. In the text processing systems, great effort is taken to resolve syntactic ambiguity before attempting to answer the question. Whether either of these approaches to resolving problems of ambiguity will prove successful remains to be shown.

8.7.3 Semantic Analysis. The phase of a question answering program devoted to semantic analysis is often not clear-cut and usually merges into the syntactic analysis and matching phases. In the data base systems, the meaning of a word is usually the denotation of either a data category or of a subroutine. This meaning is typically a coded entry associated with the word in a dictionary. In the text processing systems, the meaning of a word is generally a list of attribute codes (as the Roget cluster numbers in the Householder-Thorne ALA). By controlling syntactic correspondence, the correlation or commonalities of meaning for corresponding words in two statements can be measured in terms of corresponding codes and can be accumulated across the sentences.

While semantic analysis is much more clearly understandable in terms of the data base systems, it is apparent that not all subtleties of language can map onto an unambiguously defined data structure. The matter of coding the meanings of words and calculating the meanings of sentences is an area in which only the dimmest of understanding currently exists. However, theoretical work by Katz and Fodor [28] and by Quillian [43] suggests approaches, and a direct attack on problems of meaning is probably most profitable.

8.7.4 Obtaining and Evaluating Answers. Syntactic and semantic analyses are undertaken to transform the question and the answering text into some canonical form in which they can be easily compared. Generally this form is a syntactically ordered list of the semantic units with which the system deals. In the data base systems, the standard form is a set of list names; in the text processors the units may be English words, their synonyms, or semantic codes corresponding to words or terms. Several of the more recent systems use something approaching the format of the predicate calculus as a standard form.

However, even when both question and answer exist in canonical form, there are still serious problems in comparing the two. In the data base systems, the problem is processing the data structure and, in some cases, making inferences (such as the fact that if X and Y are "offsprings" of the same parent they are siblings, or whether 300,000 is more than 100,000). In the text processing systems, good comparisons of questions and possible answers demand far better semantic coding than has been developed, plus a much increased understanding of how to order the units for comparison. Although these systems are also potentially adept at making language inferences (by generating and answering additional questions and by using dictionaries of rules of linguistic inference), actual experiments in this direction are largely lacking.

In Kirsch's PLM and Thompson's DEACON systems, the meaning of a statement is accumulated, substructure by substructure, and the result is finally tested for truth value. In Student, the portions of meaning pertinent to solving the algebra problem are accumulated until a well formed mathematical formulation is available. These systems certainly suggest the way in which meaning (as far as a particular machine function is concerned) can be extracted and accumulated. However, to generalize these suggestions to a fairly large set of English words and constructions remains a formidable task for the future.

8.7.5 Outlook.* Although research on question answering systems has been conducted for only slightly more than five years, enough important principles are understood to offer assurance that the next five or ten years will be even more rewarding. The large data base system, controlled and queried by a small subset of English that can vary freely, offers the most immediate promise. Until now data base systems have worked with a very limited variety of data. The time seems ripe to experiment with systems having a wide variety of data in their structure. Unavoidably, such systems would be rather large, but all indications of data base research to this time indicate that their problems can be mastered.

The outlook for text processing systems is also promising, but it would be overoptimistic to expect any developmental model with practical utility for some time to come. Questions of semantic coding, of accumulating and representing the meaning of statements, and of performing inference effectively are still very much in the initial research stage. The two existing general systems (Protosynthex and the ALA) are intriguing early demonstrations of ultimately valuable language processors. Systems that study question answering methods by using rules of inference are a most recent and potentially attractive feature of the language processor, but a great deal of research into rules of logico-linguistic inference and into methods of translating from English into clarifying forms such as the predicate calculus remains to be done.

In summary, steady—even rapid—progress is being made toward the development of practical question answerers and general language processors. The most difficult questions are now becoming apparent. How does one characterize the meaning of a sentence? How are ambiguous interpretations, both syntactic and semantic, to be dealt with? How are

---

*Two recent surveys that augment this work, by Simmons and by Bobrow, *et al.* have been published in the 1966 and 1967 *Annual Review of Information Science and Technology* edited by C. Cuadra.

inferences to be made without exhaustive tree searches? How are partial answers, widely separated in the text, to be combined? To what extent can we or should we translate from English into formal languages? Can these studies be attacked from a theoretical point of view or do they yield best to the empirical approach of building large question answerers and language processors as test vehicles? Even partial answers to these questions will contribute to the eventual development of high quality, general purpose language processors.

REFERENCES

1. Belnap, N. D., Jr., An analysis of questions: preliminary report, *TM-1287*. Santa Monica, Calif.: System Development Corp., June 1963.

2. Black, F. S., A deductive question-answering system. Ph.D. thesis, Harvard U., Cambridge, Mass., June 1964.

3. Bobrow, D. G., Natural language input for a computer problem-solving system, *MAC-TR-1*, September 1964. (Also available as Ph.D. thesis, M.I.T., Cambridge, Mass., 1964.)

4. Bobrow, D. G., Syntactic analysis of English by computer—a survey. *AFIPS* Conference Proceedings, v. 24, Fall Joint Computer Conference. Baltimore: Spartan Books, 1963, pp. 365-87.

5. Bohnert, H. G., Logical-linguistic studies for machine text perusal, Semianual technical status report, May-December 1963, Project LOGOS. Yorktown Heights, N. Y.: IBM.

6. Bohnert, H. G., An English-like extension of an applied predicate calculus, *AFOSR-TN-62-3*. Yorktown Heights, N. Y. : IBM, February 1962.

7. Cheatham, T. E., Jr., and S. Warshall, Translation of retrieval requests couched in a "semiformal" English-like language, *Comm. of the ACM*, v. 5, no. 1, 1962, pp. 34-39.

8. Cohen, D., A recognition algorithm for a grammar model, National Bureau of Standards Report *7883*. Washington: Department of Commerce, 1962.

9. Cohen, D., Picture processing in a picture language machine, National Bureau of Standards Report *7885*. Washington: Department of Commerce, April 1962.

10. Cohen F., What is a question?, *Monist*, v. 39, 1929, pp. 350-64.

11. Cooper, W. S., Fact retrieval and deductive question-answering information retrieval systems, *J. of the ACM*, v. 11, no. 2, 1964, pp. 117-37.

12. Copi, I., *Symbolic Logic*. New York: MacMillan, 1959.

13. Craig, J. A., Grammatical aspects of a system for natural man-machine communication, *RM63TMP-31*. Santa Barbara, Calif.: General Electric Co., July 1963.

14. Darlington, J. L., A COMIT program for the Davis-Putnam algorithm, Research Laboratory, Electronics Mechanical Translation Group, M.I.T., Cambridge, Mass., May 1962.

15. Darlington, J. L., Translating ordinary language into symbolic logic, *MAC-M-149*. Cambridge, Mass.: M.I.T., March 1964.

16. Doyle, L. B., The microstatistics of text, *Information Storage and Retrieval*, v. 1, no. 4, 1963, pp. 189-214.

17. Ford, J. D., Jr., Automatic detection of psychological dimensions in psychotherapy, *SP-1220*. Santa Monica, Calif.: System Development Corp., July 1963.

18. Gardner, M., *Logic Machines and Diagrams*. New York: McGraw-Hill, 1958.

19. Giuliano, V. E., Studies for the design of English command and control language system, Report *CACL-1*. Cambridge, Mass.: Arthur D. Little, June 1962.

20. Green, B. F., Jr., A. K. Wolf, C. Chomsky, and K. Laughery, Baseball: an automatic question answerer, in E. A. Feigenbaum and J. Feldman (eds.), *Computers and Thought*. New York: McGraw-Hill, 1963, pp. 207-16.

21. Green, L. E. S., E. C. Berkeley, and C. Gotlieb, Conversation with a computer, *Computers and Automation*, v. 8, no. 10, 1959, pp. 9-11.

22. Hamblin, C. L., Questions, *The Australian J. of Philosophy*, v. 36, no. 3, 1958, pp. 160-68.

23. Hamblin, C. L., Questions aren't statements, *Philosophy of Science*, v. 30, 1963, pp. 62-63.

24. Harrah, D., A logic of questions and answers, *Philosophy of Science*, v. 28, no. 1, 1961, pp. 40-46.

25. Harris, Z. S., *String Analysis of Sentence Structure*. The Hague, Netherlands: Moulton and Co., 1962.

26. Hays, D. G., Automatic language data processing, in H. Borko (ed.), *Computer Applications in the Behavioral Sciences*. Englewood Cliffs, N. J.: Prentice-Hall, 1962. pp. 394-423.

27. Householder, F. W., Jr., and J. Lyons, and/or J. P. Thorne, First to seventh quarterly reports on automatic language analysis, ASTIS, Indiana University, Bloomington, Ind., 1960-62.

28. Katz, J. J. and J. A. Fodor, The structure of a semantic theory, *Language*, Part I, v. 39, no. 2, 1963, pp. 170-210.

29. Kirsch, R. A., Computer interpretation of English text and picture patterns, *IEEE Trans. on Electronic Computers*, August 1964.

30. Kirsch, R. A., and B. K. Rankin III, Modified simple phrase structure grammars for grammatical induction, National Bureau of Standards Report *7890*. Washington: Department of Commerce, May 1963.

31. Kirsch, R. A., The application of automata theory to problems in information retrieval (with selected bibliography), National Bureau of Standards Report *7882*. Washington: Department of Commerce, March 1963.

32. Kirsch, R. A., L. C. Ray, L. Cahn, and G. H. Urban, Experiments in processing pictorial information with a digital computer, National Bureau of Standards Report *5713*. Washington: Department of Commerce, December 1957.

33. Kochen, M., Adaptive mechanisms in digital "concept" processing, *Proc. AIEE*, Joint Automatic Control Conference, 1962, pp. 50-59.

34. Krulee, G. K., D. J. Kuck, D. M. Landi, and D. M. Manelski, A problem-solving system with natural language inputs, Technical Institute, Northwestern U., 1962.

35. Kuno, S., and A. G. Oettinger, Syntactic structure and ambiguity in English, *AFIPS Conference Proceedings*, v. 24, 1963, Fall Joint Computer Conference. Baltimore: Spartan Books, pp. 397-418.

36. Lees, R. B., The grammar of English nominalizations, (monograph), *International J. of Amer. Linguistics*, Part II, v. 26, no. 3, 1960.

37. Lindsay, R. K., Inferential memory as the basis of machines which understand natural language, in E. A. Feigenbaum and J. Feldman, (eds.), *Computers and Thought.* New York: McGraw-Hill, 1963, pp. 217-33.

38. MacKay, D. M., The informational analysis of questions and commands, in C. Cherry, (ed.), *Information Theory, Fourth London Symposium.* Washington: Butterworths, 1961, pp. 469-77.

39. McCarthy, J., Programs with common sense, *Proc. of Symposium on Mechanisation of Thought Processes,* Part I. London: H. M. S. O., 1959, pp. 75-91.

40. North, R. C., *et al.,* A system of automated content analysis of documents. Report by the Stanford Studies in International Conflict and Integration, Stanford U., Stanford, Calif., March 1963.

41. Ogden, C. K., *The General Basic English Dictionary.* New York: W. W. Norton and Company, 1962.

42. Phillips, A. V., A question-answering routine, Memo *16.* Cambridge, Mass.: M.I.T. Artificial Intelligence Project, May 1960.

43. Quillian, R., A notation for representing conceptual information: An application to semantics and mechanical English paraphrasing, *SP-1395.* Santa Monica, Calif.: System Development Corp., October 1963.

44. Rankin, B. K., III, A programmable grammar for a fragment of English for use in an information retrieval system, National Bureau of Standards Report *7352.* Washington: Department of Commerce, June 1961.

45. Raphael, B., SIR: A computer program for semantic information retrieval, *MAC-TR-2,* also available as Ph.D. thesis, M.I.T., Cambridge, Mass., June 1964.

46. Reichenbach, H., *Elements of Symbolic Logic.* New York: MacMillan, 1947.

47. Robinson, J. J., Automatic parsing and fact retrieval: a comment on grammar, paraphrase and meaning, *RM-4005-PR.* Santa Monica, Calif.: The RAND Corp., February 1964.

48. Sable, J. D., Use of semantic structure in information systems, *Comm. of the ACM,* v. 5, no. 1, 1962, pp. 40-42.

49. Salton, G., Manipulation of trees in information retrieval, *Comm. of the ACM,* v. 5, no. 2, 1962, pp. 103-14.

50. Sillars, W., An algorithm for representing English sentences in a formal language, National Bureau of Standards Report *7884.* Washington: Department of Commerce, April 1963.

51. Simmons, R. F., and D. Londe, Namer: a pattern recognition system for generating sentences about relations between line drawings, *TM-1798.* Santa Monica, Calif.: System Development Corp., March 1964.

52. Simmons, R. F., S. Klein, and K. L. McConlogue, Indexing and dependency logic for answering English questions, *Amer. Doc.,* v. 15, no. 3, 1964, pp. 196-204.

53. Simmons, R. F., and K. L. McConlogue, Maximum-depth indexing for computer retrieval of English language data, *Amer. Doc.,* v. 14, no. 1, 1963, pp. 68-73. (Also available as SDC document *SP-775.*)

54. Simmons, R. F., Synthetic language behavior, *Data Processing for Management,* v. 5., no. 12, 1963, pp. 11-18.

55. Spiegel, J., E. Bennett, E. Haines, R. Vicksell, and J. Baker, Statistical association procedures for message content analysis, Information System Language Studies, monograph Number 1, *SR-79.* Bedford, Mass.: MITRE Corp., October 1962.

56. Stone, P. J., R. F. Bayles, J. Z. Namerwirth, and D. M. Ogilvie, The General Inquirer: a computer system for content analysis and retrieval based on the sentence as a unit of information, *Behavioral Science*, v. 7, no. 4, 1962, pp. 1-15.

57. Swanson, D. R., Interrogating a computer in natural language, in C. M. Popplewell (ed.), *Information Processing 1962, Proceedings of IFIP Congress, Munich*. Amsterdam: North Holland Publishing Co., 1963, pp. 288-93.

58. Thompson, F. B., Semantic counterpart of formal grammars. Santa Barbara, Calif.: General Electric Co. (Mimeographed)

59. Thompson, F. B., *et al.*, DEACON breadboard summary, *RM64TMP-9*. Santa Barbara, Calif.: General Electric Co., March 1964.

60. Thorne, J. P., Automatic language analysis, Final Technical Report, 1962, ASTIA no. *297381*.

61. Travis, L. E., Analytic information retrieval, in P. Garvin, (ed.), *Natural Language and the Computer*. New York: McGraw-Hill, 1963, pp. 310-53.

62. Uhr, L., and C. Vossler, A pattern recognition program that generates, evaluates, and adjusts its own operators, in E. A. Feigenbaum and J. Feldman, eds., *Computers and Thought*. New York: McGraw-Hill, 1963, pp. 251-68.

63. Walker, D. E., and J. M. Bartlett, The structure of languages for man and computer: problems in formalization, *Proc., First Congress on the Information System Sciences*. MITRE Corp., November 1962.

64. Williams, Y. M., R. F. Barnes, and J. W. Kuipers, Discussion of major features of a restricted logistic grammar for topic representation, Laboratory Report *5206-26*. Lexington, Mass.: ITEK, February 1962.

65. Williams, T. M., Translating from ordinary discourse into formal logic: a preliminary study, ACF Industries, September 1956, ASTIA no. *98813*.

9

Translating Languages

E. D. Pendergraft

Automated language processing, in the broad sense exhibited by current research, had its origin in concern with mechanical translation. The fact that translating languages was both the earliest objective and the progenitor of an ever widening field of interest has made it difficult to maintain an objective perspective of mechanical translation research. As a consequence, the pioneers who set out bravely to manipulate natural language in relatively small computers more often gained the scars than the plaudits of their victories.

According to the historical account by Locke and Booth [20], interest in translating languages followed close upon the heels of the new computer technology stimulated by World War II. By 1946, that development had progressed sufficiently to excite speculations about using computers for purposes other than numerical analysis.

Considering post war circumstances, it is not illogical that mechanical translation should have emerged as the first objective of these early speculations. Warren Weaver found fertile ground when, in 1949, he proposed that mechanical techniques analogous to those used in breaking enemy codes might have peacetime application in decoding natural languages: "...a multiplicity of languages impedes cultural interchange between the peoples of the earth, and is a serious deterrent to international understanding" [20, pp. 15-22]. Weaver suggested "the possibility of contributing at least something to the solution of the world-wide translation problem through the use of electronic computers of great capacity, flexibility, and speed." This provocative paper, which Weaver reportedly sent to 200 of his acquaintances in various fields, appears almost single handedly to have launched mechanical translation as a scientific enterprise. It offered not only a plan and rallying point bolstered by his and Shannon's work in communication theory [32], but high purpose.

The war had just dramatized the pragmatic value of scientific knowledge and of military intelligence. Analogously, the scholar could reason that his own storehouse could be augmented through access to knowledge in other tongues. The scientific and intelligence communities were quick to recognize the implications of automated language processing, not only for the communication of information but for information management [14]. As a result, speculative dreams of mechanical translation experimentation soon became realities.

But even compelling motives might not have succeeded without a somewhat naive initial estimate of the difficulties involved in the task. The small international assemblage of mechanical translation enthusiasts that first came together at the M.I.T. conference of 1952 [20] tried to guard against overoptimism. Nevertheless, the following decade was characterized by an overvaluation of potential practical applications and an undervaluation of the efforts by which such applications would be secured.

No criticism of the origins of automated language processing is contained in these observations. Our best reference to the spirit of the times is the enthusiastic response that Vannevar Bush addressed to Weaver in 1949:

> Far from the multiple meaning of words being a barrier to your project, it seems to me it is an opportunity. Certainly a machine can make a choice in the light of a group of simultaneous impressions. I do not think it would be difficult at all to make the translating machine exercise as good judgment in picking the right word as is exercised by many human translators, particularly when they get to translating in a subject which they do not understand. Another thing is word order, and here it seems to me also there might be something rather interesting. A machine might easily store its translation of a sentence until it came to a period, whereupon I do not think it would be beyond the realm of reasonable possibility to force it to follow certain rules of word order before it emitted the result. All in all, I think the job could be done in a way that would be extraordinarily fascinating. [20, p. 4]

Norbert Wiener, whose work in cybernetics [36] gave special importance to his opinion, was a noteworthy dissenter. He responded to Weaver's attempt in 1947 to interest him in mechanical translation with this prophetic evaluation:

> ... as to the problem of mechanical translation, I frankly am afraid the boundaries of words in different languages are too vague and the emotional and international connotations are too extensive to make any quasimechanical translation scheme very hopeful. ... At the present time, the mechanization of language, beyond any such stage as the design of photoelectric reading opportunities for the blind, seems very premature. [20, p. 18]

9.1   WORD-FOR-WORD TRANSLATION

The "quasimechanical translation scheme" to which Wiener referred was at base the mechanization of three operations commonly attributed to the process of translation. According to this earliest conceptualization of the problem, the computer was required to simulate the presumed behavior of a human translator who would:

a. look up in a bilingual dictionary the individual words identified in a given text of the first language,

b. select equivalent words among possible alternatives that the dictionary made available in the second language, and

c. rearrange the chosen equivalents as necessitated by differences of word arrangement in the first and second languages.

Subsumed under the rearrangement operation were the manipulations needed to reorder, insert, or delete words in the output if a strict word-for-word correspondence would be inappropriate between the original text and its translation.

As Bush pointed out in his comments to Weaver above, it helped the conceptualization to visualize a translator who was unfamiliar with the subject being translated. This tended to externalize the operation of dictionary lookup, and to extenuate faulty simulation of the cognitive operations of selection and rearrangement. The propriety of his stratagem has been demonstrated by subsequent experience. Those parts of the operation of dictionary lookup that were accessible to external observation proved relatively easy to simulate mechanically, while the cognitive operations needed to identify, select, and rearrange words are still inadequately consummated in a computer program.

The mechanical capabilities required to identify words, either in the spoken or written forms used immediately in communication, were so clearly beyond the reach of early investigators that they concentrated upon discourse that had been transcribed into machine-oriented formats, usually by means of card punch or tape perforator. Since transcription of the material to be translated involved manual operations, word identification and, consequently, the operation of dictionary lookup were only partially automated.

Locke had argued [20] that translation of spoken language would be least difficult because of the supplementary information provided by accent and intonation. However, because a card punch operator or typist preparing perforated tape need only scan* written or printed texts in

---

*In the sense of recognizing characters, not necessarily meaning.

order to transcribe them into machine form, the contingencies of partially automated identification were less demanding for written than for spoken language. Considerations of transcription and of sponsorship focused attention upon technical texts, especially those published in Russian. There was a plausible belief that the precision of technical vocabularies would diminish problems of word selection.

The considerable effort entailed in automating the operations of word selection and rearrangement was likewise acknowledged from the start, to the extent that various proposals were made toward minimizing these problems or bypassing them entirely.

Erwin Reifler came forward in 1950 with the concepts of pre-editing and post editing [20]. In his scheme, the automated translation process would have two human ancillaries. The first, a pre-editor, would facilitate the mechanical operation of selection by adding diacritical marks to words in the text given for translation. The pre-editor need not be bilingual; he could have only knowledge of the language being translated. The second ancillary, a post-editor, would carry out the rearrangement operation. The post-editor could have knowledge only of the language conveying the results of translation. The whole task, therefore, would be done cooperatively by the pre-editor, the partially automated dictionary lookup, the automated but facilitated operation of selection, and the post-editor.

An "automatic Russian-English technical dictionary" proposed by Anthony Oettinger in 1954 essentially eliminated the pre-editor and the facilitated selection operation [20]. Instead of attempting a choice among the possible alternatives located in the bilingual dictionary, the automated part of the process bypassed the selection operation entirely. All of the recorded equivalents were listed in the output in a manner that also preserved the word order of the original text. The post-editor thereby was given a dual responsibility of word selection and rearrangement.

A commendable feature of Oettinger's scheme, apart from the contributions that it made to the technical problems of mechanically storing and retrieving word stems and affixes, was its conceptual simplicity from the standpoint of the user. All pertinent information recorded in the bilingual dictionary was displayed for the post-editor or, if desired, for the reader. There could be no suspicion of faulty word selection or rearrangement by the automated process.

However, Victor Yngve was critical of attempts to deal with the mechanical problems of word selection and rearrangement by avoiding them. He considered that one of the greatest difficulties with word-for-word translation was the possibility for a multiplicity of meanings in the output language for a single word in the input language. Supplying alternative meanings, and instructing either the reader or a post-editor to choose the appropriate one, leads to an average of three or four meanings per word and a consequent heavy burden on the reader or the post-editor. This opinion was evidently symptomatic of a wide dissatisfaction with partially automated translation. Bar-Hillel, in his influential 1959 survey of the state of mechanical translation research, had this complaint:

> In general, the intention of reducing the post-editor's part has absorbed so much of the time and energy of most workers in MT, that the problem of whether partially automatic translation, even with such a large amount of participation on behalf of the post-editor as would be required under present conditions, is not nevertheless a desirable and feasible achievement has not received sufficient discussion. I fully understand the feeling that such an achievement is not of very high intellectual caliber, that the real challenge has thereby not yet been taken up, but I do not think that those agencies, for whom any reduction of the load imposed at the moment on the time of highly qualified expert translators is an important achievement, should necessarily wait with the installation of commerical man-machine translation outfits until such a time when the post-editor's part has become very small, whatever the amount of satisfaction the MT worker will get from such an achievement. [2, pp. 7-8]

Opinion had divided among those who believed that short range objectives could produce immediately useful results and those who did not. One faction consisted of the researchers who, like Yngve, set their sights on the ideal of completely automated translation, to be attained by long range basic research. A second faction, with Bar-Hillel, aimed at short range applications, though in some cases without renouncing complete automation as an immediate objective.

As attention turned in earnest to the mechanization of word selection and rearrangement, the disparities encountered in mapping words one-for-one between languages made it more appropriate to speak of the conceptualized process as "word-by-word translation."

9.2   THE HARDWARE APPROACH

At least one agency was in accord with Bar-Hillel's conclusions in 1959 regarding the utility of partially automated translation. The U.S. Air Force during this period added its support to a "general purpose table lookup machine for the processing of natural languages" then being developed by Gilbert King and his associates at IBM. The basic mechanical concepts of the new machine, ". . . a very large fast memory and an integral address procedure for lookup . . .," [7, v. 7, p. 64] were reminiscent of an approach Bar-Hillel had suggested about five years earlier.

One of the major problems in automating word selection and reordering had been cited especially in the following passage from Bar-Hillel's
1955 paper on monolingual and bilingual idioms:

> Let us assume that, by one method or another, a word-by-word
> machine transformation of a given text from the input language into
> some output language will be technically feasible in the near future, on
> a time, cost, and precision scale that can compete with a human trans-
> lator. The number of possible translations in the output language for
> a given word in the input language will sometimes be considerable, as
> can be ascertained from any good bilingual dictionary. For a given sen-
> tence in the input language, therefore, there will generally be many sug-
> gested word sequences in the output language, with their numbers
> easily reaching into the billions. However, various methods have been
> evolved for reducing these numbers to a size that can be handled. I am
> concerned at the moment not so much with how to select from the huge
> number of tentative translations the one (or the few) appropriate one
> (or ones), as with what to do if *none* of the translations offered is ap-
> propriate. When such a situation arises with a human translator, one is
> likely to explain it by saying that the input-language sentence is some-
> how *idiomatic,* either grammatically or semantically or both. [20, pp.
> 184-85]

Thus Bar-Hillel suggested that "bilingual idiom" could be defined
operationally on the basis of a specific dictionary and set of grammatical rules. More exactly, one might regard as a bilingual idiom any input expression for which a grammatically or semantically satisfactory
translation could not be derived by lookup of its constituent words in
a given bilingual dictionary and by subsequent manipulation of the
recorded equivalents according to a given set of rules for word selection and rearrangement.

A first approximation to the definition of "monolingual idiom" could
be given similarly, namely:

> An expression in a given language L is idiomatic within $L,$ with re-
> spect to a given monolingual dictionary and a given list of grammatical
> rules if, and only if, none of the word sequences correlated to the given
> expression by the dictionary and the list of rules is (sufficiently) synony-
> mous with it. [20, p. 186]

Bar-Hillel noted that "(sufficiently) synonymous" had additional rel-
ativizations similar to those contained in the expression "(semantically)
satisfactory" used in the characterization of bilingual idioms. But this
did not undermine his scheme.

In essence, Bar-Hillel proposed to add to Oettinger's automatic bilingual dictionary two capabilities. The first would be mechanical means
of word selection and manipulation. The second and salient feature would
be a means for processing idioms, the exceptional expressions not other-

wise translated in a satisfactory way by the existing word-by-word operations of lookup, selection, and rearrangement. In particular, his extension of the automatic bilingual dictionary would include:

> A set of instructions indicating the transformations to be performed on the rough output. These instructions will be partly grammatical-syntactical, such as the following (using a self-explanatory *ad hoc* symbolism): noun-adjective $\rightarrow$ adjective-noun; *go* $+$ past tense $\rightarrow$ *went;* they will be partly idiomatic-semantic, such as: *roter Hering* $\rightarrow$ *Finte.* These instructions will have an *operational* form. [20, p. 190]

The idiomatic rule which Bar-Hillel used as his example would be needed to render into German the English sentence, "Truman declared that the whole affair was a red herring." The idiomatic expression "red herring" would first appear in the output as "roter Hering," but would be replaced according to the idiomatic rule by "Finte."

In proposing a mechanism for processing idioms, Bar-Hillel stressed "the overwhelming importance of the time-cost-capacity triangle" for mechanical translation. A fast, economical machine with the capacity to process a large number of idioms could obviously reduce the requirements of mechanical word selection and rearrangement.

The important characteristics of King's system, therefore, were its large data capacity and its specialized circuitry for performing not only the lookup, selection, and rearrangement operations of word-by-word translation, but the operations needed to process idioms [15]. Data capacity was achieved through the use of a photoscopic disk or "photostore" that held the dictionary and the operational rules. Idiom processing was mechanized primarily through an identification procedure that operated on the basis of individual character matching rather than comparison of words. With this extended identification capability, the bilingual dictionary could contain either words or idiomatic expressions.

In its original model, the system consisted of the photostore and a specialized computer often referred to as "Mark I." A modification of that machine, "Mark II," has the distinction of being the first computer to perform Russian-English translation on an interesting scale for a sponsoring agency. A full and objective study has not been made of its output by researchers in mechanical translation theoretics. In its present form the machine realizes only an interim translation process, as Bar-Hillel visualized. Yet it is a Russian-English translation process in hand, and one being extended in current research to other languages, especially Chinese [7, v. 11, pp. 202-4]. "Mark III," a second modification of the machine intended to improve its capabilities of selection and rearrangement through a multipass mode of operation, appears for the present to have been abandoned by its sponsor.

9.3 THE EMPIRICAL APPROACH

While King and his associates were trying to minimize the requirements of word selection and arrangement, a frontal assault was launched on these problems by methods which were at once straightforward and audacious.

Leon Dostert had been an invited participant at the M.I.T. conference on mechanical translation in 1952. Active in the instruction in simultaneous translation given at Georgetown University, he appraised the 1952 meeting from the perspective of a specialist in translation. He concluded that a plausible approach to the general problem involved recognition that its linguistic aspect is the primary one, and is therefore the one on which the main effort had to be focused. And rather than attempt to resolve theoretically a rather vast segment of the problem, he believed more fruitful an actual experiment, "limited in scope but significant in terms of broader implications." [20, p. 125]

In late 1953, as a result of the M.I.T. meeting, Dostert's empirically oriented approach to mechanical translation was initiated in a small scale cooperative experiment between Georgetown and IBM [8 and 20]. There were only 250 Russian words in the bilingual dictionary, each with one or two English equivalents. Some sentences in the field of chemistry were translated, first by manual simulation of the translation process and then by computer. After the experiment, Dostert gave a general work plan for further research:

> A corollary of this second conclusion—on which the Georgetown idea was based, and which guided the subsequent joint experiment with IBM and later research—is that, after the first test, the experiment would develop into a series of progressively larger and more complex tests. It is assumed that each succeeding progressive test will yield a certain number of verified conclusions, and that these in turn will serve as the foundation for hypotheses or theories to guide the advance toward the next experiment. [20, p. 125]

The fundamental elements in Dostert's scheme were diacritical codes or marks similar to those used by Reifler's pre-editor in the translation process mentioned above. Dostert had extended the concept of translation diacritics, however, in several important ways [8].

Dostert's diacritics were not to be assigned by a pre-editor to Russian words in the text given for translation, but were to be associated with each Russian word in the bilingual dictionary. Presumably the dictionary lookup operation for a given Russian word would gain access both to the English equivalents of that word and to its associated diacritics. The diacritics would thus be available, as in Reifler's scheme, to facilitate the selection of an equivalent.

Dostert had not found a way to automate Reifler's pre-editor solely by means of the extended dictionary lookup operation. The information provided to the selection operation within the two schemes was considerably different. Although both methods attached diacritics to the Russian word under consideration, the diacritical marks assigned by Reifler's pre-editor gave information about the word-event (instance, token), while those obtained from Dostert's dictionary gave information about the word-design (pattern, type).

Dostert's selection operation, in consequence, could not merely take into account the diacritics of the Russian word under consideration. That would be the case in Reifler's scheme if the pre-editor's diacritics summarized all pertinent information about the context of the word-event. But Dostert's word-design diacritics would necessarily summarize pertinent information about various possible contexts. The choice of an English equivalent would involve the recognition of the particular context containing the Russian word being considered. Selection of an English equivalent for a given Russian word in the text would be made on the basis of mechanical searches of Russian word-designs preceding or following that word, or of their diacritics.

Clearly, then, Dostert's intention was to automate the work of the pre-editor by means of the dictionary lookup of Russian word-design diacritics together with the ensuing context searches. As we have already noticed, the pre-editor's task could be explicated in these operational terms. Theoretically at least, each diacritical mark used by the pre-editor in classifying word-events could represent the satisfaction of a particular set of search conditions among the contextual word-designs or their diacritics.

Dostert also proposed to automate the work of the post-editor along with that of the pre-editor. He set out to feed in the normal language at the input, without prior human processing; and aimed at obtaining clear, complete statements in intelligible language at the output. He also expected certain *stylistic* revisions to be required, just as when translation is done by human beings [20, p. 126].

Dostert gave a theoretical justification for his methods and objectives in the following linguistic assumptions:

> Two basic operations characterize the transference of meaning in mechanical translation, even as they do when translation is done by a human being. These are the operations of (1) selection and (2) manipulation. Selection signifies here choosing the item in the output language corresponding correctly to the item in the input language. Selection therefore deals primarily with the lexical data. The second basic operation is manipulation or rearrangement: i.e., the modification of the sequence of

items in the input text to fit into the structural pattern of the output language. Manipulation deals with syntactic or structural sequence. The lexical operation thus involves a series of steps for the recognition of the word elements of the language of the input; the syntactic operation involves a series of steps for the proper syntactic arrangement or sequence within the structural frame of the language into which we are translating. [20, p. 126]

To realize his aims computationally, Dostert constructed a Russian-English Dictionary containing diacritical codes of three types. He called them "program-initiating," "choice-determining," and "address" diacritics [8].

The program-initiating diacritics for a given Russian word signalled to the computer which rules of selection or rearrangement were to be used in processing that word. There were six diacritical codes of this kind in the initial scheme; they had the following interpretations in the translation process:

0. The order of the original text to be followed.
1. There is to be a difference of order in the translation from the order in the original, and an inversion is necessary.
2. There is a problem of choice; the choice depends on an indication which follows the word under consideration.
3. There is a problem of choice; the choice depends on an indication which precedes the word under consideration.
4. A word appearing in the original text is to be dropped, and no equivalent will appear in the translation.
5. At a point where there is no equivalent word in the original text, a word is to be introduced into the translation. [8, p. 4]

Choice-determining diacritics for a given Russian word had two basic functions in the translation process. They signified to the computer those indications by which different contexts of that word might be distinguished. Or they gave indications about that word as part of the various contexts of other Russian words.

Address diacritics associated with Russian words gave "... the locations in the computer at which the information was stored which was to be used with the first two types of codes" [8, p. 4]. They were a housekeeping device within the translation routine, and will not concern us further.

In addition to these three types of diacritics used to mark Russian words in the bilingual dictionary, there were machine generated codes by which the results of lexical and syntactic searches were recorded during operation of the translation process.

In summary, Dostert's translation scheme contains these operations:

a. Dictionary lookup, by which a Russian word-event identified in the text would be compared with Russian word-designs in the dictionary to obtain the recorded English equivalents and diacritics of that word.

b. Lexical searches (signalled by program-initiating diacritics 2 or 3 above), by which word-designs or choice-determining diacritics in the context of the Russian word would be recognized. The designs or diacritics to be recognized would be specified by choice-determining diacritics of that word, and the results of the searches would be recorded by specific machine-generated diacritics.

c. Syntactic searches (signalled by program-initiated diacritics 0, 1, 4, or 5 above), by which stretches of word-designs or choice-determining diacritics involving the Russian word would be recognized and marked with machine-generated diacritics or, similarly, conditions for word insertion or deletion.

d. Selection, the actual choice of an English equivalent for the Russian word, through reference to the results of lexical searches.

e. Rearrangement, the reordering of English equivalents and actual insertion or deletion of words, through reference to the results of syntactic searches.

The first three operations, concerned with recognizing the Russian input, were usually referred to at Georgetown University under the general term "analysis," while the last two, concerned with producing the English output, were called "transfer." These are generalizations, however, because the empirical approach led not to one translation scheme but many.

Some of the technical variations that evolved out of Dostert's scheme, and the organizational difficulties those variations entailed for the empirical approach, can be inferred from Dostert's general report covering the full span of his study, from 1952 to 1963. Dostert has been candid in describing the activities of researchers in a group effort—an aspect of translation research which in other projects has largely gone unreported. "Despite the public interest awakened by the Georgetown-IBM experiment," Dostert wrote of his situation in 1954, "little official interest was aroused, and there was no official support for further research" [8, p. 5].

From 1954 to early 1956, the work was continued by a small group of linguists and engineers who shared Dostert's enthusiasm. The Institute of Precision Mechanics and Computer Technology of the U.S.S.R. Academy of Sciences announced at that time the translation of English into Russian by means of their BESM computer. More important, the Russian researchers acknowledged the relationship between their undertaking and the Georgetown-IBM experiment.

In June 1956, the National Science Foundation awarded a substantial grant to Georgetown University for intensive research in translation of scientific materials from Russian into English. The project was organized with more than twenty research workers under Dostert as the director. A good part .of the grant had in fact come from the C.I.A., as did later support for the project.

Dostert's organizational plan for his project called for two research groups: one to perform "translation analysis" and the other "linguistic analysis." The translation analysis group was to assume responsibility for the transfer operations by which the English output would be produced. The linguistic analysis group was to concentrate upon those operations concerned with recognition of the Russian input. A programmer was added to the staff "... to keep the research workers fully aware of the situations which their linguistic formulations would encounter when subjected to programming processes ..." [8, p. 6]. Intense training and orientation then began in the specific activities assigned to each group, and in procedures of group coordination.

The translation analysis group concentrated on the preparation of consistent translations as a basis for the Russian-English dictionary. For example, elegant variations were removed from translations published commercially by the Soviet Union, so that "... each word in Russian had, where reasonably possible, one translation in English. However, the original Russian was modified neither in substance nor in structure. Only the English was affected by the selection of the guide translation and this selection was intended only to minimize the inconsistencies of human translation ..." [8, p. 6].

The linguistic analysis group began its work with a detailed study of the Georgetown-IBM experiment. According to Dostert's record of its deliberations, the following decisions were made:

a. The system of transliteration was to be replaced by the Cyrillic alphabet.

b. No dictionary entries were to be split into base and ending.

c. The method of coding dictionary entries according to program-initiating diacritics and choice-determining diacritics was to be reworked and expanded.

d. The six original programs were to be recast and subdivided.

e. A corpus of eighty sentences was selected for study. Some of the problems found in this text were to be solved *ad hoc*; other existing problems were to be ignored.

The purpose of the study was to discover and solve the problems of vocabulary selection and sentence arrangement, and secondly, to refine and generalize as far as possible the translation operations employed in the original procedure. Problems were to be solved one at a time and completely. However, very little effort revealed that problem interrelationship made the piecemeal approach impractical. An over-all approach was necessary and a plan for the constant modification of what had been done to accommodate what had to be done.

After only a few months, Dostert observed that "... there was a considerable divergence of point of view ..." in the linguistic analysis group. He decided to make the most of the situation by fostering this divergence in the hope that free competition would give each analysis method a chance to prove its mettle. It became his policy "... to allow the broadest latitude to diversity of approach and of methods with the understanding that, when the various methods were tested, the one which responded best in a practical situation would be favored over the others" [8, p. 8].

Through further discussion it was decided what the test should be. A "prepared text" chosen from a Soviet publication, *The Journal of General Chemistry*, would be translated by each analysis method, together with a "random text" from the same source. The prepared text could be studied beforehand to any degree, but the random one would not be revealed before the demonstration. The tentative date of the test was set for early 1958.

There were four analysis groups at Georgetown University by early 1957, each named on the basis of the analysis method it advocated. A "code-matching" method was proposed by Ariadne Lukjanow, a "sentence-by-sentence" method by A. F. R. Brown, a method of "general analysis" by Michael Zarechnak, and "syntactic analysis" by Paul Garvin.

Zarechnak's group was the only one ready for any sort of test on the agreed date, a noteworthy event in the light of Dostert's description of the intricacies of "general analysis":

> General analysis ... works with a sentence at a time. Each sentence is analyzed into translation units whose presence, absence and positional relationship to each other are all important. The analysis is carried out at every level that will elicit useful information. Word formation (morphology) is the first level. This also includes word-collection (idiom). Word-grouping (syntagmatic processes) is the second level. This includes the agreement of adjectives with nouns, the government of nouns by verbs, or other form classes, and the modification of adjectives, verbs and other

adverbs by adverbs. The organization of word-groups into sentences (syntax) is the third level. This is specifically the relationship of subject to predicate. The possibility that there are other levels is not precluded. [8, p. 8]

But the 1958 demonstration of Zarechnak's method (by then called the General Analysis Technique) was far from convincing. One sentence of chemical text had been selected for the test, because it exhibited a number of difficulties the General Analysis Technique could handle—such as reflexive verbs, inversion of subject and predicate, the interpolation of case relationships for numbers in numeral form, prepositional government, agreement stretches, and modification by adverbs. *Ad hoc* procedures were added and an acceptable translation was obtained. Without the *ad hoc* measures, the translation would not have been acceptable.

Three of the proposed analysis methods were finally compared experimentally toward the middle of 1959. The General Analysis Technique was used again, this time to translate an "examined text" about 100,000 words in length and a "random text" of 1,500 words. Both of these Russian texts were in the field of organic chemistry. The examined text was checked beforehand against the bilingual dictionary so that words missing from the latter could be entered. A chemist who had no connection with the project examined the output; by Dostert's report, this stalwart "... concluded that the texts conveyed the essential information although their style was clumsy and the reading of them was time-consuming" [8, p. 11].

Dostert found this second demonstration of Zarechnak's method "... a marked advance." And it seems significant that, at this point, the name "General Analysis Technique" was changed to "Georgetown Automatic Translation."

But Brown's "sentence-by-sentence" method was still in the running. In Dostert's own words, it was "... undoubtedly the most novel approach to machine translation attempted at Georgetown." Brown's chief contribution was a system of programming which could be used directly by the linguist, without the intervention of a programmer [4 and 8]. The original name of his method was derived from the manner in which his programming system would be applied in mechanical translation research.

Brown was to translate one sentence of French into English, listing and filing all of the information and procedures involved. He would revise and add to his file by translating a second sentence, so that the adjusted system would translate both sentences, and so on, adding and revising in this way until the system no longer required modifications or additions to handle new sentences.

Brown did not suggest that his approach should be applied universally; he noted that "... for translating Japanese into English by machine, this optimistic approach would be worthless." [8, p. 190] He renamed his method in 1959, when it was also tested and compared by Dostert with Zarechnak's. Brown now called his system the Simulated Linguistic Computer. He translated an examined text of 200,000 running words and a random text of 10,000 running words. Although the tests on the examined text were as successful as those of the General Analysis Technique, the test on the random text was not as conclusive. There was, however, a transfer of information from the random French text into English. Dostert concluded, "... the test of the Simulated Linguistic Computer is no less significant than the test of the Georgetown Automatic Translation." [8, p. 11]

The "code-matching" method proposed by Lukjanow was tested soon afterward, though on a sample of Russian text only ten sentences in length. Throughout the competition, Lukjanow had expressed strong convictions about the value of her scheme. Dostert describes it dispassionately like this:

> Code-matching begins with the coding of each Russian dictionary entry of each English meaning. The codes represent the various grammatical and associative functions which each word can fulfill. After the words of a Russian text have been looked up in the dictionary and the codes copied, the analysis proceeds word-by-word through the text—always from left to right except for occasional regressions of one word to the left. The one function of the form which is applicable in each environment is arrived at by a comparison of the codes of contiguous words, those which are the same are selected and grouped; the others are disregarded in that context. Certain modifications are necessary, of course, when none of the codes of contiguous words match. The translation is effected by applying various mathematical processes to the strings of codes selected and to the codes of the English meanings. [8, pp. 7-8]
> The translation was excellent. No information was provided as to how it had been achieved. Other workers at Georgetown hazarded the guess that the procedures were almost entirely *ad hoc*, and information derived later from some members of the group indicated that this was the case. Miss Lukjanow was reticent in discussing her methods and did not produce a translation of either a random text or a prepared text of greater length. [8, p. 11]

A review was made of Lukjanow's methods, after which the Georgetown project "... repudiated the code-matching technique as a total solution of the problems of machine translation." Dostert gave these reasons for his decision:

> While it seems certain that code-matching must be in any case a necessary part of machine translation, any attempt to rely only on code-matching seemed unsophisticated in view of the unavoidable clumsiness of the

system of coding. The attempt to translate by a single word-by-word pass from left to right through the text seemed to involve unnecessary restriction. [8, p. 12]

The "syntactic analysis" technique proposed by Garvin was not tested, since its proponent left Georgetown University in 1960 to pursue it elsewhere. Dostert observed that, in an account of the (fulcrum) method published subsequently, "... Dr. Garvin had found it necessary to expand it beyond the limits of the original theory of syntactic analysis."

Syntactic analysis is performed one sentence at a time and centers around immediate constituent analysis. Each major constituent is considered an item, which serves as a fulcrum in the process of "prying out further information from the remaining item."

With Garvin's departure the contest had officially narrowed to a choice between Georgetown Automatic Translation (GAT) and Brown's Simuated Linguistic Computer (SLC). Yet the latter remained largely the special concern of its proponent. The SLC programming system, initially coded by Brown in attenuated form on the ILLIAC at the University of Illinois, was reprogrammed for the IBM 704 in 1958 and for the IBM 709-7090 in 1959. The numerical formats provided for linguistic coding in these early programs were extended in 1961 by a "symbolic coding language," and by an assembler to process the symbolic codes back into the numerical forms required by the SLC interpreter. Brown seems to have done most of this work himself, though occasionally we find SLC holding the breach when the more cumbersome programming methods used in GAT had proved embarrassing to the project.

GAT, therefore, became the symbol and principal embodiment of the empirical approach, and Dostert displayed enormous ingenuity in funding its development. Computer time for assembling and testing the GAT system was made available without charge by the U.S. Air Force at the Pentagon, by the European Atomic Energy Commission (Euratom) at Ispra, Italy, and by the U. S. Atomic Energy Commission at Oak Ridge, Tennessee. The initial GAT system, coded by Toma [34] for the IBM 705, was later extensively redesigned for the IBM 709 and 7090. A demonstration of the system was given for representatives of government agencies at the Pentagon in January of 1960, and again at Oak Ridge in October of 1962. By 1963, Dostert considered the GAT system completely operative and able to translate routinely texts in several scientific and technical disciplines from Russian to English. Nevertheless, GAT was not accepted for use by its sponsoring agencies, and the Georgetown project has been practically disbanded.

9.4 THE THEORETICAL APPROACH

The most persistent of the criticisms launched against the empirical approach is the claim that Dostert's scheme lacked proper foundations in linguistic theory. Still we have seen that Dostert gave a linguistic justification for his translation methods, and with slight effort his terminology and undoubtedly his conception can be traced to that paragon of linguistic authority, Leonard Bloomfield.

Writing in 1933, Bloomfield had said in his famous study, *Language:*

> The meaningful arrangements of forms in a language constitute its *grammar*. In general, there seem to be four ways of arranging linguistic forms.
>
> (1) *Order* is the succession in which the constituents of a complex form are spoken. The significance of order appears strikingly in contrasts such as *John hit Bill* versus *Bill hit John.* ...
>
> (2) *Modulation* is the use of secondary phonemes. Secondary phonemes ... are phonemes which do not appear in any morpheme, but only in grammatical arrangements of morphemes. A morpheme like *John* (d_3ɔn) or *run* (rʌn) is really an abstraction, because in any actual utterance the morpheme is accompanied by some secondary phoneme which conveys a grammatical meaning. ...
>
> (3) *Phonetic modification* is a change in the primary phonemes of a form. For instance, when the forms *do* (duw) and *not* (nɔt) are combined into a complex form, the (uw) of *do* is ordinarily replaced by (ow), and, whenever this happens, the *not* loses its vowel, so that the combined form is *don't* (dow nt). ...
>
> (4) *Selection* of forms contributes a factor of meaning because different forms in what is otherwise the same grammatical arrangement, will result in different meanings [3, pp. 163—64].

Dostert's assumption that the transference of meaning in translation is characterized by the basic operations of lexical selection and syntactic manipulation is seen to be potentially harmonious with Bloomfield's doctrine, or with a simplification of it. A precise distinction was not needed, in Dostert's concept of lexical selection, between forms and alternates resulting from phonetic modification. Mechanically, these choices in the transference of lexical meaning were quite similar, as were the mechanical requirements in translating order or modulation by rearranging forms or morphemes. Manipulations of both kinds participated in Dostert's conceptualization of the transference of syntactic meaning.

There was within Dostert's scheme the implicit assumption that lexical meaning recognized in one language would be produced lexically in another, and that syntactic meaning so recognized would be produced elsewhere syntactically, or nearly so. Even if this were usually true among languages, the handling of exceptions would be troublesome. For these were instances in which words or other lexical units had to be inserted or deleted during the translation.

This difficulty revealed itself especially in the translation of particles, which frequently convey in a language those constitutive relations given syntactically in another system. Insertion of the English articles which have no lexical equivalent in Russian, for example, remained a problem throughout the study. According to Dostert, rather than a single structural class conveying the effect of English definite and indefinite articles, Russian conveys the effect in morphological, syntagmatic, syntactic, and semantic features. In spoken language, the hearer must adduce the information from the circumstances rather than the language elements.

The insertion of English articles and similar hard cases came to be handled "statistically," that is to say, by lexical or syntactic rules which produced satisfactory results only part of the time. Clearly, it was more desirable to have a rule that worked nine times out of ten than to have none at all. This view was not popular, and even Philip Smith, who worked on the problem of article insertion within the GAT system, voiced his misgivings:

> Indeed, one may question whether article insertion, at the present stage of machine translation, is justifiable at all. If the writer could claim 90% "satisfactory" article insertions (to be determined, say, by a panel of native English speakers) for his routine, he would be very happy. But even at the high level of 90% who will be satisfied with 10% actually wrong and misleading article insertions? At present we must say that article insertion is little more than an exercise, a stunt perhaps, and that, while extremely interesting, it serves a doubtful purpose. [8, p. 170]

Statistical rules were not only misleading; in the eyes of Dostert's critics their use encouraged the neglect of established sources of linguistics knowledge. On this second point, Bar-Hillel wrote in his 1959 report:

> Gathering of statistics is regarded by many MT groups as being part of a more general methodological approach—the so-called *empirical approach*. Adherents of this methodology are distrustful of existing grammar books and dictionaries, and regard it as necessary to establish from scratch the grammatical rules by which the source-language text will be machine analyzed, through a human analysis of a large enough corpus of source-language material, constantly improving upon the formulation of these rules by constantly enlarging this corpus. With regard to dictionaries, a similar approach is often implemented and a dictionary compiled from translations performed by bilingual members of the group or by other human translators considered to be qualified by this group. I regard this approach as unnecessarily wasteful in practice and as insufficiently justified in theory. It seems that the underlying distrust has been caused by the well-known fact that most existing grammars are of the normative type, hence often of no great help in the analysis of actual writing (and to an

even higher degree, of actual speech), and that existent dictionaries are of such a nature that quite often none of the presented target-language counterparts of the source-language word are satisfactory within certain contexts, especially with regard to terms used in recently developed scientific fields. However, even in view of these facts, I believe that the baby has far too often been thrown away with the bath water. No justification has been given for the implicit belief of the 'empiricists' that a grammar satisfactory for MT purposes will be compiled any quicker or more reliably by starting from scratch and deriving the rules of grammar from a large corpus than by starting from some authoritative grammar and changing it, if necessary, from observations of actual texts. The same holds *mutatis mutandis* with regard to the compilation of dictionaries. [2, p. 11]

Thus, if we are to believe Bar-Hillel, the empiricists' heady willingness to face new difficulties as they came, to use *ad hoc* and, if necessary, imperfect procedures, had led them to prefer improvisation to available resources. On the other hand, if existent knowledge of language was imperfect, it could in time be rounded out and made perfect. The theoretical approach, whether through lesser confidence or greater discipline, called precisely for that patient labor.

Victor Yngve became an early proponent of this strategy and, in the succeeding years, its steadfast defender. Yngve had also participated in the 1952 M.I.T. conference on mechanical translation and, like Dostert, laid bare his assumptions from the start. He contended that "most of the languages of interest for mechanical translation divide a section of discourse, such as a sentence, into about as many words as English does ... (and that) words of various languages can be found that have substantially the same meaning as certain English words."

Here again was the observation that motivated early mechanical translation researchers: Lexical meaning in one language would usually be given lexically in another. As Yngve put it, "... word-for-word translations are not nearly so perfect as sentence-for-sentence translations would be ...," but, on the other hand, "... word-for-word translations are surprisingly good—tantalizingly good ..." Consequently, there was the ring of agreement with Dostert when Yngve concluded as his first methodological postulate:

> Since a strict sentence-for-sentence translation is entirely impractical, and since word-for-word translations are surprisingly good, it seems reasonable to accept a word-for-word translation as a first approximation and then see what can be done to improve it. [20, p. 208]

What Yngve had in mind, however, was improvement of the theoretical foundations of mechanical translation without immediate concern for utility. There would be, in something more than a decade of research under his direction at M.I.T., neither the scramble for applications nor the preoccupation with practicality that charged the atmosphere at IBM and Georgetown University. Yngve, by taking the contrary of Dostert's postulate, had evidently found greater satisfaction in attempting to resolve theoretically a rather vast segment of the problem, instead of making experiments, limited in scope but significant in terms of broader implications.

His inclination to regard mechanical translation as a scientific rather than an engineering problem was received with suspicion. After all, if word-for-word translations were surprisingly good, then a little ingenuity and fixing up was needed—practicality not theory. Significantly, the major support for Yngve's research came from the National Science Foundation and not from agencies professing an immediate internal need for translation applications.

The theoretical objectives he set for himself were not ostensively dissimilar from Dostert's. Yngve began from the now familiar assumption that information for resolving a multiple-meaning problem resides in context. His goal was to find out how the pertinent information could be extracted by identifying the "location" of this information and the length of context needed to identify it.

He observed that a context of nearly an entire sentence is needed for transforming the separable prefix in German to English. Cases in which a context longer than a sentence is needed to resolve some ambiguity are known. However, he decided to limit his base to a context of a sentence length, in the belief that most problems of multiple meaning could be resolved in a context of that length.

Regarding the location of the information needed to resolve problems of multiple-meaning, Yngve cited an earlier observation by Zipf, that frequently used words have the largest number of meanings [40] and argued, heuristically, that since the 50 most frequent words account for about one half of the running words in a text, a solution to the multiple-meaning problem for the 50 most frequent words would represent a solution to much more than half of all multiple-meaning problems.

> Let us look at these common words and see what they are. They are mostly grammatical words—articles, prepositions, conjunctions, auxiliary verbs, pronouns, and so on—the words that have so aptly been called the cement words. These are the words that provide the grammatical structure in which the nouns, verbs, adjectives, adverbs are held. This clue leads us to believe that a solution of grammatical and syntactic problems in translation—and this takes care, to a large extent, of the multiple-meaning problem of these most frequent words—would also be a solution for considerably more than half of all of the multiple-meaning problems. [20, p. 210]

Yngve's concept of "grammatical meaning" was illustrated by the following partial English translation in which the grammatical words and affixes, as well as the word order of the original German text were preserved. German compounds were hyphenated in the translation. His concept was approximate, he said, because "... the dividing line between what should and what should not be translated might have to be moved."

> Die CONVINCINGe CRITIQUE des CLASSICALen IDEA-OF-PROBABILITY IS eine der REMARKABLEen WORKS des AU-THORs. Er HAS BOTHen LAWe der GREATen NUMBEREn ein DOUBLEes TO SHOWen: (1) wie sie IN seinen SYSTEM TO INTER-PRETen ARE, (2) THAT sie THROUGH THISe INTERPRETATION NOT den CHARACTER von NOT-TRIVIALen DEMONSTRABLE PROPOSITIONen LOSEen. CORRESPONDS der EMPLOYEDen TROUBLE? I AM NOT SAFE, THAT es dem AUTHOR SUC-CEEDED IS, den FIRSTen POINT so IN CLEARNESS TO SETen, THAT ALSO der UNEDUCATED READER WITH dem DESIR-ABLEen DEGREE-OF-EXACTNESS INFORMS wird...." [20, p. 211]

And concerning the residual problems of word selection Yngve conjectured that use of specialized field glossaries would result in very few multiple-meaning problems remaining. Field glossaries were, of course, specialized dictionaries intended to isolate the meanings appropriate to individual technical fields.

Surely these speculations were not remarkably different from those that occurred at Georgetown University. Nor would Dostert disagree with Yngve's conclusion that a solution of the grammatical multiple-meaning problem requires a solution of the syntactic problems, including the changing of word order upon translation [20]. Dostert's analysis group made a similar decision in its first few months of deliberation.

What distinguished the theoretical approach was the decision to use formal rules as a means of language description. This does not imply that the tenets of the empirical approach could not have been formalized, but that they were not.

To be more specific, Yngve accepted while Dostert neglected the techniques that had been provided by the impingement of logical positivism upon linguistics, as exhibited notably by the work of Zellig Harris [12] and his students, for example by Chomsky [6] and later by Pike [27]. This emergence has been discussed elsewhere more fully by Winfred Lehmann and the author [19]. With regard to the contrasting techniques of *descriptive formalization* within linguistic methodology—the construction of formal "metalanguages" with which to describe "object languages" having historical existence—and of *prescriptive formalization* and its legitimate use in theoretical linguistics for the construction of such descriptive metalanguages, we said:

> The illusive distinction between prescription and description was re- solved in logic and mathematics only after protracted debate. Because at base it merely reflects the specialized interests of theoretical and ex- perimental science which have already emerged in other fields, the con- sequences of its approaching resolution in linguistics can be predicted with reasonable confidence. [19, p. 88]

The theoretical linguist is concerned with the study of metalanguages, much as the descriptive linguist is concerned with existent object lan- guages. The construction of descriptive metalanguages is an effective means by which the theoretician may formulate linguistic explications, as is the construction of mathematical models. Models are based on an- alogy, however, while descriptive metalanguages achieve their purpose through the symbolization of structural relations. In either case it is the explication, not the empirically given language being explicated, that is brought into existence. Formalization for the theorist is, accordingly, pre- scriptive.

The descriptive linguist, on the other hand, must decide before his exper- iment upon a particular metalanguage with which to record language patterns. Quite naturally he will resist the theorist's desire to change the very basis of description, provided it seems satisfactory. He will mis- interpret the latter's engrossment with prescription, finding in it an at- tempt to impose unwarranted relations upon empirical data, rather than relations which are merely less familiar but potentially more useful than those currently imposed. Frequently, he will come to regard his metalan- guage as part of the phenomena he is describing.

This tendency—to confound prescription of the metalanguage with de- scription of the object language, hence to regard formalization as an im- position upon language data and not as an adjunct to precision in the basis of description was exhibited in the following comment by Dostert:

> Natural languages, unlike conventional sign systems such as those of chemistry or mathematics, are culturally based. Natural languages are structured and can be and are being increasingly formally described. The systems of notation used to represent the nature and functions of language signs may be such as to make them appear to be mathematical formulas. But linguistics is obviously not a part of mathematics, though the algo- rithmic representation of some generalized usages or 'rules' may give that impression. Also, in our language manuals, when we speak of 'rules,' we are in fact describing the habits confirmed by 'proper' usage among the largest groups of users of a given language. [9, p. 93]

Dostert was not alone in this tendency. Those who embraced formalization were caused, in their break with custom, to fix tenaciously upon other dogmas. To the theoreticians, the offense of the empirical approach was one of omission. The decision to rely on *ad hoc* means was seemingly the choice of forging ahead without a definite hypothesis, of experimenting endlessly to discover rather than to test a theory, and of not finding one. The last, we have noted, was more damaging as a comment on willingness than ability.

To what extent were these criticisms justified? Certainly the theoretical approach has improved the basis of linguistic description. Yngve recently observed—about the field as a whole, though unmistakably from his own perspective—that interaction with linguistics has already produced several small revolutions in methodology, point of view, insight into language and standards of rigor and exactness [37].

The most passionate of these revolutions has centered on the transformational theories of Noam Chomsky, the stratificational theories of Lamb [17], the dependency theories of Hays [13], and on others now literally too numerous to mention but including, of course, the theories of Zellig Harris, whom we noticed in the vanguard. It would be difficult, indeed, in the face of today's activity, not to acknowledge the triumph of the theoretical approach, or, more precisely, of formal rules as the preferred successor of lexical and syntactic search algorithms in linguistic description. At the same time, common sense should remind us that hypothesis-making is not the whole of science, and that discipline will be needed if the victory is to contribute more than a haven from the rigors of experimentation.

Notwithstanding, an exodus is occurring from mechanical translation. The departures have been solemn and sometimes accompanied by the thesis that mechanical translation is not, after all, really worth doing, because it will be too difficult and its benefits too limited. Bar-Hillel, for example, in reviewing the past development and future prospect of mechanical translation, said recently in his book, *Language and Information:*

> In spite of this rapid development, there are some who feel that MT has reached an impasse from which it is not likely to emerge without a radical change in the whole approach. It seems now quite certain to some of us, a small but apparently growing minority, that with all the progress made in hardware, programming techniques and linguistic insight, the quality of fully autonomous mechanical translation, even when restricted to scientific or technological material, will never approach that of qualified translators and that therefore MT will only under very exceptional circumstances be able to compete with human translation. [1, p. 182]

The "pessimistic" view of mechanical translation has been propounded by Rhodes [29]. That its latest advocates are Bar-Hillel and Oettinger — researchers formerly most optimistic about the short-range prospect of partially automated translation — is therefore worth noting. Bar-Hillel goes on to say:

> This 'pessimistic' evaluation is based on various considerations, only one of which is presented here, and even this, for obvious reasons, only very shortly and therefore dogmatically. Expert human translators use their *background knowledge*, mostly subconsciously, in order to resolve syntactical ambiguities which machines will have either to leave unresolved or resolve by some 'mechanical' rule which will every so often result in a wrong translation. The perhaps simplest illustration of a syntactical ambiguity which is unresolved by a machine except by arbitrary or *ad hoc* rules is provided by a sentence, say, "...slow neutrons and protons ...", whereas, in general though by no means always, the human expert reader will have no difficulty in resolving the ambiguity through utilization of his background knowledge, no counterpart of which could conceivably stand at the disposal of computers. Similarly, there are innumerable semantical ambiguities which nothing but plain, factual knowledge or considerations of truthfulness and consistency will resolve, all of which are beyond the reach of computers. [1, p. 182]

Yngve's estimate of the state of mechanical translation differs from Bar-Hillel's not as markedly in estimation of the remaining obstacles as in desire to attack them. Syntactic analysis and synthesis, he believes, have been understood in a gross but extensible way. And through his "depth hypothesis," which accounts for variety of expression in language in terms of limitations upon the memory of the speaker, something has been learned of style [38].

He admits that his position is almost exactly the reverse of what it was in the beginning. He had hoped to get the meaning across, but had thought correct grammatical structure and style would be too difficult. In contrast, he came to think that the grammatical structure and even the style could be recovered, but that meaning constitutes a much more difficult problem [37].

We have gained in knowledge of where the information is and how to extract it. But, paradoxically, this is understanding of the formational syntax of language, the system by which language signs are constructed, and not of meaning. It brings us to the threshold of syntactic translation — to the possibility of translating by transfer of syntactic structure — as Yngve has suggested [39].

The Arabic sentence diagrammed below was translated syntactically into English by Arnold Satterthwait [37].

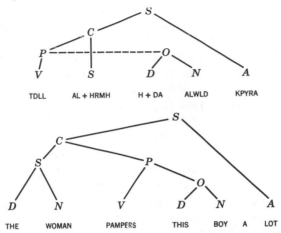

The units mapped interlingually are not words or other lexical units; transference of meaning is accomplished through the replacement of individual syntactic rules or structures of such rules. Lexical selection occurs only indirectly, because the equivalent words or lexical units are mentioned by the equivalent rules in the interlingual mapping. In Satterthwait's translation, the Arabic rule "$V \rightarrow$ TDLL" is replaced by the English "$V \rightarrow$ PAMPERS," and "$S \rightarrow$ AL + HRMH" by the syntactic structure consisting of the entailment of the three rules "$S \rightarrow D + N$," "$D \rightarrow$ THE" and "$N \rightarrow$ WOMAN." The Arabic rule "$P \rightarrow V + \cdots + O$" is one of the formal type which Yngve uses to describe discontinuities; its equivalent is the continuous English rule "$P \rightarrow V + O$."

The changing of word or lexical order upon translation occurs, similarly, because the equivalent rules mention the equivalent orderings. Thus, part of the interlingual description is concerned solely with manipulation, in that some of the syntactic rules mention the ordering of classes but not of individual lexical units. For instance, the Arabic "$C \rightarrow P + S$" becomes "$C \rightarrow S + P$" in English, but "$S \rightarrow C + A$" is the same in both languages and conveys no change of word order. Or the rules corresponding interlingually might mention individual lexical units in just one of the languages. Although not illustrated, that situation would cause the addition or deletion of lexical units during syntactic translation.

Syntactic translation is fundamentally different from lexical translation, regardless of the particular metalanguages used for lexical and syntactic description, or indeed regardless of the issue of formalization, since syntactic rules can be expressed informally. In lexical translation the units identified in the input and then replaced in the output are basic units of speech or writing; their descriptions are couched as sequences of phonemes or graphemes, for example, in the same metalanguage used to describe spoken or written discourse. The units identified and then replaced interlingually in syntactic translation are units of formational information; that is, they are the informational units by which the conventional constructions of lexical units are recognized or produced within a given syntactic system. Their descriptions are couched as syntactic rules or structures of rules in the syntactic metalanguage.

The identifiable units of formational information for a given utterance or text are described by the structures of syntactic rules resulting from syntactic analysis of the transcription of that lexical input. Once identified, the units can be replaced interlingually by equivalent units of another syntactic system. The replacement is implemented mechanically through selection of the equivalent syntactic rules or structures. These, in turn, delimit the formational units that will participate in syntactic synthesis to produce the lexical output.

Yngve's translation scheme therefore contains essentially three operations:

a. Syntactic analysis, resulting in the structures of syntactic rules that identify the formational units for the lexical input.
b. Interlingual transfer, the replacement of syntactic rules or structures by those describing the equivalent formational units of another syntactic system.
c. Syntactic synthesis, delimited by the equivalent formational units, and resulting in production of the lexical output.

The progression from lexical to syntactic translation can be traced in the schemes we have reviewed. Lexical translation was best represented by Oettinger's automated bilingual dictionary. Its method was simply the replacement of lexical units. Satterthwait's Arabic-English translation would have been implemented essentially by transfer rules of the form "TDLL $\rightarrow$ PAMPERS," "AL + HRMH $\rightarrow$ THE WOMAN," and so on. The next step was represented by our glimpse of Bar-Hillel's scheme and then that of Dostert. Aside from the handling of idioms, which are the exceptional rather than the essential features of translation method, we saw the introduction of syntactic analysis for two purposes.

The first use of syntactic analysis was to categorize lexical events as an aid to selection of their equivalents. This innovation can be illustrated by transfer rules of the form "TDLL$_V$ $\rightarrow$ PAMPERS," "AL + HRMH$_S$ $\rightarrow$ THE WOMAN," and so on, where the diacritical marks "v" and "s" signalled contextual clues to be taken into account. Dostert referred to this use as "lexical analysis," and with good reason, since his attention was focused on improving the interlingual lexical replacement by making it context-sensitive.

The second use of syntactic analysis, we recall, was to identify syntactic sequences—strings consisting of individual lexical descriptions or their diacritics—as a basis for syntactic manipulation. This use introduced transfer rules essentially describing interlingual transformations. The rule "$V + S \longrightarrow S + V$," for example, might postulate an *ad hoc* solution to the inversion of subject and verbal elements in Arabic-English translation, though its import for linguistics would not be exciting.

Dostert came to realize that his transfer method had a severe limitation. In theory, it would matter little whether syntactic manipulation were performed before or after lexical selection, because all of his data were referenced to the syntactic system of the input language. That is why he had conceptualized translation as consisting of only two major operations: analysis and transfer. Synthesis, involving access to the formational units of the output language, was provided in the GAT system only for morphology. Thus Dostert said in his final report:

> While the rearrangement operation is strong in theory, the routine is rather weak in practice. This is not due to any intrinsic features of the routine itself, but to the circumstance that it is the last routine and so is dependent on all that goes before it. A slight flaw in the morphology, in the syntagmatic analysis, or, most especially, in the syntactic analysis can completely disrupt the rearrangement routine output. [8, p. 179]

With the production of the English output attached precariously to Russian formational units, Dostert considered "self-organization" in the interlingual transfer necessary. He thought the transfer would be more acceptable if synthesis, insertion, and rearrangement were linked to the identity of the English glosses selected, rather than to the identity of the Russian. Each English gloss recorded as an equivalent in the bilingual dictionary would be coded with its own diacritics, these referenced to English syntax. If this were done

> ...the English synthesis need no longer be restricted to the morphological level, but expanded to include syntagmatic, syntactic and semantic features as well. The process of translation would become less a transfer from Russian into English with the attendant possibility that the English will be affected to a large extent by the peculiarities of the Russian, than an analysis of the Russian to extract all possible information followed by a synthesis of English in a pattern of self-organization so as to preserve all of the information, but to frame it in a purely English setting. [8, p. 180]

Dostert's goal apparently can be reached through syntactic translation. But this requires another innovation in transfer technique, exemplified by the following Arabic-English transfer rules:

$V \rightarrow$ TDLL $\longrightarrow V \rightarrow$ PAMPERS
$S \rightarrow$ AL $+$ HRMH $\longrightarrow S \rightarrow D + N, D \rightarrow$ THE, $N \rightarrow$ WOMAN
$D \rightarrow$ H $+$ DA $\longrightarrow D \rightarrow$ THIS
$N \rightarrow$ ALWLD $\longrightarrow N \rightarrow$ BOY
$A \rightarrow$ KPYRA $\longrightarrow A \rightarrow$ A LOT
$P \rightarrow V + \ldots + O \longrightarrow P \rightarrow V + O$
$C \rightarrow P + S \longrightarrow C \rightarrow S + P$
$O \rightarrow D + N \longrightarrow O \rightarrow D + N$
$S \rightarrow C + A \longrightarrow S \rightarrow C + A$

These are not transformational rules in the sense of Harris or Chomsky; they describe the replacement of formational units in one syntactic system by those in another.

Thus, the principal import of syntactic translation is in the observation that syntactic structures may be substituted for one another in ways that equate meaning. Syntactic rules, as a result, may describe significant units as well as the informational units by which language is produced or recognized. Substitutability based on shared modes of designation is as characteristic of language signs as producibility and recognizability within a syntactic system. It seems plausible, therefore, that with syntactic rules of an appropriate formal type we may discover how to transcribe language signs [24 and 33].

On this subject Dostert suggested that automatic translation is essentially a problem of sign-substitutions: formulation and programming of a substitution procedure such that the signs of the target language are selected and arranged to convey the information contained in the signs of the source language [8]. We might have agreed with this conclusion had we not found that, with a few exceptions, the empirical approach treated words as signs, reflecting the naive view that *words have meaning.*

There is now room for skepticism on a second count, since Yngve has just pointed out that even the prospect of sign-for-sign translation may leave us almost where we began with word-for-word.

> Work in mechanical translation has come up against what we will call the semantic barrier. Even when we have programs which can give grammatical analyses of the incoming sentences, we still cannot make adequate translations because of the large amount of remaining ambiguity. We have come face-to-face with the realization that we will only have adequate mechanical translations when the machine can 'understand' what it is translating. [37, p. 279]

In brief, our translations will read better, but the information for the resolution of the multiple-meaning problem still resides in the context.

But Yngve may have missed the semantical implications of syntactic translation, since his transfer operation is still incompletely formalized. The distinction between transformational rules and rules substituting formational units was made explicitly in 1959 by Solomonoff when he observed that translation could be formalized by means of a single language consisting of pairs of expressions from two different syntactic systems that were described by a grammar consisting of pairs of syntactic rules. Solomonoff suggests that, given two languages L_1 and L_2, such that there exists a translation between L_1 and L_2, a third 'language,' L_3, be constructed. 'Acceptable sentences' in L_3 are to consist of ordered pairs of sentences. The first sentence in each pair is a sentence from L_1; and second is the corresponding sentence in L_2.

> To speak of L_3 as a 'language' implies a certain generalization of the concept. The 'words' of L_3 may be pairs of ordinary words; the 'phrases' of L_3 may be pairs of ordinary phrases—or there may be no useful way to divide the sentences of L_3 into words and phrases.
>
> Knowing the grammar of L_3 will then be equivalent to being able to translate from L_1 to L_2. Here, we interpret 'knowing the grammar' to mean that if a proposed sentence pair is given us, we can use the grammar rules to determine whether that sentence pair is in L_3 or not. Another, more useful kind of grammar would be one that would give methods to determine all possible legal sentences that could contain a certain fixed phrase as part of them. In this latter case, we need only present the grammar rules with a sentence from L_1, and if the grammar rules are to complete this partial sentence of L_3 to form an acceptable complete sentence in L_3, they must give us the translation in L_2 of the sentence in L_1. [31, pp. 10-12]

If the grammar rules of L_3 are not unreasonably complex, and if L_1 and L_2 are phrase structure languages, then it is possible for L_3 to be a phrase structure language. For example, to show how L_3 may be phrase structure language, a set of substitution rules is given for L_3, and sentences in L_3 are generated by using them. In Figure 9.1, the capital letters refer to words in L_1, or to words that will eventually become phrases in L_1. Similarly, the small letters refer to L_2. The lines between the capital and small letters connect equivalent words or phrases.

If $A \ B \ D \ B, \ b \ b \ a \ d$ is an acceptable sentence in L_3, and $b \ b \ a \ d$ of L_2 is the translation of $A \ B \ D \ B$ of L_1, the sequence of diagrams in Figure 9.1b illustrate the application of Solomonoff's substitution rules.

The substitution rules for L_3 contain an important innovation that is still missing in Yngve's syntactic translation scheme, namely, the vertical or diagonal lines associating the individual symbols within each rule.

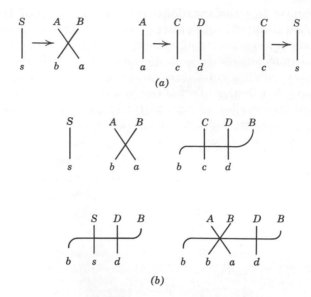

Figure 9.1 Generating Sentences in L_3 from Sentences in L_1 and L_2

Alternate notations for the rules Solomonoff uses in his example would be the following:

$$S \rightarrow A^1 + B^2 \twoheadrightarrow s \rightarrow b^2 + a^1$$
$$A \rightarrow C^1 + D^2 \twoheadrightarrow a \rightarrow c^1 + d^2$$
$$C \rightarrow S^1 \twoheadrightarrow c \rightarrow s^1$$

Because the left-most symbols of the paired syntactic rules are always associated in Solomonoff's scheme, the associations among the remaining symbols can be indicated by superscripts or any similar device giving the corresponding places of substitution.

The role of the superscripts is not unlike that of Quine's predicate schema [28]. The Arabic sentence "YVJB ALBLD ALWLD," which Yngve would translate as either "The town pleases the boy" or "The boy likes the town," requires a choice between the English predicates (1) PLEASES (2) and (2) LIKES (1). That the second rendition translates the Arabic *subject* as the English *object* and the Arabic *object* as the English *subject* is of no concern. The information about places of substitution is now carried by the superscripts.

A substitution algebra for syntactic rules with superscripts was developed by William Estes, Andrew Holley, and the author early in 1960 [10]. Essentially, we noted that Solomonoff's scheme could be used to describe monolingual as well as interlingual relations among language expressions without recourse to transformational rules in the sense of Harris or Chomsky. As a corollary, equivalence or inclusion relations could be described among the expressions of a language in terms of equivalence or inclusion relations among the syntactic rules. This possibility, together with the observation that syntactic rules may be descriptive of signs, led in 1961 to the construction of a formal semantical theory which describes a distributional classification of syntactic structures much as formal syntactic theories describe a distributional classification of language expressions. The general form of these "semantic rules" is indicated by these examples:

$$\alpha \rightarrowtail S \rightarrow A^1 + B^2$$
$$\alpha \rightarrowtail s \rightarrow b^2 + a^1$$
$$\beta \rightarrowtail A \rightarrow C^1 + D^2$$
$$\beta \rightarrowtail a \rightarrow c^1 + d^2$$
$$\delta \rightarrowtail \alpha/\beta$$

The "alphabet" in the semantical theory consists of the individual syntactic rules. The syntactic rules in the semantic classes α and β are "concatenated" to form the members of the semantic class δ. Concatenation is taken in the extended sense that each rule in β will be applied to each rule in α at the place of substitution marked by the superscript "1." The resulting rules in the class δ are $S \rightarrow C^1 + D^2 + B^3$ and $s \rightarrow b^3 + c^1 + d^2$. Thus, there are several possible types of concatenation symbolized by "1", "2" and so on. All rules in a given class are required to have the same number of superscripts.

The sense in which "semantical" may be applied to such a theory has been explained by R. M. Martin in *Truth and Denotation* [22]; in particular in his discussion of semantical metalanguages based on the relation of "comprehension." Similar theories have recently come from J. J. Katz and J. A. Fodor [16].

Although too intricate to present in detail, these theories and their use in large-scale translation experiments at the University of Texas have been described from a linguistic point of view by Wayne Tosh in his book, *Syntactic Translation* [35]. In addition to providing a generalized algorithm for syntactic translation, the theories will make possible an interlingual mapping of the structures resulting from automatic semantic analysis. The semantic translation algorithm differs from the syntactic translation algorithm much as the syntactic differs from the lexical. Semantic analysis will aim specifically at better resolution of multiple meaning through the interlingual substitution of "semantic rules."

Investigations concerned with the problem of structural transfer as a basis for translation have been pursued elsewhere, principally by Ceccato

[5] and Glassersfeld [11] in Italy, by Masterman [23], Needham, Parker-Rhodes and Sparck Jones in England [26], and by Itiroo Sakai [30] in Japan. An early unpublished approach based on the theory of semigroups was developed at the University of Michigan by William Smoke and Andreas Koutsoudas. Experimentation with structural transfer based on Harris' technique of "string analysis" is in progress at the University of Pennsylvania, and has been described by Ilse Langerhans [18].

REFERENCES

1. Bar-Hillel, Y., *Language and Information*. Reading: Addison-Wesley Publishing Co., and Jerusalem: The Jerusalem Academic Press, 1964.

2. Bar-Hillel, Y., Report on the state of machine translation in the United States and Great Britain, prepared for the U. S. Office of Naval Research, Information Systems Branch, under contract NONR-2578 (00). Jerusalem: Hebrew U., 1959.

3. Bloomfield, L., *Language*. London: George Allen & Unwin Ltd., 1933.

4. Brown, A. F. R., *Manual for a Simulated Linguistic Computer*. Washington: Georgetown U., 1960.

5. Ceccato, S., Mechanical translation: the correlational solution. Milan: Centro di Cibernetica e di Attivita Linguistiche, 1963.

6. Chomsky, N., *Syntactic Structures*. The Hague: Mouton and Co., 1957.

7. *Current Research and Development in Scientific Documentation*. Washington: Government Printing Office, semiannual.

8. Dostert, L. E., and R. R. MacDonald, Georgetown University machine translation research project, general report 1952-1963. Washington: Georgetown U., 1963.

9. Dostert, L. E., Machine translation and automatic language data processing. *Vistas in Information Handling*. Washington: Spartan Books, and London: Cleaver-Hume Press, 1963.

10. Estes, W. B., W. A. Holley, and E. D. Pendergraft, Formation and transformation structures. Austin: U. of Texas, 1963.

11. Glassersfeld, E. V., MULTISTORE, a procedure for correlational analysis. Milan: Institute Documentazione della Associazione Meccanica Italiana, 1965.

12. Harris, Z. S., *Structural Linguistics*. Chicago: U. of Chicago Press, 1947.

13. Hays, D. G., Dependency theory, a formalism and some observations, *Language*, v. 40, no. 4, October-December 1964.

14. *Hearings Before the Special Investigating Subcommittee of the Committee on Science and Astronautics, U. S. House of Representatives, Eighty-Sixth Congress*. Washington: U. S. Government Printing Office, 1960.

15. International Business Machines Corp., Final report on Computer Set AN/GSQ-16 (XW-1). Rome, N. Y., Information Processing Laboratory, Rome Air Development Center (AFSC), 1960.

16. Katz, J. J., and J. A. Fodor, The structure of a semantic theory, *Language*, v. 39, 1963.

17. Lamb, S. M., *Outline of Stratificational Grammar*. Berkeley: U. of California, 1962.

18. Langerhans, I., *Transformational Translation: English to German*. Philadelphia: U of Pennsylvania, 1963.

19. Lehmann, W. P., and E. D. Pendergraft, Structural models for linguistic automation, *Vistas in Information Handling*. Washington: Spartan Books, and London: Cleaver-Hume Press, 1963.

20. Locke, W. N., and A. D. Booth, *Machine Translation of Languages*. New York: Technology Press of M.I.T. and John Wiley and Sons, 1955.

21. Lukjanow, A. W., *Statement of the Proposed Method for Mechanical Translation*. Washington: Georgetown U., 1957.

22. Martin, R. M., *Truth and Denotation*. Chicago: U. of Chicago Press, 1958.

23. Masterman, M., Semantic message detection for machine translation using an interlingua, presented to the First International Conference on Machine Translation of Languages and Applied Language Analysis, Teddington, England, 1961.

24. Morris, C., *Signs, Languages and Behavior*. Englewood Cliffs: Prentice Hall, 1946.

25. Moyne, J. A., *Georgetown Automatic Translation, General Information and Operation Manual*. Washington: Georgetown U., 1962.

26. Parker-Rhodes, A. F., A new model of syntactic description, presented to the First International Conference on Machine Translation of Languages and Applied Language Analysis, Teddington, England, 1961.

27. Pike, K. L., Taxemes and immediate constituents, *Language*, v. 19, pp. 65-82.

28. Quine, W. V., *Methods of Logic*. London: Routledge and Kegan Paul, 1952.

29. Rhodes, I., A new approach to the mechanical syntactic analysis of Russian, *Mechanical Translation*, v. 6, 1961.

30. Sakai, I., Syntax in universal translation, presented to the First International Conference on Machine Translation of Languages and Applied Language Analysis, Teddington, England, 1961.

31. Solomonoff, R. J., *The Mechanization of Linguistic Learning*. Cambridge: Zator Co., 1959.

32. Shannon, C. E., and W. Weaver, *The Mathematical Theory of Communication*. Urbana, Ill.: U. of Illinois Press, 1949.

33. Spang-Hanssen, H., Recent theories on the nature of the language sign, *Travaux du Cercle Linguistique du Copenhague*, v. 9, Nordisk Sprogog Kulturforlag, 1954.

34. Toma, P., *Serna System*. Washington: Georgetown U., 1959.

35. Tosh, W., *Syntactic Translation*. The Hague: Mouton and Co., 1965.

36. Wiener, N., *Cybernetics*. New York: Technology Press of M.I.T. and John Wiley and Sons, 1949.

37. Yngve, V. H., Implications of mechanical translation research, *Proc. of the Amer. Philosophical Soc.*, v. 108, no. 4, August 1964.

38. Yngve, V. H., A model and an hypothesis for language structure, *Proc. of the Amer. Philosophical Soc.*, v. 104, 1960.

39. Yngve, V. H., A framework for syntactic translation, *Mechanical Translation*, v. 4, 1957.

40. Zipf, G. K. *Human Behavior and the Principle of Least Effort*, Cambridge, Mass.: Addison-Wesley, 1949.

10

Designing Artificial Languages for Information Storage and Retrieval

C. H. Kellogg

As the dialog between man and computer becomes more intense, the problems associated with communication between them become more apparent. This result has stimulated a large amount of current research in natural language data processing and in the field of programming languages and systems. Intermediate between these two focal points of activity is an area, with which this chapter deals, concerned with the problems of interrogating and controlling computer based information stores with languages that are less procedure oriented than are programming languages, yet less complex and variable than are the natural languages.

Developments in artificial languages for information storage and retrieval draw upon insights into natural language behavior and construction, upon practical advances in program language design and data description techniques, and upon tools and techniques of document retrieval (i.e., reference providing) systems.

The significant features of languages for data providing systems are discussed principally in terms of examples drawn from existing and proposed systems. Three separate yet related categories of systems are identified: data based systems; logic based systems; and (on-line) cooperative systems. Initial remarks are directed at contrasting natural and artificial languages and sketching some of the concepts and tools used by the language designer.

10.1 ARTIFICIAL LANGUAGE SYSTEMS

The following operational definition of an artificial language will serve our purposes:

An artificial language is a system of signs deliberately constructed by a person or a small group of people, over a comparatively short interval of time, for a particular purpose.

History provides us with many examples of the creation of artificial languages. As Ohlman remarks,

> ... before there were machines to do our intellectual dogwork, persons like Delgarno, Wilkins, Leibnitz, and Spencer were designing languages to suit their own conceptions. They wanted to improve upon natural languages because the latter lack universality, precision and logic, and these are just the characteristics we would like our information retrieval languages to have.
>
> However, universes are hard to come by, precision of meaning would increase our vocabulary requirements an order of magnitude, and logic cannot adequately describe our highly probabilistic, plural, and illogical world. Perhaps this is why all artificial languages created to be of universal application have failed—and it is not for lack of trying, for there have been some 400 attempts. [56, p. 8]

Ohlman's words should warn us of past mistakes and pitfalls to be avoided. They should not, however, keep us from exploiting the newly available tools from logic, linguistics, and other disciplines that may help in constructing improved language systems.

LINCOS and LOGLAN are two artificial languages, developed for purposes other than information retrieval (IR) or computer applications, which illustrate some of the typical features of artificial languages—features that might prove useful to the information retrieval language designer.

Freudenthal, at the University of Utrecht, developed LINCOS (lingua cosmica), a logic based language, to serve as a vehicle for cosmic intercommunication. Freudenthal explains,

> My purpose is to design a language that can be understood by a person not acquainted with any of our natural languages or even their syntactic structure. The messages communicated by means of this language will contain not only mathematics, but in principle the whole bulk of our knowledge. I shall assume that the receiver of these messages has understood their language if he is able to operate on it. He will be able to do so only if he has grasped the meaning of the expressions of this language, because it will be a moderately formalized language that cannot be handled on the ground of formal rules only. [28, p. 13]

Such a project raises a number of interesting logical, linguistic, and communication issues. A complete script for a cosmic broadcast is not given, but an extensive set of abstracts of LINCOS "program texts" covering major aspects of mathematics, time, behavior, space, motion, and mass are given.

The artificial language developed by Brown, called LOGLAN (LOGICAL LANGUAGE) [10, 11], has the following interesting characteristics:

a. Phonemes are represented proportionally from the eight major languages.

b. Syntactic ambiguity is absent—"...it is impossible to write a grammatical sentence in LOGLAN that can be legitimately interpreted in more than one way." [10, p. 131]

c. Spoken and written forms of LOGLAN are isomorphic (punctuation, spaces between words, etc., are spoken as well as written).

LOGLAN was developed to provide an experimental vehicle to test the Whorf hypothesis (that language determines the structure of human thought) and to explore certain questions about language learning and about communication across cultural boundaries. Two features of natural language—the capability for productive novelty and transmutation—are singled out for particular attention by the author:

> If, as it appears, human thought is a by-product of these two evolving features of the human language game—its capacity to produce new ideas, on the one hand, and to check them by deduction against the body of the old, on the other—and it is true that these performances are in any sense dependent on, or functions of, the structure of the game itself—then it behooves us, now and then, to tinker with the rules. This is what LOGLAN does. [10, p. 137]

LINCOS and LOGLAN—efforts concerned with novel communication situations and changing the rules of the communication game—manifest some of the spirit behind current attempts at developing improved means for man-machine communication.

10.1.1 The Emphasis on Natural Language. Information science researchers are focusing increasing attention on the problems involved in computer processing of natural language expressions. Practical as well as theoretical reasons have influenced this research direction, among them the availability of natural language text, need for mechanical processing, and utility of natural language for communication.

Large quantities of natural language text are available in diverse formats and many subject areas. To make such text available for computer processing involves development of appropriate keypunching procedures, keypunching, and validation. Operational character recognition devices may soon be expected to facilitate the input of natural language text to computer systems. The alternative to computer processing of natural language is conversion, prior to computer processing, of natural language text into formatted data or artificial language text. However, the conversion itself may be so difficult and expensive that it is not necessarily more economical than development of the capability directly to process natural language text by computer.

Natural languages have evolved and have been refined over the centuries. Billions of people understand the basic rules of at least one natural language well enough to generate meaningful utterances. The ability to represent the same idea in many ways (rich paraphrase resources) and the redundancy of a natural language facilitate communication. Formal or artificial languages are likely not to possess these capabilities. Nevertheless, many specialized languages have been developed to fulfill particular needs, and some of them (e.g., in the areas of mathematics and logic) have clearly demonstrated their superiority for the purposes for which they were designed.

The very richness and complexity of a natural language, its emotive components, features causing frequent ambiguity and vagueness, pervasive ellipsis, heavy reliance on context for successful communication of meaning, etc., all complicate the research task involved in developing methods for processing natural language by computer.

10.1.2 Possible Advantages of an Artificial Language.   Some of the possible advantages of artificial languages are precision, conciseness, suitability for computer processing, and inferential power. Artificial languages are consciously developed and tailored for a particular function or purpose. The developer of an artificial language has control over the degree of precision in the language. The domain of discourse can be restricted and described precisely. Rules determining structure of expressions in the language and rules indicating permissible language content can be created and presented explicitly and completely. For a natural language, on the other hand, such rules have to be discovered.

The economy of expression inherent in an artificial language often facilitates automation and inferential power as well as the conservation of storage space. Inferential power is one of the most important potential benefits from suitably constructed artificial languages. Artificial languages may contribute to drawing inference from data and text in two ways: (1) by facilitating human inference (drawing conclusions from graphs, ordered data, precisely formulated premises, etc.), and (2) by facilitating machine inference.

10.1.3 Programming Versus IR Languages.   The design and implementation of programming languages has resulted in a large amount of literature; some of it is pertinent to the design and construction of computer interpretable IR languages. Construction of compilers for converting programming language source statements into target language expressions directly interpretable by machine has been documented extensively.* The objective in translating a programming language is to gen-

---

*See for example Rosen [60] and Knuth [41] for surveys of recent work in this area. The bibliography in [60] is useful as an entrance to the relevant literature.

erate efficient sequences of machine instructions. In translating a retrieval language, sequences of machine instructions must similarly be generated but the translating machine is likely to have to perform much more analysis to discover what search and processing algorithms must be realized by the sequences of instructions. This additional analysis is required because the source statements, i.e., the statements being translated, are not procedurally organized.

Translation is typically a multistage process, usually consisting of one stage during which the source statements are syntactically analyzed and one or more stages during which the required statements in the target language are synthesized. Syntax directed compilers [12, 26, 44, 47, 53, 70] use a recursive syntax analyzing algorithm operating on a formal description of the source language supplied in tabular form. In Section 10.2, a retrieval language is described that is translatable by means of a syntax directed compiler. Bobrow [6] suggests that these compilers could be used for parsing natural language expressions. Syntax specification metalanguages such as those described by Backus [2] and Gorn [29] may be used in specifying and describing a wide variety of programming, retrieval, and other kinds of artificial languages.

Programming language developments have led to advances in data description techniques as well as advances in techniques for specifying processes. Iverson [48] details a number of considerations involved in specifying and manipulating structured operands such as trees, vectors, or matrices of data items. Steel [64] and Smith [63] describe generalized arrays. Most of these data organization techniques aim at the concise arrangement of more or less homogeneous data in a manner that permits efficient sequential processing of data sets. They also permit the ordering of information in terms of objects or entities, properties of objects, and associated data values. However, only data values are usually stored explicitly. Objects and properties usually are implicitly represented by indices or other devices specific to the program or its adjuncts. This is a serious defect for information retrieval purposes.

Two of the more formally developed frameworks for describing and manipulating information are the Information Algebra and LISP. The Information Algebra, developed by Bosak and the CODASYL Language Structure Group [9], is an abstract formulation of data types in terms of point set theory, and procedures to be applied to these types can be defined in terms of operations on collections of point sets. The Information Algebra may very well prove useful in specifying IR storage languages and search processes.

LISP [50] provides a precise means of specifying symbolic expressions and computable functions of symbolic expressions. The definition of complex recursive functions is comparatively straightforward in LISP, which might consequently provide a useful vehicle for the expression of complex retrieval algorithms and search strategies.

Colilla and Sams [17] present an illuminating account of information structures, especially tree structures, for information processing and retrieval. In Bobrow and Raphael [5], the various list processing languages are reviewed and compared. A relatively complete survey of data processing languages and data description techniques is presented by McGee [51].

There is a significant degree of overlap among the design problems that occur in specifying programming and those that occur in specifying information storage and retrieval languages. A great deal of effort has been expended in the design and implementation of programming languages, and the resultant fund of knowledge can serve as a valuable source from which to draw selectively in constructing artificial IR languages.

10.1.4 Languages and Calculi; Algebraic Linguistics and Symbolic Logic. Algebraic linguistics and symbolic logic are the bases of theoretical developments of relevance to the construction of language systems. *Algebraic linguistics* deals with the abstract systems realized by the syntactic descriptions of languages, i.e., their grammars. These abstract systems involve rules for successively replacing language symbols with other language symbols until a well formed formula or sentence is generated or recognized. Systems differ from each other with respect to the kinds of rules permitted to implement the symbol replacement operation. Work in the field has led to the identification of a hierarchy of language families or abstract grammar types, which vary in their capability to generate linguistic expressions and provide adequate syntactic descriptions. The four most widely known of these abstract systems, in order of increasing generality, are finite state, context free, context sensitive, and unrestricted rewriting system grammars [see Chomsky, 14]. Most programming languages and most of the English grammars implemented on computing machines are at the context free level. According to Bach, "It can be demonstrated that finite state and context free phrase structure grammars are essentially inadequate to describe a language like English" [1, p. 173].

For a discussion of the impact of some of these concepts of algebraic linguistics on computing languages, see Elbourn and Ware [23]. Excellent discussions of relevant automata theory are provided in McNaughton [52] and Kirsch [40].

The field of logic is concerned with the study of correct inference. Suppes states that,

> For over two thousand years mathematicians have been making correct inferences of a systematic and intricate sort, and logicians and philosophers have been analyzing the character of valid arguments. It is, therefore, somewhat surprising that a fully adequate formal theory of inference has been developed only in the last three or four decades. In the long period extending from Aristotle in the fourth century B. C. to Leibnitz in the seventeenth century, much of importance and significance was discovered about logic by ancient, medieval and post-medieval logicians, but the most important defect in this classical tradition was the failure to relate logic as the theory of inference to the kind of deductive reasonings that are continually used in mathematics. [65, p. xv]

A *logical calculus* is a language system that permits explicit and precise deductive inference by the manipulation of symbols according to exactly formulated rules. The definition of a calculus includes specification of inference (transformation) rules as well as grammar (formation) rules. The sentence is the smallest symbolic unit that may have a truth value associated with it. The sentential (propositional) calculus permits the construction of complex sentences from simpler sentences and connectives. The predicate (functional) calculus deals with the inner structure of sentences. These two and other logical calculi have been applied successfully to the study of the foundations of mathematics and to certain theoretical issues in the philosophy of science.

IR research involving applied logical calculi will be discussed in a later section. A major reason for implementing a calculus rather than just a language is the possibility of developing and using mechanical theorem proving techniques in conjunction with a computer file of information.

An *interpreted language* is a language for which there exists a formal or informal semantic description as well as a syntactic description. Many unsolved theoretical and practical problems remain in the study of semantics, but recently some significant contributions have been made toward solving the problem of precisely specifying and displaying interpretations of ordinary language expressions. See, for example, Katz and Fodor [35], Kay [36], and Robinson [59].

An *interpreted calculus* requires three sets of rules for its description: syntactic, semantic, and inference. The field of formal semantics is concerned with interpretable calculi. Work currently in progress at the theoretical level may provide results applicable to constructing more useful and powerful artificial calculi.

10.1.5 Summary. Insight into the behavior of languages and calculi and means for constructing them can stem from numerous activities at the theoretical-formal level and at the applied-descriptive level. Work on both levels in various degrees has concerned itself with specifying characteristics of grammar, inference, and meaning. On the first level, we have alluded briefly to relevant work in algebraic linguistics and symbolic logic. The former field is concerned with language systems and the kinds of rules required for characterizing phrase composition and decomposition. The latter field goes beyond this interest in rules for forming expressions to concern itself with inference rules for use in deducing consequences from certain kinds of given expressions. In addition, both linguists and logicians have proposed various means of making explicit and manipulating the meaning of symbolic expressions.

This theoretical work has been applied to the description of natural languages and the specification of programming languages. Work on storage and request languages for data providing systems, the subject of this chapter, has been influenced by the theoretical work and its previous applications; moreover, it seems evident that an increasing awareness of contributions in these related areas will be required for further progress in the design and implementation of storage and request languages.

10.2   DATA BASED LANGUAGE PROCESSING SYSTEMS

The area of greatest activity in the design and construction of artificial information storage and retrieval language systems is one in which the basic information to be stored and retrieved is structured in the form of ordered sets of data items packed into fields, records, files, list structures, etc. In this section, we discuss and compare, as far as practical, certain features of nine systems that have been constructed or proposed for computer retrieval of information from structured data bases.

In discussing IR language systems, we will adopt from logic, and use in an informal sense, the term *domain of discourse*. The primary entities about which information is stored in a particular system will be referred to as *objects* or *members* of the domain of discourse. Where a system is intended for general use, representative examples of members will be listed.

The several systems to be considered are distinguishable not only in terms of variety and complexity of their domains of discourse but also in terms of content and structure of their request and storage languages. Principal features of these artificial languages for formulating queries and for representing stored information are outlined and contrasted in Figure 10.1.

System	Domain of Discourse	Storage Representation		Request Representation
		Language File	Data File	
(1) Descriptor	*Examples:*		inverted file (descriptor-object records, or direct file (object-descriptor records)	descriptors, Boolean combinations of descriptors
(2) IDL	people documents parts	thesaurus (a) index list (term vs. record) (b) glossary (term, term number)	records describing objects, relations among objects	generic descriptions of objects, object relations
(3) GIRLS	arbitrary objects	dictionary containing information defining file record and field formats	records containing data values	formatted requests describing record selection and report preparation criteria; Boolean combinations of such requests
(4) RECOL				interrogation statements composed of SELECT, NAME, ASSOC, EDIT, SUM orders
(5) ACSI-Matic	objects of military interest	glossary and index files	raw, intermediate, and formal data files, multiplets linked to natural language fragments via geographical, date, subject, and source characteristics	not specified in available literature
(6) ALERT		fact language files (a) term glossary (b) question/ identifier index (c) question/ identifier list structures	fact data file, fact descriptions and their geographical, date, subject, and source associations	formatted requests describing objects, fact context and data range; Boolean combinations of such requests
(7) Baseball	American League Baseball games in 1959	extensive dictionary for natural language to specification list translation, includes: (a) syntax codes (b) semantic codes (c) question-word, idiom-identification codes	each game described by six sets of attributes: year ——— month——— place——— game——— team——— score ——— team ——— score ———	English requests, conversion to intermediate search language, iterative derivation of required data from file
(8) Walker and Bartlett	Airfields	dictionary for natural language to IR language translation, tables defining property-value constraints	arrays of object-property value triplets	
(9) QUERY	objects of military interest	formation-rule syntax description, tables defining data constraints	not specified	English-like requests, parsing algorithm driven by formation rules, syntax ambiguities resolved via data base semantic constraints

Figure 10.1. Data based language processing systems

The computer readable files in these systems are of two principal kinds, differentiated here as "language files" and "data files." Elements of information (terms, rules, etc.) that specify permissible structure and content of request and storage languages will be considered as part of a *language file*. Specific stored expressions that represent facts about members of the domain of discourse form the contents of a *data file*.

The several systems can be most conveniently considered and discussed in terms of the following five subjects:

a. Descriptor systems, in which descriptors (index tags, property names) are directly associated with a representation of an object (document, electronic part, person, etc.) to be described. The coordinate index is one popular system of this type.

b. Data file retrieval systems, developed to retrieve and manipulate information stored in conventional magnetic tape record formats.

c. Military information systems that required fairly extensive efforts (1) to determine the system users' information requirements, (2) to develop techniques to represent these requirements in computer files to aid in the extraction of specific information from source documents, and (3) to provide flexible storage and retrieval capabilities.

d. Data searching techniques, which demonstrate interesting methods for deriving information from data files.

e. English-like query systems, in which queries formulated in a restricted form of English are translated into file search instructions through the use of syntax directed compiler techniques.

10.2.1 Descriptor Systems.   Descriptor systems constitute the least complex and most widely used kind of information retrieval systems.* The information within such systems is exclusively in the form of expressions that associate one or more descriptors with a member of the domain of discourse. A descriptor language consists of a vocabulary of descriptors (single words or phrases) D_1, D_2, $\cdots$, D_n, which are used to describe a set of members I_1, I_2, $\cdots$, I_m. Described members may be documents, people (in personnel record systems), machine parts (in inventory control systems), or any of a wide variety of well defined object classes. The problem of constructing information expressions to go into the file of a descriptor system is one of selecting appropriate descriptors and assigning them to the document or object in question. As descriptor vocabularies become large, various degrees of order are introduced to facilitate this selection process. For example, descriptors may be ordered alphabetically; they may be partitioned into classes and subclasses ac-

*The literature concerning such systems is vast; see Herner [32], for example.

cording to function and/or meaning; or relations between descriptors may be displayed utilizing tree or lattice structures. Weights may also be introduced to represent the relative importance of descriptors or the confidence of some reporter of information into the system that he has correctly applied a descriptor.

The unordered assignment of descriptors leads typically either to a direct descriptor-under-object or inverted object-under-descriptor file organization. The latter is often referred to as a coordinate index.

In a descriptor system, requests are usually expressed in terms of a Boolean combination of descriptors. The inadequacies of this kind of request, where the objects concerned are documents, have been discussed frequently in the literature [68]. However, it can be and is being used effectively in a variety of applications.

A descriptor system using more sophisticated kinds of requests is that discussed by Sable [62]. He has proposed an Information Description Language (IDL) utilizing a vocabulary of terms arranged in a "discrimination tree"—a semantic structure in which relations between the meanings of terms are explicitly represented by links between nodes of the tree. Each node represents one term. Each node is assigned a term number that serves as its address. The meaning of a term is represented by the set of nodes that can be reached from the node representing the term. This set is called the *scope* of the term. A generic-specific relation between meanings of the corresponding terms is implied by a node having another in its scope. In a tree of this type, the greater the depth, the finer the degree of semantic discrimination. For example, the more general terms are represented by the higher nodes in the tree, more specific terms by intermediate nodes, and the names of objects in the domain of discourse by terminal nodes. IDL terms may designate not only one-place properties of objects (descriptor terms) but also relations among objects (relational terms). Sable proposed an experimental procedure for determining scope relations between terms. His procedure consists of asking a system user to indicate the pertinence or nonpertinence of a term occurring in a document to a term in a query. A response indicating pertinence results in a positive value being inserted in the appropriate cell of a scope matrix. The scope matrix can be reduced to yield a connection matrix for the tree structure. The tree thus defined can then be used both for storing and for requesting information.

A discrimination tree is represented in explicit form by Sable as a thesaurus file. The thesaurus file associates terms with their corresponding term numbers, and includes a coordinate index connecting terms with records in which they are used. The record file contains a record for each information-carrying expression applying terms to objects.

Consider the named objects "Brown" and "Smith" for example. These object names might constitute terminal nodes on a discrimination tree within the scopes of the descriptors "Sgt." and "Pvt." respectively. The rank relationship between them could be expressed by a relational term "is superior to." The term numbers representing the two objects and this relationship would form a part of the thesaurus files and the index would supply the identification of records that utilized these terms in an expression such as "Sgt. Brown is superior to Pvt. Smith."

The IDL request language differs in several significant ways from a request language in a simple descriptor system. First, subtrees common to the scopes of two separate but generically related descriptors can be used to determine much more sensitive responses than is possible in systems which contain no information about how the meanings of separate descriptors are related. Second, terms are not limited to designation of nonrelational properties but can be used for storage and retrieval of information about relations holding among members of the domain of discourse.

10.2.2   Data File Retrieval Systems. The Generalized Information Retrieval and Listing System (GIRLS) developed by Postley and Buttell [57], when supplied with a dictionary defining the format of a computer data file, will accept and respond appropriately to request statements that list search criteria and criteria specifying the format of a report to be generated. Several such requests may be batched and processed against a file at the same time. Each record of the file is examined and, if it meets the search criteria, required data are extracted and placed on tape. This intermediate tape is used to prepare the specified reports.

Another general file interrogation system is RECOL (Retrieval Command Language) [16] designed by Climenson. Like GIRLS, it utilizes file description information stored in a dictionary to control search of magnetic tape files. RECOL interrogation statements may be composed of a combination of several kinds of interrogation orders. These orders can effect record selection (SELECT), delimitation of classes of records (NAME), association (ASSOC), editing (EDIT), and summarization (SUM). Some constraints are imposed on the arrangement of these orders in a request, but a very large number of order combinations is possible.

The distinctive feature of systems of this kind is their ability to search and manipulate any of a wide variety of existing magnetic tape data files. The dictionaries that constitute their language files permit search and selection on the basis of the names of objects or properties as indicated by data values stored for the objects.

In GIRLS and RECOL, we are faced with a somewhat more complex retrieval situation than in descriptor systems. Boolean operations are still much in evidence but their use is different and more complex. The scope of Boolean conjunction, disjunction, and negation operators is expanded to cover entire request statements in GIRLS. In RECOL, these operators may range over name-value pairs or sequences of nested pairs, which form proper parts of SELECT or NAME orders. A GIRLS request must be composed within a preformatted request form by filling in appropriate columns and rows. RECOL interrogative statements may take the form of any of a wide variety of legitimate order sequences. Both systems permit the specification by means of a sequence of sort and tabulation instructions, of search and editing operations.

In both systems the influence of compiler techniques on request translation is apparent. There is a close connection between schemes for translating higher order programming languages into sequences of machine instructions and schemes for translating retrieval requests into searching and processing routines. Knuth [41] has pointed out that modern compiler algorithms may be visualized as being composed of two basic components: (1) a part that parses input formulas and coverts them to prefix notation, and (2) a part that translates from the prefix notation to machine instructions. In RECOL, logical condition expressions are translated into prefix forms, which, in turn, are scanned to generate closed routines to represent the desired search test. These subroutines are inserted into a precoded executive routine that executes the searching and processing operations.

GIRLS and RECOL represent an interesting and fruitful "marriage of convenience" between information retrieval and conventional business data processing techniques. While neither system would be as efficient for a particular application as specially coded searching and processing programs, the generality and convenience of the systems more than offset this loss of efficiency in many applications.

   10.2.3   Military Information Systems.   A group associated with Radio Corporation of America and working for the Office of the Assistant Chief of Staff for Intelligence (OACSI), Department of the Army, developed ACSI-Matic [31, 54], a large scale, computer based information retrieval system.* The major purpose of the system is "... building up a research file of complete information on particular subjects. This file must contain highly formalized data-limited relations between certain classes

---

*This description of ACSI-Matic is based on information contained in the two reports on the system available in the published literature. It is understood that the system actually implemented differs in some respects from these published accounts.

of items—as well as background information which can best be expressed in a relatively free style" [31, p. 260].

Several important system requirements had considerable influence on the design effort.

> The inputs in most cases are fragmentary in nature. The machine programs had to be designed therefore to help fill in the formal categories by piecing together and associating new and previously received data. ...
>
> It is necessary that there be considerable human analysis and decision making required with respect to the data being processed ... moreover, man-machine communications were to be provided to allow for manual control over processing and file maintenance where desired. [31, p. 261]

The input information for the ACSI-Matic system consists of statements in natural language plus certain kinds of auxiliary data, such as identification of source, security classification, and date. Several levels of input information formalization were developed. The first and most basic level of formalization involved the development of a set of attributes or descriptor classes. Specification of values for these attributes provides a description of a member of the system's domain of discourse. Members of descriptor classes are termed descriptees, and a set of descriptees constituting a piece of input information is referred to as a multiplet. A multiplet has the form:

$$(A, X: B, Y: C, Z: ...)$$

where A, B, C represent chosen descriptor classes (for example, person, location, job title) and X, Y, Z represent descriptees from the chosen classes (for example, Joe Smith, Detroit, President).

Multiplets are the main information items subjected to extensive computer manipulation. A second level of stored information is the previously mentioned auxiliary data. Additional levels contain fragments of the natural language text from which multiplets were derived and index tags that characterize the fragments and associate them with particular multiplets.

There are five major kinds of files in the system: glossary, index, raw data, intermediate data, and formal data. The original input is stored in the raw data file. Next, the input fragments are indexed and stored in intermediate files. Glossary files display term relations and are used to develop and standardize descriptee entries. A series of index files associate individual index tags and descriptees with multiplets. Once multiplets are authenticated, they are stored in formal data files.

A second military information system is called ALERT (for Automated Linguistic Extraction Retrieval Technique) [38]. This is a fact retrieval system in which major emphasis is placed upon the detailed description and development of the system user's basic information requirements.

In ALERT, suitably formulated information requirements are stored in computer memory and utilized in joint man-computer procedures (1) to extract information items from source materials for subsequent computer manipulation and storage, (2) to prepare reports, and (3) to retrieve facts from the computer's store. ALERT was developed for an information handling situation in which prime requisites were timely derivation and systematic filing, for immediate availability, of large quantities of factual information from source materials.

A study of the kinds and types of information of interest to the system user indicated that much of the required information could be expressed by and with a series of questions formulated in a simplified version of ordinary English. A standard language was developed to facilitate the explicit and unambiguous expression of these questions. The basic standard language component—the question identifier—is used in two ways. In a computer question-asking mode, it elicits appropriate input information. When associated with a response, it serves as the identifier component of a stored information unit, i.e., a "fact."*

Question identifiers are composed of standard language terms, each of which might consist of several English words. There are five term classes (parts of speech), and a series of syntax rules delimiting permissible term combinations.

Just as rules had to be developed for combining terms of different classes into statements (question identifiers), other rules were necessary for combining sequences of these statements into list structures. The statements in a particular structure pertain to a specific subject identified at the beginning of the structure. They are ordered generically within a particular structure. These list structures form the principal mechanism for eliciting information and labeling it for subsequent retrieval.

Consider as a simple example a possible question identifier for a list describing activities at an airport: "Number of aircraft being refueled by tanker trucks?" By replacement of the question mark with a numerical datum and indication of the circumstances surrounding this event, a fact can be specified.

ALERT is capable of unambiguous description of events involving certain kinds of complex objects. A fact consists of three major components: (1) an identifier component, (2) a datum component associated with the identifier, and (3) a context component. The context component provides a reference frame or environment for the described fact.

*For further discussion of the notion of "fact" see Section 10.3.1. A discussion of facts in the context of a business information system is given in Kellogg [39].

For example, it associates the identifier and datum with a specific object at a certain moment in time and a certain point in space and with one or more subject categories that serve to further characterize the object.

As shown in Figure 10.1, the ALERT language file consists of a term glossary, a question identifier index, and the question identifier list structures. The function of the glossary is to aid in translation from nonstandard English to standardized terms. Terms in and outside of the language are arranged in a crossreference scheme to facilitate the location of appropriate standard terms.

Standard language terms are linked to identifiers in a second section of the language files through a coordinate index. This index enables the discovery of identifiers in which given terms co-occur. The question identifiers make up the third portion of the language files. Each identifier is associated with an address that relates the identifier to its neighbors and to associated subject categories. This address is used as a key to link together elements of language and data files and to form specific fact descriptions.

The request language developed to facilitate the search of the ALERT fact file permits the expression of interrogatory statements concerning objects and their attributes, and imperative statements that describe operations to be performed on retrieved data. All elements of a basic request statement are connected by logical conjunction. Basic statements may be connected conjunctively or disjunctively to form requests of requisite complexity. A statement may consist of one or more of the following kinds of elements: (1) object oriented elements, which may name particular objects or specify regions of space or time in which relevant objects may occur; (2) identifier oriented elements, which are specified by coordination of terms from the standard language vocabulary, by subject category, or by generic level; or (3) data elements, which specify bounds on the desired data or operations to be performed on selected data, such as summation, counting, etc. A request composed of such statements, when entered into the computer, results in a compilation of a special routine, which, in turn, searches the file and prints out the desired information.

Additional information about military data base systems may be found in Reference 21.

10.2.4 Data Searching Techniques. The Baseball system developed by Green, Wolf, Chomsky, and Laughery [30] involves a domain of discourse restricted to baseball games played in the American League in 1959. The system is programmed in IPL-V, a list processing language, and consists of two basic parts. The first part, a *linguistic analysis routine,* analyzes English questions using a dictionary of terms, idioms, and question words. Based on this analysis, the meaning of the question is represented as a list that specifies attributes and associated values relevant for identifying an answer. For example, the question, "Where did the Red Sox play in July?" would yield the specification list:

$$\text{Place} = ?$$
$$\text{Team} = \text{Red Sox}$$
$$\text{Month} = \text{July}$$

The second part of the Baseball routine, the *processor*, uses an interesting technique for searching the data base to find answers to the questions posed in terms of specification lists. If the answers cannot be found directly, the necessary information may be derived indirectly from the file. For example, the meaning of a question concerning the number of teams playing in five places during the month of August could be represented by the following specification list consisting of three attribute-value pairs:

$$\text{Team (no. of)} = ?$$
$$\text{Place (no. of)} = 5$$
$$\text{Month} = \text{August}$$

The processor first attempts to answer directly with data in the file. In the example, it cannot, since the first two attributes are modified by the qualifiers "no. of" and the required data are not directly available. Actually, three more specification (hereafter called "spec") lists must be generated before one is found that is directly answerable from the file. The first of these derived spec lists results from deletion of the team qualifier, the second from replacement of the place qualifier by a question mark, and the third from matching of "team" with each team at each place in August. Each derived spec list is placed on top of its predecessor in a "stack" or pushdown list. Lists of data that match the topmost derived spec list are checked against the spec list at the next level in the stack and this process is repeated for each spec list on the stack. In our example, a list is generated for each team that played in August and the places at which it played. This, in turn, is scanned and processed to yield the number of places for each team and, finally, a list of teams that played exactly five games in August is generated.

Walker and Bartlett [69] describe a more ambitious natural language question answering system. They conceive the problem mainly as one of proper formalization: formalization of natural language question analysis, formalization of suitable IR searching and storage languages, and the step-by-step development of an algorithm to translate between the two formalized representations.

Given the wider scope of this project, more powerful and general techniques for data retrieval are required than those available in the Baseball processor routine. Walker and Bartlett's preliminary formalization of certain IR techniques may be summarized as follows: data structures, to be useful, (1) must be able to represent or symbolize virtually anything in the world (just as natural language does), (2) should be capable of yielding related structures when subjected to standard transformations, and (3) should display properties that permit the formation of effective (performable) data retrieval algorithms. The initial first-order data structure arrived at to approximate this set of conditions is termed an object-property-value matrix. The matrix rows represent classes of objects (objects having certain structural features in common), and the columns represent properties of the objects. Row-column intersections indicate specific values of properties for particular kinds of objects. Matrix operations are given that may be combined to yield suitable search algorithms.

10.2.5 An English-Like Query System. Cheatham and Warshall [13] describe the development of a grammar and a procedure for translating requests posed in an English-like language into a program for searching a structured data base. The authors first point out that, in the case of translating a program language input string into machine language, the formation rules of the program language have semantic significance and, consequently, given a parse of the input string, the semantic interpretation of the string is straightforward.

> Similarly, if one had a parse of an English data request in which those words which referred specifically to the domain of discourse were tied to descriptions of the nature of the data in a dictionary, and in which formation rules corresponded to semantically interesting commands to the retrieval procedure, then automatic retrieval driven by this parse would at least be possible, although achieving efficient performance would still be a major problem. . . . it is in fact possible to define a useful set of such statements in terms of a collection of formation rules of the familiar kind. However, in contrast to the case of algebraic compilers, an application of one of these rules does not in general correspond to a semantically meaningful act. [13, p. 36]

As here indicated, they are faced with the well-known ambiguities, syntactic and semantic, that plague man-computer communication in English and near-English languages. In describing their retrieval language, called QUERY, they discuss a method for syntactically analyzing request statements and possible means for resolving certain kinds of ambiguities.

The QUERY language is defined by fourteen word classes and, by means of formation rules, an expression of relations between these words classes and higher order syntactic classes. The formation rules are stated in Backus Normal Form [2], a metalinguistic notation commonly used in specifying the grammars of programming languages. The data base consists of fictitious information about the status of military forces and resources. Request statements typically involve an imperative, such as "count" or "list," a noun naming the object of inquiry, prepositional phrases, and relative clauses. An example of the syntactic analysis of a simple QUERY request "Count bases in Boston" according to these rules is illustrated in Figure 10.2.

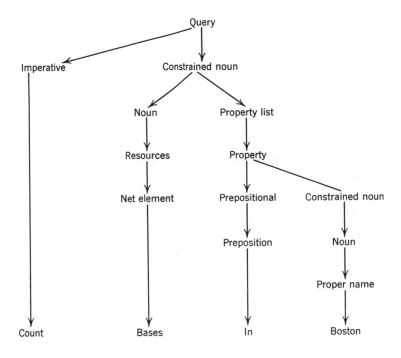

Figure 10.2. QUERY Syntactic Analysis

In this example, the principal components of the question are an *imperative* and a *constrained noun*. The constrained noun phrase "bases in Boston" is further broken down into a noun and a property list and, ultimately, into a *net element*, preposition, and proper name. This kind of analysis can be performed automatically by a syntax directed compiler provided with a table of rules representing the grammar expressed in Backus Normal Form.

A method is proposed by Cheatham and Warshall to resolve syntactic ambiguities in queries by introducing certain semantic information into the system. For example, they resolve the ambiguity of the query, "Count all planes on bases that are B-58's" by introducing the information that the term "B-58's" is subordinate to the term "plane," not to "bases." This information is introduced from a resource net, which consists of the names of classes of things mentioned in the data base and attributes of these classes. Their method for semantic resolution of syntactic ambiguity calls for a modified parsing or syntax analysis program, which references the resource net whenever a property list is recognized.

10.2.6 Data Base Input Techniques. Two major categories of practical problems are involved in getting information into a large computer based storage file: input, and input qualification. A marked difference between the language of storage and the source material language introduces the problem of translating from one language into the other. This task of language transformation may be performed manually by input editors or reporters, automatically by machine, or cooperatively by man and machine.

The problems of automatic conversion of source language to storage language may range from simple transliteration of one artificial language into another that is isomorphic in structure but different in coding to the much more difficult translation of natural language sentences into formalized expressions.

Between fully manual and fully automatic solutions to the input problem there is a wide range of variation. The cycle-and-string-association process in ACSI-Matic provides an example of cooperative action between man and machine in developing and preparing information for storage. Some ACSI-Matic input messages may be incomplete, incorrect, redundant, or contradictory in nature. A major processing task is the comparison of incoming multiplets with those already on file. A preliminary stage of input processing involves the standardization and development of a complete set of descriptor terms. This is performed with the aid of computer stored glossaries. Once information has been properly formatted, related multiplets can be retrieved from the file. Computer procedures permit the association of input multiplets with multiplets already filed. Two multiplets are considered to be associated if they have in common a "biunique" descriptee that identifies a "major" informational element of the system.

The objective of multiplet association is to find cycles and strings. A cycle of multiplets consists of an ordered set of multiplets in which each individual multiplet is associated with its predecessor and successor in the ordering (the successor of the last multiplet being taken as the first multiplet in the ordering). An example of a cycle is shown in Figure 10.3. Cycles, therefore, are closed chains of related multiplets concerning major subject areas of interest. A string of multiplets is similarly defined but, in this case, the association required to close the chain is lacking.

Cycles and strings of multiplets can be displayed to a human analyst

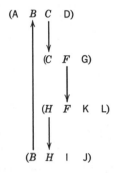

Figure 10.3   A cycle linking four multiplets

for additional processing and verification, and the analyst may call up related information fragments from the file as required to pass judgment on the displayed data. This type of processing facilitates the location of obsolete data and thus aids in file purging as well as in item association.

Getting the right input information at the right time from the right source may be as important and difficult a task as precise conversion of information to storage language form. The solution of this problem revolves around some sort of characterization of the system user's regular information requirements.

Automated question asking is utilized in ALERT [38] and is discussed in Kellogg [39] and Travis [67]. It permits a computer based information retrieval system to keep track of its user's needs, of sources that can provide information to meet these needs, and of the particular circumstances under which sources might be interrogated. A possible advantage of automated question asking is rigid control over type and form of information admitted into the system. Input responses may be required to fall into a particular format according to the type of information required. Some of the restrictions in language flexibility apparently resulting from a technique of this type may be mitigated by providing for the input of free text comments in addition to prescribed responses. The computer may sequence questions based on human input response. Thus can be effected a kind of question and answer sequence that proceeds from the very general to the very specific.

10.2.7 Overview. The data based language processing systems surveyed vary widely in domain of discourse and in vocabulary and means of vocabulary combination permitted in requests. From the design point of view, these systems can be characterized in terms of *structure*—i.e., the representation of request and storage language information internally within language and data files—and in terms of *process*—i.e., the retrieval algorithms required to operate upon requests and cause the output of desired data. A fairly coherent body of structural patterns and process characteristics becomes evident when examining and comparing these systems, despite their differences in subject and request scope. Much of the similarity among systems undoubtedly stems from the considerable influence that EDP file processing and programming language compiler techniques have had upon the design and implementation of data based language processing systems. Structural and process similarities are principally seen in the use of highly ordered and rather inflexible storage arrays, in extensive use of glossaries and term coordination to find subsets of relevant items, and in the processes involved in decoding request expressions involving Boolean operators into file searching routines. However, reflection upon the *differences* in process and structure may provide clues for use in constructing improved data based systems.

Notice the entries under the data file heading in Figure 10.1. Most of the internally stored information (e.g., in GIRLS, RECOL, ALERT, Baseball, and Walker and Bartlett) is ordered into structures that describe objects in each system's respective domain of discourse. Each structure constitutes a record in the data file, and relations between objects become explicit only as a result of applying a retrieval process. Internally stored descriptions in IDL and ACSI-Matic, however, do not fit this pattern. IDL expressions either may describe a particular object in isolation or may express relations among several objects. In the ACSI-Matic storage language, the description of an object may be distributed among several records in several files (for example, the description of the activities of a General Smith at a particular time might involve several multiplets cross-referenced to several natural language fragments and to date, place, information source, and other data).

Tree structures are often used to express relations among components in the language files. In IDL, for example, the glossary specifies a semantic discrimination tree in which each term number identifies an entrance into the tree. The ALERT glossary also specifies a discrimination tree, but one in which syntactic as well as semantic distinctions are made. Semantic distinctions between question identifiers of a generic nature are displayed in the question identifier list structure. Coordination of terms by means of the question identifier index permits linkage between components of the two tree structures.

Turning our attention to the request representation column of Figure 10.1, we can detect three principal kinds of requests: (1) requests that are simple Boolean combinations of terms, (2) requests formulated as procedurally organized programs in some intermediate search language, and (3) requests in an English-like language. The Boolean requests and their associated output lists fall into four distinctive groupings. Requests composed of Boolean combinations of descriptors result, in a simple descriptor based system, in the output of a list of objects that satisfy the stipulated conditions. In an IDL type system, Boolean combinations of one-place descriptors and relational terms could be composed of, and the associated output would consist of, object descriptions subsumed within the scope of request terms. GIRLS and RECOL request languages admit Boolean combinations of record selection, association, and editing criteria; requests activate dictionary lookup and file searching routines that select and generate appropriate lists of data. In ALERT, the scope of Boolean operators is enlarged, to include the specification of *spatial and temporal* constraints. The output is a set of fact descriptions containing terms used in the requests and describing facts that satisfy the specified constraints.

The search strategies used in Baseball, and those described by Walker and Bartlett, are important pioneering attempts that can be expected to stimulate the development of more complex strategies. The Walker and Bartlett method of successively selecting, reducing, and expanding matrices of data according to a program of matrix manipulating instructions is closer to strategies used in some of the other data base systems. It requires the synthesis of an appropriate program in order to provide correct output data. The Baseball search method, on the other hand, automatically attempts the derivation of more specific specification lists, which might be satisfiable, if a given specification list cannot be directly satisfied with data in explicitly stored form.

10.3 LOGIC BASED LANGUAGE PROCESSING SYSTEMS

The concept of logic based language processing systems is used to emphasize the difference in orientation and approach of the work described in this section from that of work on the data base systems just reviewed.

Logic is centrally concerned with the precise definition and use of concepts of symbolic structure. If some of these concepts can be adapted successfully to the design of artificial IR languages, higher levels of precision, clarity, and utility may result. In a properly formalized system, automatic procedures may be used to provide a significant degree of automatic inference capability. None of the research here surveyed has yet resulted in the construction of a complete operational system. However, a brief indication of the progress made so far is in order, if only to illustrate some of the problems and potentials in this area of rapidly growing interest.

The concept of a *function* is important in the field of logic just as it is in mathematics.

> In mathematics and logic, an *n*-adic function is a law of correspondence between an ordered set of *n* things (called arguments of the function, ...) and another thing (the value of the function, ...), of such a sort that, given any ordered set of *n* arguments which belong to (the function's) domain, the value of the function is uniquely determined. [15, p. 113]

This concept of function is centrally involved in the research to be discussed below.

Two major threads of development may be distinguished in the efforts covered in this section. All of the work depends on concepts drawn from the logic of the propositional and predicate calculi and from abstract set theory. However, differences in purpose and in the kind of information-carrying units utilized serve to differentiate the first effort discussed from the others.

10.3.1 A Definition of 'Fact.' Travis has developed a logical explication of the notion of "fact" and discusses a number of theoretical and practical problems involved in constructing fact retrieval languages and systems [67]. After a brief comparison of document and fact retrieval systems, in which he concludes that document retrieval can be construed as a special type of fact retrieval, he narrows the field of systems and system features to be covered to exclude fact retrieval systems with capabilities for structural reorganization, inductive inference, and learning, and focuses on what he calls structurally fixed question answering (SFQA) systems.

Travis considers a "fact" as a nonarbitrary association between a member of a domain of discourse and a datum, where "member" and "domain of discourse" have their usual meanings (see Section 10.2) and a datum is a sequence of symbols. For example, let us consider the domain of major league baseball teams. The idea of a nonarbitrary association is made more precise by introducing the idea of a "fact function." This notion is defined as follows: "By 'fact function' we mean a grouping which associates, for each moment of time, and according to some definite rule, each member of a domain of discourse (or each n-tuple of members for some n) with one and only one particular datum type" [67, p. 319]. A fact function whose domain consists of the baseball teams might be presented by listing a series of ordered argument-value pairs that associate baseball teams and the date on which games have been played, with corresponding data. Such a grouping is of little practical interest, however, until the meaning of "a definite rule" is clarified.

The definite rule involved in a fact function is determined by the meaning of some word or string of words that constitutes a predicate—a symbol designating some property or relation applicable to, in the case of our example, baseball teams. A typical predicate for the baseball team domain might be "seventh-inning score" designating a certain relation among two baseball teams, an interval of time, and numerals representing "score." Travis devotes considerable attention to examining the problems involved in satisfactorily defining predicates for use in SFQA systems.

Three additional concepts are defined: "variable," "constant," and the "existence" of specific facts. A "fact functor" is formed from a predicate by associating appropriate variables with it to stand for members of the domain of discourse and for the time argument. The replacement of these variables with constants (such as proper names for teams and dates) yields a "datum identifier."

An example of a fact functor is "seventh-inning score (X, Y, T)." To assert the existence of a particular fact, a statement composed of a datum identifier and a datum, e.g., "seventh-inning score (Yankees, Angels, 6-3-64) is '5/3' " is used. Such a statement is called a "fact assertion."

The notion of "fact" can now be characterized more precisely, as follows: A fact is a member of some set of ordered pairs that constitutes a fact function. The significance of the association between the components of a fact is determined by the meaning of a predicate. The existence of specific facts is asserted with fact assertions.

Many variations of this basic fact structuring scheme are possible. For example, consider again the fact assertion example "seventh-inning score (Yankees, Angels, 6-3-64) is '5/3'." This characterizes an event in time. The event can be further characterized with another fact assertion "game location (Yankees, Angels, 6-3-64) is 'Los Angeles'." For some domains it might be more appropriate to handle space-time regions more explicitly by incorporating a space as well as a time argument within each functor.

One of the several extensions of this initial framework is the concept of a "fact history." This notion is introduced to deal with some of the difficulties inherent in referencing continuous and discrete intervals of time. For example, one kind of fact history assigns a data sequence, rather than a single datum, to a datum identifier. Thus, a fact history involving the arguments of the example above might be that at any moment of time during the seventh inning, on the date and for the game mentioned, the score was "4/2," "5/2," or "5/3."

The pragmatic test of a series of formalized constructs such as those just sketched is their utility in uncovering and clarifying issues that were vague, and their ability to lead to additional fruitful constructs. Among the problems related to SFQA language system design is specification of two principal kinds of information and structuring of computer files in order to organize this information. *Interpretive information* must be supplied to define predicates, permissible relations among predicates, and terms in the system's vocabulary. Also included in this concept of interpretative information is the specification of data characteristics required to control the associations of predicates with the second principal type of information—*representative information.*

Files containing interpretative information are subject to extensive manipulation in SFQA systems since they provide the principal means for implementing inferential retrieval (i.e, the retrieval of answers implied by information in the system but not directly stored). Inferential retrieval requires the use of (1) interpretative data that characterize the logical properties of predicates (e.g., transitivity), their syntactic structure, and their generic-specific relationships, and (2) interpretative data that define datum properties such as type, units, and datum length.

Files of representative information contain the separate data that, when associated with appropriate datum identifiers, constitute facts. For proper interpretation of such stored data, additional information must be stored in these files to indicate associations of the data with domain of discourse members or with parts or complexes of members, and with possible second-order information about reliability, source, and age of data. Files for storing interpretative information are called "language files," and those for storing representative information, "data files."

Rudimentary formulation of the notion of fact, language files, and data files emerged during development of the ALERT system; Travis has succeeded in formalizing and greatly extending the scope of these ideas. The result is a development, in some detail, which can provide a logical rationale for the design and construction of fact storage and retrieval systems. For too long has such design and construction been effected by haphazardly combining a set of *ad hoc* principles and techniques which happen to work, though often not well, for some particular case. Travis' conceptual analysis, based on the notions of fact and fact function, serves, at least partially, to bridge the gap between data base systems and the systems to be described next whose stored assertions involve only two kinds of datum: truth and falsity. Here the emphasis shifts to the well known logical calculi, means for interpreting them, and algorithms for translating English sentences into well-formed expressions manipulatable within these calculi.

10.3.2 Fact Retrieval within an Aristotelian System. Cooper [18] has described an experimental system, implemented on an IBM 7090 computer, centering around a somewhat different concept of fact retrieval. He views the basic problem of fact retrieval as the development of a systematic capability for logical inference using natural language sentences. Recognizing the long-range nature of this goal, he has proposed and constructed a small-scale system, with modest question answering and deductive inference capabilities, as a step toward better understanding of the problems involved. Seen from the point of view of the variety of data available for output in response to a question, this kind of fact retrieval might not seem impressive. Such a system is capable of "retrieving" only a "yes" or "no" or, equivalently, "T" or "F" response. The "data file" would thus have a trivial structure. Corresponding "language files," however, might be far from trivial. Further, very many requests for information can be phrased as yes or no questions. (Work on the logic of questions may lead to the eventual relaxation of the restriction to yes-no type questions. See Belnap [4].) Cooper's system is based on traditional Aristotelian logic that deals with classes, class defining properties, and forms of syllogistic reasoning. The basic statement types in this logic have the forms "All X's are Y's," "no X's are Y's," "some X's are Y's," and "some X's are not Y's."

From this starting point, Cooper constructs an English-like language "L" in which statements are formed as certain restricted combinations of nouns, adjectives, verbs, and adjectival phrases. Examples of typical statements are, "Fuel burns" and "Ferrous sulphide is a dark gray compound that is brittle." A translation algorithm is given that will translate statements of this kind into another language L^*, which implements an Aristotelian syllogistic system admitting basic forms of the kind described above. L^* is a calculus having inference as well as formation rules. This feature permits a measure of deductive question answering capability. Questions of a yes-no type that are within the system's purview can be interpreted, and their logical compatibility with stored statements determined automatically. For example, the system was able to deduce that "gasoline is a fuel that burns" from the L^* representations of the statements "gasoline is a fuel," "gasoline is combustible," and "combustible things burn." Cooper recognizes the search problem inherent in this kind of deductive system and, to limit the otherwise enormous number of subsets of stored statements that would have to be considered, he arbitrarily restricts the program so that it uses no more than three stored statements as premises at a time. This has the effect of increasing question answering speed, at the expense of possibly missing a set of stored statements that would result in an affirmative response.

10.3.3 Logical Paraphrase. Williams [71] describes a series of procedures for the logical paraphrasing of natural language sentences. Her technique, termed F-translation, illustrates many of the problems to be solved in constructing a logic based language processing system. F-translation involves the step-by-step conversion of natural language sentences in context into logical statements that can stand alone as propositional functions with truth values. One statement may be composed from several sentences. Conversely, one sentence in different contexts may yield different statements. Williams' sentence-to-statement conversion procedure involves three stages: developmental paraphrase, analytic paraphrase, and symbolization. She outlines techniques for the developmental paraphrase of simple declarative sentences and some kinds of nonsimple sentences. Analytic paraphrase and symbolization involve the more complex aspects of logical analysis: semantic interpretation, quantification, grouping procedures, and reduction to final symbolic form.

Developmental paraphrase, the area to which she devotes most of her attention, involves the reformulation of sentences in context and their representation in terms of a sentence pattern and a sentence key. A sentence pattern expresses the basic structure of the sentence in a modified predicate calculus notation. This structural pattern is linked to the sentence key, which serves to define the predicate and other component expressions in the sentence pattern. These component expressions result from a logical factoring of the original sentence and are made more precise, when necessary, by consulting the sentence context, incorporating information about the source of the sentence, and defining the tense of the predicate expressions. As an example of the development of sentence pattern and key from a simple sentence, we might consider the following sentence: The pilot landed the airplane at the airport at about noon.

Williams does not define a precise mechanical algorithm for the paraphrasing procedure. Instead, she describes, largely through examples, requirements for an adequate paraphase. The above sentence would be

sequences from its expressions, and it provides a structural foundation for the construction of more expressive languages. Consider, as an example, a sentence in ordinary English given by Bohnert: "Client-12 prefers the rich to the poor." This might be symbolized using conventional predicate calculus notation as:

$$(X)\,(Y)\,(R(X).\sim R(Y) \supset P(C12, X, Y))$$

The equivalent spelled-out LAMB statement would be:

FOR-EVERY PERSON-1 FOR-EVERY PERSON-2 IF BOTH PERSON-1 RICH AND NOT PERSON-2 RICH THEN CLIENT-12 PREFERS PERSON-1 PERSON-2

An important feature of the LOGOS approach to a logical analysis of English linguistic devices and structures is the potentially useful byproducts. These byproducts would be well-behaved, precise, artificial English-like languages incorporating some of the powerful grouping and descriptive devices available in English, yet structured precisely and explicitly enough that the powerful inferential techniques of formal logic are applicable. Recent work by Bohnert [7] on the logic of English determiners, grouping devices, relative pronouns, tense, and spatial-temporal object descriptions suggests that logic based English-like languages adequate for some military and business system purposes may be feasible in the not too distant future.

In addition to the English language systems described above, some interesting work is being performed in the Soviet Union by Kuznetsov [43] and his colleagues in developing an information language for geometry and an algorithm for Russian-to-geometry language translation.

10.3.5 Summary. The import of the work described for future logic based language processing systems resides mainly in its relevance to the construction of procedures for machine inference. Automatic decision procedures already exist for large classes of expressions formulatable within the predicate calculus, but most of them are too inefficient for direct use within a practical question answering system. For practical systems, efficient techniques for discovering inference chains must be invented, both for classes of expressions for which formal decision procedures exist and for classes for which they do not. The important thing about such techniques is that they be efficient and that they succeed most of the time. Even though the invention of such techniques is different from the logician's traditional goal of inventing formal decision procedures, formalization is none the less essential. Additionally, use of the various concepts of formal logic serves to clarify the statement of the

problems involved even if it does not directly contribute to their solution.

Williams's work illustrates the scope and difficulty of the problems involved in developing logically precise statements that represent English sentences. Cooper and Bohnert direct their efforts at the representation of small portions of English within the frameworks of certain traditional logical calculi. Bohnert has outlined a systematic plan for step-by-step extending the size of these portions. Travis' work extends the application of logic to fact functions not limited to "true" or "false" data values and thus to problems in data base system design where the stored information may not be in the form of linguistic expressions. He also focuses attention on the importance of constructing more adequate means for internal representation of the meaning of predicates.

10.4 COOPERATIVE LANGUAGE PROCESSING SYSTEMS

We now briefly consider systems where man and computer might directly interact to effect efficient information retrieval and consider the languages needed to enable such interaction. The systems and languages discussed up to this point* have been directed mainly toward the following type of problem: given a query expressed as a string of alphabetic characters, a machine is to interpret it and then search out and output the requested information. Man-machine communication modes made possible by recent developments in time sharing systems, light pens, display devices, and programming languages allow for much closer cooperation between man and machine with the man monitoring and assisting the machine's interpretation and the machine helping the man focus and make explicit his exact needs for information. We shall outline some recent efforts in conceptualizing and constructing on-line problem solving systems and suggest an approach possibly useful in the development of language data processing techniques for on-line interactive information retrieval.

10.4.1 On-line Problem Solving Systems. Papers by Licklider [45, 46] and Englebart [24] present convincing arguments for the potential importance of on-line man-computer cooperation. Licklider outlines goals and details requirements, some of which (e.g., time sharing of large central processing units, on-line programming languages, and sophisticated display consoles) are now met in certain experimental systems. Englebart presents a conceptual framework that focuses on co-

*The exceptions are ALERT and ACSI-Matic, which make some use of on-line input and retrieval techniques.

operative systems as a means for augmenting human intellectual capabilities. A recent indication of an "augmentation effect" was reported in which an experienced programming language designer was able to develop an on-line programming language, using the M.I.T. Project MAC time-sharing system, in six weeks rather than in the year estimated to have been required without the use of such a system. Additional evidence that such an effect occurs and markedly so is available from the work of Culler and Fried [19], and of Sutherland [66].

Culler and Fried [19, 20] have developed a cooperative system for solving a difficult mathematical problem whose method of solution may not be completely known at the start but may be discovered as a result of interaction between a mathematician and a computer. Sutherland [66] has developed a graphical communication system (SKETCHPAD) that facilitates creation and modification of line drawings. Ross and Rodriguez [61] have described a system for the on-line solution of engineering design problems. Mooers [55] has defined a language (TRAC) that includes interesting features for the input, retrieval, and rearrangement of text strings entered from on-line typewriter. The text strings may be mixtures of data and program control information. Englebart and Huddart [25] are also developing procedures for on-line text manipulation.

Work directly concerning on-line retrieval includes the ALERT and Acsi-Matic efforts, the work of Doyle [22], Ford and Holmes [27], and Kochen [42]. Doyle has proposed and implemented techniques for generating "association maps," i.e., machine-manipulated and-displayed networks of descriptors that may be helpful to the human information seeker in making critical semantic discriminations during the process of selecting search terms. Kochen has proposed a system that, through use of a display console, permits retrieval of simply structured information items. Ford and Holmes have invented a "term diagram" technique, which might be of use to a person in assimilating information from an on-line display console.

10.4.2 An Approach to On-line Fact Retrieval.   Much more powerful retrieval procedures than those presently available will be required as basic components of most future on-line problem solving systems. There is no doubt of the importance and utility of developing a capability to query a computer in ordinary English or to exploit the precision inherent in formal artificial languages. However, natural languages and most formal artificial languages have developed over the years without regard for the particular characteristics of computers and the environments in which they are used. Therefore, it seems appropriate to seek out language techniques particularly suited for communication between man and computer (and very likely outside the scope of contemporary programming languages, which require procedural organization of requests made of computers). Natural languages have developed in an environment that presupposes certain commonalities in communicant backgrounds [34]. The dissimilarities between humans and computers provide not only a barrier to efficient communication, but also a challenge: exploiting them could result in more effective communication procedures.

We are particularly concerned with the development of techniques for improving communication between a human requestor and a machine-stored data file in situations where the human may wish to probe the file intensively. In most retrieval systems, request formulation is a function performed by humans, while request interpretation, file search, and data transformation and presentation are carried out entirely by computer. The proposal is to let the formulation, interpretation, and presentation problems be jointly solved by man and computer. One potentially very important possibility is help to the requestor in expanding and reformulating a request on the basis of information quickly fed back to the requestor from the file, i.e., help in bringing the request into accord with what is actually available from the file.

In the area of man-machine interactive information retrieval, we may expect the gradual evolution of languages having some of the convenience of natural language, some of the precision of formal languages, and some new characteristics that are due to particular capabilities of computers and their associated input-output equipment. In this regard, we should seek to exploit maximally the availability, in the computer store, of information that helps to narrow request focus and direct attention to pertinent aspects of the file. Among the aids that might be provided a requestor are (1) guidance, (2) control option cues, (3) browsing opportunity, (4) detection of communication discrepancies, and (5) mechanical means for direct communication.

A computer provided with sufficiently explicit information about the structure and content of its files can examine a request and guide a requestor's attention to appropriate regions of the file and to file parameters. In effect, the computer can instruct unskilled requestors in certain aspects of the request language and in the contents and arrangement of the file. A network of guidance "prompts" might be interposed between file and user to permit varying degrees of computer guidance based on the knowledge and skill level of the requestor.

As distinct from guidance prompts, control option cues would indicate various options of control available to the requestor. These cues might signal procedures that could be selected to manipulate displays or implement various clerical procedures. Such cues might be very helpful if selectively presented to the requestor in the appropriate context at the appropriate time.

A browsing capability would permit call-up of relevant file information during the request formulation and interpretation stage—information that might have an important bearing upon more precise specification of the request. On-line browsing may be the only means of ensuring exactly delimited retrieval for certain kinds of applications or request situations. An adequately formulated recognition grammar would be capable of detecting incorrectly formed statements. Information about such occurrences fed to the requestor on an appropriate display could assist in rapid correction of syntactic misunderstanding. Innovations such as light pen and light button languages show promise for communication of complex decisions without the need for natural language input.

The author has outlined a series of techniques for improving on-line retrieval capabilities [37] that may be briefly reviewed here. The techniques are applicable within a system consisting of a computer fact store and several communication channels, on each of which is imposed certain linguistic, device, and technique constraints. There are two alternative means of communicating queries to the computer. Empirical investigations will attempt to determine desirable characteristics of the communication channels in various combinations, through the use of graded sets of questions and problem situations. As results are obtained, the communication scheme will be modified and more empirical studies will follow. This step-by-step procedure is expected to yield qualitative and quantitative information concerning desirable communication characteristics and useful techniques for achieving man-computer rapport. The test vehicle may be considered as composed of (1) a communication interface, (2) a translation control algorithm, and (3) a fact store.

The communication interface includes three computer generated visual display forms and two user information entry devices (light pen and typewriter). The typewriter may be used to enter a request in conventional form, i.e., as a string of English words to be interpreted by the computer. The light pen serves as a device to select one or more light buttons (special display characters that, when selected, trigger a specific computer action). Thus, a communication cycle consists of computer display of information in one or more of the three possible forms and the user's response by selecting light buttons and/or typing in data or strings of English terms. The formulation of a complex request requires a number of such cycles in which the computer must store and operate upon the information successively entered by the user. The result of the computer operation appears as updated information on the display forms. The three display forms present control information, request formulation information, and fact-store information. Displayed to the user are, respectively, (1) lists of control and search alternatives—decision points represented by light buttons—to serve cueing and guidance functions; (2) a representation of the request as it is structured so far; and (3) summary information about file data that have been referenced. Appropriately organized displays of these kinds should prove a distinct aid in formulating request problems, testing hypotheses, and implementing browsing operations.

The light pen and typewriter equipment represent complementary entry procedures. Initial versions of light button (LB_1) and typewriter (TW_1) query specifying languages have been constructed. LB_1 is a system of signs called decision points. At certain times during the interaction process, the computer may select and present an ordered subset of these signs, and the user, in turn, responds by choosing and arranging members of this subset. Data to be associated with LB_1 selections may be entered using TW_1. Practically, LB_1 vocabulary and syntax are defined using a signed, directed graph that admits cycles. The use of LB_1 is controlled by a cycling program that operates upon this directed graph structure. Pushdown lists are used to control the procedures and parameter values defining appropriate computer actions for some of the decision points.

Each decision point corresponds to a node in the network defined by this directed graph structure. Each node is associated with four things; node identifier, label, procedure, and successor-node set. All of the information may be stored conveniently as three list structures encoding the connection matrix for the network, the labels that identify decision point functions in English, and the procedures that represent decision point machine meanings. LB_1 consists of a network of about 160 decision points. The network is subdivided into sets that characterize certain general search and control techniques. These techniques include methods for modifying the structure and content of LB_1 itself, TW_1, and the fact store. A technique called "constraining" is used to modify the machine meaning of nets according to the context of their use. This feature eliminates the need for a large number of nodes.

TW_1 is a more conventional query language. It can be characterized as English-like, since its vocabulary is composed of ordinary English terms. However, the system of syntactic categories used for structuring statements in this language is quite unlike traditional grammar developed for analysis and description of conversational language. The syntactic categories are task oriented and are based on certain general relations between the functions of English words and the structural aspects of the fact store. TW_1 is defined by means of a dictionary—in which each vocabulary term is associated with syntactic and semantic codes—and two tables that connect the syntactic and semantic codes. The machine meaning of a TW_1 query is a sequence of canonical operations that form a file searching program. The semantic codes specify these operations, and the ones to be used for the interpretation of any query are determined by the syntactical structure of the query and then by the meaning of this structure according to the tables.

The chief difficulty in translating TW_1 queries is in ensuring the selection of the correct syntax code and semantic code for each term from the several possibilities that are usually present. The translation/control algorithm performs this function through recursive application of the rules in the syntax and semantic tables. This algorithm is the major computer program component of the experimental test vehicle. Its three basic parts consist of cycling, analysis, and synthesis programs. TW_1 queries are parsed by the analysis program, a table driven, phrase structure, syntax analysis routine. The synthesis program uses results of the analysis to generate a sequence of canonical operations. After a check to determine the validity of the sequence of operations, appropriate subroutines are called to form a file search algorithm.

The functioning of the LB_1 language is controlled by the cycling and synthesis programs. The specification of a query using LB_1 results in an output list similar to that provided by the syntax analysis of a TW_1 query. This list, in turn, serves as input to the synthesis program. LB_1 functions, other than file searching, are controlled directly by the cycle program. In particular the functions associated with selection of a new subset of relevant decision points.

The canonical operations that comprise a search program successively operate upon elements in the language and data files. A series of these operations selects subsets of file elements and combines and manipulates these elements to present, in the end, the requested fact or set of facts.

10.4.3. Summary. The designer of cooperative language processing systems is faced with a number of challenges and opportunities that differ in degree and kind from those involved in other kinds of systems. He is faced with a series of severe time constraints: acceptable processing time for analyzing queries and searching information stores may be measured in seconds. Making parsing and searching algorithms more efficient is a major design problem. Because of requirements for increased responsiveness, traditional file organization patterns and file maintenance procedures can be expected to be replaced by others (such as those made possible with list processing) that facilitate frequent modification of the structure and content of information stores.

Design of cooperative language processing systems may progress along three principal dimensions: serial, parallel, and structural reorganization aspects of on-line communications. *Serial aspects* have to do with exploiting computer provided feedback as a means for aiding decision formulation processes, through provision to the user of sequential cues and the processing of hierarchies of sequentially dependent inputs. *Parallel aspects* have to do with the possibility of providing users with a choice, at any point in time, between attending to any of several displays and using any of several input response mechanisms. Finally, future on-line language processing systems can be expected to provide means for adaptively reorganizing the structure as well as modifying the content of information stores.

10.5 CONCLUSIONS

The request languages discussed in this chapter are those in which statements are simple Boolean combinations of descriptors; those in which statements involve some of the logically more complex features of ordinary English; and those that exploit a new generation of man-machine communication artifacts. No inference should be drawn, however, that the newer and more sophisticated request languages are necessarily best for all applications or better on all counts than older and simpler ones.

If we contrast the Boolean and English-like request languages, we see that the former are operational, are adaptable to a wide range of subject matter, and have proven their utility. The latter remain in the research and development sphere, have so far been applied only to subject areas of limited scope, and have yet to prove they are worth the extra implementation and operation costs. It may be that no practical request language can meet all of the goals of being nonprocedural, nondiscursive, and unambiguous, yet easy to use and of great power and scope. We can find out how far we can go only by trying. For some applications, a compromise involving the use of several complementary languages (such as those described in Section 10.4.2) may be the best solution.

Three of the request languages covered are characterized explicitly in terms of their formation rules. Of these three, those constructed by Bohnert and Cooper involve explicit specification of inference rules to enable a degree of machine deduction capability. This capability is used to determine whether a problematic statement is true or false given stored statements as premises. None of the operational systems surveyed involves an explicit listing of semantic rules for dealing with the meaning of statements. Semantics is the least understood, most difficult, and most important area for further research and development in IR language design. Work in formal semantics as well as empirical, semantical studies of natural languages must be drawn upon.

We see at least as much variety in internal information structures as in request languages. Several broad levels of information representation are apparent, and it might be useful to characterize them. At a first level above that of basic machine language, we can identify units such as fields, records, files, and lists. This is the level upon which currently operational file manipulation systems principally operate in fetching data according to the identifying information in a file dictionary. On a second level we can place entities such as vectors, trees, and the various forms of rectangular and generalized arrays. Second level entities can be embedded into first-level units and, in turn, serve as a means of representing higher level structures. At a third level the notions of predicate, term (descriptor), individual identifier, datum, etc., occur. Finally, on a fourth level we might place "fact assertions" and complex expressions of various kinds.

At the third and higher levels, information structures are no longer programming or computer oriented. The emphasis changes from concern with efficiently accessing and economically storing information to a focus on the descriptive capability of the information carrying units. Restrictions are imposed deriving from the human's view of the world and events that occur in it. That is, the information structures possible at these levels form a subset of those theoretically possible at lower levels. That this limitation in potential descriptive capability is not worrisome but is, in fact, a fruitful way of proceeding is a basic assumption behind much of symbolic logic. The question of providing additional or "better" information representation structures at the third and higher levels is fundamental but beyond the scope of this chapter.

A design problem of considerable practical importance centers around methods for embedding higher level units into lower level units, to preserve descriptive capability, and to maintain efficient and economical storage.

Documentation tools such as thesauri, coordinate indices, and generic-specific listings appear in several of the systems described. When an information store reaches a certain size and degree of complexity, these kinds of ordering and searching aids become essential. A great deal of work on translation algorithms has gone on for both natural and artificial languages. Most attention, however, has been paid to syntax analysis and much less to the serious problems involved in synthesizing suitable output strings. Additional work in techniques for synthesizing search programs and means for combining selected units once they have been found is clearly desirable. The synthesis problems range from simple tabulating operations to those of mechanizing deductive inference.

When an on-line retrieval capability is desired, the information retrieval language designer is faced with new problems that stem from the language requirements essential for achieving effective man-computer interaction. These include problems associated with specifying requests precisely (computer aided request formulation), with synthesis of expressions to be stored (as a result of the computer's questions to a human reporter, for example), and with preparatory processing of output information in a way that facilitates human information assimilation.

We have surveyed a variety of operational and proposed language processing systems for retrieving information from computer files. Principal emphasis has been placed on artificial information storage and retrieval languages, which are significantly less complex than natural languages, yet different in structure and function from procedure oriented computer programming languages. These artificial languages offer the advantages of increased precision, inferential power, economy, and communication efficiency for certain purposes and classes of users. A wide range of tools and techniques has been used in efforts to design IR languages, stemming from such diverse areas as documentation, compiler development, and mathematical linguistics and logic. Operative in this diversity of approaches to language are evolutionary forces not unlike those that have been at work for so long in the area of man-to-man communication. We can expect an acceleration of the evolutionary processes as the volume of man-machine dialog increases. Issuing from the processes will be languages that are "natural" and effective for communicating queries and commands to and from computing devices, though languages possibly quite unlike those that have evolved as "natural" and effective for man-to-man communication.

REFERENCES

1. Bach, E., *An Introduction to Transformational Grammars.* New York: Holt, Rinehart and Winston, 1964.

2. Backus, J. W., The syntax and semantics of the proposed international algebraic language of the Zurich ACM-GAMM conference, ICIP, Paris, June 1959, PP. 125-31.

3. Bar-Hillel, Y., Discussion of the paper by Dr. J. McCarthy, *Proc. of the (1958) Symposium on Mechanization of Thought Processes.* London: H. M. S. O. 1959, pp. 85-7.

4. Belnap, N. D., Jr., An analysis of questions, *TM-1287.* Santa Monica, Calif.: System Development Corp., June 1963.

5. Bobrow, D. and B. Raphael, A comparison of list processing languages, *Comm. of the ACM,* April 1964.

6. Bobrow, D. G., Syntactic analysis of English by computer—a survey, *AFIPS Conference Proc., 24.* Baltimore, Md.: Spartan Books, 1963, pp. 365-87.

7. Bohnert, H. G., Logical-linguistic studies for machine text perusal (Project LOGOS), Semiannual Technical Status Report (1 May 1963-31 December 1963), Contract AF 49(638)-1198, Air Force Office of Scientific Research.

8. Bohnert, H. G., Research summary, Project LOGOS, *Comm. of the ACM*, July 1962.

9. Bosak, R., *et al.*, An information algebra, *Comm. of the ACM*, April 1962.

10. Brown, J. C., LOGLAN and the machine, *Computer Applications*. New York: Mac-Millan Co., 1961, pp. 128-40.

11. Brown, J. C., LOGLAN, *Sci. Am.*, v. 202, no. 6, June 1960, pp. 53-63.

12. Cheatham, T. E., and K. Sattley, Syntax directed compiling, *AFIPS Spring Joint Computer Conf.* Baltimore, Md.: Spartan Books, 1964, pp. 31-57.

13. Cheatham, T. E. and S. Warshall, Translation of retrieval requests couched in a "semi-formal" English-like language, *Comm. of the ACM*, January 1962.

14. Chomsky, N., Formal property of grammars, in R. D. Luce, R. R. Bush, and E. Galanter, eds., *Handbook of Mathematical Psychology II*. New York: John Wiley and Sons, 1963, pp. 323-418.

15. Church, A., Definition of "function," in D. D. Runes, ed., *Dictionary of Philosophy*. Littlefield: Adams and Co., 1961, p. 113.

16. Climenson, W. D., RECOL—A retrieval command language, *Comm. of the ACM*, March 1963, pp. 117-22.

17. Colilla, R. A., and B. H. Sams, Information structure of processing and retrieving, *Comm. of the ACM*, January 1962.

18. Cooper, W. S., Fact retrieval and deductive question-answering information retrieval systems, *J. of the ACM*, v. 11, no. 2, 1962, pp. 117-37.

19. Culler, G. J., and B. D. Fried, An on-line computing center for scientific problems, Internal Report *M19-3U3*. Canoga Park, Calif.: Thompson Ramo-Wooldridge Inc., January 1963.

20. Culler, G. J., and R. W. Huff, Solution of nonlinear integral equations using on-line computer control, *Proc. Spring Joint Computer Conf.*, May 1962.

21. Development and management of a computer-centered data base, *Proc. of the Symposium*. Santa Monica, Calif.: System Development Corp., January 1964.

22. Doyle, L. B., Semantic road maps for literature searchers, *Comm. of the ACM*, v. 8, 1961, pp. 553-78.

23. Elbourn, R. D., and W. H. Ware, The evolution of concepts and languages of computing, *Proc. of the IRE*, May 1962, pp. 1059-66.

24. Englebart, D. C., Augmenting human intellect: a conceptual framework, Stanford Research Inst., Contract AF49(638)-1024. October 1962.

25. Englebart, D. C., and B. Huddart, Research on computer-augment information management, Contract AF14(628)-4088 Report *ESD-TDR-65-168*. Menlo Park, Calif.: Standford Research Institute, March 1965.

26. Floyd, R. W., The syntax of programming languages—a survey, *Trans. on Electronic Computers*, v. EC-13, no. 4, August 1964, pp. 346-53.

27. Ford, J. D., and E. H Holmes, A comparison of human performance under natural languages and term diagram procedures for the production of report summaries, *TM-662*. Santa Monica, Calif.: System Development Corp., 6 February 1962.

28. Freudenthal, H., *LINCOS Design of a Language for Cosmic Intercourse*, Part I. Amsterdam: North Holland Publishing Co., 1960.

29. Gorn, S., Specification languages for mechanical languages and their processors, a baker's dozen, *Comm. of the ACM*, December 1961.

30. Green, B. F., A. K. Wolf, C. Chomsky, and K. Laughery, Baseball, an automatic question answerer, *Proc. Western Joint Computer Conf.*, v. 19, 1961, pp. 219-24.

31. Gurk, H., and J. Minker, The design and simulation of an information processing system. *J. of the ACM*, April 1961.

32. Herner, S., Methods of organizing information for storage and searching *Amer. Doc.*, v. 13, no. 1, January 1962, pp. 3-14.

33. Humby, E., Rapid write—a new approach to COBOL readability, *Computer J.*, v. 4, 1962, pp. 301-4.

34. Katter, R. V., Language structure and interpersonal commonality *J. of Verbal Learning and Verbal Behavior*, v. 3, no. 2, April 1964.

35. Katz, J., and J. Fodor, The structure of a semantic theory, *Language*, v. 39, no. 2, April-June 1963, pp. 170-210.

36. Kay, M., Rules of interpretation—an approach to the problem of computation in the semantics of natural language, *Proc. of the IFIP*, 1963, pp. 318-21.

37. Kellogg, C. H., Investigation of man-computer interaction in retrieving information from a computer-based fact file, unpublished note, System Development Corp., 1963.

38. Kellogg, C. H., *et al., ALERT-1 Reference Series* (four volumes). Canoga Park, Calif.: Ramo Wooldridge Div. of Thompson Ramo-Wooldridge, Inc., 1961.

39. Kellogg, C. H., The fact compiler, a system for the extraction, storage, and retrieval of information, *Proc. of the AFIPS Western Joint Computer Conf.*, Spring 1960.

40. Kirsch, R. A., The application of automata theory to problems in information retrieval, National Bureau of Standards Report *78821*. Washington, D.C.: Dept. of Commerce, March 1963.

41. Knuth, D. E., A history of writing compilers, *Computers and Automation*, v. 11, no. 12, December 1962.

42. Kochen, M., Statement in *Current Research and Development in Scientific Documentation No. 11*. Washington: National Science Foundation, November 1962, pp. 114-16.

43. Kuznetsov, A. V., E. V. Paducheua, and N. M. Ermolayeva, On an information language for geometry and a translation algorithm from Russian into this information language, *Information Storage and Retrieval*, v. 1, pp. 147-65.

44. Ledley, R. S., and J. B. Wilson, Automatic-programming-language translation through syntactical analysis, *Comm. of the ACM*, March 1962.

45. Licklider, J. C. R., and W. E. Clark, On-line man-computer communication, *Proc. of the Spring Joint Computer Conf.*, May 1962, pp. 113-28.

46. Licklider, J. C. R., Man-computer symbiosis, *IRE Trans. on Human Factors in Electronics*, March 1960.

47. Irons, E. T., A syntax directed compiler for ALGOL 60, *Comm. of the ACM*, January 1961.

48. Iverson, K., *A Programming Language*. New York: John Wiley and Sons, 1962.

49. Maron, M. E., A logician's view of language data processing, in P. L. Garvin, ed., *Natural Language and the Computer*. New York: McGraw-Hill, 1963, pp. 128-50.

50. McCarthy, J., *et al., LISP 1.5 Programmer's Manual*. Cambridge, Mass.: M.I.T. Press, 1962.

51. McGee, W., The formulation of data processing problems for computers, in F. Alt (ed.), *Advances in Computers,* v. 4. New York: Academic Press, 1963.

52. McNaughton, R., A survey of automata theory, in F. Alt (ed.), *Advances in Computers,* v. 2. New York: Academic Press, 1961.

53. Metcalfe, H. H., A parameterized compiler based on mechanical linguistics, *PRCR-311.* Planning Research Corp., March 1963.

54. Miller, L., J. Minker, M. Reed, and W. Schindle, A multilevel file structure for information processing, *Proc. of the Western Joint Computer Conf.,* May 1960.

55. Mooers, C., and L. Deutsch, TRAC, A text handling language, *Proc. of the 20th ACM National Conference,* August 1965.

56. Ohlman, H., Comments on "Discussion: the pros and cons of a special IR language," *Comm. of the ACM,* January 1961.

57. Postley, J., and T. D. Buttell, Generalized information retrieval and listing system, *Datamation,* December 1962, pp. 22-25.

58. Reichenbach, H., Analysis of conversational language, in *Elements of Symbolic Logic* New York: McMillan, 1947, pp. 251-354.

59. Robinson J., Automatic parsing and fact retrieval: a comment on grammar, paraphrase and meaning, *RM-4005 PR.* Santa Monica, Calif.: The RAND Corp., February 1964.

60. Rosen, S., Programming systems and languages, *AFIPS Spring Joint Computer Conf.,* 1964. pp. 1-15.

61. Ross, D. T., and J. E. Rodriguez, Theoretical foundations for the computer aided design system, *AFIPS Spring Joint Computer Conf.,* 1963, pp. 305-322.

62. Sable, J. D., Use of semantic structure in information systems, *Comm. of the ACM,* January 1962.

63. Smith, L. W., Information and transformation on general arrays, *16th National Meeting ACM,* 1961.

64. Steel, T. B., The foundations of a theory of data processing, *16th National Meeting ACM,* 1961.

65. Suppes, P., *Introduction to Logic.* Van Nostrand, 1957.

66. Sutherland, I.E., SKETCHPAD: a man-machine gaphical communication system, *AFIPS Spring Joint Computer Conf.,* 1963, pp. 95-105.

67. Travis, L. E., Analytic information retrieval, in P. L. Garvin (ed.), *Natural Language and the Computer.* New York: McGraw-Hill, 1963, pp. 310-53.

68. Verhoeff, J., W. Goffman, and J. Belzer, Inefficiency of the use of Boolean functions for information retrieval systems, *Comm. of the ACM,* v. 4, no. 12, December 1961, pp. 557-58.

69. Walker, D. E., and J. M. Bartlett, The structure of languages for man and computer: problems in formalization, *First Congress on the Information Sciences,* 20 November 1962.

70. Warshall, S., Summary of a method for the automatic construction of syntax directed compilers, *AFCRL-62-955.* Computer Associates, December 1962.

71. Williams, T., Translating from ordinary discourse into formal logic, *AFCRC-TN-56-770,* ACF Industries, November 1956.

11

An Application of
Language Processing

Harold Borko

As the title indicates, this entire book reports the state-of-the-art in automated language processing, i.e., the use of computers to translate from one language to another, to answer questions, to analyze writing styles, and to abstract, index, and classify collections of documents. Each chapter reports on the research that has been performed and the progress that has been made in one or more of these respective areas. As a conclusion, this chapter has a slightly different format; it describes an application of automated language processing that has been used in the preparation of the book itself. The techniques used are experimental-not in the sense of a controlled laboratory experiment, but in the sense that they are uncommon and unproven. We are convinced that as the effectiveness of these techniques is demonstrated, through applications such as this one, they will become common. With this in mind, we will describe what we did and how we did it.

11.1 PREPARING A MACHINE-READABLE RECORD

Before a computer can be used to process a document or to study the characteristics of language, the text that is to be analyzed must be in machine-readable form. Comparably, to do a statistical analysis of test scores, these data must be punched on cards as input to a computer. However, there is an important difference between keypunching test scores for numerical analysis and keypunching textual data for language analysis. The difference is in cost. There are many many words in as large a document as a book, and it is both expensive and time consuming to keypunch an entire text for machine processing. If language data processing is to become practical for large-scale operations, a way must be found to reduce the cost of preparing the machine-readable record. To a large extent, as this application demonstrates, machine code can be produced as a by-product of the original typing.

From the very beginning it was planned to use this book as a data base for research in language analysis. Obviously, we were going to need a machine-readable record, and we wanted to prepare this code efficiently and as economically as possible. To save time and money, we wished to avoid keyboarding the same material more than once. We adopted as our cardinal principle that data were to be keyboarded one time and only one time. Thereafter, the data were to be processed by machine to provide the various outputs that would be required in the different stages of the preparation of the book and for subsequent analysis.

This principle was applied throughout the production cycle, and while its implementation required a great deal of machine manipulation, it proved to be both desirable and feasible.

The physical preparation of a manuscript normally involves substantial typing and retyping of the original manuscript and its many revisions. To expedite the typing task and to simultaneously prepare a machine-readable record, the first editor-controlled draft was typed on a Flexowriter. Since the authors of the individual chapters did not have a Flexowriter available, their rough manuscripts, when received by the editor, were sent to a Flexowriter operator who in one operation prepared a typewritten copy and a punched paper tape. This copy was considered to be the first draft. It was reviewed by the editor and an editorial assistant who, at this time, were primarily concerned with assuring a uniform style in chapter headings, bibliography, etc. A review for content would come later. The necessary stylistic changes were marked on the manuscript for incorporation into the second draft by the Flexowriter operator.

This second draft was to be returned to the authors for their substantive review of content and coverage. Since this book is an edited volume made up of the work of a number of authors, it was important that each person see and review not only his own work but also the work of his colleagues, to avoid any undesirable overlap and the possibility that some material would not be covered at all. In effect, each author served as a reviewer and needed a complete copy of the manuscript.

Because many copies were needed, a decision was made to facilitate reproduction by preparing the second draft on multilith masters. Whereas normally, the preparation of a reproducible master would have been expensive and would have required a complete retyping of the manuscript, we were able to produce one at very little additional cost. The Flexowriter operator used the paper tape prepared during the typing of the first draft She used master sheets in the Flexowriter instead of typing paper. Most importantly, the operator did not have to retype the entire manuscript. She simply monitored the tape-controlled keyboard operation and, when appropriate, she typed in the editor's changes to the original manuscript. The final output was a stencil, ready for duplication, and a punched paper tape that contained, in machine-readable code, all of the words in the text. It was thus possible to send a copy of the complete mansucript to each author, to other reviewers, and to the publisher for their comments.

11.2 COMPUTER TYPESETTING AND COMPOSITION

While these reviews were going on, the editor, with the assistance of the staff at System Development Corporation, had the paper tapes converted to a magnetic tape for use in future research studies in automated language processing and particularly in automated indexing.

As a demonstration of applied language processing, the editor and the publishers agreed to have the manuscript typeset by advanced automated techniques. Although there were many obstacles to overcome, we are pleased to report that the book you now have in your possession was produced by a process that involved the use of computers for typesetting and composition.

The first obstacle was to find an organization that would be willing to undertake the job and to work with the machine-readable record of the manuscript that had been prepared by the editor. This latter point is important for we did not wish to violate our principle that data should be keyboarded once and only once. When this principle is applied to the writing of books, it means that the typing of the manuscript produces a machine readable record that is changed, corrected, and edited but never retyped in its entirety—not even in the composition process.

For obvious reasons the actual coding techniques and processes used by the compositor are proprietary and cannot be described in detail. But it doesn't really matter, for automated typesetting is changing rapidly and today's techniques are sure to be obsolete tomorrow. It is the philosophy of book production by automation that deserves emphasis and explanation.

The punched paper tape, together with the second draft of the manuscript were sent to the compositor. This was done early in the production cycle in order to allow him ample time to become acquainted with the materials that were to be used and to check out the system and the computer programs. In actuality, this took a great deal longer than anticipated, for new procedures had to be developed and new programs written.

Meanwhile, the reviewers were making changes in the content of the book and the publisher was editing the manuscript and specifying headings, font style, and other printer's instructions. We were now ready to prepare the third draft which would be the galley proofs. This proof copy is prepared by the printer. Whereas normally, this would be done by re-keyboarding the entire manuscript and setting the type in lead, this time it was done by adding the revisions and instruction codes to the paper tape and then converting to magnetic tape. The tape is processed by computer program into measured and justified lines and pages.

Although the last statement was made in a single sentence, the programming processes involved are exceedingly complex. The words of running text must be divided into lines of equal size. The programs that justify lines automatically must account for indentations, ligatures, changes in type font, the presence of mathematical formulas, hyphenation of words, and a host of other variables. (A detailed description of computer typesetting procedures involving equipment, programs, applications and prospects is contained in Barnett (1).)

A computer printout of this complexly coded magnetic tape serves as the equivalent of the galley proofs. These proofs are returned to authors and publisher for checking. They are printed in upper and lower case format, but the type font used is that of the print-chain and not the one in which the book would be printed. Furthermore, the character set is limited and the proof contains many special instructional codes that would be needed for final composition but do not appear in print. Difficult proof to read and edit, it could probably be eliminated.

After proofreading and checking, the magnetic tape is prepared for input to the photon. This machine selects the proper type fonts and exposes each line on photographic film to compose the book pages. The film chips are developed automatically and from these, page proofs are prepared for final editing. As is always the case, some changes are made at the page proof stage. The magnetic tape needs to be updated to reflect these changes and, where necessary, new films are made. The book is printed, by photo-offset, from these films. On a production basis the process described is faster and more efficient than setting pages by Linotype or similar procedures.

11.3 PROSPECTS AND TRENDS

The book you hold in your hands is an example of the application of automated language processing to book publishing. The final product is not too different from the conventionally printed book. Analogously, the first automobiles resembled the more conventional conveyances of the day and were called "horseless carriages." Nevertheless, they were the forerunners of a transportation revolution. By implication, it can be predicted that our society is now approaching a revolution in communication media sparked by automated language processing. This book is only one of many examples of the changes taking place. Newspapers are being typeset by computer as are various scientific journals. But publication is only one aspect of the total communication process, which also includes the storage and retrieval of documents and data. These other aspects are also being affected by the technological revolution and are changing radically and rapidly.

The American Chemical Society, which is one of the largest printers and disseminators of scientific documentation, is moving toward an integrated communication system. Original scientific contributions are typeset by computer and printed as journal articles. The same tape–or rather portions of it, for it must be reprocessed–is used to publish Chemical Abstracts and other secondary publications. And this same tape, again reprocessed, will be used as a data base in an information storage and retrieval system that chemists will be able to search and from which they will retrieve relevant information. Similar systems are being developed by the American Biological Society, by the National Library of Medicine, by the Library of Congress and by a host of other government and industrial organizations in the United States and throughout the rest of the world.

To provide the necessary research and theoretical structure upon which these systems will be built, a new acadamic discipline, called Information Science, is emerging and is beginning to appear in the course catalogs of many universities. The state-of-the-art reports published in this book provide a basis for future research in Information Science.

1. Barnett, M. P., *Computer Typesetting: Experiments and Prospects.* The MIT Press, Cambridge, Mass., 1965.

Index